D0401677

WHAT THEY <u>DIDN'T</u> TEACH YOU ABOUT WORLD WAR II

MIKE WRIGHT is an Emmy-winning television writer. Wright was born in 1938 and grew up in Norfolk and Portsmouth, Virginia. Wright began working in radio while enrolled at William and Mary College in Virginia. During his long career in television he was a reporter, anchor, and producer. For 17 years he was a producer with NBC in Chicago. Wright retired from television in 1991 and is the author of the *What They <u>Didn't</u> Teach You* series which includes *What They <u>Didn't</u> Teach You About World War II, What They <u>Didn't</u> Teach You about the American Revolution,* and *What They <u>Didn't</u> Teach You About the Wild West.*

AVAILABLE NOW

Helmet for My Pillow
The General
March to Glory
By Robert Leckie

Samurai!
By Saburo Sakai with Martin Caidin
and Fred Saito

Thunderbolt!
By Robert S. Johnson and Martin Caidin

Zero
By Masatake Okumiya and Jiro Hrikoshi
with Martin Caidin

Fork-Tailed Devil: The P-38
The B-17: The Flying Forts
By Martin Caidin

When Hell Froze Over
By E.M. Halliday

The World War II Reader
By the Editors of *World War II* magazine

Vietnam: A Reader
By the Editors of *Vietnam* magazine

The Civil War Reader: 1862
By the Editors of *Civil War Times Illustrated* and
America's Civil War

Operation Vulture
By John Prados

The Battle for Jerusalem
By Lt. General Mordechai Gur

Company Commander Vietnam
By James Estep

The Yom Kippur War
By The Insight Team of the *Sunday Times*

Manhunt
By Peter Maas

What They Didn't Teach You About The Civil War
By Mike Wright

WHAT THEY <u>DIDN'T</u> TEACH YOU ABOUT WORLD WAR II

By
MIKE WRIGHT

ibooks logo
new york
www.ibooks.net
DISTRIBUTED BY SIMON & SCHUSTER

An ibooks, inc. Book

Distributed by Simon & Schuster, Inc.
1230 Avenue of the Americas, New York, NY 10020

ibooks, inc.
24 West 25th Street
New York, NY 10010

The ibooks World Wide Web Site address is:
http://www.ibooks.net

ISBN: 0-7434-4513-9
First ibooks printing December 2002
10 9 8 7 6 5 4 3 2 1

Share your thoughts about *What They Didn't Teach You About the World War II*
and other ibooks titles in the ibooks virtual reading group at
www.ibooks.net

To Lin
Together we will sing the ancient ways.

Above all, this book is not concerned with poetry,
the subject of it is war, and the pity of war.
—Wilfred Owen, Poems

Contents

Acknowledgments

Writing is among the most solitary of professions, which does not mean anyone writes alone. Many people and organizations aided the preparation of these essays, and while any mistakes are mine, I would like to thank those who helped me along the way. My thanks to researchers at the Chicago Public Library, the Newberry Library in Chicago, the Portsmouth, Virginia Public Library, and the Bradbury Science Museum at the Los Alamos National Laboratories. I especially thank the docents at the Smithsonian Institution's Paul E. Garber facility of the National Air and Space Museum, those volunteers who, on a hot summer afternoon, guided my wife and myself through warehouse after warehouse full of historic aircraft; the center is in Suitland, Maryland and houses, restores, and cares for more than 100 aircraft. Curator Michael J. Winery and Assistant Curator Randy Hachenbury of the U.S. Army Military History Institute's photo archive section at Carlisle, Pennsylvania graciously helped wade through thousands of photographs to find many reproduced in the following pages. Similarly, the staff at the National Archives Still Photo section rescued me as I stumbled through their files. Historians at the Statue of Liberty shared information about the statue's manufacturer, and Rangers at Ft. Sumter National Monument answered questions regarding a time not generally associated with that fort's history.

I thank my friend of many years George "Butch" Cook for all his help; my brother of even more years, Richard L. Wright, Sr., did the same. Thank you both. Strangely, none of us have aged over the past 50 years.

Many shared their experiences of World War II; I remember them all and thank you, especially Roger Harris, who told me of those days so long ago at Iwo Jima.

To Publisher Bob Kane and his son Richard, thank you for suggesting this book, and thank you E. J. McCarthy, Executive Editor at Presidio, for early, often, and constant enthusiasm about this project.

Mainly, I am proud once more to thank my wife Lin Drury. I believe she understands.

Chronology of World War II

1922
October 28: Benito Mussolini becomes head of Italian government.
1923
November 8–9: Adolf Hitler attempts to seize power in Beer Hall Putsch.
1931
September 19: Japanese troops seize Chinese territory; Manchurian incident.
1933
January 30: Hitler becomes Chancellor of Germany.
March 4: Franklin D. Roosevelt becomes president of the United States.
1935
October 3: Italy invades Ethiopia.
1936
March 7: Germany remilitarizes the Rhineland.
1938
March 28: Germany annexes Austria.
September 29–30: Munich Agreement; Chamberlain declares "peace in our time."
November 9-10: Anti-Semitic Kristallnacht, (Crystal Night), in Germany.
1939
September 1: Germany attacks Poland; World War II begins.
November 4: FDR signs Neutrality Act.
1940
January 8: Food rationing begins in Britain.
May 10: German Blitzkrieg in Europe; Churchill becomes British prime minister.

June 4: Dunkirk evacuation saves 300,000 British and French troops.

June 14: German troops enter Paris.

June 22: French surrenders; Hitler declares "the war in the West is won."

July 10: Battle of Britain begins.

September 27: Japan, Germany, and Italy sign Tripartite Pact.

October 16: More than 16,000,000 Americans register under Selective Service Act.

November 5: FDR wins third term as president.

December 29: FDR calls on Americans to turn nation into an "arsenal of democracy."

1941

May 6: At March Field, California, Bob Hope headlines USO show.

May 10–11: More than 2,000 fires started, 1,212 people killed in heaviest raid of Blitz.

June 22: Germany launches offensive against Soviet Union.

July 26: FDR halts trade with Japan, freezes Japanese assets in U.S.

August 7: FDR and Churchill draw up Atlantic Charter.

October 18: Gen. Hideki Tojo becomes premier of Japan.

October 20: German troops reach outskirts of Moscow.

October 31: German submarine sinks U.S. destroyer *Ruben James* off Iceland.

November 26: Japanese fleet departs the Kuril Islands to attack Pearl Harbor.

December 7: Japanese bomb U.S. base at Pearl Harbor, Hawaii.

December 8: U.S. declares war on Japan.

December 8: Britain declares war on Japan.

December 11: Germany and Italy declare war on the United States.

December 21: U.S. and Britain determine "Germany first" prosecution of war.

December 23: Wake Island falls.

December 27: U.S. rationing begins; the first item—automobile tires.

1942

January 20: Germany begins "final solution" of the "Jewish problem."

January 23: Japanese submarine shells oil refinery near Santa Barbara, California.

February 20: Lt. Edward "Butch" O'Hare becomes first U.S. fighter ace of the war.

February 28: Ceiling set on all U.S. wholesale prices.

March 11: MacArthur leaves Corregidor by PT-boat; declares "I shall return."

April 1: U.S. begins forced relocation of Japanese-Americans to internment camps.

April 10. Bataan Death March begins.

April 18: Lt. Col. James Doolittle launches first bombing raid against Japan.

May 6: Japanese capture Corregidor.

May 7–8: U.S. defeats Japan in the Battle of the Coral Sea.

May 14: U.S. Women's Army Auxiliary Corps (WAAC) created.

May 15: Gas rationing begins on U.S. East Coast.

June 4–5: U.S. defeats Japan in the Battle of Midway.

June 13: FDR creates Office of Strategic Services (OSS), forerunner of CIA.

August 7: U.S. 1st Marine Division lands on Guadalcanal in the Solomon Islands.

August 19: Allied troops fail in invasion of German-held port of Dieppe, France.

August 23: In USSR, history's last cavalry charge.

August 23: Germany begins assault on Stalingrad, USSR.

November 4: Gen. Bernard Montgomery leads breakthrough at El Alamein, Egypt.

November 8: Lt. Gen. Dwight Eisenhower leads Allied attack on North Africa.

December 2: Enrico Fermi achieves the first nuclear chain reaction.

1943

January 12: Soviet forces raise the siege of Leningrad.

January 14: FDR flies to Casablanca, Morocco, for meeting with Churchill.

February 7: Shoe rationing begins in America.

February 23: Rommel defeats U.S. forces at Kasserine Pass in Tunisia.

April 1: Nationwide food rationing begins in U.S.

July 9: Allied amphibious landing on Sicily.

July 22: Palermo, Sicily, surrenders to Gen. George Patton's Seventh Army.

July 25: Italian dictator Mussolini overthrown and arrested.

September 8: Italian government surrenders to Allies.

October 1: U.S. Fifth Army enters Naples, Italy.

October 7: Last 100 American POWs remaining on Wake Island are executed.

October 13: Italy declares war on Germany.

November 28: FDR, Churchill, and Stalin meet in Tehran, the first Big Three meeting.

December 24: Eisenhower named commander of up coming Operation Overlord.

1944

May 3: Meat rationing ends in U.S.

June 4: U.S. Fifth Army troops enter Rome.

June 6: Operation Overlord: D day on the French coast at Normandy.

June 13: First German V-1 buzz bombs fall on London.

June 15–16: First bombing raid of Japan since Doolittle attack in April 1942.

August 8: U.S. troops complete capture of the Mariana Islands.

August 25: Allied troops enter Paris.

September 8: First V-2 missiles launched against Britain.

September 14: U.S. troops take Aachen, first great German city to fall to the Allies.

September 17: Allied airborne troops begin ill-fated Operation Market-Garden.

October 25: First Japanese Kamikaze attacks on U.S. warships.

November 7: FDR reelected to fourth term of office.

December 21: Germans encircle U.S. troops at Bastogne, Belgium.

1945

February 4–16: Allied leaders meet in Yalta Conference, second Big Three meeting.

February 13-15: Allied bombing destroys Dresden, Germany.

February 23: Flag raised on Mount Suribachi, Iwo Jima.

March 7: American troops seize Remagen River bridge over the Rhine.

March 9–10: Nearly 300 B-29 Superfortresses bomb Tokyo.

March 27: Last V-2 rocket hits London.

April 1: U.S. Tenth Army lands on Okinawa, the final amphibious landing of the war.

April 10: German ME-262 jet fighters shoot down ten U.S. bombers near Berlin.

April 11: U.S. Ninth Army reaches Elbe River.

April 12: President Franklin Roosevelt dies at Warm Springs, Georgia; Vice-President Truman becomes president.

April 23: Soviet troops enter Berlin.

April 29: U.S. forces free 32,000 surviving inmates at Dachau concentration camp.

April 30: Adolf Hitler commits suicide; cremated in Chancellery garden.

May 2: Berlin falls.

May 8: V-E Day in America.

June 26: United Nations charter signed in San Francisco.

July 16: Near Alamogordo, New Mexico, the first atomic bomb is detonated.

August 6: B-29 Superfortress *Enola Gay* drops atomic bomb on Hiroshima, Japan.

August 8: Soviet Union enters war against Japan.

August 9: B-29 Superfortress *Bockscar* drops atomic bomb on Nagasaki, Japan.

August 10: Japan sues for peace.

August 10: Soviet Union invades Korea.

September 2: Japan surrenders. World War II is over.

INTRODUCTION

A World Gone Mad:
But What if Tomorrow Never Comes?

Shortly before the middle of the twentieth century, the world lost its mind. Beginning in 1931, the people of one Asian nation invaded another Asian nation; it remained a local war until the Japanese claimed that their invasion of China was part of a new order (the Greater East Asia Co-prosperity Sphere) to rid East Asia of the detested white race.

Beginning in 1939, the people of one European nation invaded another European nation; it remained a local war until the Germans claimed that their invasion of Poland was partly a need for living space *(Lebensraum)* and partly to rid Western Europe of those they detested as a race of inferior beings.

From September 18, 1931, (in Asia) and September 1, 1939, (in Europe) until May 7, 1945, (in Europe) and September 2, 1945, (in Asia), the world turned to war. We killed more people and did more physical and psychological damage than ever before in history. If we are lucky and we work at it, we will never break our own record for death and ruin.

For most of history, when people fought other people it was their *world war,* because their worlds did not yet go beyond boundaries written by waterways or mountains or deserts. When their worlds expanded, so did their wars, and they were forced to find a new way to name those wars.

Gone were the days of fancy or fanciful names: the War of Jenkins' Ear (in 1739, Spanish revenue agents cut off the ear of an English seaman named Robert Jenkins; a member of Parliament displayed Jenkins's pickled ear in England's House of Commons), The War of Austrian Succession (which grew, so to speak, out of the War of Jenkins' Ear), and The Hundred Years' War (a good name, although it lasted more than a hundred years, from 1337 to 1453).

Even the American Revolution and the Civil War had definitive names.

The start of the twentieth century saw the Great War, which only later we called the World War. The next time we got into trouble, all we did was give the war a number: World War II. It was the largest war the world has ever known. By giving it a number, not a name, we admitted that we were doing it all over again.

During World War I, Britain's prime minister, David Lloyd George, bitterly commented, "This war, like the next war, is the war to end all wars." Each time we hope it *is* "the war to end all wars." So far, we've been wrong.

Americans were called out of factories, out of offices, and out of schools; called to pick up rifles, get behind cannons, get into tanks or airplanes; called to ride bucking destroyers in the dead of a North Atlantic winter and slip their carriers over a sun-flattened ocean somewhere in the South Pacific. They fought under seas and along stormed shores. Others kept factories rolling, continued growing corn and raising cattle, and saw to the millions of items needed to stay alive.

Those who fought often fought alongside their British and Canadian and Australian cousins who had been doing the same things longer and at greater costs. All the while, our more distant relatives, who looked and sounded a bit different from us, overran Manchuria and Korea or goose-stepped their way through France and the Netherlands. To their shame and the world's sorrow, too often they cut off prisoners' heads or herded victims of their hatred into showers of death-spewing gas.

In 1940, the United States had a population of 131,669,275. Even before Germany's attack on Poland, many Americans realized that they, and the world at large, soon would be at war. Neither the Neutrality Act nor the self-proclaimed isolationists of the America First Committee (really just those who were anti-British, anti-Roosevelt, and anti-Semitic) could keep the nation out of what would become the first truly global war. Already, the army, navy, marines, and Coast Guard were expanding.

December 7, 1941, became the "date which will live in infamy," and neither the United States nor the world in general would ever be the same.

To paraphrase Winston Churchill, never before had so many fought so hard, so far away; never before had so much of a nation's soul been put into a war effort. Even America's Civil War, which took more American lives than any other conflict the country had been in, did not match the atrocities, the changes in lifestyles, the often total reversal of fortunes of World War II.

In the course of forty-five months—the duration of U.S. involvement in the war—disbelief, despair, confusion, and chaos changed to confidence and hope, organization and order. It was a time when old enemies became friends and old friends became enemies. In the axiom of politics, our enemy's enemies became our friends. At least temporarily.

World War II was like just about any other war in at least one respect. Most of the time it was not an adventure; it was a time of loneliness and boredom and fatigue. Action and danger were the punctuation marks.

Still, in its ferocity, World War II was like no other war anyone has ever seen. Let's hope it stays that way.

CHAPTER ONE

Greetings:
Moments To Remember

I was in the class of '41, the last high school class. You see? By that winter Leslie Bidwell would be dead at Pearl Harbor. My class would be dying.
— Betty Basye Hutchinson, resident of Oroville, California

Say what you will, nothing can make a complete soldier except battle experience.
— Ernie Pyle, United Features Syndicate, August 23, 1943

In September 1940, as Congress debated America's first peacetime draft, a fistfight broke out in the Capitol, the first in fifty years. Outside, women protestors burned in effigy Sen. Claude Pepper, who had championed the draft bill.

Congress also created a two-ocean navy and, in a case of extreme, virtually unprecedented liberality, allocated $660 million for the army in the coming fiscal year. The War Department had asked for only $460 million. It did not, of course, refuse the extra $200 million.

The United States operated 6,500 local Selective Service Boards, called draft boards. October 16, 1940, was registration day, "R Day." America's young men reported to their local boards and registered for the draft. Some thought they'd be going into the army right then; a man in Davidson County, Tennessee, was so sure he'd be heading off to war that he took along his hunting rifle. It didn't work that way, of course; there were several steps involved in the process.

From the moment the men stepped into the Selective Service Board office, the military confronted them with paperwork. First came DDS Form 40, an eight-page questionnaire. Because neither the military nor the bureaucracy spoke any normal language, many registrants needed help filling out the form.

Question: Have you ever been in an institution?
Answer: Yes, the hospital when I had my appendix taken out.
Question: Have you ever been found guilty of a crime?
Answer: Yes.
Question: Give particulars.
Answer: An automobile accident.

When the men walked out of the draft board office, they carried an item they were never supposed to be without under penalty of the law: DDS Form 2, better known as the draft card. By mail, registrants received draft lottery numbers ranging from 1 to 7,836. They were ready to go to war—not always willing or able, but generally ready.

Secretary of War Henry Stimson stood blindfolded beside a ten-gallon glass bowl, the same bowl used to hold World War I draft lottery numbers. Now, on October 29, 1940, the bowl was back in action.

Newsreel cameras rolled; radio microphones picked up the words. America and the world waited. Stimson reached in, drew out a blue capsule containing a number, and handed it to President Roosevelt, who read out the number for the first draftee: number 158. In the watching crowd, a woman screamed, "That's my son." Six thousand one hundred seventy-five other young men held lucky number 158. Western Union message boys around the nation hopped on their bikes and pedaled off to deliver telegrams from the Selective Service Board. The first line said it all: "Greetings."

Inductees reported to their local draft board in the predawn darkness, with large groups of boys (truly, they were boys, not yet men) who stood in grim silence. Often with them were virtuously sobbing girlfriends, openly crying mothers, proud fathers, and noisy younger siblings who thought it was a gas for brother Bill to go off to be a soldier.

The inductees stood around and waited, some of them shy, some boisterous, some still drunk or hung over from the previous night's farewell party. Unless the drunkenness got too out of hand or the hangover was so severe that it "spilled" onto other inductees, the army didn't care. Finally, all the inductees climbed into a bus and were taken to an induction center, where they stood around some more.

Inside the center, an officer ordered the draftees to strip to their shorts, socks, and shoes. Most of the men were uncomfortable standing there in their underwear, especially with businesslike nurses walking among them. The army knew they'd be uncomfortable and realized that a man often sheds his defenses with his clothing. A sergeant issued tags for the inductees to wear around their necks, another sign that the military cared more for numbers than for names.

About the time that the men had given up expecting anything more to happen, a team of physicians marched in and examined the inductees one by one, poking and prodding them, checking them for irregular heartbeat and any outward signs of ill health. A nurse handed out specimen bottles and ordered the half-naked men to take them to a rest room and urinate. Those with the smallest specimen bottles invariably wound up farthest away from the urinals.

Inductees had to be at least five feet tall and weigh a minimum of 105 pounds. That appears small today, but the average World War II draftee was an inch taller and eight pounds heavier than the average in his father's war, the War to End All Wars.

Recruits' vision had to be correctable, and they had to have at least thirty-two natural teeth and not have flat feet, hernias, or venereal disease. The rule about teeth was left over from the Civil War draft, when a soldier needed most of his teeth in order to bite the end off a paper cartridge before loading his musket. The rule was dropped in mid-1943. The current concern was over the wretched state of the inductees' teeth. It may have been due to the Great Depression and its long-lasting poverty.

In all, men drafted from the West and the Dakotas were, by far, the healthiest. Those from the South were the most likely to be rejected for health reasons.

If the inductees thought the physicians were quick in checking them over, the next group to have a go at them was even faster: psychiatrists. As World War II began, nearly 100,000 World War I veterans remained in government hospitals, still diagnosed as "shell

shocked." In the 1940s, such individuals were termed "neuropsychiatric" undesirables. After Vietnam, the term would be "post-traumatic stress disorder." By whatever name, the military wanted to
avoid having to hospitalize the men at government expense when
World War II was over, so it screened inductees for any predilection
toward neurosis. The psychiatric examination, however, usually was
brief: "How do you feel?" "Are you nervous?" "Have you ever been
nervous?" One psychiatric examiner saw 512 men in one day, which
in an eight-hour day gave him less than one minute per inductee,
not counting time off for lunch. Only after the war did the military
admit that "the army's standards on mental defects were inadequate
and ineffectively administered." In fact, although the army rejected
1,846,000 men for neuropsychiatric disorders, it had to discharge an
additional 330,000 for the same reason. As draft board head Gen.
John Hershey put it, the men whom the psychiatrists rejected were
"no queerer than the rest of us."

If the inductees passed the limited physical and mental examination, they were classified I-A and sworn in to the military. The story
goes of draftees at an induction center who were milling around,
pushing, and complaining about how they'd been checked out like
horses at the Kentucky Derby. An old sergeant who'd seen and heard
it all stood on a table at the front of the room: "Gentlemen, gentlemen! Calm down. Let's have some quiet here, please. Gentlemen,
please be quiet!" Once he got their attention, he turned the inductees over to a young officer who administered the oath. From that
point on, Uncle Sam owned the recruits. The old sergeant let them
know it as soon as the young officer left the room. "Shut up, damn
it. You're in the army now."

The recruits would be allowed a final furlough to put their lives
in order, then they had to report to a reception center. To make certain they showed up at the center, the military read them the 58th
and 61st Articles of War, which said they had to return or be declared
AWOL, absent without leave, and subject to military trial and punishment. Later, they'd have the entire list of Articles of War read to
them so often they would memorize it. Years later, many World War
II veterans could still remember the Articles of War, along with their
military serial number.

• • •

At first, only about 10 men from each local draft board were called up per month. That was 10 men out of a pool that averaged about 3,000 registrants for each local board. The number called increased, but for December 1941, the month of the Pearl Harbor invasion, only 20,000 men were called up nationwide. The army had reached its quota of 900,000 men and wasn't prepared to take any more.

Initially, men between the ages of 21 and 36 were called. For some on the higher end of this scale, it was double duty; if they'd lied about their age they might have served in the Great War. Congress changed the law to limit inductees to ages 21 through 27, but after Pearl Harbor they changed it again and gave the president power to draft men by age group. Less than a year after America's entry into World War II, men as young as 18 were drafted; the upper range was returned to 37, where it remained for the rest of the war. By the time Japan surrendered in 1945, more than 34 million American men had registered for the draft, with 10 million ordered to report for induction.

In both the United States and Canada, the armed forces were seen as a good way to get a job in a depressed economy. The unemployed thought more kindly of the draft than did, say, college students and those with steady jobs. Teenage boys tried growing mustaches to look older. Older men tried using shoe polish to cover up gray hair; in Canada a 76-year-old man who tried this was rejected.

All told, approximately one-sixth of all American males served in the military during the war, and draftees made up 10 million of the 16 million members of the armed forces. In the beginning, it was a white man's war. The large contingent of blacks who had served so well in the Union Army during the Civil War were forgotten and not replaced. Virtually no blacks served on southern draft boards. A postwar report on South Carolina's Selective Service system tried to explain it by obfuscating in the best style of political rhetoric: "We did not put any Negroes on the Local Boards or Appeal boards, the reason for which was explained to their satisfaction"—whatever that means.

When the National Association for the Advancement of Colored People (NAACP) campaigned for the integration of the armed services, Secretary of War Henry Stimson wrote in his diary: "What these foolish leaders of the colored race are seeking is at the bottom social equality." Dwight Eisenhower, a brigadier general on the General Staff's War Plans Division, told the War Department that he'd found no country where black troops would be welcomed. A year later, after more lobbying by the NAACP, army chief of staff George Marshall said, "Quit catering to the negroes' desire for a proportionate share of combat units. Put them where they will best serve the war effort." Generally, that meant that black draftees received little specialized training and were assigned to units behind the lines. Blacks in the navy usually were messboys or hospital orderlies or worked dockside or as cargo handlers; most drivers of the navy's ship-to-shore vehicle, the DUKW, were black. Blacks drove trucks in the army, and a large percentage of drivers in the Red Ball Express were black. Blacks were also construction workers; black engineers and workers helped to build the Alcan Highway, the Alaska-Canada highway that ran from the railhead at Dawson Creek, British Columbia, to the Richardson Highway about a hundred miles from Fairbanks.

During the 1940s, blacks made up 10.6 percent of America's population, but the American military never came close to having 10.6 percent of its forces black. Other ethnic groups whose representation didn't match population figures had different complaints. When a large number of draftees on the Chicago list carried Polish names, Polish American residents accused the local board of calling up too many from that one group; the area then, as now, had a major segment of first- and second-generation Poles. Chicago area Poles and others of Eastern European extraction believed that they (meaning Christians) were being drafted while others (meaning Jews) were deferred, because those others "knew somebody on the draft board." The belief was totally without basis, but it didn't stop them from assuming that it was fact. Many still do, "knowing" their ethnic group was drafted far more often than any other ethnic group, "knowledge" that seems to be shared by every other ethnic group.

Cherokee Indians in North Carolina wanted their own draft board. In the Southwest, draft lists were loaded with Spanish names, and few were ever exempted.

One of the first to be drafted under the new law was John Larson, of Chicago. He was inducted on January 4, 1941. He and his girl back home, Marjorie Griffith, planned to marry after John, or Jonathan as she sometimes called him, had served his one-year hitch.

> Dearest Jonathan:
> We see the future, and in it, America will play a big role. . . . Wouldn't it be a good idea to save what we can now, so outside of what expenses we will have on furloughs, we might have a little to go and buy a piece of America. . . . Huh, Johnnie?
> I often think of the Army, hope and pray you will not be changed by association with a lot of men who indulge in coarseness to different degrees. I know you won't tho'. And I appreciate that you do not deceive me. . . .
> Good Night, my Johnnie
> Marjorie Elizabeth

Marjorie Elizabeth Griffith and John Larson didn't wait for his one-year enlistment to be completed; they were married on June 27, 1941.

Despite stories about men trying hard to fail their physical examinations and be exempted from the draft, it usually worked the other way. Some who perhaps should have been exempt tried hard to be accepted. It became a point of pride, not to mention worry over what the folks at home might say if they didn't make the grade. "Funny thing about the medical examination," draftee Marion Hargrove wrote in his best-selling book about life at Fort Bragg, North Carolina. "Before you get to it, you're afraid you'll pass. When you go through the examinations, you're afraid you won't."

Still, 50 percent of the inductees were rejected as IV-F (4-F, in common terms). Of the first lucky holders of draft lottery number 158, that left about 3,100 standing. Subtract another 10 percent as being functionally illiterate (another holdover from the Depression years), and the number was down to about 2,800 men.

Occupational deferments could declare individuals as "holding an essential occupation," which sometimes simply meant they performed some labor that no one else could. Usually, occupational deferments were granted for certain agricultural and industrial occupations, which the government deemed vital for the war effort. In some cases, workers—miners are a good example—spent the war years in the same jobs they'd had before the fighting. Even some of those who volunteered to go were still rejected.

There were thirteen draft classifications:
IA—Fit for general military service
IB—Fit for limited military service
IC—Member of the armed forces
ID—Student fit for general military service
IE—Student fit for limited military service
IIA—Deferred for critical civilian work
IIIA—Deferred due to dependents
IVA—Already served in the armed forces
IVB—Deferred by law (such as draft officials)
IVC—Alien
IVD—Minister
IVE—Conscientious objector
IVF—Physically, mentally, or morally unfit for service

In the early days of the war, local civic or social groups—the Elks or Moose or Eagles—hosted flag-waving celebrations sending their "brave young men" off to war with a going-away present of a carton of cigarettes, a ten-dollar bill, and a fifth of whiskey. The inductees smoked the "butts", pocketed the "sawbuck," and took the "booze" along on trains or buses packed with other recruits on their way to the reception centers. Such buses and trains often held the remnants of farewell celebrations. Some less than sober men often did considerable damage; other recruits quietly reflected on what lay ahead.

Directly ahead lay a large installation, the reception center, where once again inductees were ordered to undress. This time, it was for what troops called "shortarm inspection," but what the Medical Department referred to as a "short physical inspection." By whatever name, inductees were examined to determine whether they had contracted any venereal disease since they'd last been checked. From there on out, every time they changed a military post—even more frequently in the navy: whenever they left port—they'd be given a shortarm inspection. The examination, in the jargon of the times, was conducted by a "pecker checker," a "pricksmith," or a "penis machinist." Recruits also got the 1940s version of a sex lecture: "Flies spread disease, so keep yours buttoned."

As the men moved from spot to spot, from test to inspection, old-timers (those who had been in as long as a week) shouted and jeered at the newcomers. "Get out while you can!" as if they had much choice. "You'll be sorry!" as if the inductees already weren't more than just a little sorry.

Next, they took the Army General Classification Test, or AGCT. It consisted of 150 multiple-choice questions that tested basic abilities: math, verbal skills, and spatial (that is, nonverbal) reasoning. It didn't measure intelligence but, rather, was a test of what people had done with the intelligence they'd been born with—"social experience," psychologists called it. The military wasn't so much interested in whether a recruit was a genius (actually, they didn't know what to do with someone whose intelligence was greatly above normal) but *how* quickly does this guy pick up new information and use it. How high you scored on the AGCT might determine what you did during military life and, in fact, how long you might live. As an example, a recruit needed a score of 115 or better to get into officer candidate school (OCS).

If the AGCT didn't get you, a fifteen-minute classification examination might. It came next. Stories, rumors, and apocrypha abound about the classification tests. Few inductees, goes the claim, wound up doing in the military anything for which they had experience in civilian life. A civilian banker might become a military baker because the interviewer misspelled the word.

Examiners used the *Index and Specifications for Occupational Specialists* to determine the proper peg for the proper hole—medical, transportation, or telephone installation, for example. Sometimes it worked; sometimes it didn't. As General Hershey put it, "I haven't seen a draft questionnaire yet in which the guy said he shot people for a living." When all other classification failed, inductees were deemed fit for "any arm of service" and usually became infantrymen–foot soldiers who slogged around the world.

The British military version of the fifteen-minute classification exam checked for what was called "combat temperament," the higher, the better. By 1943, the U.S. Medical Corps suggested a similar system to cull those men who possessed not only stamina but the ability to adjust to an unfavorable environment, a man who would show aggressiveness and initiative. One psychiatrist advised looking for men who possessed a spirit of adventure, a love of competition, and "a love of blood sports."

The next step consisted of inoculations—smallpox and typhoid "injections." The many stories of inductees passing out at the first sign of a hypodermic needle led reception center personnel to wait until all other tests were completed before they subjected draftees to what everyone knew were square needles.

The inductees' stay in the reception center lasted an average of nine days. During this time they were not only tested and poked, injected and scorned, they were given remarkably quick and remarkably short haircuts, remarkably free of charge. They got uniforms, which of course always fit perfectly, despite the saying: "the military has two sizes—too big or too little."

Men traded uniforms to find something close to fitting, and men who had never before put needle to thread tried shortening or lengthening pants. Others, such as Elliot Johnson, found another way around the problem.

I found out that there were some very enterprising people in the world. One of the men who had been drafted had set himself up as a tailor. The pants I was issued dragged at least a foot beyond my shoes onto the sidewalk, and for fifty cents that enterprising young man altered my pants and made them fit.

In the beginning, many uniforms were left over from World War I. They often came complete with IDs of long-dead soldiers and names of long-gone girlfriends tucked away in moth-eaten pockets. The primary uniform was a floppy olive-drab outfit called "fatigues," topped with an equally floppy hat.

An army may march on its stomach; it certainly marches on its feet, and boots were a major item for recruits. For a while, the government issued leftover World War I puttees, khaki-colored strips of canvas that soldiers laced around their lower legs and ankles. Puttees were designed to help keep the Doughboys' feet dry in World War I trenches.

World War II GIs hated puttees and left them off whenever they could get away with it. They were so tedious to put on that soldiers sometimes left them on for long periods of time, so long that many developed the condition known as trench foot—the flesh looks deathly white and wrinkled and breaks out in sores.

"It is an awesome experience," wrote columnist-cartoonist Bill Mauldin, "when a man with three stars on each shoulder steps out of the bushes and demands to see your bare feet." The three-star general who inspected Mauldin's feet was Lt. Gen. Walter Krueger, who commanded the Third Army at the start of the war and was known for surprise foot inspections.

Finally, troops received boots that looked like lace-up, high-top shoes, with a top section that strapped around the ankle.

Author Marion Hargrove wrote about being issued shoes:

> My shoe size, the clerk yelled down the line, was ten and a half.
> "I beg your pardon," I prompted, "I wear a size nine."
> "Forgive me," he said, a trifle weary, "the expression is, 'I wore a size nine.' These shoes are to walk in, not to make you look like Cinderella. You say size nine; your foot says ten and a half."

In an effort to give recruits properly fitting boots, the army used an X-ray device known as a fluoroscope. You stood with your feet inside the machine, wearing what the quartermaster sergeant assured you was the correct size boot. A television-type screen displayed a live, eerily green X ray of your feet, boots clearly outlined around them. You really could see if your boots fit! You really could, and sometimes did, get an overdose of X rays. For several years following the war, the fluoroscope was a favorite of shoe store owners, and also kids who wanted to see their foot bones wiggle.

Another method of shoe sizing was to have recruits try on their new boots while carrying buckets loaded with sand. Supposedly, the sand represented the 105-pound pack they'd later have to tote all over camp and all over the world.

At the start of the war, American troops still used World War I British army-style "tin hats." They were so heavy that they often gave the wearer a stiff neck and didn't do much to protect him from shell fragments thrown up from the ground. It took a while, but the Quartermaster Corps came up with the M1 helmet, a two-piece combination of steel pot and liner, which together weighed three pounds. According to specifications, the new helmet would protect the wearer from a .45-caliber bullet fired five feet away. The liner was constructed of laminated phenolic resin–impregnated fabric. By itself, the liner could be used in parades and gave an appropriately military look. Really neat for cadets in the Reserve Officers' Training Corps (ROTC).

The steel pot was a miracle: a washbasin, a mixing bowl, a cooking pot, a table, a pillow, or even a short stool to sit on. Its visor rim not only kept rain off the wearer's face, in a pinch it could be used like a shovel blade to dig a hole. An army nurse said she found twenty-one separate uses for the new helmet.

The M1 helmet had a chin strap, but was generally worn unfastened. In fact, Gen. George Patton said he'd fine any man twenty-five dollars if he caught him with his chin strap fastened. Patton claimed to have lost an aide in Tunisia who had his helmet strapped on. A concussion from a shell snapped the man's head back and broke his neck.

If there was anything wrong with the new M1 helmet, it was its appearance. Some critics claimed that it looked too much like the German helmet. When U.S. troops were sent to Northern Ireland, they had to go back to the 1917 tin hat to keep from scaring the natives. The army stuck with the M1 helmet until the late 1980s, when it went over to a model that *really* resembled a German helmet. It's made of the same material used for police bulletproof vests, and it comes with a variety of camouflage-pattern covers. It cannot, however, be used as a cooking pot.

Later on, recruits were issued a lot of other gear, everything from athletic sneaker–type boots to be worn in the jungles (they were never satisfactory) to "shoepacs," boots now commonly seen gracing the pages of hunting and outdoor gear catalogs: rubber bottoms with leather tops. They got shelter halves (an idea left over from the Civil War; you joined your shelter half with a buddy's and made a tent), packs, barracks bags, sleeping bags, and ammunition carriers. The government issued jungle troops eighteen-inch-long machetes to allow them to cut through miles of brush without causing blisters.

The army also issued a marvelous invention called the "entrenching tool," a folding shovel. You could dig with it when it was unfolded, chop with it when it was partially closed, and use it as a weapon in hand-to-hand combat. After the war, the tool saved many a former GI from getting his car bogged down in heavy snow. It became an almost standard accessory for postwar auto trunks.

Many consider the quartermaster's greatest success to be the field jacket. In the mid-1930s, the army issued millions of short, windbreaker-type jackets, but in February 1943, the Quartermaster Corps started giving troops of the 3d Division in Italy longer field jackets, and the troops loved them. Warm, waterproof, and lightweight with loads of pockets, they were perfect for the cold, wet Anzio area. When the rest of the Fifth Army saw the new field jackets, they clamored for their own. It became the favorite coat of soldiers in World War II. Thanks to postwar stores specializing in used military gear, field jackets lived on as the coats of choice among men on street corners and college campuses. In the 1960s and 1970s, they became virtually a uniform for antiwar protestors.

It was the first time away from home for many draftees, and most of them enjoyed the experience, at least in the early stages of their military careers before the shooting started. One young man from North Carolina, however, went a bit overboard in writing his buddies at home about the joys of army life.

> Tell all of the boys to come on down for the Army is all right they are good to you down here for they will serve you breakfast in bed if you want them to all you have to do is tell them the night before and they fixt you right up it is so easy.

A draftee from Texas told the folks at home one reason he liked army life: "They let you sleep till 5:30."

• • •

The World War II draftee was likely to have some high school education, know how to drive a car, and be proficient in the jitterbug, the big apple, or the lindy. He was not as likely as his father and grandfather in earlier wars to have ever shot a rifle. Hopefully, he would learn.

In the early days of the war, technical specialties got the cream of the draftees, with the army air forces right behind. Because the navy and the Marine Corps thrived on volunteers only (later, they welcomed draftees), "the army ground forces got the dregs," as one general put it. By the second year of the war, that changed; toward the end of the war, the quality of army ground units was actually improving.

The average American soldier in World War II was 5 feet 8 inches tall and weighed 144 pounds. He had a 33½-inch chest and a 31-inch waist; his shoe size was 9½D. During basic training he gained 6 to 9 pounds, added at least an inch to his chest, and his shoe size rose to 10D. Officers, who frequently came from a better educated and wealthier part of society, were somewhat taller and heavier than enlisted personnel.

On the other side of the war, where nutrition was also a factor, the average Japanese officer was only 5 feet 6 inches tall and weighed 128 pounds. That put Allied officers a good 30 pounds heavier and several inches taller than their opposite numbers.

CHAPTER TWO

Camp Life:
You're In The Army Now

There's the right way, the wrong way, and the Army way.

—World War II saying

This is the Army, Mr. Jones!
No private rooms or telephones!
You had your breakfast in bed before,
But you won't have it there anymore!

—Words and music by Irving Berlin,
1942, *This Is the Army, Mr. Jones*

One hot summer day in 1941, a truck convoy from the 110th Quartermaster Regiment rolled by a Memphis, Tennessee, golf course. Seeing several women golfers on the course, the troops called out in typical army fashion, with whistles, shouts, invitations, and wolf calls. They saw a casually dressed man about to tee off and cried out, "Yoohoo," "Fore," and "Hey, buddy, need a caddy?" "Buddy" was sixty-two-year-old Lt. Gen. Ben Lear, commander of the Second Army. He was in civilian clothing, indulging in his favorite pastime of a round of golf.

Lear ordered the troops to behave, but they, having no idea who he was, told him to butt out, using slightly different and more obscene language. They found out who the aging duffer was when he ordered them to dismount and take a hike, literally—fifteen miles in record-breaking Memphis heat. The *Arkansas Gazette* got hold of the story and played it up big. The national press picked it up, and it became the "Yoohoo Crisis." The War Department and General Lear were flooded with letters from indignant parents of draftees. One U.S. senator, Missouri's Bennett Clark, got into the act and tried to prevent Lear from being promoted. It didn't work, and "Yoohoo" Ben Lear went on to become Eisenhower's deputy in Europe.

• • •

Author Marion Hargrove wrote of a fictitious letter home going around the barracks at Fort Bragg.

Dear unfortunate civilian friend:

I am very enthusiastic about Army life. We lie around in bed every morning until at least six o'clock. This, of course, gives us plenty of time to get washed and dressed and make the bunks, etc., by 6:10. At 6:15 we stand outside and shiver while some [deleted] blows a bugle. After we are reasonably chilled, we grope our way through the darkness to the mess hall. Here we have a hearty breakfast consisting of an unidentified liquid and a choice of white or rye crusts.

After gorging ourselves with this delicious repast, we waddle our way back to the barracks. We have nothing to do until 7:30 so we just sit around and scrub toilets, mop the floors, wash the windows and pick up all the matchsticks and cigarette butts within a radius of 2,000 feet of the barracks.

Soon the sergeant comes in and says, "Come out in the sunshine, kiddies!" So we go out and bask in the wonderful North Carolina sunshine—of course, we stand knee-deep in the wonderful North Carolina sand. To limber up, we do a few simple calisthenics, such as touching your toes with both feet off the ground and grabbing yourself by the hair and holding yourself at arm's length.

At 8 o'clock we put on our light packs and go for a tramp in the hills. The light pack includes gun, bayonet, canteen, fork, knife, spoon, meat can, cup, shaving kit, pup tent, raincoat, cartridge belt, first-aid kit, fire extinguisher, ten pins, rope, tent pole, hand ax, small spade, and a few other negligible items. Carrying my light pack, I weigh 217¼ pounds. I weighed 131 pounds when I left home, so you can see how easy it is to gain weight in the Army.

When the draftees reached their training centers, their lives began to change dramatically. For some, the time in service represented years of lost opportunity. For others, the military itself was an opportunity.

For recruits and their loved ones, it was a time of sorrow. Karl Jensen, of Caldwall, New Jersey, had been gone only a short time when his wife, Sigrid, wrote him this letter:

> My Darling:
> You've only been gone a few hours and already the house is waiting for you. I came back from driving you out to the avenue and began mentally putting away our life together to make room for the new one. The main difficulty is there is too much of you here. Your magazines, your books, your ash receiver, your papers still where you dropped them last night, your clothes spilling out of your closet, and even your pajamas flung on the bed. But it wasn't till I picked up the shirt you'd worn last night that the feel of you was unbearable. . . . I stood there holding the shirt thinking it must go to the laundry. But I couldn't put it in the hamper. I couldn't even lay it down. . . .
> It's not yet 10:15, but I'm going to bed—I'll pretend we're together, and that every once in a while I must nudge you to make you move over, or stop snoring! And if I dream about you, tomorrow will be a lovely day.
> I love you,
> Sigrid

A divisional camp needed 40,000 acres of varied terrain. It needed a good supply of water, good roads, and good rail facilities. Training camps spotted the country, with every state having at least one or two. The majority were on the West and East Coasts and in the South; land in the South literally was dirt cheap, so many camps were built there.

In 1945, Fort Benning, Georgia, was the largest of all the training camps; with 95,000 men, it was as large as many cities. Fort Jackson, South Carolina, had 65,000 men; Fort Bragg, North Carolina, had 76,000. Farther south were Fort Blanding, Florida (54,000), Fort Claiborne, Louisiana (55,000), Fort Hood, Texas (68,000), and Fort Shelby, Mississippi (86,000).

Wherever they were, camps all looked pretty much alike. Usually they were built from the Quartermaster Corps' 700 Series plans, which were drawn up in the 1930s: bare, angular, wood construction two stories high—"nothing above two stories except the flagpole"—

housing bunks for sixty-three occupants with banks of toilets, lava-
tories, and showerheads. The original plans specified unpainted
buildings, but Eleanor Roosevelt once visited an army post and she,
with help from the Painting and Decorating Contractors of America, succeeded in getting the buildings painted—all the same color.
Mrs. Roosevelt's suggestion to curve camp streets to make them more
pleasant failed, however. The sameness made it difficult to tell one
military camp from another, one camp street from another. Recruits
often got lost.

In the beginning, the nation's military training machine ran a bit
wobbly. Improperly trained men were unfamiliar with either the system or their weapons. The story goes of a new replacement plunked
down in a firefight near the Rapido River in Italy. With the Germans
only ten yards away, he looked at his M1 rifle and shouted, "How
do you load this thing?" In America's Civil War, Union general
Ulysses S. Grant once complained that his men, too, were so green
that they didn't know how to load their weapons. The more things
change. . . .

In World War II, entire National Guard units often were feder-
alized, leaving entire towns wondering what would happen if their
young men didn't come home again. Many divisions, however, were
a hodgepodge of ethnic, regional, and economic backgrounds. Still,
amidst this hodgepodge, recruits found friends. An Italian American soldier might find himself surrounded by other Italian-speak-
ing draftees; the same held for many other ethnic groups. Without
trying too hard, you could get together a group of musicians—jazz,
country and western (hillbilly, it was called then), or even classical.
Card and dice games were everywhere, even though the military officially frowned on them. A former New York bartender said he'd
"seen all kinds of characters, but this place has got me doubled in
spades."

Just as letter receiving became the major way that draftees kept
up with life back home, letter writing became a major way to let the
folks know how great or bad or tough or easy life was in the training
camps. Because many training camps were in the South, northern

recruits often wrote home about being stationed in "Tobacco Road" or "somewhere in the damn Alabama woods."

When new recruits found themselves thrown in among others, they learned how different a world it was beyond their hometown. The guy in the next bunk could be just about anybody, especially if you believed tales reminiscent of boys' camps. One soldier wrote home about his new buddy who'd been an elephant trainer in the circus; another told of having met someone who "knows the Lone Ranger personally." And, of course, there was the almost daily re-fighting of America's Civil War, with each side easily identified by their accents and each side giving the other hell when the barracks' lights went out at night.

As a college graduate, Elliot Johnson (the man who'd had his new army pants tailored for fifty cents) was sent to officer candidate school at Fort Sill in Oklahoma. It was, he said, "my first real taste of the South." He remembers reporting to his battery commander, saluting, and saying, "Lieutenant Johnson reporting for duty as ordered, sir!" His commander waited, not returning his salute, while Johnson stood rigid, sweat "rolling down my forehead" and a "fly on the end of my nose." Finally, after a very long time, the officer asked, "Northerner or Southerner?" Johnson said, "I'm a Westerner, sir." The commander threw him a salute and said, "Relax, you'll do."

Sooner or later, barracks became much like small villages. As in a village, small talk and gossip were among the means of diversion, often with persons as the objects of conversation. Each barracks had its share of wise guys (know-it-alls who spoke out about everything in a degrading manner) and sad sacks (generally inept and unlucky individuals). Former Walt Disney artist George Baker had a cartoon strip in *Yank* magazine featuring Sad Sack, a soldier who became the epitome of incompetence.

One thing that recruits grew competent in was the fine art of cursing. Words that to a later generation became known as "the seven words you can't say on television" were environmentally acceptable. Words they'd never thought of using at the corner drugstore became commonplace, to the extent when they went home on furlough or leave they often caught themselves saying the wrong thing at the wrong time. "I get stuck with a lot of chickenshit duty," a new soldier might complain in a letter home, not even thinking about how the word likely would shock mom, who'd refuse to let the recruit's younger siblings read the letter. Snafu (situation normal, all fucked up) and tarfu (things are really fucked up) were accepted in the barracks but weren't customary at a soldier's or sailor's dining table back home. A recruit would shock the folks he'd grown up with by asking for "more fuckin' peas." It caused consternation around the dining table on Elm Street, but it didn't bother most recruits in the mess hall.

This change in language mores shocked mom and amazed sociologists and psychologists, experts who never could agree on why the "sociologically obscene" became everyday words and phrases. Some claimed that it was the recruits' way of getting around a lack of vocabulary in their new life; others called it an "aggression against all of those who accept the taboo." Most social scientists had trouble writing of the phenomenon because they were afraid to use the words that concerned them.

Cursing essentially was a way of getting along with a recruit's new friends, a way of becoming accepted by your barracks mates, and a way of protecting your sanity in a new social order. Subconsciously, you all knew you'd need one another when the pretend war of training turned to the real thing of killing and being killed.

GIs exchanged civilian clothing for uniforms and accepted military demands and orders, but at heart they remained pretty much as they had been before receiving the government's "greetings."

They took physical education (PE) and ran obstacle courses, the most grueling aspects of basic training. PE varied in intensity from camp to camp. For all personnel under the age of 40, the army prescribed a mandatory 25-mile road march with full equipment. Sometimes, troops did more. The 351st Infantry Regiment once covered 62 miles in full gear in a 29-hour period; nobody fell out, and General Marshall gave them a special commendation. At the 351st's training center, the culmination of physical training was the requirement that the soldier with rifle and 30-pound pack negotiate a 1,500-foot obstacle course in three and a half minutes. Specific requirements were that he take off with a yell (yelling or singing frequently accompanied physical activity), mount an eight-foot wall, slide down a 10-foot pole, leap a flaming trench, weave through a series of pickets, crawl through a water main, climb a 10-foot rope, clamber over a five-foot fence, swing by rope across a seven-foot ditch, mount a 12-foot ladder and descend to the other side, charge over a four-foot breastwork, walk a 20-foot catwalk some 12 inches wide and seven feet off the ground, swing hand over hand along a five-foot horizontal ladder, slither under a fence and climb another, and cross the finish line at a sprint. Recruits learned how to climb ropes, read maps, and survive a tear-gas attack. They learned how, when, and what to salute; when in doubt or if it moved, they saluted it.

They trained with old Springfield .275-caliber rifles because the army didn't have enough of the new Garand M1 gas-operated, semi-automatic rifles. The M1 was their dream weapon. If a soldier could eject and reload eight-round clips fast enough, the M1 fired twenty .30-caliber rounds a minute. The U.S. Army loved the M1; a lot of U.S. Marines did not. It had passed the army's tests, but because some Marine Corps noncommissioned officers (noncoms, or NCOs) didn't like it, they found a way to make the M1 jam; they dropped the ammunition clips in the sand, and the sand jammed the rifles. One reason that Marine Corps noncoms didn't like the Garand M1 was that it meant requalifying for expert rifleman under a more difficult marksmanship course, which they would rather not have taken. Yet an expert rating was worth five dollars a month, and to NCOs making thirty dollars a month before the war broke out, five dollars a month more was worth getting upset about.

Sure, the M1 had problems—"seventh-round stoppage," when the seventh round in the eight-round clip jammed, and a rear sight that had a tendency to jump up—but it was effective at 550 yards and was generally noted for its reliability and accuracy. The army adopted the Garand M1 in 1936, but it wasn't until 1942 that the Marine Corps gave in and adopted it over their NCOs' objections. More than 4 million M1s were produced during World War II, but its developer, John Cantius Garand, never got a penny in royalties. He was a government employee at the Springfield, Massachusetts, U.S. Armory and as such couldn't take out a patent on his invention.

Quickly, recruits learned that the M1 was a "rifle," not a "gun." Call it a gun and you might be ordered to report outside the barracks, naked except for helmet, socks, and boots. Carrying your rifle at port arms, you'd shout and point at appropriate locations—weapon or groin—"This is my rifle; this is my gun. This is for shooting; this is for fun."

Recruits also learned to drive tanks and jeeps, the latter, for some unknown reason, referred to as "peeps" by General Patton. Before it became a copyrighted word, *jeep* apparently stood for the letters *GP,* indicating a general-purpose vehicle.

Recruits drove trucks: the 4-by-4 half-ton, Ford-built vehicles that the drivers called "Our Darling" and the 6-by-6 from General Motors. With its six wheels on three axles, it became the truck of choice for the Red Ball Express in Europe, rolling along with supplies that fed the army and its machines.

Troops learned how to fight with bayonets and knives, how to fight dirty, because, "The guy you'll be fighting ain't gonna fight clean." They learned about land mines and booby traps, how to toss a hand grenade. They learned how to field-strip a cigarette butt: tear the paper into tiny bits, shred the tobacco, then spread them around. A drill sergeant who saw a recruit toss away a cigarette butt without field-stripping it ordered the recruit to strip the butt and bury it in a 6-by-6-by-6 foot hole. Later, the sergeant asked the recruit, "What brand of cigarette was it?" Of course he couldn't accept the recruit's claim and made him dig up the butt to show him, then rebury it in another 6-by-6-by-6 foot hole.

Recruits learned how to pitch a tent and how to camouflage their camp, how to make up a bed so tightly that a quarter would bounce on the top blanket. They learned how to peel potatoes and scrub garbage cans. They learned how to survive on what the army called food.

Troops met "nice girls" at USO-sponsored events, and they patronized prostitutes in nearby red-light districts. They learned to use the "Pro Station," the prophylactic station, where they tried to wash off and be cured of any and all diseases they might have carried back to the base with them. Troops also sat through hours of gruesome movies showing what syphilis could do to a man who was less than careful. Time for another shortarm inspection.

Let's face it, wherever there are soldiers or sailors, marines or airmen, prostitutes are likely to be found nearby, along with bars and tattoo parlors. In 1942, the *Washington News* ran the headline: "Enough VD Cases in D.C. to Overflow the Stadium." The venerable Griffith Stadium seated 30,000 fans. The *News* claimed, "There are fifteen thousand more cases [of VD] than there are [stadium] seats."

Cities sometimes tried to rid themselves of prostitutes by setting aside districts for their use. Sometimes whole sections of houses of prostitution were set up, either just out of town or in the same city but set apart. It was a way for a city to put, if you will, all of their bad eggs in one basket. Such areas became known as "The Strip," "GI City," "Boomtown," or something of the sort. The saying was that "If you have to ask what kind of place The Strip is, you don't belong there."

With Jefferson Barracks and a slew of army air forces facilities in the neighborhood, St. Louis's city fathers thought of instituting such a plan. St. Louis's city mothers didn't go for it, and the plan never came about.

Norfolk, Virginia, tried setting aside an enclave of sin known as East Main Street. Stretching from the Norfolk-Portsmouth ferry landing to Norfolk's Union Station, East Main Street was notorious: with glaring neon lights and blaring jukeboxes. It was fitted out with "everything a sailor could possibly ask for except peace and relaxation." It held the dingy Gaiety burlesque theater, where sailors could get a close-up revelation of feminine charms. There were penny arcades with peep shows and shooting galleries and stands where an accurate baseball thrower could knock a girl out of bed. There were tattoo parlors and flophouses. Everywhere there were barrooms. There was plenty of wine, women, and song to be had for the right price.

On stage at the Gaiety, Anne Corio and Gypsy Rose Lee strutted and stripped as the crowd cheered its appreciation. Tavern waitresses would double as B-girls, offering to sit with any customer who'd buy them seven-dollar bottles of "champagne"; they'd slip ticket stubs into tight-fitting dresses and, at the end of the evening, split the profits with the bar owner. A B-girl usually made multiple dates with sailors, knowing that most would be so drunk they'd forget about it. At the end of the evening, however, there'd often be a line outside the front door, waiting for her. Fights among drunken servicemen were not unusual. It was the job of the navy's shore patrol to control things; Norfolk city police had handed over to the military any problems that came up on East Main Street.

An ex-sailor named China Solly ran an establishment near the Norfolk Naval Base called The Stars and Stripes Forever. Its inside walls were complete with paintings of fire-belching battleships. Because Virginia law at the time banned the sale of liquor by the drink, China Solly got around it by claiming that his was a "club" serving members only. At its height, The Stars and Stripes welcomed weeknight crowds of 12,000 or more sailors; Saturday nights were *really* busy.

Joints by the hundreds catered to the military: the "Krazy Kat" and "Arab's Tent" among them. On the windows of bawdy houses, working girls put up signs, using the titles of recent movies to get their point across: *Boys' Town, It Happened One Night,* and *All That Money Can Buy.*

It was the same at camps, forts, and military bases all over the country. Near the training camp for the 3d Armored Division at Camp Polk, Louisiana, off-duty GIs patronized the Red Dog Saloon, the Tip Top Inn, and the Roof Garden. About ten miles west of Columbus, Georgia, an entire Alabama town was built to service Fort Benning's paratrooper trainees. According to one report, "The principal industry of the small town of Phenix City, Alabama, is sex, and its customer is the Army. . . . The town is at least eighty percent devoted to the titillation and subsequent pillage of that group it affectionately calls 'Uncle Sam's Soldier Boys.'"

Military trainees went looking for girls who were easy, but they also looked for someplace to meet decent girls in real companionship. Often, they confided this to USO dance hostesses or chaperons at church socials, who were themselves "decent girls." It was the old story of soldiers wanting to date a girl with round heels but insisting that her heels be on the square for marriage.

"It was . . . a very hectic, exciting time," Patricia Livermore remembered. She followed her fiancé to San Diego, hoping to see him before he shipped out.

There were girls in San Diego marrying servicemen right and left during the war, partly because they felt sorry for them. The other reason was the serviceman's fifty-dollar-a-month allotment—that's what the government gave the wives. A girl would marry a man. He'd go overseas and make out the allotment to her before he went. While he was gone, she'd go down to Tijuana, Mexico, and marry another serviceman, get another allotment.

The military had a name for such ladies: "Allotment Annies." Pat Livermore says she knew of one girl who married six men that way. She was "very true to the first one, until she met the second, and true to the second until she met the third."

Everywhere recruits went, they marched. They drilled, went on bivouacs, and stood inspection. Training during 1942 took up forty-four hours over six days; Sunday they were off and many went to chapel, even though it wasn't compulsory. It was almost as if, with the deadly reality of war facing them, they were repeating what they'd done in high school or college: cram for their final exams, with ministers, the "Holy Joes," ready to help them study.

Reveille was at 6:10 A.M. and lights out was at 9:45 P.M. Officers in charge of the Army Ground Forces Replacement and School Command admitted that the training schedule was too tight, the programs were too full, the days were too concentrated, and the men were too seldom able to relax, so they were not fresh and fit each day for the training they were to receive. Men agreed and wrote home about it, often complaining that basic training was "hot and tough." Frequently, they added, "I hope I have guts enough to really take it like I should."

An Indiana soldier wrote about camp life in Texas:

I cannot picture everything clearly to you, for I cannot send you a box of Texas dust to pour liberally over your whole body. I cannot send you a long, hot road and a fine set of blisters or a pair of heavy G.I. shoes to be broken in. I cannot send you an overcoat which you will not be allowed to wear at reveille when it is freezing, but which you will be required to wear during the sweltering afternoon.

• • •

Soon, the hard part of basic training was over. Soon, all they had to do was fight for their lives.

The American military man complained about his food, yet in general it was far superior to that eaten by other armies around the world. The basic meal of troops in garrison was the A ration, with about 70 percent made up of fresh foods. They ate B rations, which were much like A rations but had canned meats, fruits, and vegetables, and even those delectable items, powdered eggs and potatoes. A too-frequent mess hall item was chipped beef on toast, known universally as "shit on a shingle."

Each B-ration pack was supposed to provide enough food for ten men for three meals for one day, so it sometimes earned its nickname the "10-in-1."

The famous C ration was the canned variety that contained ten different meat combinations—chicken and vegetables; franks and beans; ham, eggs, and potatoes; ham and lima beans; meat and rice; meat and vegetable stew; and meat and spaghetti. C rations also provided cereal, crackers and jam, powdered coffee, and sugar. They even included powdered lemonade for vitamin C, but few soldiers drank it. Instead, they used it as a stove cleaner or for the finicky a hair rinse. In 1937, the Hormel Meat Company came out with SPAM—chopped ham and pork shoulders, or so the manufacturer claimed. GIs learned not to ask what SPAM really was made of. But, then, military troops didn't get the real SPAM; instead, they got a cheap imitation cooked up by the army Quartermaster Corps. As part of Lend-Lease, tons of SPAM were shipped to the Soviet Union, where it was fondly (believe it or not) referred to as "Roosevelt sausage."

C rations contained toilet paper and even a small pack of cigarettes, usually an unknown brand. "Lucky Strike Green Has Gone to War," the advertising slogan went. The government needed the green ink for metal production, so the package became the current white with a red bull's-eye. Luckies or Camels or Chesterfields, themselves, hardly ever showed up in C rations.

All military rations were well packaged and at least semi-impervious to humidity and immersion, which was both the good news and the bad news: good news in times of war, bad news when the military wanted to store its leftovers. Unused crates of C rations were stored in warehouses until years later when someone declared millions of them spoiled, begging the question, "How can you tell?" By the Korean War, cigarettes left in stored C rations were so dry they burned faster than the match it took to light them, burned so fast that soldiers often tossed them aside or used packs of them for target practice.

D rations, the so-called "iron rations," were 600-calorie emergency meals, vitamin-packed chocolate bars, marked off in segments that troops were told could last for a day each, if the damned thing didn't break their teeth. They were hard as a rock and took from forty-five minutes to an hour and fifteen minutes to gnaw through.

Troops going into combat took K rations, individual meals carried for breakfast, dinner, or supper. Unlike C rations, which were meant to be heated (with the aid of a pocket-sized paraffin heater) to bring them close to an edible state, K rations could be eaten cold, while a man was huddled in a foxhole. A typical K-ration breakfast was a fruit bar, powdered lemonade mix for hair rinsing, crackers, and a can of ham and eggs. K-ration lunch and dinner was the same: a can of potted meat or cheese, crackers, more powdered orangeade or lemonade, sugar, chocolate, dessert, salt tablets, and chewing gum.

There was something referred to as "kennel rations": meat loaf, but certainly not the kind mom made back home. Mom (and girlfriends, too) sent boxes of goodies, everything from cookies to salami to fruitcakes, and now you know where that fruitcake you got last Christmas originated.

Probably the most treasured item for many World War II soldiers was the small, folding can opener that was supposed to come with every C and K ration but often didn't. In Vietnam, you'd frequently see a soldier wearing a can opener hanging from his dog tag chain.

Each man carried an individual two-piece aluminum mess kit. It had a folding handle and included a three-piece set of utensils—knife, fork, and spoon; hook the utensils to the mess kit handle and immerse them in hot water for cleaning. Standard issue also called for an aluminum canteen and a form fitting cup with a folding handle for use with hot beverages. The canteen hooked onto the soldier's web belt; the mess kit and utensils went into his backpack.

Neat. They later became standard, if unauthorized, camping gear for postwar Boy Scouts.

Army rations have changed little in the past fifty years. Not until the Persian Gulf War and Operation Desert Storm in 1991 were they replaced by something called MREs, meals ready to eat. They, too, can be stored for years, and they, too, in years to come will be remembered, sometimes fondly, by American service personnel. Like C and K rations, they will be the subject of strange, late-night cravings by those who suffered and enjoyed them at an earlier date.

A telegram got the soldier into the army by announcing "Greetings." Another telegram to many folks back home became an epilogue: "The Secretary of War desires to express his deep regret that your son, Private John Doe, was killed in action in defense of his country. . . . A letter follows." The telegram was signed by the adjutant general.

A follow-up letter might come from the late man's unit commander, explaining how he died. Another came from the government, explaining that, as the man's beneficiary, the recipients would receive six months' worth of their son's pay, as well as proceeds from the $10,000 insurance policy he'd signed up for the day he was inducted.

Occasionally, long after the initial telegram and follow-up letters went out, friends and relatives would receive letters from the dead man. If they'd been postmarked after he died, it inspired hope that the official report was an error. Sometimes it was; more often it was not.

CHAPTER THREE

Now We Begin:
Canned Goods Gone Bad

This nation will remain a neutral nation.... I have seen war and ... I hate war.... I hope the United States will keep out of this war. I believe this is wise.
       —Franklin Delano Roosevelt, Fireside Chat, August 14, 1936

Never tolerate the establishment of two continental powers in Europe.
       —Adolf Hitler, prior to invading Poland, 1939

On September 18, 1931, China attacked Japan. A group of middle-grade Japanese officers said so. Chinese saboteurs, they claimed, had tampered with the roadbed of the Japanese-owned South Manchuria Railway, so Japanese troops marched into China to defend the railroad's property against the Chinese.

The incident was manufactured by members of the Japanese officer corps, apparently without approval of the Tokyo regime. While the government debated the issue, wavering between inaction and doing nothing, troops seized the Chinese city of Mukden (now known as Shenyang) and launched a major campaign in northeastern China. It became known as the Mukden Incident. With the civilian government still not taking any action regarding the incident, the Japanese army set up a puppet state. They named it Manchukuo and installed a puppet emperor, Henry P'u-i', who had been China's last emperor but who'd been forced to abdicate in 1912. The Japanese military then claimed that Manchukuo was independent of China and declared it under the protection of the Japanese government.

Japan's takeover of Manchuria was in direct violation of the Kellogg-Briand Pact, which Japan signed in 1928, not that it mattered to the Japanese. It was more important to the rest of the world, but the rest of the world took little notice of the Mukden Incident and even less action to stop it. The world took only slightly more interest in the next international incidents involving Japan.

On December 12, 1937, Japanese warplanes bombed the U.S. Navy gunboat *Panay* along with three American tankers while the ships were at anchor on the Yangtze River about sixty miles north of Nanking. The *Panay* was well identified and flew the American flag. An American sailor and an Italian journalist were killed in the bombing, and fourteen others on board were critically wounded. The Japanese claimed that it was an accident and said they were sorry.

The apology came on December 14, one day after another incident. On December 13, Japanese troops again invaded China, this time attacking the capital city of Nanking. To that date, it was the worst incident of the coming war. The "Rape of Nanking" shocked the world. Japanese planes flew more than a hundred air raids against Nanking. Some of the raids lasted eight hours and demolished much of the city.

Japanese soldiers beheaded Chinese citizens and used live prisoners for bayonet practice. On December 15, a Japanese soldier recorded in his diary: "Recently, when we were very bored, we had some fun killing Chinese. We caught some innocent Chinese and either burned them alive or beat them to death with clubs."

Nanking may be the single largest massacre in world history, but it is one of the least known or studied. Japanese troops slaughtered at least 50,000 Chinese citizens. The number may be much higher, but that is all historians are able to document. Also documented are more than 20,000 rapes inflicted by Japanese soldiers on Chinese women at Nanking.

After Nanking, Japan attacked Shanghai. Oliver J. Caldwell, an American born in China, was an agent with the Office of Strategic Services (OSS), precursor to the CIA, during the war. He wrote:

> For weeks the air trembled with the sound of distant artillery. We saw planes flying between us and the city. [Caldwell and his family] were evacuated from the mountain to a coastal port where we boarded a British passenger ship. An American destroyer convoyed us to the mouth of the Hwangpu River below Shanghai. We arrived in the middle of a tremendous naval and ground attack on the Chinese positions; there appeared to be about one hundred Japanese warships offshore bombarding the Chinese army.

The Japanese went on to capture Shanghai. The American public gave little thought to Japan's invasion of China and the resulting devastation it laid on the Chinese people and their nation.

Not much thought was given to another event in 1937: Adolf Hitler said that Germany was not to blame for World War I. He repudiated the Versailles Treaty, which had ended the Great War. Since Germany wasn't to blame for that war, why not go ahead with another one and not be blamed for it, either? He did. On August 31, 1939, Poland sttacked Germany. Hitler said so.

Eight days earlier, much to the surprise of the world, Germany and the Soviet Union announced a nonaggression pact. For years Adolf Hitler and Josef Stalin had shaken their fists at each other; now they shook hands. With the pact, historian A. J. P. Taylor says, Hitler believed that "he would score another Munich over Poland"—that is, a more or less peaceful dividing up of a neighbor the way the earlier Munich Pact divided up Czechoslovakia. According to Taylor, Stalin thought he had "at any rate escaped an unequal war in the present, and perhaps even avoided it altogether."

Whatever Stalin thought, Hitler had already made other plans. More than five months before the nonaggression pact, on April 3, Hitler's aides had planned Operation Case White, the invasion of Poland. As part of the operation, Gestapo chief Heinrich Müller, Reichsführer-SS Heinrich Himmler, and Obergruppenführer Reinhard Heydrich set up Operation Canned Goods. On August 22, 1939, Hitler told his leading generals, "Close your hearts to pity. Act brutally." The West, he predicted, would not intervene to save Poland.

German SS troops under Col. Alfred Naujocks gathered in the town of Gleiwitz (now Gilwice), on the German side of the border with Poland. On the night of August 31, according to Nazi propaganda, Polish troops marched into Gleiwitz and attacked the town's small German-operated radio station.

As proof of Poland's culpability, Germany later showed off the bodies of several dead Polish soldiers found around the radio station and in a wooded area near the village of Hochlinde. A militaristic Poland, Hitler claimed, had invaded peace-loving Germany.

It was, of course, a fake and didn't really fool anybody. Naujocks's SS troops had taken thirteen German concentration camp inmates from Oranienburg, dressed them in Polish army uniforms, and used them to attack the Germans' own radio station and kill their own people. To avoid any of the "Polish" soldiers blowing the whistle, the SS injected them with poison, leaving their bodies where they could easily be found, "proof" that Poles had attacked Germany. The SS even left one dead inmate inside the radio station studio and faked an announcement claiming that Poland had invaded Germany.

Fake or not, it served Hitler's purpose. Similar fake attacks followed at other points along the border. World War II was under way.

Hitler's invasion of Poland rendered moot President Roosevelt's promise to "remain a neutral nation." The question became not if but rather when the United States would go to war.

Years later, Colonel Naujocks deserted to American troops and testified at the war crime trials in Nuremberg:

> I received the code word for the attack which was to take place at eight o'clock that [August] evening. I had a man laid down at the entrance to the [radio] station. He was alive but unconscious. I could recognize that he was alive only by his breathing. I did not see the gun wounds, but a lot of blood was smeared across his face. We seized the radio station, as ordered, broadcast a speech, fired some shots and left.

Later, Naujocks was imprisoned but escaped. The man who planned the raid that started World War II was never heard from again.

At 4:45 A.M. on September 1, in retaliation for this "unprovoked attack" by the Poles, Germany invaded Poland, pouring across the border men and materiel that just happened to be waiting nearby. At 6 A.M., German planes bombed Warsaw. From the north, south, and west German troops rolled, all heading for the Polish capital. Hitler ordered his troops to "kill without pity or mercy all men, women, and children of the Polish race or language."

William C. Bullitt, the U.S. ambassador in Paris, telephoned President Franklin Roosevelt at the White House with news of the German invasion. "Mr. President," he said, "several German divisions are deep in Polish territory. . . . There are reports of bombers over the city of Warsaw." Roosevelt replied, "Well, Bill, it has come at last. God help us all." It was 2:50 A.M. in Washington, D.C.; the president ordered all navy ships and army commands to be notified at once.

Fifty-three German divisions smashed across the Polish border, pushing back an army half its size. The German army used a tactic called blitzkrieg, a "lightning war," combining rapidly moving ground forces and devastating air attacks: fast motorized infantry, troops on motorcycles, dive-bombers, and tanks. Its fundamental principle was *einheit,* unity, not merely cooperation but integration of armed combat teams at the lowest level. The Germans had practiced this air and ground coordination in the Spanish Civil War in 1936. In worked in Spain, and it worked in Poland.

The blitzkrieg, however, created logistical headaches. The German army quartermaster had to supply quickly advancing columns with everything from food to fuel, weapons to ammunition. As an example, in 1941 it took more than twenty-two tons of fuel to move a Germany army panzer (tank) division a hundred miles; a panzer division included a total of 2,600 other kinds of vehicles, all needing fuel. Which all shows another point about the blitzkrieg: it was so logistically difficult and so expensive, it was used only on rare occasions. Simply put, Germany could not have afforded to blitz all of Europe the way it did Poland in the beginning. It was fear of blitzkrieg that cowed other nations.

To fight off the onrushing German blitzkrieg—in what had to be one of the most fruitless gestures of all time—12 brigades of Polish horse cavalry charged against the German tanks and armored cars. In 1939, the Polish army had a single armored brigade with two battalions of six-ton minitanks. The German army, which under the Versailles Treaty had been limited to 100,000 men, had more than 2 million men under arms, including six heavy tank divisions with more than 2,000 tanks. The German army also had three mountain divisions, four light divisions, and a cavalry brigade.

Germany, which under the Versailles Treaty wasn't even supposed to have an air force, had the largest in the world—1,500 bombers, 1,100 fighter planes, and numerous transport planes. Among its aircraft were the Messerschmitt 109 and 110 fighters, the best in the world. The Polish air force, on the other hand, had 900 aircraft, about half of them biplanes left over from the World War I era.

On the morning of the German invasion, Winston Churchill met with British prime minister Neville Chamberlain. The prime minister, Churchill later wrote, "told me that he saw no hope of averting a war with Germany. . . . " England *had* tried, *had* appeased Hitler, *had* sat by while Czechoslovakia was partitioned at Munich, *had* watched as German troops annexed Austria. But, none of it had worked. Chamberlain mobilized British forces that afternoon.

For two days, both France and Great Britain dithered frantically but did not act. Both nations had promised to protect Poland if it were invaded by *anybody*. Finally, they sent Germany an ultimatum to withdraw and begin peace negotiations. Hitler didn't even bother replying. At 11 A.M. on Sunday, September 3, the ultimatum expired. Fifteen minutes later, British prime minister Chamberlain announced that a state of war existed between Britain and Germany.

That same afternoon, a message was flashed to all British ships: "Winston is back." Churchill, the cigar-chomping, brandy-drinking son of a famous if not particularly wealthy family, was back as First Lord of the Admiralty, a post similar to America's secretary of the navy. It was a job that Churchill first held in 1911. As such, he'd been responsible for making the British navy the best in the world.

In October, a month after Germany invaded Poland, Hitler denounced Churchill as a warmonger and claimed that as for himself, all he had done was redress punitive measures of the 1919 Versailles Treaty.

The night that Britain declared war, the German submarine *U-30* torpedoed and sank the British liner *Athenia,* carrying 1,100 passengers as it passed 200 miles west of the Hebrides. One hundred twelve passengers were lost, including 12 Americans. The European war was under way; only later would it become known as World War II.

On September 5, the United States declared it would stay out of the war despite President Roosevelt's desire to help Poland. Four years earlier, in 1935, Congress had passed the Neutrality Act. In another speech, Roosevelt said of Hitler and Mussolini, "Force is the only language they understand, like bullies." A hero of World War I, Sgt. Alvin York, put it much more vividly if simply: "Hitler and Mussolini jes' need a good whippin'."

Adolf Hitler obviously didn't care what Sergeant York said for that matter. Didn't much care what anyone said. On August 22, 1939, while planning the invasion of Poland, Hitler repeated his pledge to exterminate all Poles. No, their deaths didn't matter, he said; no one would care. As he put it, "After all, who remembers the Armenians?"

We remember Poland, but most of us *have* forgotten the Armenians. Hitler's comment referred to the extermination of thousands of Armenians by Turkey in the seven-year period beginning in 1915. This Turkish genocide was primarily confined to adult Armenians who refused to convert to Islam. Children young enough to forget their Armenian heritage were allowed to live as long as they were reared as Turkish Moslems.

All a generation of Americans remembered about Armenia was that when, as young children, we declined to clean our plates at dinnertime, we were told to think of all the starving Armenians.

In 1921, a year after Turkey took control of Armenia, crop failures were widespread throughout the Soviet Union, due in part to drought, in part to the harsh transition to communal farming, and in part to Moscow's unrealistic economic policies. By midyear, as many as 25 million Soviet citizens faced starvation. Everywhere, crowds of peasants clogged streets and roads, begging for food. An estimated 500,000 children were orphaned by the famine; in the harsh winter of 1921–22, thousands of destitute youngsters plodded through the countryside in a desperate search for something to eat. Many froze to death along roads and in fields and huddled in cities. All together, despite an international relief effort (headed by U.S. president-to-be Herbert Hoover), millions of Russians—and Armenians—starved to death. Think of all the starving Armenians, we were admonished as children.

History must note not everyone starved in 1921. On May 5, French designer Coco Chanel presented to an anxiously waiting world her newest concoction: Chanel No. 5.

Sixteen days after Germany invaded Poland from the west, the Soviet Union sent in its own troops from the east to aid its "blood brothers" living in Poland. By August 28, Warsaw had fallen to German troops, and Germany and the Soviet Union had signed another agreement, this one dividing the spoils of Poland. Between them, the Germans and Soviets took at least 900,000 Polish prisoners. In Lublin, Poland, Hitler established his first Jewish ghetto.

Winston Spencer Churchill sometimes wore jumpsuits that needed only his name embroidered over the pocket to make you want to say: Check my oil and water. At other times, he wore marvelously flamboyant bow ties, right out of a 1920s' Hollywood film, and heavy three-piece suits with gold watch chains flashing across his ever-increasing girth Hats? Unbelievable. Everything from bowlers to peaked naval officers' caps to wide-brimmed sombreros.

Winston Churchill braced the free world and scared the hell out of Hitler. He wasn't all that big, except in the ways that count. He was an alcoholic with an alcoholic's rheumy eyes, a snub nose that seemed too small to let him take a proper breath, and a square chin made even more determined by the huge cigars he constantly gripped between his teeth. A photograph taken of Churchill after he addressed the Canadian Parliament in 1942 shows him glaring pugnaciously at the camera. Just seconds before snapping the picture, the photographer snatched Churchill's cigar out of his hand, and the big man wasn't too happy. Beautiful picture. It's exactly as many would like to picture him—defying devils, disdaining those who dared cross him or his countrymen, ready to take on anyone, anytime.

England, and its sixty-six-year-old prime minister, confounded Adolf Hitler. Nazi Germany rolled over Poland, the Netherlands, France, and most of the rest of Europe. It might have kept on rolling, but Hitler had a love-hate relationship with the land of Shakespeare and Chaucer and the Magna Carta and, of course, Churchill.

Nazi propaganda films portrayed England as a tattered and broken-down lion. They showed Churchill as pudgy, a bit tipsy, scarred, and just barely holding on. Well, the British *were* tattered, but they *weren't* broken down. Winston Churchill *was* a heavy drinker, but like the bulldog he resembled, he had a good grip and wasn't about to let go.

CHAPTER FOUR

Women At Home, Women At War:
Fighting for the Right to be Second Class Citizens

The problem that has no name—which is simply the fact that women are kept from growing to their full capacities—is taking a far greater toll on the physical and mental health of our country than any known disease.
— Betty Naomi Friedan, *The Feminine Mystique*

Suddenly I saw something I hadn't seen before. My sister became Rosie the Riveter. She put a bandanna on her head every day and went down to this organ company that had been converted to war work. . . . It became more than work. There was a sense of mission about it. Her husband was Over There.
— Mike Royko, columnist, *Chicago Tribune*

At the height of World War II, Germany imported maids to keep civilian homes neat and sparkling. Not just high Nazi Party officials' homes, either, but homes of ordinary citizens as well.

At the same time, German laborers still did not have to work nighttime shifts. Plant owners and party officials apparently didn't believe they had to. In comparison, many American plants worked two and sometimes three shifts, turning out aircraft, warships, jeeps, tanks, and just about every other item needed in a two-ocean war. As a result, the American effort produced unprecedented quantities of weapons and other materiel needed to win the war. Even Soviet premier Josef Stalin recognized this. At the 1943 Tehran Conference, Stalin raised a toast to American war efforts: "To American production, without which this war would [be] lost."

American workers didn't suffer from this, at least not financially. Not only did many work their regular day shift but some added either the "swing shift" (4 P.M. to midnight) or the "graveyard shift" (midnight to 8 A.M.). On top of this, wages increased.

The average hourly wage for production workers rose from 66¢ in 1940 to $1.02 in 1945. By 1945, coal miners were paid $1.20 an hour, up from the prewar 85¢. Still, there were problems. In 1945, more than 3 million workers staged more than 4,600 labor strikes. Just as coal miners led in wages, they also led in strikes.

Money may not have been rolling in for the average American worker, but with the cost of living kept low during the war, workers were more than able to keep ahead of inflation. The Great Depression was over.

At the beginning of World War II, a private in the army was paid $21 a month; in the summer of 1942, his pay more than doubled, up to $50 a month. In 1997 dollars that amounted to about $750 a month (in 1997 dollars, officers received about $2,200 a month). U.S. troops were the highest paid in World War II.

The prewar pay for a good, solid civilian job was about $25 a week. Even if an army private sent home half of his wartime salary, it didn't give his wife much to live on. In 1942, Congress passed the Servicemen's Dependents Allowance Act; however, the allowances were insufficient to run a household, especially if the household were in a large city. For many women, that meant getting a job outside of the home, something they had never done before.

On the eve of World War II, women made up only about 25 percent of the American labor force. By 1944, Rosie the Riveter (as women workers were often called no matter what their job) constituted 36 percent of the workforce. Housewives who had never before worked outside the house got their first paychecks. Some "Rosies" left jobs as maids and cooks to work in defense plants. Both private industry and the government actively recruited women workers, and women responded—white, black, and Hispanic, single and married, college educated and school dropouts.

They pumped gas, became lumberjacks, maybe lumberjills, and drove trucks, buses, and tractors. They built bombsights and fighter planes. Most were successful. Most experienced some form of sexism on the job.

At least one Rosie the Riveter was familiar with war. She was the widow of Confederate army general James Longstreet, the man whom Robert E. Lee referred to as his "Old Warhorse." At the age of eighty, Mrs. Longstreet worked at the Bell Aircraft factory in Marietta, Georgia.

In 1944, the Labor Department surveyed Rosie the Riveter and her sisters; 80 percent wanted to stay on the job. When the big show ended, however, many women—often reluctantly—gave up their jobs and returned to domestic life. Their daughters weren't that willing. Rosie and her sisters had set a precedent, and when their daughters came along, the workforce blossomed with women wanting to do it all, and in most cases succeeding.

There really was a Rosie the Riveter—two of them in fact. One was an aircraft worker named Rosina B. Bonavita, who, with a coworker, inserted 3,345 rivets on the wing of a Grumman Avenger in six hours. Another was Rose Will Monroe, who posed for the "We Can Do It!" painting, a woman with her head wrapped in a polka-dot bandanna, sleeves rolled up, muscles flexed, and a determined look on her face. Rose Will Monroe was born in Pulaski County, Kentucky, but moved to the Detroit area during the war. She worked as a riveter building B-24 and B-29 bombers at Ford's Willow Run Aircraft Factory in Ypsilanti, Michigan. She was asked to star in a promotional film about the war and to pose for that painting. "They found Rose," her daughter Vickie Jarvis said. "She was a riveter and she was the one who fit the profile for the 'Rosie the Riveter' song. So she happened to be in the right place at the right time. . . ."

Rose Will Monroe didn't go back to the kitchen when World War II ended. Instead, she became a taxi driver, then ran a beauty shop, and owned her own construction company in Indiana—Rose Builders. She died at the age of seventy-seven in mid-1997.

Probably the most famous, and undoubtedly most unusual, World War II Rosie the Riveter was an attractive brunette who worked in an aircraft plant in Bakersfield, California. Her personal problems began early. Sadly, they also ended early.

As a child, she went from orphanage to orphanage. She asked why, because she knew she had a mother. However, her mother was mentally unstable and had been institutionalized. At age sixteen the girl married an aircraft factory worker named James Dougherty. Not long afterward, she herself went to work in the plant, and it was there that her life began to change.

A photographer from *Yank* magazine took her picture; after it was published, she was offered some small modeling jobs in the area. She divorced her husband, changed her hair color, and changed her name—from Norma Jean Baker to Marilyn Monroe.

• • •

Women fought in the American Revolution dressed as men. During America's Civil War, it was again the only way they could fight. During World War I, the U.S. Navy enlisted women as yeomen clerks. They didn't fight, and after the war, all women were discharged and no more were enlisted. By the time World War II started, the only women in the American armed services were nurses. As one historian points out, they "wore uniforms and were under military control, but they lacked military rank, equal pay, retirement privileges, and veterans' rights."

When World War II broke out in Europe, women's groups, with Eleanor Roosevelt and Congresswoman Edith Nourse Rogers lending their support, demanded that women be allowed to enter the service. In 1941, the War Department began planning for women "so that when it is forced upon us," an official wrote, "we shall be able to run it our way." That "way" kept the Women's Army Auxiliary Corps (WAACs) just that— "auxiliary." For servicewomen, both pay and benefits were inferior to that of servicemen. Only in late 1943 would the WAACs become the WACs, the Women's Army Corps, with full rank, pay, and status.

In May 1942, Gen. George Marshall said, "I want a women's corps right away and I don't want any excuses." He got it. The first director was Col. Oveta Culp Hobby, nicknamed "Miss Spark Plug" because of the way she got things done. She later became the first secretary of the Department of Health, Education, and Welfare.

Then, as now, Congress had mixed feelings about women in the service. They liked them but refused, for example, to give Colonel Hobby a general's star, even though she commanded more troops than were included in an army field corps.

From an initial group of 727 WAACs, the WACs ended the war with 5,746 officers and 93,542 enlisted women, none of whom was allowed to serve in a combat role. About 10,000 served overseas. There were many unfounded rumors about WACs, rumors of rampant sexual promiscuity and women soldiers having to be shipped home from overseas because they were pregnant. Simply, the rumors weren't true. Still, WACs often lived in guarded, barbed-wire compounds to protect them from what the army believed were sex-starved GIs. They moved about in groups, escorted by armed guards, and even went to the movies in formation. About the only off-duty activities allowed them were unit parties.

It didn't help dispel the rumors when General MacArthur's controversial chief of staff, Brig. Gen. Richard Kernes Sutherland, tried to have his part-time secretary and full-time girlfriend commissioned an officer in the WAACs. Apparently, Sutherland didn't even care that she was an Australian. He claimed that MacArthur himself wanted her commissioned, and pushed it through over the objections of Colonel Hobby. Finally, MacArthur heard about it and the lady was sent back to Australia "with all the suddenness of the circus man shot from a cannon."

WACs were technicians, secretaries, supply clerks, and mechanics. At New York's Fulton Fish Market, a sign told of the number of employees then serving in the Armed Forces: "170 and one WAC." By the end of the war, 70 percent of America's soldiers thought and spoke highly of women in the army.

For women in the army air forces, the jumble of acronyms gets confusing: WAAFs, WAFs, and WASPs. WAAFs were members of the Women's Auxiliary Army Air Forces. WAFs were the Women's Auxiliary Ferrying Squadron. WASPs were the Women's Air Force Service Pilots. Both WAFs and WASPs ferried aircraft—both light aircraft and heavy bombers—within the United States and from America to England and Europe. Eventually, all these groups merged into the WASPs.

Sometimes, WASPs towed targets for gunnery practice, an occupation that seems almost as dangerous as combat. Sometimes, they accidentally on purpose got into combat and killed or were killed by the enemy. At least thirty-eight died in training or on ferrying missions.

WAVES were the Women Accepted for Voluntary Emergency Service, the women's navy reserves. It was established in mid-1942, and its numbers grew quickly. By the end of the war, 86,000 women were in the WAVES, not including the more than 11,000 women in the navy nurse corps.

For much of the war, WAVES, other than nurses, were not allowed to serve outside the continental United States. In late 1944 that was changed a bit, when they were permitted to serve in Alaska, Hawaii, and the Caribbean. Not with Adm. Chester W. Nimitz, however. He refused to allow women at his headquarters until, as CINCPAC (Commander-In-Chief Pacific), he moved his headquarters to Guam. Finally, WAVES were assigned to Pearl Harbor.

In 1948, Congress passed the Women's Armed Forces Integration Act. It gave women the prospect of a military career, albeit mainly in nursing, health services, and administrative fields. It would be years before women would be integrated into the mainstream military, and even in the late 1990s they officially are not allowed to serve in combat.

Only one woman has even been awarded the Congressional Medal of Honor. During the Civil War, Dr. Mary Edwards Walker (whom, at first, the army didn't even want to recognize as a surgeon) was awarded the medal. In 1919, the year of her death, Congress tried to take away her award, but she refused to give up her medal. She was buried holding it in her hands. Not until 1977 did Congress reward Dr. Walker the medal, and the U.S. Post Office issued a stamp in her honor.

SPARs were women members of the U.S. Coast Guard, their name derived from the Guard's motto *Semper Paratus*, always ready. About 10,000 SPARs were on active duty when the war ended, stationed either on the mainland or in Alaska or Hawaii.

Women also served in the Marine Corps. About 300 women served in World War I; during the first year of World War II, more than 13,000 joined the ranks in administrative, supply, training, and control tower jobs. At the end of the fighting, there were 820 officers and 17,640 enlisted women marines. They never really had a name such as WAC or WAVE; they were simply women marines or women reservists. Writer and editor H. L. Mencken claimed the navy had its own special term for women marines, though it may have been Mencken himself who coined the phrase: BAMs, or "broad-assed marines."

In England, where young women today often are referred to as "birds," during World War II women in the Royal Navy were called WRNs, pronounced "wrens," as in "birds."

Germany had Hanna Reitsch, a flyer (aviatrix was the term then) who test-flew jets and rocket-propelled aircraft. Reitsch, born in what now is Jelenia Géra, Poland, was the daughter of an ophthalmologist. She was attractive, fair haired, blue eyed, and brave. She also was fanatical over *der Führer,* Adolf Hitler.

Hanna Reitsch was studying medicine but dropped out to take up gliding and flying. She went on to hold several world records—the longest time for a woman in a glider (11½ hours) and the highest altitude for a woman (9,134 feet). In 1934, when helicopters were just coming into being, she demonstrated the aircraft's ability by flying an experimental model inside an enclosed building—a difficult job, considering the swirls of air stirred up by the helicopter. In 1942, she became the only woman to be awarded Germany's Iron Cross.

Reitsch was injured while testing an early jet-propelled aircraft. She emerged from months of hospitalization with such a fear of falling that she couldn't even sit in a chair. Gradually she overcame her fear and resumed her career.

On February 24, 1945, as it became increasingly obvious that the days were numbered for the thousand-year Reich, Hanna Reitsch was called to Hitler's mountaintop hideaway near Salzburg known as Eagle's Nest, in Berchtesgaden. It was just two months before Allied troops would overrun the retreat.

Reitsch wanted to fly a jet-powered V-1 rocket. Normally unmanned, the craft had been flown by two other pilots—both men—but they died when their planes crashed.

"Those other two [pilots]," she told Hitler, "did not know how to bring down fast planes." Hitler believed her, and she made a successful test flight in a V-1. Reitsch, however, wanted more. She wanted to fly a buzz bomb to London, and she proposed a suicide squad to do just that. She even wrote and signed an agreement: "I hearby voluntarily apply to be enrolled in the suicide group as pilot of a human glide-bomb. I fully understand that employment in this aspect will entail my own death."

Plans for manned V-1 flights never materialized, however, when the increasingly erratic Adolf Hitler moved on to other projects.

During the final days of Nazi Germany, Reitsch and Gen. Ritter von Greim flew a single-engine plane into Berlin and made a daring landing on a shell-torn street in order to say good-bye to Hitler. As they flew over the German capital, Soviet troops laying siege to Berlin opened fire on the small plane. Von Greim was wounded, but Hitler appointed him to head the Luftwaffe, replacing the disgraced

Hermann Göring. A few days later, Reitsch flew von Greim out of Berlin.

After Germany surrendered, Hanna Reitsch was captured and interrogated by the Allies. For fifteen months they questioned her, then she was released with no charges brought against her. She returned to her flying career and continued to win championships and set records. In 1962, she opened a school for gliding in the African nation of Ghana.

The Soviet Union had between 800,000 and 1 million women in its army during what it called the "Great Patriotic War," its war with Germany. Women had served in the Soviet air force since 1911 when a Russian princess became a reconnaissance pilot. In 1941, when the air force ran short of pilots, it called on women to form a special women's flying corps. It had three regiments of women pilots, the only all-women air regiments in the world, the Soviets liked to say. One was the 586th Fighter Squadron, which flew Yak-1 fighters, a plane that by 1942 was obsolete. Still, in September 1942, Valaria I. Khomyhakova became the first woman to shoot down an enemy aircraft in aerial combat, downing a German Ju-88 over Saratov on the Volga River in the Soviet Union.

Another Red air force women's unit flew the Pe-2, a light bomber, but it was a difficult plane and called for a lot of muscle to pilot it. The third all-women unit, the 46th Guards Tamansky Night Bomber Air Regiment, flew the Po-2, one of the last biplanes to be built for military service. The night-flying women pilots became known as the "Night Witches"; they flew their final combat mission on May 5, 1945, two days before V-E Day.

Two women Soviet pilots were aces. Lilya Litvak, who shot down twelve German aircraft, was awarded the Order of the Red Banner and the Order of the Patriotic War. She died in September 1943 when her own plane was shot down.

Katya Budanova was the Soviet Union's second-highest-scoring female fighter pilot. For flying sixty-six combat missions during the Battle of Stalingrad in 1942 and shooting down eleven German aircraft during the war, she became a Hero of the Soviet Union.

CHAPTER FIVE

The Children of War:
When Daddy Went Away

We were on our way to the movies on Sunday afternoon. I was twelve at the time.... [The] car radio was on. "Oh my God!" my father said. "Pearl Harbor!" I said, "What's a Pearl Harbor?"

—Jean Bartlett, quoted in Studs Terkel, *The Good War*

This war we are fighting now is not a new thing. In 1776, in 1812, in 1917, earlier generations of Americans fought the very same battles we are fighting now. Because they won those battles, you today have something for which to fight. The end of this war will not mark the end of the fight of the democratic peoples for a free way of life.

—Lyle M. Spencer and Robert K. Burns, *Youth Goes to War*

The war years were full of Memorial Day music, Fourth of July speeches, and quiet moments on Armistice Day. A people who had struggled through the Great Depression now watched newsreels, read newspapers, and nervously listened to their radios. "Good evening, Mr. and Mrs. North America and all the ships at sea. Let's go to press!" "This . . . is London." Huddled by the radio, Americans listened to Walter Winchell and Edward R. Murrow. Don't forget H. V. Kaltenborn and Gabriel Heater.

By the hundreds of thousands, husbands and brothers, children and fathers were called to go where no one was really certain and to stay for how long was anybody's guess. An intensity unknown for years enveloped the nation. Moments of happiness were mixed with times of fear; periods of patriotic enthusiasm were matched with intervals of nail-biting concern.

The horror of war was seen on newsreel films and examined in the graphic pages of *Life* and *Look* magazines; the radio amplified it. "Mom," the question went, "what was on the radio before the war started?"

Radio was an important source of news for adults during World War II. For good little boys and girls, it was a time when make-believe adventure heroes chased down Nazi spies, fought the war in exotic places, and saved democracy for us all.

Radios that were tuned in to Kaltenborn and Murrow by parents were tuned in by children to *Tom Mix, Little Orphan Annie, Captain Marvel, The Shadow, Hop Harrigan,* and *Terry and the Pirates.* Radio adventure shows moralized on good and evil and proved to young Americans how truth and justice would prevail, even if it took several serial chapters to do it. Clearly, the Japanese and the Germans were the bad guys; Americans and the English (along with an assortment of others) were the good guys. No doubt about it.

Radio exhorted children to confront the enemy, to combat waste, and to collect scrap materials. Before confronting the Nazis and Japanese, while sprawled on the floor in front of the Philco or Stromberg Carlson or RCA Victor, American children were told that Ovaltine was the drink for "young, red-blooded Americans." They were told to "Eat Wheaties, the Breakfast of Champions." Captain Midnight had children sending away cereal box tops for a secret decoder ring, which decoded a message telling them to "Buy War Bonds," not to mention buying more cereal. "If your grocer doesn't carry Kellogg's Pep, ask him to order it." Superman, after all, ate Kellogg's Pep. "Look! Up in the air! It's a bird, it's a plane, it's Superman!"

A study conducted in the 1940s showed that children between the ages of four and seven began "to take an active, continuous interest in radio entertainment." By six, a child was "a habitual listener" who would "enter freely into fantasy and whimsy" in which radio was "an exciting realm for imaginative wanderings."

While Daddy was away fighting the war and Mom off riveting B-17 Bombers, wartime radio stimulated childish imaginations. Too much so, some psychologists and educators believed. They, along with other radio critics, complained there was too much murder, too much robbery, sabotage and arson, even too much drug peddling. Radio sound effects may sound weak and tinny to 1990s' ears, but to those in the 1940s, they often were too real, leaving "nothing to the imaginations."

It wasn't just young boys, either. "On a whole," a survey reported, "girls were almost as interested in crime and mystery shows as boys." Girls, however, as usual got slighted. There was *Little Orphan Annie,* but most boys liked her as well. *Jack Armstrong—All-American Boy* had his all-American sidekick girl, and later on there was a *Mary Marvel* to go along with the Captain. Usually, however, "superheroes and su-persleuths" were only one sex: male. Adult females had *Our Gal Sun-day*, *Ma Perkins*, and *Stella Dallas*, but there were no heroines for the teen or preteen set.

On the East and West Coasts and near defense production areas, children sometimes wore I.D. tags. In the San Francisco area, the tags were stamped with numbers, and local civil defense officials kept lists of the numbers in the event of an evacuation. New York City kids not only wore dog tags, they were also fingerprinted.

Children in wartime boom areas were given special inoculations, because who knows what disease the newcomers brought in with them? In Hawaii, where another Japanese attack was always a con-cern, youngsters were issued gas masks, and subjected to occasional testing. Their classrooms would be filled with tear gas. The students would be told to quickly put on their masks so an army officer could check the fit. Usually, as the children filed out of the room, the of-ficer would tell them to open their masks to get a whiff of the tear gas, just so they'd know how it smelled.

To a child, the war often came in stages. Dad (or less often Mom) would hear about a job in some strange city and leave home to find work. For a while, the family would stay behind until Dad or Mom found a place for them to be together again. Once in a new city, the family likely as not it would live in a crowded apartment or a house still being built even as they moved in. In these new communities, streets would, at best, be mud puddles or clouds of dust.

Kids are tough, and such things as dust and mud don't matter that much. At least the family would be together; at least Dad was safe at home until he was called off to fight the war. Many kids, of course, were not so safe, physically or emotionally. Those old enough to know about the war faced the trauma of losing a parent to the fight-ing. They heard their parents talk about the draft, and often they worried as much as their parents.

Early in the draft, being married kept a man on the civilian side of life. Sometimes, couples who had dated each other before the war were worried about surviving the coming fight and pushed ahead their plans for marriage. If a couple married too soon after Pearl Harbor, however, the local draft board might look closely at the relationship. The rule of thumb was that the couple had to be "courting" for at least a year if the marriage was to carry any weight with the draft board.

The marriage boom led to the baby boom. From 1940 to 1950, America's population increased 13.7 percent; from 1950 to 1960 there was another 18.8 percent jump.

While men might marry to avoid the draft, women might marry to avoid spinsterhood. Supposedly, after all, America's prime supply of men was going off to war. "If this shortage keeps up," one young woman said, "the government will have to start rationing husbands." As sociologist James H. S. Bossard put it in 1943, "Many women are today picking husbands like they shop on bargain days. They do not exactly want the article which is selling so rapidly, but if they do not buy it, someone else will, and besides, one may need it later on."

"War marriages," declared many, including President Roosevelt's wife, Eleanor, "were doomed to divorce." Mrs. Roosevelt advised college women not to enter into a hasty marriage simply "because their beau was going into the army." Instead, she suggested, women should remain at school where they could "gear their present work to real preparation for the future."

Not that any sociologist or president's wife ever stopped anybody from marrying. Soldiers, sailors, and airmen married hometown girls or girls they met at dances organized by the Salvation Army, the YMCA, or the USO. They married them whether in the States or overseas, with or without the government's permission. Just as many feared, quickie marriages often did lead to quickie divorce. In rare cases, they also led to polygamy. Partners of either sex occasionally married someone else without the niceties of a divorce.

For the first three years of the Selective Service system's operation, fathers were classified as III-A and protected from induction. To ensure something approaching a nonmarried military, while also ensuring adequate numbers, draft boards lowered the draft age and began drafting men who were "less well qualified"—both physically and educationally—rather than induct fathers. Politicians of the day suggested that the Selective Service system should fill its quotas by drafting "unmarried men who shun work and are found in pool rooms, barrel houses, and on the highways and byways. . . . "

It wasn't enough. By late 1943, the Selective Service system abolished class III-A and began inducting fathers. First to go were those fathers whose children were conceived *after* Pearl Harbor. If there was any question, draft boards demanded that the prospective draftee get a note from his doctor, or at least his wife's doctor, stating when the child or children were conceived. By April 1944, more than half of all inductees were fathers.

This meant that a lot of military wives and children were left at home. In mid-1945, the Office of Dependency Benefits awarded family allowances to 2.8 million army wives, plus 1.8 million children. Another 3.8 million men were in the navy and marines, with about 35 percent of them married, so there were an additional 1,350,000 navy and Marine Corps wives and 900,000 children also receiving benefits. At about the time the war in Europe was winding down, the United States had 5,150,000 military wives and 2.7 million children wondering when daddy was coming home.

The wives, of course, did more than sit and wonder. Some went to work, but with Mom gone, what happened to Baby? And here the story gets rough to tell, because in World War II, as in all other wars, it was Baby who suffered most.

In the October 1943 issue of *Woman's Home Companion* magazine, Gretta Palmer put it simply, "Pregnancy is America's Number One industrial health problem today." With the baby boom in full swing, ways had to be found to deal with children.

Occasionally, Baby was aborted, a procedure illegal in the United States at the time but nonetheless often carried out. Dr. Morris Fishbein, one-time head of the American Medical Association, estimated that during the first two years of World War II, abortions increased by 20 to 40 percent. As one midwife-abortionist admitted, "There's an abortion boom. . . . I had 45 patients on Saturday. The girls like Saturday because that gives them the weekend to rest. They come here straight from the factory, in slacks and overalls."

Abortion wasn't talked about in public, but among working women it was a major issue. As a woman worker at a Buffalo, New York, aircraft plant put it: "There are only three subjects we discuss in the women's rest room—'my operation'; how to keep from getting pregnant if you aren't; how to get rid of the baby if you are."

Usually, illegal abortions were performed under the worst possible conditions, and not surprisingly, the death rate from abortions was high, 17 percent in 1942.

In addition to abortion, the later war years saw a growth in the black market sale of babies. The price among "baby brokers" was up to $2,000 in some markets, much lower in others. During World War II, fewer than half of the states had laws to prosecute baby brokers. The director of the California Division of Social Welfare at the time admitted that San Francisco had one of the highest numbers of black market babies, both among married and unmarried women: "It is the old, old story all over again. The sweethearts of servicemen will come to San Francisco for a 'last good-bye.' They will remain here to have their babies and leave them before they return to their hometowns."

Some who sold their babies were married but not to the baby's father. Frequently, the husband was overseas, and the woman tried to place the baby in a good home, whether through an adoption agency or by selling the child to another family before her husband found out about it. Baby brokers advertised openly.

In many respects, World War II was the "grandparents' war." With father off to the war and mother off to the factory, children on the home front often were left with grandmother and grandfather. Grandma nourished and cared for the children, while Grandpa taught the boys how to play baseball, and read comics to girls.

It was a solution long acceptable to African-Americans; now it became commonplace for other ethnic groups.

For families where dad was still at home, *Parents* magazine had a suggestion: "Let your child invite Jimmy or Jane whose father is overseas to dinner one night. . . . Competent as any mother may be to direct her child's energies and activities, there is simply no escaping the fact that when a man takes a hand in the youngsters' games, a sort of rough and ready masculinity adds to the fun."

Where there was no grandparent, working mothers had few choices: leave the children to fend for themselves or put them in day-care centers. Women who had been skeptical about day-care before the war now saw it as a viable and satisfactory answer. As the war progressed, public subsidization of day care rose to a point where, in late

1944, a woman could leave her two-year-old child at a center and pay only fifty cents a day. Included in the price were lunch, morning, and afternoon snacks.

The government struggled on both sides of the child-care issue. The Federal Works Agency, which controlled funds given to areas where defense plants greatly increased the population (it was called the Lanham Act), favored group-care facilities. On the other hand, the Federal Security Agency, along with the Children's Bureau and the U.S. Office of Education, opposed day care. Opponents warned that children required full-time mothers who could give youngsters "a push here and a lift there." "There is a need," a spokesperson claimed, "for day to day adjustment. . . . If the mother works, this must be regarded as insoluble—[his] care should not be sacrificed to anything."

In 1943, Democratic senator Elbert Thomas of Utah introduced a bill to end the Federal Works Agency's group child-care programs and to finance foster homes and individual child-care plans on a dollar-for-dollar basis with states. Under Senator Thomas's bill, the states, not the localities, would be responsible for initiating child care. The Senate passed the bill, but the House turned it down before it could get out of committee. The purse strings remained with federal, not local, authorities.

By 1944, enrollment in federally funded day-care centers was rising, thanks to a decision to make funds available for the care of children under two years old. By early May, 2,512 federally funded child-care agencies were in operation, enrolling 87,406 children. By July, the numbers were even higher—3,102 centers with 129,357 children enrolled.

It wasn't just the federal government doing the job, either. One of the most innovative ideas came from private industry, specifically Edgar F. Kaiser, whose father, Henry J. Kaiser, headed up steel and aluminum mills as well as shipyards in Portland, Oregon. The younger Kaiser was the manager of two of the shipyards, employing about 25,000 women. Already he'd built a "company town," Vanport City, just outside Portland. It was one of the country's largest civilian housing projects of the war.

Kaiser turned to child-development experts to help build day-care facilities, constructing them "not out in the community, but right at the entrance to the shipyards, convenient to mothers on their way to and from work." Centers had classrooms, fully staffed kitchens, wading pools for the children, benches where parents could sit and visit their children during breaks, and large windows where youngsters could see where their mother worked. Trained workers and nurses cared for the children. The centers not only prepared meals for the children while they were there, they cooked take-home meals for mothers to pick up as they came off their shift; the cost per portion was fifty cents.

Kaiser and his staff ran the centers, with the company adding the costs of operating them (after deducting a nominal sum paid by the mothers) to its cost-plus fee contracts with the government. The only problem, it seems, was that fewer mothers took advantage of the centers than had been hoped for and planned. The two centers had a combined peak enrollment of 1,005, far short of the estimated 1,125-person enrollment for each center. Why the centers weren't greater utilized by Kaiser's Rosie the Riveter isn't certain.

Federal Bureau of Investigation director J. Edgar Hoover got into the act and claimed women were rejecting their children by working outside the home. "Millions of Americans," he wrote in 1943, "are not fighting or moving toward the battlefronts, [they] labor on day, night, and midnight shifts in factories," often leaving children unattended at home. Hoover believed these children faced a dismal future of "stumbling into the dreaded maze of delinquency and disease, of reformatory and prison, or, if they are not apprehended, of maiming and plundering. America's leaders must realize . . . as should every American that boys and girls are our most priceless national asset, that their preservation is as important as any objective in this war."

By early 1944, 1,360,000 American women were working outside the home while their husbands were in the service. Of this number, 280,000 had children under the age of 10.

Still, more women remained at home rather than join Rosie the Riveter. In 1941, about 30 million women were homemakers with no outside employment. "The housewife," says historian D'Ann Campbell, "not the WAC or the riveter, was the model woman" in the 1940s.

Not all kids were lucky enough to stay with grandma or go to a day-care center. World War II saw a sharp rise in the number of "latchkey" children, youngsters who took care of themselves and, in many instances, took care of other children as well.

Agnes E. Meyer, the journalist wife of the *Washington Post* publisher, toured the nation to report on America at war. It was, she wrote, a "journey through chaos."

> In Los Angeles a social worker counted 45 infants locked in cars in a single parking lot while their mothers were at work in war plants. Older children in many cities sit in movies, seeing the same film over and over again until mother comes off the evening "swing" shift and picks them up. Some children of working parents are locked in their homes, others locked out.

Sometimes, children six to seven years of age were kept out of school to take care of younger siblings.

Finally, there was the last-ditch method. If grandparents or day-care centers were not available, working mothers sometimes gave their children to orphanages.

The 1940s was a time of jingoism, nationalism, and patriotism—patriotism that today often sounds a bit corny. The Council Against Intolerance in America created a poster with a young woman proudly holding an American flag: "One Nation—Indivisible 1943–1944." Another read, "We CAN'T win this war without sacrifice on the home front, too." A political campaign-style button showed Uncle Sam hanging Hitler: "Let's Pull Together." Other buttons read, "To Hell with *Hitler*" and "Kick 'em in the Axis." And everywhere, "Remember Pearl Harbor—Buy War Bonds." The Office of War Information, which replaced an agency with an even more telling title—the Office of Facts and Figures—produced a radio program titled "You Can't Do Business With Hitler."

In the book *Youth Goes to War,* published in 1943, authors Lyle M. Spencer and Robert K. Burns, of the Science Research Associates, wrote:

> World War II started . . . when the Mikado's Nipponese legions first attacked the peaceful Chinese. [Now]we make more guns, tanks, shells, bullets, and other munitions than they

do. . . . We have something else the Axis warlords do not have—plenty of *food*. We may ration some of it to reduce waste and keep the supply even all around, but there will be no real hunger to cripple the workers in the armies and factories of America.

The book assured youngsters that "You are on *loan* to your school until you are prepared for a war job." The youth of the 1940s could prepare for the big jobs ahead by selling War Bonds, working with the Victory Corps to raise crops and livestock, and helping in salvage drives.

For those who might not make it into the military, *Youth Goes to War* outlined the possibilities of service on the home front. "Where Do You Fit?" it asked.

With but few exceptions, all boys will be inducted for service soon after they reach the minimum fighting age of eighteen. Many will volunteer at seventeen. This means that most American boys will have to postpone their peacetime career dreams for the duration and buckle down to mastering the fighting tools of war.

Girls, on the other hand, "for the most part will be concerned with home front war work. . . ." Young girls could look forward not only to the traditional homemaker role but to jobs in industry. "The sight of women driving transcontinental trucks. . . or working on giant railroad locomotives would have been strange indeed a few short months ago. . . ." Not in the new world of the 1940s. Thousands of women are "invading the transportation field," it said, showing a decidedly hefty woman about to step into the driver's compartment of an over-the-road truck. Other women, decidedly not hefty, were shown as nurses. "Most hospitals," the book claimed, "are clamoring for girls to go into nurses' training, so that they can take the places of the nurses who have entered the Army and Navy."

Winning the war will be difficult, the book reminded youngsters.

Though the early odds in this war may be against us, we will not be stopped. The Nazi schools have drilled their goose-step-ping German youth long and hard in preparation for this war. The Fascist groups of Italian boys have grown into black-shirted warriors, trained by Mussolini with but one object in mind— to destroy us. And the treacherous rulers of Japan plotted long for the chance to deliver the smashing sneak blow at Pearl Harbor. . . .

Upon the youth of today depends the kind of world we will live in tomorrow. You will be in the driver's seat. What will you do with this responsibility?

During World War II, young children heard their parents rage against the dirty sons-of-bitch Nazis in Europe and the yellow-bellied-Japs who bombed Pearl Harbor. Parents used racist stereotypes, and children followed right along, copying them epithet for epithet. "I'd like to take a machine gun to those bastards," a child would hear a drunken neighbor say, and when it came time to play, the child took a toy machine gun to imaginary enemies, those "yellow-bellied sons of bitches."

Across the country, boys improvised toy weapons because commercially made toy guns were in short supply; metal and rubber were needed for war and were scarce. Often with the help of a parent, they built guns out of cardboard, wood, tree branches, and clothespins. Walkie-talkies (actually, handy talkies) printed on cereal boxes were cut out and became "real" with string hung between corn flakes and puffed rice.

No longer did children play Cowboys and Indians or even Cops and Robbers. Now, they "shot up" Nazis with wooden guns and "bombed" Japs trying to invade their hometowns. In some areas, whole gangs divided up to play "guns," roaming streets and alleys, taking part in pretend street fights just as their fathers and uncles and brothers took part in real ones. One side would be the Americans and the other would be the "dirty Japs" or the "rotten Nazis." Younger sisters and girls next door played nurses.

Boys tossed beanbag grenades at cardboard Hitlers, climbed trees and shouted "Bombs away!" as they released water-filled balloons on unsuspecting enemies. "Shoot the Japs!" "Bomb the Nazis!" Too late, psychologists and child guidance experts tried to discourage the activity.

In *Daddy Goes to War*, historian William M. Tuttle, Jr., quotes letters and nursery rhymes and advertising signs:

> Whistle while you work,
> Hitler is a jerk.
> Mussolini is a weeny,
> And Tojo is a jerk.

> Three blind rats, three blind rats,
> Hitler, Benito and the Jap.

> Slap
> The Jap
> With
> Iron
> Scrap
> Burma-Shave.

In one southern city, just as the war ended, a gang of more than a hundred young boys planned and executed a two-day "battle," using an abandoned and half-demolished house as headquarters, sneaking across overgrown fields to capture the enemy's fort—last year's Christmas trees carefully hoarded and stacked. When the battle was over and the winner declared, the dead came alive and both sides celebrated by setting fire to the Christmas tree fort. The year-old trees were brown, except for one that some enterprising resident had painted white; it stood as the centerpiece of the fort and was lit first.

Neighbors wandered out into the night and stood gossiping in the light of the burning trees. Fire- and policemen showed up, and they joined the gossiping crowd.

It was a helluva time, folks

It was the great "Battle" of the war, and like World War II itself, it came to an end.

CHAPTER SIX

Rationing America:
Getting Along With Less

Use it up, wear it out;
Make it do, or do without.

—New England maxim

Spartan simplicity must be observed. Nothing will be done merely because
it contributes to beauty, convenience, comfort, or prestige.
—Office of the chief signal officer, U.S. Army

The old saying is it "Takes a heap of living to make a house a home." It certainly took a large heap of food to keep the military going in World War II. While army and marine troops in the field had to make do with an alphabet of rations, our boys at sea ate well. Take the stores on board a U.S. battleship during World War II. For the crew of about 2,000 officers and men, two-weeks' rations ran something like this: 1,500 pounds of smoked ham; 20,000 pounds of frozen beef; 4,000 pounds of frozen veal; 500 pounds of luncheon meat; 1,000 pounds of frozen fish; 1,000 pounds of rhubarb; 37,000 eggs; 2,400 pounds of lemons (to make the navy's popular lemon pie); 1,700 pounds of cucumbers; 2,400 pounds of lettuce; and 1,800 pounds of sweet potatoes. Add to that several tons of ice cream and two to four tons of coffee to wash it all down. The records don't list it, but sick bay must surely have stocked bicarbonate of soda by the hundreds of pounds.

In 1934, the Henningsen Company opened an egg-drying plant in Denison, Texas. It was a seasonal, part-time operation, because the market then was confined to a few large baking companies. Beginning in March 1941, with the enactment of the Lend-Lease program, Great Britain became the Henningsen Company's largest customer. Business boomed. By the end of 1941, Denison, Texas, proclaimed itself the "Egg Breaking Capital of the World." The company's plants ran day and night, with shifts of workers breaking 1.5 million eggs a day on average. According to historian Lee Kennett, "Some of the workers were so adept that they could break two eggs in each hand."

Soon, the Henningsen Company's products went not just to Great Britain, but to the United States military. Out of Denison, Texas, came the illustrious, if not beloved, powdered egg.

In August 1941, the U.S. government established the Office of Price Administration (OPA), which the following year became an independent agency. Effective May 1942, OPA froze prices on almost all everyday goods, including about 60 percent of food items. It took a presidential directive to give the OPA rationing authority, a power that Congress only reluctantly approved.

The word *rationing* comes from the Latin *ratio;* the idea was to provide for fair distribution at home while guaranteeing supplies to the war effort. Generally it worked. Only seldom were there any real shortages. Before the war was over, the government had rationed nearly everything. It may be the most remembered consequence of the war for many Americans.

In the beginning, rationing on the home front was on a voluntary basis, but early in the war the government got serious about it. In May 1942, the OPA issued "War Ration Book One," dictating how much any one person could buy of any one item. One member of the family was supposed to be in charge of the family's ration books. Each book came with instructions and a severe warning: "Punishments ranging as high as *Ten Years' Imprisonment or $10,000 fine, or Both* may be imposed under United States Statutes for violation thereof arising out of infractions of Rationing Orders and Regulations." There were, needless to say, numerous attempts to counterfeit ration stamps.

Sugar was the first food item to be rationed, and it remained rationed until the end of the war. A lot of sugar went to provide Coca-Cola for the military. The company's president, Robert Woodruff, had pledged, "We will see that every man in uniform gets a bottle of Coca-Cola for five cents, wherever he is and whatever it costs." It's estimated that American military personnel drank 10 million bottles of Coca-Cola. Coke was so popular that when the army stepped ashore in North Africa in late 1942, it took along several fully equipped bottling plants to quench the GIs' thirst. The British didn't particularly like Coca-Cola, and they liked even less the idea of filling valuable cargo space with the soft drink.

Coffee required ships to get it from Brazil to America, and coffee became the next to be rationed in November 1942. The OPA pulled coffee stamps from ration books issued to children under age 15, but by July of the following year, coffee was back on the shelves. It remained in short supply, however, for the duration.

Prices on canned meats and fish were frozen in early 1943, about the same time that the OPA issued "War Ration Book Two." That one contained blue and red stamps, each worth ten "points." Red stamps were for meat, cheese, butter, canned milk, and canned fish. Blue stamps were for processed food—canned vegetables, juices, baby food, and dried fruit. A pound of ham might cost fifty-one cents and eight points. Baked beans might carry a ten-point sign along with the price. Chicken was not rationed. You knew you were buying black market meat if the dollar and cents price remained the same but it took fewer ration points to make the purchase.

If you were hospitalized for a period longer than ten days, you were expected to turn your ration books over to the person in charge of the facility. If a family member died, his or her ration book was to be returned to the OPA.

Used fat was valued for its glycerine, which was used in manufacturing powder, dynamite, paint, tanning leather, and even the Plexiglas windows of military planes. You could earn meat and cheese points by saving fats, such as cooking grease, and turning them in to your local butcher: two extra red points for every pound of meat drippings and other fat turned in. An OPA recommendation read: "Remember to fry out trimmings cut from your meat. Chunks of fat should be fried out and strained. Remember, too, that odors do not affect the glycerine properties. The fact that onions or fish have been cooked in the fat makes no difference. Pour into any clean tin can, keep it cool and take it to your meat dealer when a pound or more has been accumulated." Over time, the OPA came out with red and blue fiber tokens to take the place of the stamps. One token equaled one stamp and could be used over and over at an annual savings to the government printing office of $35 million.

Nonfood items were also rationed and the first one was rubber. After the Japanese seized rubber plantations, which supplied 90 percent of America's raw rubber, farmers in California and Texas tried growing a plant called guayule, the seeds of which were used in making synthetic latex. By the end of the war, more than 200,000 acres of guayule had been planted and 1,500 tons of "rubber" were made from the seed oil. The Russian dandelion, Kok Sagyz, was grown in some areas and turned into a rubberlike substance.

The government called on Americans to contribute every bit of scrap rubber possible. President Roosevelt asked for "old tires, old rubber raincoats, old garden hose, rubber shoes, bathing caps, gloves—whatever you have that is made of rubber." To conserve tires not currently being used, the government asked the owners to turn them in under the Idle Tire Purchase Plan. The OPA issued leaflets on "What You Must Do to Qualify for Gasoline and Tires," which included having your tires inspected between December 1, 1942, and January 31, 1943: "You will be denied Mileage Rations if you or anyone in your household owns any passenger tires (including scrap tires) not mounted on motor vehicles or equipment. You must sell or give such tires to the Government under the Idle Tire Purchase Plan."

Rationing boards could deny anyone rubber or gasoline: "If you do not have your Tire Inspection Record signed during every inspection period. If you abuse your tires and tubes. If you violate the 35 miles-per-hour speed limit. If the serial numbers on your tires are not the same as those on your Tire Inspection Record, unless you have been authorized to buy another tire and have Part D of a Tire Certificate showing any serial number not listed."

Used golf balls were collected for recycling, and baseballs "went to war." Prewar baseballs used cork centers, but wartime baseballs substituted less precious rubber for the even more precious cork. The rubber for baseballs came from old golf balls.

Beginning in December 1942 gasoline was rationed. The OPA issued various types of rationing stickers (to be affixed to the car's windshield) for different occupations or auto uses. The "A" sticker (issued to owners whose use of their cars was nonessential) was good for four gallons of gas per week, but that dropped to three as the war continued. Anyone driving with an "A" sticker who was found "pleasure driving" was penalized by the loss of the gas ration. Police found the penalty almost impossible to enforce, so the ban against pleasure driving was lifted eight months later. The "B" sticker was for essential driving—traveling salesmen were included as "B" sticker drivers—and gave a supplemental allowance. "C" stickers went to physicians, ministers, and mail carriers; because "C" provided the largest ration of gasoline for personal use, they were the most widely counterfeited and sold on the black market. Truckers used "T" stickers, with unlimited fuel available. Members of Congress and some others received "X" stickers, indicating that they were Very Important People and could buy as much gasoline as they wanted. The OPA had estimated that about 1 percent of the nation's driving population would need "X" stickers; in Washington, D.C., alone, 12 percent of the city's population claimed them. OPA administrator Leon Henderson had only an "A" card himself (he and Eleanor Roosevelt had conspicuously applied for them) and because the number of "X" card holders was so high, Henderson made their names public. Several hundred people reassessed their needs and returned their "X" cards.

Americans had not yet grown used to hopping in the car and driving off to the shopping mall (indeed, there were no shopping malls in the 1940s) or around the block for an ice cream cone. They seldom took the family on Sunday afternoon drives or cross-country vacations by car; a July 1943 Minnesota Tourist Bureau ad suggested that people "Select a cabin in the woods. Stay put! Fish, canoe, sail and swim in the waters of a Minnesota lake."

Intercity buses, railroads, and airplanes became popular modes of transportation. In addition, people joined driving clubs, a term that changed to "car pools."

With tires and gasoline rationed, automobile production was stopped in early 1942. The supply of new cars dried up quickly, and former auto dealerships turned their attention toward auto repairs. If they could get the parts to do the job.

Metal containers for many goods were replaced by cardboard boxes and glass bottles. Just prior to the war, beer began to be sold in cans; brewers quickly went back to glass bottles, which could be more easily recycled. You couldn't buy a new bird cage, lobster forks, even a spittoon. They were considered nonessential. Beginning in 1944, even beer and whiskey grew scarce.

When the navy needed rope for its ship hawsers, the government paid farmers to grow *Cannabis sativa* to make hemp. More than 50,000 acres of *Cannabis,* better known as marijuana, were grown under government orders.

Save, salvage, and survive: "Get In The Scrap: Save Waste Paper and Old Rags." Old newspapers were collected. Washed and flattened tin cans were turned in. In one month, women donated 626,127 pounds of stockings for use in parachutes.

Rationing changed fashion styles. Women's slacks were slimmer and had no cuffs; blouses might have short sleeves and no sash, saving four or five yards of material. Men's outlandish zoot suits were out before a cool cat could say hubba hubba to a slick chick.

World War I cannon that once graced the front yards of VFW posts and county courtyard squares went to the World War II scrap pile. Bicycles and toy cars were melted down for the war effort. America saw a true reversal of a Bible verse. Men beat their plowshares into swords, their pruning hooks into spears. Nations lifted up their swords against other nations; they learned war forevermore.

CHAPTER SEVEN

Rendezvous With Death:
Confidence Gained, A Generation Lost

I know war as few other men now living know it, and nothing to me is more revolting.
— General of the Army Douglas MacArthur,
April 19, 1951, address to Congress

Cry "Havoc!" and let slip the dogs of War.
— William Shakespeare, *Julius Caesar*, III, i

Economic superiority does not necessarily mean victory in war. The United States confidently approached World War II, but initially it wasn't certain we could do what we eventually succeeded in doing.

Many believed that America's economy, once we began producing war goods, could outproduce any other nation on Earth. Some who believed this, however, obviously forgot that the nation, along with much of the rest of the world, was still clawing its way out of the Great Depression; for years, the American economy had failed to vault the nation out of Wall Street's gigantic collapse. Now it was to produce a war victory? Madness.

Many forgot also that, in World War I, it wasn't the United States that produced most of the war materiel for the fight against Germany; it was England and France. Overconfident Americans failed to remember that tens of thousands of troop uniforms in the Great War bore labels that read "Made in England." Clearly, in that War to End All Wars, the United States did *not* outproduce Germany. In fact, the last time the United States *had* managed to perform the economic task of outproducing an enemy was when the Union defeated the Confederacy.

As 1941 drew to a close, the United States readied itself for war. The nation shipped so many of its goods on Lend-Lease to England, France, and even the Soviet Union that many of our own troops lacked weapons. Some new GIs trained with broomsticks as make-believe rifles and used eggs in place of grenades. They pretended to fire fake cannons and fought fantasy battles against old trucks carrying signs that read "TANK." The trucks themselves likely were four-cylinder vehicles left over from World War I. Real rifles and cannon and tanks were still on the assembly lines, the men were told. When they didn't have pistols, some American officers took to stuffing rolls of toilet paper into their holsters. "Surrender, or I'll...."

Four months prior to Pearl Harbor, Congress debated whether to pass a one-year renewal of the draft law. Hoping they'd be going home soon, short-timers in the army wrote on barracks walls: "OHIO," meaning "Over the Hill In October." The one-year draft extension passed by one vote.

Well, we got there. We truly did outproduce the enemy, but it took us a while. In the beginning we didn't have enough trained soldiers much less enough troops. There weren't enough men to turn *into* trained soldiers. (This was, of course, generations before the country began considering women as combat capable.)

Let's put it into numbers. In mid-1941, President Roosevelt asked the War Department to determine how many men it would take to win the war in Europe. At the time he thought only about an Atlantic war, not one in the Pacific Ocean as well. Roosevelt wanted a "Hitler first" strategy, in which nations allied against Germany would engage and defeat Nazi troops before they could be redeployed from their eastern-front war with the Soviet Union. FDR wanted the War Department's best guess for "overall production requirements [needed] to defeat our potential enemies."

The job of coming up with this best guess went to an officer on the General Staff, Maj. Albert Coady Wedemeyer, the Omaha-born son of parents who had emigrated from Hannover, Germany. Wedemeyer graduated 270th in 285 in the class of 1919 at the U.S. Military Academy, served in China for a couple of years, then attended the *Kriegsakademie*, Germany's war college. Forty-four years old, tall, suave, able, and ambitious, Wedemeyer was married to the daughter of Lt. Gen. Stanley D. Embick, the head of the Defense Commission. Wedemeyer worked closely with his father-in-law in preparing what was unofficially known as the Victory Plan. Only four copies existed and had to be signed for before being read.

Unfortunately, one of the four copies fell into the hands of Robert R. McCormick, publisher of the anti-Roosevelt *Chicago Tribune*. On December 5, 1941, two days before you-know-what, the *Trib* printed the salient points of the newly promoted Lieutenant Colonel Wedemeyer's plans, claiming Roosevelt was planning to go to war. True but not quite the way the *Trib* put it.

All of this—son of German immigrants, recent graduate of the German war college, the Victory Plan leaked to the press—made Albert Wedemeyer look suspicious enough to warrant an FBI investigation into, at best, lax security, and, at worse, spying. Investigators never discovered who leaked the fourth copy of the Victory Plan, but in the fall of 1943, Albert Wedemeyer was promoted to major general and, as he himself said, was "eased out to Asia," where he served as deputy chief of staff to Britain's Lord Louis Mountbatten.

In putting together the Victory Plan, Wedemeyer took many things into consideration, especially conventional military wisdom that said that one side needed a two-to-one margin to win. If, as he believed, Germany could field 400 infantry divisions by 1943, the Allies would need 800 divisions. A division included 15,000 combat troops plus another 25,000 behind-the-lines troops: 40,000 men per division times 800 divisions comes to 32 million troops. The War Department went along with Wedemeyer in figuring that the Soviet Union was pretty much out of it, which of course wasn't true, but for figuring's sake they thought Joe Stalin and his boys were gone.

The battered British Empire, what was left of France, and anybody else who could or would join in would contribute, say, 100 divisions. That left the United States with only 700 divisions to supply. In other words, 28 million men. At the time, the U.S. population was something like 135 million, including 67.5 million males of all ages. Wedemeyer knew that the War Department could take only about 10 percent of the male population; someone had to stay home to build tanks and airplanes or to grow wheat and cattle, not to mention just grow up. Again, not counting women and after giving the navy, marines, and air corps* their share of draftees and recruits, the army

*In June 1941, the army air corps became the army air forces, which it remained until September 18, 1947, when it became a separate service, the U.S. Air Force.

at its peak could muster 8.8 million men, a far cry (about 19.2 million too few) from the number needed. Instead of 700 divisions, the U.S. Army would be able to muster only 216 divisions to get the job done.

If Germany would have 400 divisions, the Allies would, under this scenario, have only 316 divisions, not only *not* twice the number as conventional wisdom required we have, but not even as many as Hitler and his bunch could put in the field. The Victory Plan, however, claimed that this *would* be enough. How? We'd make up for it with airpower, mobility, and firepower, which would allow us to shove 5 million men ashore in Europe, then push on to Berlin.

To get these 5 million men and the necessary equipment ashore in Europe would require at least a thousand ships. Building the ships alone would take two years. Meanwhile, America would recruit and draft an army, invent and build the weapons that these men would need, and keep the country and the rest of the world afloat with an economy still whimpering from the Great Depression. Confidence was certainly the name of America's military game, but Hi-Ho, Hi-Ho, it's off to work we go—asDisney's Seven Dwarfs put it.

One of the nation's first big war-era achievements was the Liberty Ship, a mass-produced cargo ship that was the nautical equivalent of a stripped-down, bargain-priced car. It was based on an 1879 English design for a "tramp" steamer. President Roosevelt, whose naval background was extensive, called them "ugly ducklings." The motto could have been, Build 'em fast, build 'em cheap, and build a lot of 'em.

Beginning with the *Patrick Henry* on September 27, 1941 (13 others were launched within hours), 19 shipyards in the United States produced about 2,700 liberty ships. Fact is, no one is really sure just how many *were* built. However many, we more than doubled the number called for in Wedemeyer's plan.

The record for building one ship was just seven days, 14 hours, and 23 minutes on the building ways and another two weeks for fitting out. The secret to high-speed building was welding the plates for the hulls, not riveting them. Liberty ships were 445 feet long and carried about 11 tons (equal to 300 railroad freight cars) at a speed of about 11 knots. The "ugly ducklings" may have saved the world, and when the war ended, many of the surviving liberty ships were used to help rebuild merchant fleets around the world.

As for the army, America eventually came up with 90 divisions, with 8.3 million men and women in Europe, more than 2.5 million of them ground forces—not the numbers that Albert Wedemeyer believed were needed, but they got the job done in spades. Army officers no longer had to pack toilet paper in holsters because they lacked pistols. Trucks no longer had to be driven around with "TANK" signs. And recruits no longer had to do close order drill shouldering broomsticks. America's self-confidence had paid off with the greatest war machine ever known.

During World War II, the world proved that if we could be born we could be murdered and we could murder others. Those years saw the most incredible mass suffering and death in history—by rifle and mortar, cannon and bomb, land mine and booby trap; by lethal gas and hanging and decapitation. By starvation.

We will never know the exact number of casualties in World War II, but we can make a rough guess, one both frightening and appalling. More than 26 million died—soldiers, sailors, marines, and airmen. How to compare this incredible number of deaths? In the 1980s, a theme park was built north of Chicago. The site was selected because more than 20 million people lived within a two-hour drive. World War II killed 26 million men, women, and children—6 million *more* than within that two-hour drive of Chicago.

More were *wounded* in World War II than *lived* in the United States at the time of America's Civil War: 34.5 million people.

Together, the dead and wounded of World War II (60.4 million) almost equaled the entire turn-of-the-century population of the United States: 63 million. Truly, this was a generation lost.

The death toll includes 403,399 American soldiers, sailors, marines, and airmen; another 671,846 were wounded. Members of the British Commonwealth suffered 544,596 deaths. Seven and a half million citizens—military and civilian—of the Soviet Union died. From France, the toll was 210,671. China lost 2.2 million.

Germany suffered 3.5 million military deaths; between 3,450,000 and 4,150,000 German civilians were killed by Allied bombing. More than 300,000 Italians and 1.5 million Japanese died.

Add to this more than 6 million Jews, Poles, Gypsies, the mentally ill, homosexuals, and (for reasons only Hitler could fathom) Jehovah's Witnesses slaughtered by the Germans in concentration camps and death camps.

Twenty-six million dead, 34.4 million wounded. Appalling is too weak a word to describe this human devastation.

World War II lasted almost six years, about 10 weeks, from September 1931 (Japan's invasion of China) to 1945 (Japan's surrender). Based on our casualty estimate, one that many will consider too low, there were about 166,455 deaths per week, more than 23,779 every day the war lasted.

If World War I was "The Great War," what was World War II?

When the war began depended on where you were.

For the Chinese, war began on September 18, 1931, the day Japan launched an attack on Mukden. But there had been civil war since 1912, when China's last emperor had been forced to abdicate, so China might believe that 1912 sounded the opening bell of war.

For the Abyssinians of Ethiopia, war began on October 3, 1935, the day Italy invaded their nation. But the Italians had been trying to take over that small northern African nation since the late nineteenth century; so Ethiopians might set the start date earlier.

For Poland the war started on September 1, 1939, the day Germany launched its attack. But back in 1921 border wars had broken out between Poland and Germany.

For England and France, September 3, 1939, was the day they declared war on Germany because of its attack on Poland.

For the Soviet Union, the defensive war began June 22, 1941, the day Germany launched Operation Barbarossa from the Black Sea. But in a very real way the Soviet's war with Germany began on September 17, 1939, the day that Moscow invaded Poland in conjunction with Russia's then comrades, Hitler's Germans.

They were all major events, but localized fighting did not become a world war until December 7, 1941, the day that Japan bombed America's Pearl Harbor; we had been emotionally preparing for it for years.

France shrugged off Hitler's March 7, 1936, parade into the Rhineland, confident behind its concrete Maginot line, which stretched from Luxembourg to Switzerland. Essentially, the line was a trench built in an area that had seen much of World War I's trench warfare. In the parlance of the 1990s, the Maginot line was the mother of all trenches. Not just a hole in the ground, either. The French built above-ground forts, pillboxes from which they could watch the enemy and fire machine guns, barbed-wire entanglements, aircraft hangars, hospitals, storerooms, a subway, and even a theater. Much of it was air-conditioned, something relatively new and certainly unusual for the times. It took millions of dollars and many years to build what France's military experts predicted would be an impregnable defense against a German attack.

Obviously, they were too confident. A *Life* magazine photo taken in late fall 1939 shows an overweight, contented French soldier sitting in a straight-back chair, his rifle on the ground beside him; he is secure and bored, smoking a cigarette as he faces the Maginot line. He doesn't worry about the Hun, as many still called the Germans.

War came to France on May 10, 1940, with 155 German divisions, including 10 tank divisions, simply roaring around the Maginot line, outflanking it, and leaving that now not-so-bored French soldier still facing eastward. In fact, *all* of France's guns faced eastward, *away* from the German army—shocking, although fully expected by nearly everyone except the French. The German army quickly pushed into the heart of the country. Winston Churchill, who was in France at the time, was stunned when told that the French had no strategic reserve force: "It never occurred to me that any commanders having to defend five hundred miles of engaged front would have left themselves unprovided with a mass of manoeuvre. No one can defend with certainty so wide a front; but when the enemy has committed himself to a major thrust which breaks the line one can always have, one *must* always have, a mass of divisions which marches up in vehement counterattack at the moment when the first fury of the offensive has spent its force."

On May 15, French cabinet member Paul Reynaud telephoned Prime Minister Winston Churchill in London and, speaking in English, told the British leader, "We have been defeated." Once again, Churchill was stunned: "Surely it can't have happened so soon?" Reynaud replied, "The front is broken near Sedan; they are pouring through in great numbers with tanks and armoured cars."

Five days it took, five! The German army went around the Maginot line, sped through the countryside, and did just what France's leaders had said would be impossible.

It wasn't long before many in the French government, afraid their justly cherished city of Paris would be destroyed, threw up their hands and said something akin to "we quit." By June 10, the French government evacuated Paris. Germany took over the Alsace-Lorraine area of France and installed a puppet government in Vichy.

Then Hitler ground France's nose in it. He fined the French $120 million for their troubles and assessed "occupation costs" of $2 million a year, about four times the annual reparations Germany paid after losing World War I.

World War I ended in 1918, in a railroad dining car at Rethondes, France, in the Compiègne forest. The dining car had been preserved as a monument to the victory over Germany. Nearly twenty-two years after the World War I armistice, Hitler forced French delegates to present themselves humbly before him in that same railway car.

And the Maginot line? In the 1950s, France converted it to another equally useless purpose. It became a fallout shelter to be used in case of an atomic attack.

CHAPTER EIGHT

Names and Faces:
A Funny Thing Happened To Me During the War

Everyone has his day and some days last longer than others.
— Winston Spencer Churchill, speech in the
House of Commons, January 1952

Look at an infantryman's eyes and you can tell how much war he has seen.
— Bill Mauldin, cartoon caption in *Up Front*, 1945

When World War II broke out, a Christian missionary from America became a field intelligence officer for Gen. Claire Chennault's Fourteenth Army Air Force. He spoke Mandarin and went to work behind the Japanese lines, in central China.

After the war, a fellow agent wrote about this twenty-seven-year-old former missionary-turned-OSS agent. "He made me very uncomfortable," said Oliver J. Caldwell. They sat at an airstrip in northern China, having lunch. There wasn't much conversation; the ex-missionary "answered in monosyllables." Caldwell wrote, "His eyes were opaque. There was no communication at all between us." The other man, Caldwell believed, "had lived among the Chinese so long he seemed in his thinking almost as much Chinese as American."

When Lt. Col. Jimmy Doolittle bailed out of his fuel-drained B-25 following his historic bombing raid on Tokyo, the missionary-turned-OSS agent was among the first to welcome him to China.

On V-J Day in August 1945, he was ordered to rush to a Japanese prisoner of war camp near Peking and demand that the camp commander surrender. The commander was infamous for his ill-treatment of Allied prisoners, and the OSS was afraid he would shoot his prisoners to keep them from testifying at a war-crimes trial. The area was already controlled by the Chinese Communists, and at a roadblock, an officer asked the agent where he was going. Instead of answering, the former missionary lost his temper and began yelling at the officer. The Communist ordered the agent shot. Hearing of the agent's death, an air force lieutenant said, "It served him damn well right." The agent, the lieutenant said, "was a sadist who loved to inflict pain, to beat the Chinese."

The death of the missionary-turned-OSS agent gave rise to a myth. He was not a sadist who loved to inflict pain; rather, the myth claims, he was a strong anti-Communist. In the 1950s that myth was ridden to fame and sometimes fortune by members of a right-wing political society, one that Jimmy Doolittle describes as "a highly vocal postwar anti-Communist organization." The group soon took the missionary-agent's name: John Birch.

In his autobiography, General Doolittle remembers meeting Birch and says that he always seemed more interested in holding church services than fighting Communists. Birch, however, according to Doolittle, "had no way of knowing that the John Birch Society . . . would be named after him because its founders believed him to be the 'first casualty of World War III.' I feel sure he would not have approved."

Oscar, the statuette awarded by the Academy of Motion Picture Arts and Sciences, contributed to the war effort. Normally constructed of a mixture of copper, tin, and antimony, then electroplated with gold, nickel, and copper, Oscar gave up his metal content during the war. From 1942 to 1945, he was made of plaster.

Even before America joined the war, one of Hollywood's brightest stars had left "to do his part." Actor David Niven still held his British citizenship, and when England went to war, he went back to England. Niven was a 1927 graduate of Sandhurst, the British equivalent of the U.S. Military Academy. He resigned his commission several years later and came to the United States to become an actor. Within months of Britain's declaration of war on Nazi Germany, Niven left Hollywood and rejoined the army as a second lieutenant in a rifle unit, later switching over to the commando section. He also worked with military intelligence.

Lieutenant Colonel Niven was assigned to the U.S. 1st Infantry Division and went ashore with them at Normandy. He was one of only twenty-five from Britain to be awarded the U.S. Legion of Merit. After the war, he returned to Hollywood, where, not surprisingly, he often portrayed military officers—veddy, veddy British officers, don't cha know.

Veddy, veddy American Henry Fonda enlisted in the U.S. Navy in August 1942 and was stationed aboard the destroyer *Saterlee*. Commissioned a lieutenant (junior grade), he was put into Air Combat Intelligence in the central Pacific; awarded the Bronze Star, Fonda was discharged in October 1945.

For years, during both summer stock theater and in Hollywood, Fonda shared an apartment with Jimmy Stewart. At the time, they were noted more for helling and womanizing than for acting. It's a far different picture from the Jimmy Stewart who won an Academy Award in 1940 for *Philadelphia Story*. A couple of years later, Stewart, as he put it, won the lottery when his draft number was pulled out of the jar and he reported for his physical. At six foot two and a half inches and weighing only about 135 pounds, Stewart was too skinny for the army, so he put on 10 pounds and qualified for enlistment. His weight gain and enlistment were covered in the tabloids.

An avid pilot, Stewart flew with the 445th Bombardment Group of the Eighth Air Force, chalked up twenty-five missions in a B-17 named *Four Yanks and a Jerk*, and won the Distinguished Flying Cross. After the war, he returned to his movie career, where he became a brigadier general in the air force reserve. In later years, when his friend Ronald Reagan spoke to crowds about Stewart, he called him a major general. Finally, Stewart told President Ronald Reagan that he wasn't a major general. Stewart said the higher rank sounded so good that he hated to correct the president. No word on why the president didn't rectify the situation right there. Stewart died in 1997 at the age of eighty-nine.

While Jimmy Stewart was piloting *Four Yanks and a Jerk*, serving under him was another soon-to-be well-known Hollywood actor, Walter Matthau. Matthau enlisted in April 1942 and as a staff sergeant won six battle stars while serving as a gunner and radio operator on board B-17s.

Ed McMahon, sidekick to former television talk show host Johnny Carson on *The Tonight Show*, also flew during the war, a Marine

Corps fighter pilot stationed for a while aboard the carrier USS *Guadalcanal.*

Former lawyer Howard Cossell, who became the best-known (not to mention the best-loved and most-hated) sportscaster of his day, served in the U.S. Army, miraculously rising from private to major. He spent the entire war at the New York Port of Embarkation.

Sportscaster Curt Gowdy joined up but ruptured a disc during calisthenics and received a medical discharge.

Television Emmy- and Hollywood Oscar-winning actor Art Carney was drafted one day after he'd served as the voice of Gen. Dwight Eisenhower on the radio program *Report to the Nation.* It was March 14, 1944, less than three months before the Allied landing at Normandy. On D day, Carney was wounded and evacuated home without ever firing a shot. He limps now as a result of his wound; Carney's right leg is three-quarters of an inch shorter than his left.

Richard Burton was a navigator in the Royal Air Force (RAF), and just prior to V-E Day he was sent to Canada for special training.

In 1942, seventeen-year-old Paul Newman enlisted in the U.S. Navy. He was sent to the naval air corps Officers' Training School (OTS) at Yale University, where he hoped to earn a commission and become a pilot. But the man whose blue eyes are among the most famous in the world is color blind, and he washed out of OTS. Instead, he fought in World War II as a radioman and gunner on torpedo planes flying the South Pacific. After the war, he was discharged and became one of an estimated 7.5 million veterans who took advantage of the GI Bill of Rights. Newman used the GI Bill to study acting.

Comedian Wally Cox was drafted into the army and sent to Fort Walters, Texas. He couldn't take the hot weather and was hospitalized several times. Finally, the army gave him an honorable discharge for medical reasons.

Before he was Charles Bronson and started beating up movie bad guys, he was Charles Buchinski. His publicity information says he flew bombers as a gunner during the war. Actually, Bronson was a delivery truck driver for the 760th Mess Squadron in Kingman, Arizona.

Betty Grable and Rita Hayworth went to war, or at least their pinup pictures did. Their pictures were the favorites of U.S. troops all through the war. That picture of Grable looking back over her shoulder, showing off those legs? She was known as the girl with the "million dollar legs," but they were insured for only $250,000. Ida Lupino served as a lieutenant with the American Ambulance Corps. So-called Hollywood "experts" claimed that all Hedy Lamarr had to do was "stand still and look stupid." She was far from stupid. Hedy Lamarr, whose real name was Hedwin Eva Mareia Kissler, coinvented a torpedo guidance system evaluated by the U.S. Navy but never adopted. Her concept involved "frequency hopping," a system widely used today in communications. It's a system by which a torpedo "might carry commands" for direction with a "receiver hopping" between frequencies in sync with the transmitter on the firing submarine to relay direction commands. The navy did not adopt her invention and Lamarr returned to acting.

Strom Thurmond, who served for a short while as governor of South Carolina and a long while as a U.S. senator, enlisted in the army just four days after Pearl Harbor. He served in the 82d Airborne Division and was wounded in the Normandy landing. Thurmond won several medals, including the Purple Heart, the Legion of Merit, and the Bronze Star. In January 1946 he was discharged as a lieutenant colonel. He was thirty-nine years old when he enlisted, just about at the far end of acceptability for military service.

At the other end was actor Sidney Poitier, who lied about his age to get in; he was just sixteen. Poitier was assigned to the 1267th Medical Detachment, an all-black unit stationed at a psychiatric hospital in Northport, Long Island. One year and eleven days after he enlisted, Poitier was discharged, *prior* to his eighteenth birthday.

Oceanographer Jacques Cousteau was a gunnery officer aboard the French cruiser *Dupleix*, then was transferred to a coastal fort where he was stationed during the German occupation in 1940. With France under Nazi control, Cousteau worked with the Resistance movement. In 1943, he developed the aqualung, the self-contained underwater breathing apparatus (scuba), and helped clear mines from the French coast along the Mediterranean Sea.

Before he was a television reporter and anchorman, David Brinkley spent two years as an army supply sergeant at Fort Jackson, South Carolina.

Before he was a Pulitzer Prize–winning author, Samuel Eliot Morison was a Harvard history professor. Selected as the official historian of the U.S. Navy in World War II, he wrote a fifteen-volume account of the war. President Roosevelt had Morison commissioned a lieutenant commander in the navy reserves in May 1942.

And before he sang to Miss America, Bert Parks enlisted in the army as a private in 1942 and was discharged as a captain. Before he strolled the Boardwalks in Atlantic City, Parks got lost behind Japanese lines in the jungles of Burma for ten days.

At just five feet four inches, actor Alan Ladd was drafted into the army (pardon the pun) at the height of his career. The announcement that the U.S. Army Air Force wanted Ladd was made on January 25, 1943, during the *Lux Radio Theater*. Ladd made training and propaganda films and conducted War Bond drives, never leaving the country.

Hollywood producer, comedian, and actor Mel Brooks was a combat engineer whose duty was to deactivate mines during the war. He even took part in the Battle of the Bulge in December 1944. Once, when German troops tried to unnerve the Americans by broadcasting Nazi propaganda over loudspeakers, Brooks stood up and did a loud imitation of Al Jolson singing "Toot-Toot-Tootsie, Good-bye."

Sterling Hayden was in the OSS, where he used his real name, John Hamilton. He went through commando and parachute training in England, but during a jump he broke his ankle, tore some of the cartilage in one knee, and injured his spine. Back in the United States, Hayden became a PT boat test pilot before joining the Marine Corps. He graduated from officer candidate school (OCS), went into the OSS, and ran arms and equipment across the Adriatic Sea from Italy to Yugoslavia, where he got to know many of Marshal Josef Tito's Communist partisans. Hayden joined the Communist Party but later, before the House Un-American Activities Committee, renounced his membership.

Rex Harrison wanted to be an RAF pilot, but he was turned down because he had a glass eye. As an enlisted man, Harrison served as a radar operator.

The "Singing Cowboy" also served. Western star Gene Autry, who battled many a bad guy at Saturday matinees (without so much as a kiss from any costar other than his horse, Champion) was an army air forces pilot. Autry enlisted as a staff sergeant in July 1942 and learned to fly on his own time. He spent most of the war flying C-47s in the China-Burma theater for the Air Transport Command.

One actor who did not fight was Fritz Weaver, a conscientious objector who served at Civilian Public Service work camps.

Christopher Lee, who went on to scare the hell out of teenagers as a horror film actor, likely sent a good number of Germans to hell or someplace like it. Lee was an RAF pilot and was decorated by the Czech, Yugoslavian, and Polish governments as well as in his native England.

Mime Marcel Marceau fought with the French underground beginning in 1944. His father was taken hostage by the Germans and executed.

Future baseball great Jackie Robinson was a civilian on board a ship leaving Pearl Harbor on the morning of December 7, 1941, watching the attack and listening to radio reports. In April, he was drafted and applied for OCS but was turned down. He was sent to Fort Riley, Kansas, where he met another black athlete, M.Sgt. Joe Louis, the world's heavyweight boxing champion. Louis telephoned Secretary of War Stimson's adviser on racial issues, Gibson Truman, and Robinson got into OCS. He was commissioned a second lieutenant and was sent back to Fort Riley, where he became a morale officer for black troops.

Robinson and Louis worked together to improve recreational facilities for black troops at Fort Riley. Once on a bus at Fort Hood, Texas, the driver told Robinson to move to the back with the other blacks. Jackie refused and, according to a report, threatened the driver. The army brought him before a court-martial but acquitted him.

Robinson was a basketball, track, and football star at the University of California. Based on ankle injuries from his days in football, Robinson applied for a medical discharge. He was discharged in 1945 as a first lieutenant. Two years later, he broke baseball's color barrier when he took the field with the Brooklyn Dodgers.

In 1936, German heavyweight champion Max Schmeling knocked out world champion Joe Louis in a nontitle match, the only person ever to do that. Two years later, they fought again in one of the most internationally significant boxing matches of all time. Schmeling was Adolf Hitler's great white hope, the German heavyweight champion whom *der Führer* had proclaimed the symbol of the Aryan race. On June 28, 1938, Schmeling and Louis met again with the world eagerly listening for the results. The day of the fight, Hitler cabled Schmeling, addressing him as "the coming world's champion." Sorry, Adolf. In two minutes and four seconds into the first round, Joe Louis scored a technical knockout over Schmeling.

On January 9, 1942, Joe Louis received his draft notice. That same day, he defeated Buddy Bear in a world heavyweight boxing title bout and gave his purse to the Navy Relief Fund. Two months later, Louis defended his title against Abe Simon and knocked out the challenger in the sixth round. Louis gave that purse to the Army Relief Fund. As a master sergeant during the war, Joe Louis visited military hospitals, bases, and ships. By the time World War II ended, he'd fought more than a hundred exhibition matches. Before he entered the army, Joe Louis was quoted as saying, "We will win because God's on our side."

Despite Hitler's proclaiming him the Aryan of all Aryans, Schmeling was not a member of the Nazi Party. In fact, he was liberal minded and had a Jewish manager. As a paratrooper in the war, Max jumped into Crete during the German takeover of the Greek island. His tour of duty on Crete didn't last long; he was hospitalized with a severe case of diarrhea. Propaganda minister Joseph Goebbels faked papers claiming Max was a hero, and Hitler awarded the former boxing champion a medal.

Schmeling was forty years old when the war ended; still, he tried to resume his boxing career and won a few fights. He retired from professional boxing in 1957 and became the Hamburg bottler of Coca-Cola.

FBI agent Melvin Purvis, who shot and killed notorious outlaw John Dillinger, was commissioned a colonel in the U.S. Army Intelligence Corps. He put together much of the evidence used against German war criminals at the Nuremberg trials. He later grew despondent and committed suicide, using the same gun he'd used to shoot Dillinger.

Folksingers Pete Seeger and Woody Guthrie sang antifascist songs that were broadcast by the Office of War Information (OWI). Seeger was drafted into the army in 1942 and spent the next three and a half years in the Special Services entertaining troops. Guthrie joined the Merchant Marine in 1943 and over the next eleven months his ships were torpedoed twice. He was drafted into the army on May 8, 1945, which happened to be V-E Day. Guthrie spent the next eight months in the army but was given a dependency discharge.

William Joyce and Arthur Pierrepoint had a brief encounter, although Joyce undoubtedly didn't appreciate it. Joyce was born in Brooklyn, New York, to an English mother and a naturalized Irish father. Before the war he joined an English Fascist organization and later founded the British National Socialist League. He and his wife moved to Germany, and during the war he broadcast propaganda for the Nazis. That's when British soldiers began calling him "Lord Haw-Haw," because he tried to use an aristocratic accent in his broadcasts. He began each broadcast: "This is Germany [pronounced 'Jairmany'] calling." Joyce was captured in 1945, taken to London's Old Bailey court, and charged with treason. Six months later he was hanged, and that's where Arthur Pierrepoint, England's chief executioner, came in. On January 3, 1946, he hanged Joyce.

Douglas Chandler was known as "The American Lord Haw-Haw." Like William Joyce, Chandler broadcast propaganda for the Nazis, using the name Paul Revere. He began each broadcast by addressing "Misinformed, misgoverned friends and compatriots." He was captured after the war, convicted by a federal court, and sent to prison.

Iva Ikuo Tuguro d'Aquino broadcast anti-American propaganda for the Japanese during the war, first using the pseudonym "Ann" (short for "announcer") and later as "Tokyo Rose." After the war, d'Aquino moved to Chicago and vehemently claimed she'd been forced to make the broadcasts. On January 19, 1977, President Gerald Ford issued Tokyo Rose a full pardon. It was his final day in office.

Another American who made propaganda broadcasts for the enemy was George Nelson Page. The nephew of the U.S. ambassador to Italy, he became an Italian citizen. Page served for a while in the Italian army before the war and became a friend of Count Ciano, the Italian foreign minister. Because of this connection, Page got a high office in the Italian Propaganda Ministry and began making radio broadcasts for Mussolini's Fascist government.

Hollywood producer Jack L. Warner had his studios near the Los Angeles Lockheed Aviation plant, and he didn't want any Japanese bombers mistaking his sound stages for those of an aircraft factory. On the roof of his studios, Warner had painted the words "Lockheed thataway" and an arrow pointing thataway. Word got out, not to Japanese pilots who never made it to California anyway, but to a not-too-happy public. The sign was painted over. Later, Warner was commissioned a lieutenant colonel in the army air forces but stayed stateside making War Department movies.

Charles Lindbergh, the first person to fly the Atlantic Ocean solo, was the son of a rabid isolationist and was, himself, fervently opposed to America's entering any war. After observing the German air force, Lindbergh believed the Luftwaffe was unbeatable; therefore, no country should bother fighting Germany. A guest of Germany's Hermann Göring at the opening of the 1936 Olympic Games in Berlin, Lindbergh was given a Nazi Party medal, although apologists say he received it only at the insistence of U.S. ambassador Hugh Wilson. As a member of the America First Committee, Lindbergh made increasingly more strident antiwar and anti-Jewish speeches, claiming American Jews had caused the war.

In its August 12, 1941, issue, *Look* magazine ran an article: "Why Congress Should Investigate Lindbergh." The magazine asked, "Is the 'Lone Eagle' a fascist?" then said, "Let's find out—democratically." Samuel Grafton, the author of the article, was said to be "one of the most emphatic . . . of newspapermen . . . who writes editorial columns." According to Grafton, "The people of the United States have put up with the Lindbergh legend long enough." The writer called for "an investigation of the combination of forces, which has lined up, screaming and clawing, behind Charles Lindbergh. I want answers," he demanded, "under oath. . . . "

Lindbergh continued making isolationist speeches until Japan bombed Pearl Harbor. Then, he said, right or wrong, America had to fight. Charles Lindbergh was a colonel in the air corps reserves when World War II broke out, but the air force declined his offer of active duty. Instead, he worked as a civilian consultant to the United Aircraft Corporation, builders of Pratt & Whitney engines and Vought Corsair fighters. In the Pacific theater, he flew fifty missions as a civilian observer. On at least one occasion, he became more than an observer. While flying a P-38, he was attacked by Japanese fighters. Lindbergh downed at least one enemy plane.

In 1932, Charles and Ann Morrow Lindbergh's infant son was kidnapped. A body, apparently the child's, was found two months later, not far from the Lindbergh home. In a highly publicized but, by modern standards, uncertain trial, New Jersey resident Bruno Hoffman was found guilty of kidnapping and murdering the Lindbergh baby.

The search for the Lindbergh baby killer was led by the superintendent of the New Jersey State Police, Herbert Norman Schwarzkopf. Superintendent Schwarzkopf had served in the U.S. cavalry in World War I and, after being wounded, resigned his commission. He returned to active military duty in 1942 as chief of the military mission to Iran. His son, also named Herbert Norman Schwarzkopf, commanded American forces in the 1991 Persian Gulf War.

During World War II, John Wayne filmed several war-based movies—*Flying Tigers, Reunion in France,* and *Fighting SeaBees* among them. In all, he appeared in fourteen World War II–set movies during his career. What he didn't appear in was a real uniform. John "Duke" Wayne, who was born Marion Michael Morrison, was 4-F.

He was in good company. Actor Marlon Brando also was 4-F thanks to a knee he injured playing football in high school that kept him out of the war. Errol Flynn acted his way through World War II as an officer and a gentleman, but a heart condition made him 4-F. Comedian Jackie Gleason's famous line was "And awaaay we go," but he didn't go anywhere; he was a hundred pounds overweight: 4-F. Liberace had an injured spine, which didn't stop him from lighting a candelabra on his piano. Van Johnson played a World War II pilot, but head injuries received in an auto accident kept him out of the real war. Cliff Robertson, who played John F. Kennedy in the movie *P.T. 109,* missed the boat with poor eyesight. Gary Cooper, who had a peculiar lope as he ambled along as a movie cowboy, was 4-F because of a displaced hip. Even the comic book character Superman was 4-F. Some felt that "it would be demoralizing to the regular fighting men to have Superman involved in the war."

Two other comic book characters, however, got into the big show; Mandrake the Magician and Joe Palooka fought for the good old United States of America.

In the television series *Hogan's Heroes*, actor John Banner played the bungling German prison guard, Sgt. Hans Schultz. In real life, Banner was a Jew who fled from Austria after the German Anschluss of 1938, and during the war he posed for U.S. Army recruiting posters.

Fellow *Hogan's Heroes* cast member Robert Clary was a prisoner of the Nazis, spending three years in a concentration camp. While he was a prisoner, the Germans tattooed a number on his left forearm: A5714.

Professional baseball gave many of its best to the war effort. Cleveland star pitcher Bob Feller was a gunner on the battleship *Alabama*. Catcher Lawrence Berra, better known as "Yogi," was a gunner on the rocket ship *Bayfield* at Normandy. Joe Dimaggio enlisted in the army air forces and was part of the physical training program; however, he spent most of his service time hospitalized with stomach ulcers. Ted Williams, who gave American league pitchers ulcers for years, joined the Marine Corps in 1942 and became a fighter pilot, flying more than 1,100 hours. Harold "Pee Wee" Reese, standout shortstop for the Brooklyn Dodgers, served in the navy from 1943 to 1945; he was discharged as a chief petty officer. Hank Greenberg of the Detroit Tigers was the first major league star player to enlist. He joined the air force just after Pearl Harbor and became an administrative officer for a B-29 unit in China.

There were many others, famous before and famous after, who served. Daniel Inouye was a member of the Japanese American 442d Regimental Combat Team. He lost his right arm in combat but later became a U.S. senator from Hawaii. Kirk Douglas was a communications officer in the navy where he received internal injuries when a depth charge exploded close to his patrol boat in the Pacific. Columnist Art Buchwald joined the marines in 1941 when he was only sixteen years old. Actor Eddie Albert was a civilian informant for army intelligence until he enlisted in the navy.

Tom Harmon's life reads like a Hollywood script. He was a college football star and joined the army air corps in 1940. His plane crashed in the jungles of South America in June 1943; Harmon was the only survivor of the seven men on board. He flew P-38 fighters over China until his aircraft crashed. Four months later, on November 30, 1943, he was shot down again parachuting to safety once more. Guerrillas smuggled him back to his base, and on August 26, 1944, he married the boss's daughter.

Harmon's plane was named "Old 98–Little Butch." *He* was "Old 98," his football jersey number. "Little Butch" was his nickname for his bride-to-be, Elyse Knox, daughter of the U.S. secretary of the navy, Frank Knox. When she married Harmon, "Little Butch's" wedding dress was made from his parachute.

Desmond T. Doss was a conscientious objector (CO) who served as a medical corpsman. He was the first CO to receive the Congressional Medal of Honor for conspicuous gallantry above and beyond the call of duty at the risk of his own life.

CHAPTER NINE

Leaders Who Went to War:
What Did You Do in the War, Mr. President?

This conjunction of an immense military establishment and a large arms industry is new to the American experience.
—Dwight David Eisenhower, radio and
television address, January 17, 1961

This will remain the land of the free only so long as it is the home of the brave.
—Elmer Davis, *But We Were Born Free*, 1954

America's first hero of World War II was a B-17 pilot from Florida, Capt. Colin Purdie Kelley Jr. Just three days after Pearl Harbor, Captain Kelley and his crew took off from Clark Field, which had also been bombed by the Japanese during that "day of infamy." Kelley's bomber attacked Japanese ships off Luzon, in the Philippines. Kelley's bomber also hit and sank a transport, but then a Japanese Zero fighter charged the American plane. His B-17 on fire, Kelley ordered his six surviving crewmen to jump; he remained on board and died when his bomber crashed.

America was hungry for heroes, and the government claimed Kelley had sunk the Japanese battleship *Haruna*. Later, it was learned that no battleships were in the area, but it didn't matter; a transport was good enough. Kelley's mother accepted his posthumous award of the Distinguished Service Cross.

A total of 12,731 B-17 Flying Fortress bombers were built during World War II. About 4,750 of them were lost in combat missions. One just got lost.

B-17 number 40-3097 was part of a flight of bombers that landed at Hawaii's Hickam Field while Pearl Harbor was being bombed. The B-17 was badly damaged, but the air force cobbled it back together with parts from other wounded B-17s and sent it flying once more. One of its first pilots, a man named Weldon H. Smith, gave it its name: *Alexander, the Swoose.* He based it on a popular song about a bird that was half swan and half goose, a swoose. As the Japanese over-ran island after island, the *Swoose,* a model B-17D, was moved from base to base.

Late in the war, newer model B-17Es began to trickle into the 7th Bombardment Group, to which the *Swoose* was attached. Soon, various parts of the *Swoose* were used to patch up damaged aircraft still flying bomb runs. Before it could be completely dismantled, Lt. Gen. George Howard Brett requisitioned it as a command plane. Its weapons and other unnecessary gear were stripped off, and the *Swoose* was removed from the line as a bomber.

Brett's pilot was Capt. Frank Kurtz, a former Olympic champion whose original plane was destroyed at the same time the *Swoose* was damaged. With Kurtz at the controls, General Brett and the *Swoose* logged an average of 150 hours a month in the air, much of it ferrying around high-ranking officers.

On one flight from Darwin to Cloncurry, Australia, the passengers included Brig. Gen. Ralph Royce, William F. Marquat, and Edwin S. Perrin. All told, about sixteen souls were on board for the trip, including lower ranked American and Australian officers, a few newspaper reporters, and, as a crewman put it, "a big, lanky guy from Texas."

About the time they should have arrived over Cloncurry, navigator Harry Schreiber looked around, surprised to learn that the *Swoose* wasn't where the *Swoose* ought to be. In fact, they were lost. Frantically, he tried to find out what had gone wrong. Meanwhile, radio operator Aubrey Fox set about trying to get a fix on a ground station, and pilot Kurtz began flying a boxcar pattern, hoping to see a familiar ground location.

Say this for the brass on board; you couldn't keep such a mistake from them. Quickly, they learned of the predicament. Just as quickly, they broke out in a sweat, especially one general who made a general nuisance of himself by pacing back and forth. The general paced one way, and pilot Kurtz had to adjust his flight trim. The general paced the other way, and copilot Marvin McAdams had to adjust the flight trim back again. All this was taking place while Kurtz and McAdams were trying to find where they were before they ran out of fuel.

The oldest member of the crew was Sgt. Harold Varner, a veteran nicknamed "The Hostess" because his duties entailed taking care of whatever brass was on board at the time. Varner had a reputation for not taking guff from anyone, general or not, especially one who disturbed a pilot who was trying to keep them all from crashing and burning. "General," Sergeant Varner said to the nervous officer, "get back there and sit down!" When the officer hesitated to do as told by a lowly sergeant, Varner escorted him back near the tail wheel, plunked the general down on a toilet, and strapped in the would-be pacer.

Finally, Kurtz saw a more or less flat spot below. Gingerly, he set down the *Swoose* in a near perfect landing close by Carris Brook Farm, about forty miles southeast of Winton, Australia. As they came to rest, the fuel-starved engines sputtered out. All on board survived without a scratch.

It wasn't long before the crew learned what had gone wrong. Because the *Swoose* no longer flew combat missions, the ground crew had removed the steel plates used to protect the pilot from antiaircraft fire. When the plates were removed, no one thought to recalibrate the compasses for the lack of metal. Kurtz and his crew could have, and may have, flown in circles because their compasses were out of whack.

Fate, however, didn't let this lost plane end its days in some Australian farmer's field, scaring away crows. Compasses adjusted to tell north from south, *Alexander, the Swoose* flew on. Later, in fact, it flew with General Brett when he took over the Caribbean Defense Command in November 1942. Finally, with the war over and the U.S. Air Force junking its other old B-17s, the *Swoose* was also headed for the wreck heap. At the last minute, however, it found a new home. The *Swoose* sits in warehouses 22 and 23 at the Smithsonian Institution's Paul E. Garber facility in Suitland, Maryland, torn apart and scattered. Yet, in a way, the *Swoose* still flies high. Pilot Frank Kurtz named his daughter, actress Swoosie Kurtz, for the old B-17.

The big, lanky guy from Texas on board the *Swoose* when it made its forced landing in that Australian farm field was a congressman then serving as a navy lieutenant commander: Lyndon Baines Johnson. As Sergeant Varner recalled, almost as soon as the lost B-17 landed and neighboring farmers began wandering out to see what was happening, President-to-be Johnson began making friends with the local constituents, discussing crops and telling them they ought to have a tariff to protect their wool market. As Varner put it, "Pretty soon, he knows all their first names...and there's no question he swung that county for Johnson before we left."

Wars are America's favorite hunting ground for future presidents, and World War II was our happiest hunting ground so far. Every president from Eisenhower to Bush was involved in the military in some way during the war.

Dwight David Eisenhower, possibly more than anyone else, determined the course of the war in Europe. He was known as Ike and was born in 1890 in Denison, Texas, long before Denison became the powdered egg capital of the world. Ike's family moved to Abilene, Kansas, when he was two years old. There were six brothers all told; despite a childhood that was barely this side of the poverty level, things worked out for them. Brother Edgar became a lawyer, Arthur was a banker, and Roy was a pharmacist. Earl was a journalist and an electrical engineer. Milton went on to become president of Johns Hopkins University. Dwight Eisenhower entered the U.S. Military Academy, where he had a promising career in football until he broke his knee. That knee almost cost him his army commission. Apparently, he'd always had knee trouble; as a fifteen-year-old boy he skinned his knee and the wound caused blood poisoning. A physician said the boy's knee should be amputated, but Eisenhower refused and the leg was saved.

Eisenhower graduated from the Academy in 1915, sixty-first in his class of 164. During World War I, he commanded a heavy tank unit but never got overseas. Instead, he served most of the time at Gettysburg, Pennsylvania. He so liked the small town that he later retired there, near the Civil War battlefield.

Ike served on Gen. Douglas MacArthur's personal staff for almost six years, most of the time in the Philippines. They didn't get along very well, and Eisenhower later said he "studied dramatics" under MacArthur. About all Eisenhower said at the time was that, when he and his wife left the Philippines, "MacArthur saw us off at the pier."

In 1942, both MacArthur and Eisenhower were nominated for the Congressional Medal of Honor. Eisenhower turned his down, saying that it was given for valor and that he had done nothing in that category. MacArthur accepted his.

When Eisenhower was summoned to the White House in the early days of the war, he was so little known that the official appointment book lists him as "Lt. Colonel Eisenhaur." He was already a brigadier general and never spelled his name that way.

His first combat experience was as commander of Allied forces in the invasion of North Africa. It found him hesitant and left him depressed, but he worked around it and was promoted to full general in the fall of 1943. He got the hang of amphibious landings at Sicily and Salerno and pushed them in plans for a cross-Channel assault on France. On June 6, 1944, he made Operation Overlord work when others doubted it.

With the war won, both the Democratic and Republican parties called on Ike to run for president, although neither party knew where he stood. He was less glamorous than MacArthur, less sure of himself than Patton, and maybe that was what the American people wanted. Often it is said we get exactly what we deserve.

In 1951, after he'd decided that he was a Republican, Dwight Eisenhower was nominated as the presidential candidate of his newly embraced party. He swept into office in 1952 on a campaign of Korea (he would go personally to end the war–police action), communism (he and his vice-presidential hopeful, Richard Nixon, were against it), and corruption, even though Harry Truman had said if Eisenhower were elected "his administration would make [Ulysses S.] Grant's look like a model of perfection." Grant was another general who swept into the White House; his administration was noted for its corruption. Truman earlier remarked that, "If you like Ike as much as I do, you will vote with me and send him back to the Army, where he belongs."

As president, Eisenhower once said, "Our government makes no sense unless it is founded in a deeply felt religious faith and I don't care what it is." Ike's opponent in both 1952 and 1956, Adlai Stevenson, said, "Some of us worship in churches, some in synagogues, some on golf courses." Dwight Eisenhower often took time off from his White House duties for a round of golf at his favorite course, the Burning Tree Country Club in Washington, D.C. When he did, his Secret Service guard naturally went along as protection, making it the first known time that rifles and machine guns were regularly carried in golf bags.

In 1952, Republicans handed out campaign buttons for their candidate: "I Like Ike." In 1956, Republicans handed out similar campaign buttons: "I Still Like Ike." Ike sometimes wasn't all that clear in his words and deeds, saying once, "The great problem of America today is to take that straight road down the middle."

John Fitzgerald Kennedy commanded several PT boats, including *PT-101* and *PT-59*. It was the *PT-109* to which he is normally linked. He was in command of *PT-109* when it was rammed and sunk by the Japanese destroyer *Amagiri* in 1943 in an area of the Pacific Ocean known as The Slot, a high-traffic area between New Georgia and Bougainville in the Solomon Islands. Two crewmen were killed; however, Kennedy helped rescue at least one badly injured man. The survivors hung onto the hull of their wrecked ship until they could make it to an atoll named Bird Island. Using a message scrawled on a coconut, and a cooperative native to get the coconut through, Kennedy sent word to an Australian secretly stationed nearby as a coast watcher. That got them all rescued and got Jack Kennedy acclaimed a hero.

Jack Kennedy was wounded in the sinking of *PT-109* and used his time recuperating to write a best-selling book, *Profiles in Courage,* though it's not certain whether it actually was Kennedy or one of his aides who put typewriter to paper. The book won a Pulitzer Prize. After the war, Kennedy was elected to the U.S. House of Representatives. Five years later, he went to the Senate.

His successful bid for U.S. president in 1960 relied heavily on his World War II career as a hero. During the campaign there was even a song about the plight of *PT-109*. A tie clip of the boat became a highly coveted campaign memento. In reality, the loss of the *PT-109* may have been due to the crew sleeping while in the middle of a war zone. Once, during a late-night campaign interview when Kennedy was asked about the incident, he told the reporter, "It was involuntary. They sank my boat." The coconut that had carried his message wound up as a souvenir, sitting on a table in the Oval Office of the White House.

Kennedy of course never completed his first term. While on a campaign trip in Dallas, Texas, he was assassinated. Oddly enough, the man he had defeated for the office of president, and who one day *would* be elected, also was in Dallas at the time. By coincidence, Richard Nixon was there on business on November 21 and 22, 1963. He left by air shortly before the shooting and said he learned of the assassination when he arrived in New York City that afternoon.

Jack Kennedy's vice president was sworn in as president even before *Air Force One,* with JFK's widow and his body on board, could take off for the return trip to Washington. Lyndon Baines Johnson said he was anxious to have the country heal.

Johnson was thirty-three years old when the war broke out, a four-year veteran as U.S. representative from Texas. He was the first congressman to join the military after Pearl Harbor was bombed. Earlier, he told his constituents that, if war started, "I'll be in the front line, in the trenches, in the mud and blood, helping to do the fighting." It was a pledge far more glorious and glamorous than LBJ's time in service proved to be. However, he did sign up for active duty, much to the chagrin of President Roosevelt, who wasn't too happy at the prospect of an American congressman being captured by the enemy. He ordered Johnson to the West Coast to inspect shipyards and production plants. Roosevelt then sent Johnson as his personal representative to report on the war in the Southwest Pacific, presumably a safe enough job.

In June 1942, Johnson flew as a passenger on the B-25 *Heckling Hare* out of Queensland, a bombing run on a Japanese air base on the northeastern coast of New Guinea. The *New York Times* said the bomber turned back because of engine trouble. Johnson claimed they were attacked by a flight of Japanese Zero fighters. A crewman backed up the future president, saying Johnson was "just as calm as if we were on a sightseeing tour," which, of course, LBJ was. Another bomber on the run apparently was shot down with another inspection officer on board. No one was injured on the *Heckling Hare,* and General MacArthur presented LBJ with a Silver Star. Johnson was the only one on board who received the honor, but then he was the only congressman on board.

Then came Johnson's touch with, if not greatness, then the semi-great *Alexander the Swoose.* It was all too much for the man in the Oval Office, and on July 9, 1942, President Roosevelt ordered all congressmen on active duty to return to Washington.

At the time, there were eight of them. Four resigned in order to remain in the armed services. That included Sen. Edward Brooke of Massachusetts, who served as an officer with the all-black 366th Combat Infantry Regiment; he was awarded the Bronze Star for bravery. Four other congressmen, Lyndon Johnson among them, resigned from the armed services and returned to the Halls of Congress. Johnson never did get into that bloody trench.

Richard Milhous Nixon was a twenty-eight-year-old lawyer from Yorba Linda, California, when World War II came along. One month and two days after the Japanese attack on Pearl Harbor, Nixon applied for a job with the Office of Price Administration in Washington, D.C., at a salary of sixty-one dollars a week. At the time, the average American salary was twenty-five dollars a week. Nixon was commissioned a lieutenant (junior grade) in the navy and was sent to the Quonset Point, Rhode Island, Naval Air Station. Four months later he shipped out to the Ottumwa, Iowa, Naval Reserve Aviation Base.

After a year in service, Nixon reported for duty at Fleet Air Command in Noumea, New Caledonia, a South Pacific island that served as a landing site for American aircraft being ferried to Australia. He was placed in charge of the South Pacific Combat Air Transport Command, and in mid-1944 (now a full lieutenant) Richard Nixon was transferred to Alameda, California, outside San Francisco. Later, he went to Washington, D.C., where for ten months in 1945 he worked at the Bureau of Aeronautics in the Navy Department. While still on active duty, he was endorsed by the Committee of One Hundred, a political group organized to decide upon a candidate to face five-term Democratic representative H. Jerry Voorhis in California. Richard Nixon was discharged from the navy on March 10, 1946 and, nine days later, filed in both Republican and Democratic primaries for Voorhis's seat in California's 12th District. That November, he was elected to Congress while still in the naval reserve.

In the middle of his first term in Congress, Nixon was named chairman of a subcommittee of the House Un-American Activities Committee (HUAC). It was a time when America's Red scare was heating up, fear of Communists under every bush or, in Nixon's case, inside every pumpkin. In testimony before HUAC, admitted Communist Party member Whittaker Chambers claimed he'd hidden microfilm of stolen State Department documents in a Maryland pumpkin patch. Nixon's spot as Eisenhower's vice president, according to historian Samuel Eliot Morison, came "as a reward for having uncovered the former communist connections of Alger Hiss. . . . He had no other qualifications."

For twenty-six years, Nixon used the Whittaker Chambers–Alger Hiss pumpkin for all it was worth. When Nixon ran for president in 1960, former president Harry Truman said that Nixon "never told the truth in his life."

Richard Nixon's first vice president was Spiro Theodore Agnew, who had been a lawyer, teacher, politician, and governor of Maryland. In World War II, he was a company commander in the 10th Armored Division and won the Bronze Star for bravery. On October 10, 1973, Agnew pleaded nolo contendere (that is, no contest) to tax evasion charges, a technicality. He had failed to pay taxes on bribes made to him while he was governor of Maryland by contractors who wanted to buy him off. Under the 25th Amendment, on October 12, Gerald Rudolph Ford became the first appointed U.S. vice president.

When Richard Nixon resigned, Gerald Ford became president without an election. Virtually the only person who voted for Ford for president in 1974 was Richard Nixon. Ford had, however, been elected to Congress thirteen times.

The man who would become our thirty-eighth president was

born Leslie King, Jr., in Omaha, Nebraska. When he was two years old, his parents divorced; his mother took little Leslie to Grand Rapids, Michigan, met and married Gerald R. Ford, who adopted the boy and gave him his own name, Gerald Rudolph Ford.

Leslie-turned-Gerald graduated from the University of Michigan in 1935 and Yale Law School in 1941. In April 1942, he enlisted in the navy, where he served on the carrier USS *Monterey* as physical education officer and assistant navigator. He was discharged in 1946 as a lieutenant commander. He returned to his Grand Rapids law practice until 1949, then was elected to Congress, where he remained for the next twenty-five years, eight years as House Republican leader. In the 1974 confirmation hearings to decide whether Ford should be named vice president, he promised that, if in some wild event he became president, under no condition would he run for the office when his term expired. He did, of course, but in 1976 was defeated by Jimmy Carter.

James Earl "Jimmy" Carter officially did not serve during the war. He was, however, enrolled in the U.S. Naval Academy at Annapolis, Maryland, graduating in 1946 *after* the war.

Ronald Wilson Reagan was the nation's fortieth president. In his case, wartime action followed the words "Lights, camera. . . ." A football player in college at Eureka, Illinois, Reagan worked as a play-by-play radio sports announcer in Des Moines, Iowa. At age twenty-six, he turned to Hollywood, where he became a model and moderately successful film actor, once referred to as "a plain guy with a set of homespun features." In 1940, Reagan married one of Hollywood's top stars, Jane Wyman; it greatly enhanced his career, and he began to take on more starring roles.

Reagan enlisted in the army on April 14, 1942, but was disqualified from combat duty because of poor eyesight. He spent the war at home in Hollywood—clean sheets and uniforms carefully pressed by servants—doing what he did before and after, making movies, the chief difference between his wartime movies and those earlier in his career being that the latest ones were aimed at recruiting, training, and building morale.

In 1944, Capt. Ronald Reagan signed the discharge papers of another actor, Maj. Clark Gable (real name, William Clark), who had served in the army air forces (Gable flew as a photographer on B-17s over Germany, causing Hermann Göring to put a bounty of $5,000 on the head of the man who had starred in *Gone With the Wind*). Following the war, Reagan's career branched out to such movies as *Bedtime For Bonzo*. He also became the host of television's *General Electric Theater*.

The Wyman-Reagan marriage ended in 1948, and Reagan later married Hollywood starlet Nancy Davis, with whom he'd costarred in a highly forgettable movie called *Hellcats of the Navy*.

For a while, Reagan was active in Democratic Party and Screen Actors Guild politics, but he switched his outlook from liberal to conservative during the McCarthy era. After turning Republican, he successfully ran for California governor and was notable for his austere attitude toward the state's funding of welfare and education. He had run on a platform for reduced government, but by the time he left office, California's debt and public employment rolls had expanded greatly.

In 1968, Reagan made a brief run for the GOP presidential nomination, but he'd entered too late to gain much support. He tried again in 1976, but this time he lost to Gerald Ford. In 1980, he won the nomination and defeated incumbent president Jimmy Carter.

Reagan's vice president, who had campaigned against him by deriding what he termed Reagan's "voodoo economics," was yet another World War II veteran, George Herbert Walker Bush.

Bush was the wealthy son of U.S. senator from Maine George Prescott Bush. At age eighteen the younger George joined the U.S. Navy, where he was said to be the service's youngest pilot. In September 1944, he was flying a TBM Avenger off the aircraft carrier *San Jacinto*. While attacking a Japanese radio station on Chichi Jima, about 150 miles north of the better known Iwo Jima, his plane was hit by enemy flak.

Bush did everything he could to avoid going down over the island, and who could blame him? A Japanese general on the island had issued orders that "captured airmen are to be killed and eaten." With his plane on fire, George Bush and his two crewmen bailed out. The others died but Bush survived and swam to his life raft, where he literally was lost without a paddle. He floated around for an hour and a half until he saw the submarine *Finback* heading his way. An amateur cameraman on the submarine filmed Bush being brought on board, film that later would be used in Bush's political campaigns. He was awarded the Distinguished Flying Cross.

After the war, Bush attended Yale University, settled in Texas, and founded an oil company. He ran for the U.S. Senate in 1964 but lost; two years later he was elected to the House of Representatives. After a stint as ambassador to China, he served as director of the Central Intelligence Agency. After losing to Reagan in a race for the Republican presidential nomination, and despite making anti-Reagan comments, he was elected vice president in 1980. Eight years later, he ran for and was elected president. His single term of office ended when he was defeated in 1992 by William Jefferson "Bill" Clinton.

Clinton was the first American president elected after 1950 who did not serve in World War II. He couldn't. He was born in 1946, more than a year after the fighting ended and both Germany and Japan had surrendered.

CHAPTER TEN

Kick 'em in the Axis:
Mussolini, Hitler, and All Their Jazz

Hitler is a monster of wickedness, insatiable in his lust for blood and plunder.
—Winston Churchill, June 22, 1941

Springtime for Hitler and Germany/ Deutschland is happy and gay.
We're moving to a faster pace/ Look out, here comes the Master Race!
—Mel Brooks, *The Producers*, screenplay, 1968

Benito Juárez Mussolini was a failure; despite propaganda to the contrary, he couldn't even get the trains to run on time. Italians listened to *Il Duce*, then finally murdered him.

Mussolini's father named him after the Mexican revolutionary leader Benito Juárez. His mother was a schoolteacher and young Mussolini was a teacher himself but was more interested in socialism than in helping his students learn. He was a revolutionary who spent five months in prison because he'd led a workers' demonstration. He was a newspaper publisher who called for Italy to join the fighting in World War I, and he was a soldier in that war but didn't even make it through basic training before being wounded by a misfired hand grenade.

After the Great War, a group of capitalists who'd turned against socialism took over his newspaper, and Mussolini was out of work. In 1919 he founded a group of black-shirted thugs he called the *Fasci di Combattimento*, the Fascist Party. That's when he began calling himself *Il Duce*, the leader. After Benito and his black shirts waded in and stopped a spreading workers' strike, King Victor Emmanuel III panicked and asked him to form a new government.

So, what was one of the first things Mussolini did? He outlawed all other political parties in Italy, pretty much standard for dictators, and he turned his black shirts into a personal army, preaching that "the prestige of nations is determined absolutely by their military glories and armed power." His Fascist party slogan was "Believe, obey, fight." His party flag carried the motto "The Country Is Nothing Without Conquest." He tried to fulfill his slogan.

In October 1935, he sent troops into Ethiopia, a small African nation that Italy had been trying to conquer since 1896. It was a war pitting a modern army against spears, but it took Mussolini seven months to send the almost indestructible if diminutive Emperor Haile Selassie into exile.

That exile led Selassie to the United States, where he appealed to both Congress and the president; neither was much help. Congress allowed him to speak before a joint session, and that made Selassie popular, albeit homeless. Roosevelt proclaimed that "a state of war unhappily exists" between Ethiopia and Italy. Selassie knew that; that's why he was in Washington. Roosevelt said the United States could do nothing about the situation because of the Neutrality Act.

That left it up to the League of Nations, which means Selassie got no help there, either. The United States wasn't even in the league, thanks to a political squabble in 1919 between Democratic president Woodrow Wilson (who had proposed the League of Nations) and Republican Senate leader Henry Cabot Lodge (who liked much of the idea in general but opposed the league specifically because his Democratic opponent had proposed it).

Without the United States in the league, all that that not-so-august body could do to help Emperor Haile Selassie was to apply partial economic sanctions on Mussolini and Italy. It didn't do any good. Mussolini just laughed it off, and that gave another European Fascist ideas of his own.

Benito Mussolini was the idol of a forty-six-year-old Austrian of somewhat confused heritage. His father, Alois Schicklgruber, was thirty-nine years old when he took the name Hitler. On April 20, 1889, Alois Schicklgruber/Hitler and his wife, Klara Poelzl (who was also Schicklgruber/Hitler's foster daughter), gave birth to their third child and named him Adolf Hitler.

Young Adolf was a failure. He wanted to be an artist, but he almost starved on an Austrian street corner trying to sell postcards.

Hitler considered himself a better than average artist and, when he was eighteen, auditioned at the Vienna Academy of Art. Twice he auditioned, and twice he was rejected. He spent the next several years knocking around Vienna and Munich, trying without much success to sell hand-painted postcards to tourists. He succeeded only in being lonely and bitter.

The War to End All Wars broke out. Hitler avoided service in the Austrian army but volunteered for a Bavarian infantry regiment. By the end of what came to be known as World War I, Hitler had reached the rank of corporal (the equivalent of private first class in the U.S. Army), had been decorated twice for bravery in action, and was wounded and hospitalized.

He took to reading books that can only be described as narrow-minded and racist. From a long-brooding, self-delusional, unsuccessful Austrian artist, he turned into a fanatically German nationalist who looked on Mussolini as a hero. In 1919, Hitler joined the German Workers' Party, which was so small that he was just its seventh member. Two years later he was the leader of this small group, and he changed its name to the National Socialist German Workers' Party, more popularly known as the Nazis. The original abbreviation of National Socialist was Nasos. Journalist Konrad Heiden coined the term *Nazi* as a word of derision, but his derision became accepted even by the Nazis themselves.

Just as Mussolini had organized his Italian black-shirted bodyguard, Hitler set out to form his own personal army; to be different, he put them in brown shirts. They were the SA, the *Sturmabteilung,* the storm troopers. Originally said to be a gymnastics and sports group within the Nazi Party, in reality they were just as fanatical as Hitler himself, just as willing to beat, bully, and kill anyone who got in their way.

The Brown Shirts' marching song was named after the Berlin leader of the SA, Horst Wessel. He was shot by a Communist in February 1930. It made him a martyr for the Nazis, even though he had earlier resigned from the party because of his love for a prostitute. His killer was a Communist all right, but he was also the prostitute's pimp.

Backed by his Brown Shirts, Hitler was ready for revolution, and he set it to begin on November 11, 1923, the fifth anniversary of Germany's surrender in World War I. He planned to take over local governments in Bavaria, seize railroads and telegraph and police stations, and arrest all Communists and labor leaders who protested his revolution. It became known as the Munich "Beer Hall Putsch."

Hitler led a group of 3,000 followers in a march under their new banner, which featured the swastika, a design that goes back to prehistoric times. Police fired on them and, in the rioting, three policemen and 16 Nazi Party members were killed.

One party member shot and wounded in the riot was Hermann Göring, a World War I flying ace. Göring's wife rescued him and took him to safety in Austria, where he was hospitalized. Doctors there introduced Göring to morphine, and he became addicted to the drug. Over the next twenty years, Göring seesawed between addiction, being confined to mental hospitals, running Germany's Luftwaffe, and suffering from venereal diseases. After the war, he was convicted of crimes against peace; he committed suicide while in prison.

The Beer Hall Putsch failed miserably initially. Hitler and nine others were arrested and tried for high treason.

Hitler obviously was the star at the trial, and he used it as a political event. He wasn't a traitor, he declared, his accusers were. He spoke for four hours one day, telling the court, "I feel myself the best of Germans who wanted the best for the German people"—this despite the fact that he wasn't a German but an Austrian.

The trial lasted twenty-four days and when it was over, Hitler no longer was the obscure leader of an even more obscure political party. During the trial he became a hero to some, a menace to many, and a national figure to just about everybody in the newspaper-reading, radio-listening world.

Ignoring his rhetoric, the court convicted Hitler, ordering him to serve five years, not doing hard time but residing in the 1920s version of a 1990s country club prison, the castle at Landsburg am Lech. The castle was known as a place where prisoners had virtually unlimited visitation privileges and where they could buy beer and wine at moderate prices. Tipping allowed.

Hitler served only nine months of his five-year sentence. During this time he wrote the first volume of a bizarre book he wanted to call "Four and a Half Years of Struggle Against Lies, Stupidity and Cowardice." A publisher talked him into changing the title to *Mein Kampf,* "My Struggle."

With Hitler in his cell at Castle Landsburg was his editor and devoted homosexual disciple, Rudolph Hess, who hadn't been convicted of anything but chose to live in prison with his idol, Adolf. It was Hess who declared, "Hitler is simply pure reason incarnate" and called him "the greatest son whom my nation has brought forth in the thousand years of its history." It was Hess who, when the war began, wrote British aristocrat, the future duke of Hamilton, suggesting peace. It was also Hess who, in May 1941, flew an unarmed German fighter plane from Augsburg to the duke of Hamilton's Scottish estate. It may have been a peace mission; it may have been an effort to trick the British. Hess may even have been crazy. Apparently, he left Hitler a note saying that if his mission failed—whatever that mission really was—Hitler could say that Hess had gone mad.

Even before he flew off to Scotland, Rudolph Hess was the subject of ridicule among some of his fellow Nazi Party members. Behind his (and Hitler's) back, they referred to Hess as "Fräulein Anna" because of his homosexuality.

Hess's mission did fail, and Hitler said his former cell mate was crazy. He kicked Hess out of the Nazi Party and replaced him with Martin Bormann.

By this time, Hess was being held by British authorities, who were baffled by his actions. They treated him just as he'd said he was—a mental case. For the rest of the war they held him in the Tower of London. Later, he was tried at Nuremberg and convicted of crimes against humanity. He and seven others were sent to Berlin's Spandau Prison. Twenty years later, Hess was the sole man remaining; all the others had died or been set free. Twenty-one years later he died himself.

Spandau Prison is gone now, torn down, a supermarket built in its place.

The third member of the Axis' terrible trio was Hideki Tojo, Japan's prime minister. "Fighting Tojo" his schoolmasters called him;

later his nickname was "Razor Brain." Scrawny, bald, and wearing thick glasses, he was an easy target for political satirists. When it was suggested that Japan withdraw its troops from China and Korea, Tojo objected vehemently: "The way of diplomacy isn't always a matter of concessions; sometimes it is oppression." Pulling its troops out of areas it had overrun would be "a stain on the history of the Japanese Empire."

After October 1941, Hideki Tojo was both prime minister and war minister, as well as the army's leading spokesman. In the fall of 1942, he assumed even more authority and became foreign minister, succeeding longtime diplomat Shigenori Togo. This gave him unquestioned control over Japan. Tojo believed that the United States was strangling Japan's economy and the only recourse was war. Historian Basil Collier, however, claims that Tojo was a "right-wing conservative rather than a revolutionary."

Tojo resigned on July 18, 1945, just weeks before Japan surrendered. When General MacArthur ordered Tojo arrested, he refused to leave his home in Setagaya. Finally, an American MP shouted, "Tell this yellow bastard we've waited long enough. Bring him out!"

Hideki Tojo attempted suicide by shooting himself in the chest. He lived, however, and after a controversial trial was sentenced to death. He was hanged on December 24, 1948.

CHAPTER ELEVEN

At War in the Air:
Off We Go Into an Even Wilder Blue Yonder

They that wait upon the Lord shall renew their strength; they shall mount up their wings as eagles; they shall run, and not be weary; and they shall walk, and not faint.
—The Holy Bible, *Isaiah* 40:31

In what distant deeps or skies
Burnt the fire of thine eyes?
On what winds dare he aspire?

—William Blake, *The Tyger,* 1, 2

Germany's war economy wasn't nearly so bad as we were told, its war production not nearly so hampered by round-the-clock bombing. In the fall of 1943, German factories turned out more fighter planes than the Allies shot down. In 1944, Germany produced 39,807 aircraft. The United States, however, turned out 96,318, almost two and a half times as many. Britain produced another 26,461; the Soviet Union, according to Josef Stalin, turned out about 40,000 planes. World War II was like every other war: the side that produced the most guns or ships or planes won.

In December 1940, Britain's royal family sent out what came to be known as "Blitzmas Cards." King George VI and his family posed in front of London's bomb-torn Buckingham Palace. The cards clearly showed where German bombs had destroyed part of the family's opulent home. It was a very effective way of saying that England, even the royal family, suffered and survived the bombing.

In February 1944, the German Luftwaffe launched what came to be called the Little Blitz. The seven days of attacks were nowhere near the scale of the 1940–41 Blitz of London, because the Luftwaffe was too weak for a major assault. Besides, the German air command knew about Berlin's next weapons.

One week after the Allies landed at Normandy, while England luxuriated in the mistaken belief it would be over soon, Germany introduced a new weapon: the *Vergeltungswaffe*. "Retaliation bombs," Hitler called them. Vengeance bombs. Officially, the Germans called them Fieseler Fi 103s. The British had less official names for them: buzz bombs or doodlebugs. They were also known as V-1s.

The V-1 was the first missile in history to be used in a large-scale attack. Four were launched against England on June 13, 1944. Three didn't make it to their targets, but the fourth exploded in the Bethnal Green section of London, killing six people and injuring nine others. More buzz bombs followed.

The V-1 was launched from a short catapult and climbed to a height of about 3,000 feet and reached a maximum cruising speed of about 400 miles per hour. It was just under 26 feet long, about half again as long as a modern, full-sized car. Carrying 1,870-pound warheads, a V-1 was more than a mere doodlebug. Its standard range was about 150 miles.

The V-1 was a pilotless aircraft powered by a pulse-jet engine, built of inexpensive materials worth about $600. A gyroscopic control unit kept the V-1 on a preset compass course. An aneroid barometer helped it maintain specified altitudes. At the nose was a small propeller that drove what's called an airlog, used to measure a programmed distance. The airlog itself wasn't new; the Wright brothers had a similar instrument on their 1903 flyer.

When the airlog counted off a preprogrammed distance, the jet engine cut out. The buzz bomb tipped over and the aircraft dove to the ground. It was this sudden stopping of its engine, perhaps as much as the actual damage the bomb did, that frightened the English. They'd hear the sputtering roar of the engine—the sound of a jet engine was strange enough in 1944—then came sudden silence. Those on the ground knew the next sound they'd hear might be an explosion near them, might well be the end of their lives.

Lionel King was an eight-year-old boy in London when V-1s landed all around him. He later recalled his reactions.

> The first came over one afternoon. . . . It gave us little warning. Ten seconds and the engine cut out directly overhead.

There was an oddly resounding explosion about half a mile away. . . .

Day after day the rush to the shelter. A cut out. A distant explosion. Back to play in the garden. One breakfast Mum rushed in from the kitchen: "One coming!" From the shelter the explosion seemed close.

One Saturday night we were awakened suddenly from our sleep in the shelter by the sound of glass fragmenting in a long crescendo, as if countless objects were slowly being slid off a ledge. It must have been about 1 A.M.

"That's our home gone!" shrieked our mother.

V-1s killed more than 6,000 people in England, most of them civilians. They seriously wounded thousands more and wrecked and damaged an estimated 1 million buildings. Winston Churchill later wrote: "This new form of attack imposed upon the people of London was a burden perhaps even heavier than the air-raids of 1940 and 1941. Suspense and strain were more prolonged. Dawn brought no relief, and clouds no comfort."

London was not the only target. Parts of Kent and Sussex were hit so often that the area became known as "bomb alley." Churchill himself was almost the victim of a V-1 missile. "One landed near my home at Westerham," he wrote, "killing, by cruel mischance, twenty-two homeless children and five grownups collected in a refuge for them in the woods." Trying to put a good light on the attack, Churchill said in Parliament, "The people at home could feel they were sharing the perils of their soldiers." In the first two weeks of the V-1 attack, an average of a hundred missiles a day fell on Britain.

The V-1 was developed at Germany's gigantic underground *Mittelwerke* factory near Nordhausen, southwest of Berlin and west of Leipzig. About 30,000 V-1 missiles were built, mainly by slave labor from a nearby concentration camp. More than 20,000 such prisoners died while forced to build Hitler's vengeance bombs.

The Allied air forces discovered where the V-1s were being built, and before the first one fell on London the American Eighth Air Force began Operation Crossbow to knock out the plant. It didn't do much good, but it resulted in more than 25,000 bombing sorties dropping more than 36,000 tons of bombs. They would have flown more, but operations were limited by the weather, at the time said to be the worst winter in Europe's history. More than 2,000 American airmen died in the effort to stop the V-1s, even as the missiles fell on London and Antwerp, the Belgium city that the Allies used to land material for invading forces.

Operation Crossbow didn't stop the V-1s but it did force the Luftwaffe to alter its plans for permanent V-1 launch sites. After July 1944, the Luftwaffe began dropping V-1s from high-flying bombers and made plans for other bombers to tow the V-1s into range. They even flight-tested a piloted version, but it never was used operationally.

The V-1 attack began in June 1944, lasting until March 1945. About one-third of the V-1s launched against England reached their targets. The rest were destroyed in the air, either by aircraft or anti-aircraft guns or barrage balloons.

Barrage balloons, those large, unmanned balloons, were anchored by steel cables and sent aloft to foul aircraft wings and propellers. Just how effective they were against manned aircraft is hard to say. However, they were cheap; they destroyed more than 200 V-1s and, in the United States, became the symbol of the Battle of Britain.

The idea for barrage balloons went back to World War I, their ancestors even further back. Such balloons led Germany's Graf Ferdinand von Zeppelin to invent a much larger balloon and name it after himself. Von Zeppelin's zeppelin first flew in 1900. By the thirties, these rigid airships, generally known as dirigibles, were all the rage. On May 6, 1937, the zeppelin *Hindenburg* attempted to land in a thunderstorm at the U.S. Naval Air Station at Lakehurst, New Jersey. It carried 36 passengers, a crew of 56, tons of mail, and 6.7 million cubic feet of explosive hydrogen gas. Lightning apparently struck either the mooring tower or the *Hindenburg* itself. Reporter Herbert A. Morrison of Chicago's WLS Radio was doing a live nationwide broadcast on the arrival of the zeppelin, and in one dramatic, unforgettable moment, the United States learned of the disaster: "Oh, the humanity . . . !" Miraculously, 57 people survived the crash; the *Hindenburg* itself was reduced to a pile of twisted steel, and that was the end of Zeppelin's dirigibles.

Now, nearly sixty years after the event, people argue over whether the *Hindenburg*'s crash was an accident of nature or an act of sabotage. It was, sabotage advocates argue, something of a Nazi propaganda coup every time zeppelins flew. The *Hindenburg*, they claim, even carried on electronic surveillance missions for Germany in that suspicious prewar time.

U.S. Navy airships called blimps were the smaller descendants of the zeppelins. They were filled with a far safer helium gas and began flying coastal antisubmarine patrols in early 1943.

How blimps got their name isn't certain. One version has it that they were named after model B "limp" British airships—blimps; however there never was any such model B airship, but it makes a good story. An equally simple, even more serendipitous, version has a British Royal Navy pilot pressing his thumb into the side of a nonrigid airship and hearing the sound it made: "blimp!"

Instead of observing submarines, modern descendants of World War II blimps observe other, sometimes equally deadly, endeavors. You can see them on almost any given Saturday or Sunday afternoon, flying high above stadiums, sending back televised pictures of groups of large human beings banging heads in a type of warfare called football.

Meanwhile, the descendants of World War II barrage balloons are the more colorful variety flown over newly opened American supermarkets.

While Londoners looked to the skies and listened for V-1 engines to cut out, Germany worked on the Fritz-X. Officially designated by Germany as the X-1, the Fritz-X was a radio-controlled glide bomb launched from high-flying bombers, not unlike cruise missiles launched today by modern warplanes.

In early September 1943, the remnants of the Italian fleet were steaming toward Malta to be surrendered to the Allies. It was one day after General Eisenhower had announced the surrender of all Italian forces to the Allies.

Dornier Do217 bombers carrying Fritz-X missiles attacked their former Italian Allies aboard the battleship *Roma*. The Fritz-X carried a 704-pound, armor-piercing warhead; it easily shot through *Roma*'s thin skin and exploded. Water rushed in, and ruptured electrical cables sparked. After the vessel fell out of formation, a second Fritz-X hit, setting off more fires and causing more flooding. One of the ship's gun turrets exploded. The *Roma* capsized, broke in two, and sank. More than 1,200 members of her 1,849-man crew died. So much for Germany's former allies.

Later that day, the *Roma*'s sister ship, the *Italia,* also was hit by a Fritz-X missile, but it got away. A week later, the British battleship HMS *Warspite* wasn't as lucky. The ship was so heavily damaged that she had to be towed to port, where she sat out the rest of the war. Miraculously, only nine men died in the attack on the *Warspite.*

An American ship, the *Savannah,* also survived an attack by a Fritz-X missile. The bomb penetrated a gun turret and exploded deep in the cruiser's interior. More than 200 men died in the attack, but it could have been worse. Water rushing in through holes made by the explosion prevented the ship's magazine from exploding.

Germany built almost 1,400 Fritz-X missiles in a 21-month period. About half of them were used in tests. The missile was dropped from an altitude of 26,000 feet and could be controlled by radio. Like some other German weapons invented during the war, the Fritz-X came too late to do much harm to the Allied cause.

The V-1 was launched by the German air force, the Luftwaffe, while the next invention, the V-2 rocket, came from the German army. It was was the most spectacular weapon of the war and the precursor to today's intercontinental ballistic missiles.

Experiments on rockets began in the 1930s. (Those launched against Britain were the fourth version of the weapon, called the A-4 by German scientists.) They successfully test-fired the first V-2 in late 1942 from Pennemünde on the Baltic Sea. It would be almost two years before the V-2 became operational, but the rain of rockets that began on September 6, 1944, saw nearly 1,200 missiles launched in the next six months.

The first two V-2s were aimed at Paris, newly liberated by the Allies. Very quickly, however, England became their prime target. After Paris, Chiswick, England, had the "honor" of receiving a German V-2 rocket. It landed at 6:34 P.M. on September 8, 1944, taking several lives. Nearly all V-2s that went up, came down in England; however, in addition to targeting London and several European cities, Germany launched V-2s at the Ludendorff railway bridge at Remagen, Germany (site of the first Allied Rhine River crossings), hoping to delay the Allied advance.

V-1 missiles sometimes were shot down by antiaircraft guns or fighters, but the V-2 couldn't be touched; it flew too high—about six miles up—and too fast—nearly 4,000 miles per hour. At that speed, it took the V-2 only three to four minutes to reach its target 200 or so miles away.

Toward the end of World War II, Londoners called the V-2 "Bob Hope," a double meaning. The radio and movie comedian aside, it meant "Bob down and Hope for the best."

The V-2 was almost twice as long as a V-1 and carried more than 2,000 pounds of explosives. Luckily for those near ground zero, much of the explosive force was absorbed by the ground because the V-2 dug in several feet before detonating. The V-1s did more damage, but V-2s gave their victims an unwanted insight into the future. They killed nearly 2,800 people in England and injured another 6,500.

Generally, the V-2 was a wingless creature, but a variant called the A-4b was developed with wings; it had more than twice the range of the wingless form. When the war ended, German scientists were working on an advanced A-10 model, a two-stage missile designed to be launched in Europe to reach America's major East Coast cities, something neither enemy bombers nor missiles were ever able to do during World War II.

Allied pilots found it difficult to locate and destroy V-2 launch sites. The missiles needed no permanent launch pad and could be trucked in, unloaded, set up, and quickly fired. The launch platform itself was easily removed and trucked to its next location.

Britain's Air Chief Marshal Sir Arthur Harris viewed the V weapons as cowardly things, "damn silly rockets." He wanted to launch a gas attack on Germany in reprisal for V-1 and V-2 attacks. Several bomber crews were trained to do the job. Eisenhower and others talked him out of it.

After Germany surrendered, both the United States and the Soviet Union rushed to take control of Nordhausen and Peenemünde along with the remaining V-1 and V-2 missiles. They captured dozens of V-2s, and the United States eventually test-fired sixty-nine of them.

The United States built a few V-1-type missiles on speculation, calling them "Yankee Doodles"; the navy planned to send them against Japan, using ships as launching pads. The navy also experimented with launching American-built V-1s from surfaced submarines, another preview of modern warfare.

For the United States and the Soviet Union, the end of World War II meant the race was on, not just to capture German rockets but to capture German rocket scientists. The Soviets occupied the coveted research site at Peenemünde, but many scientists, including Arthur Rudolph and Werner von Braun, had already surrendered to American GIs.

Two years after the war ended, the United States and Germany worked together on Operation Paper Clip, a plan aimed at clearing Nazi scientists for permanent immigration visas in America. The code name came from the way photographs of scientists were attached to incriminating documents. The photographs more easily indentified those who were to be cleared.

The United States hoped to get the scientists working as quickly as possible on American missiles, so records were doctored—sanitized, some called it—on orders from the Pentagon. America couldn't have any Nazis working on U.S. rockets, so their past was cleaned up with not a Fascist left in sight. Even Arthur Rudolph came, and he'd been an ardent Nazi, using thousands of slave laborers from the Nordhausen concentration camp.

Rudolph became the production chief for the U.S. Saturn V rocket. He, like many other German scientists whose history was sanitized, became an American citizen. However, in 1984, Rudolph denounced his U.S. citizenship after being deported to Germany to be tried for war crimes.

Werner von Braun's rockets ravaged much of London in 1944. With his record spruced up, he quickly became part of America's space effort. By 1960, he had helped produce the U.S. Jupiter-C and

Saturn rockets. Twenty-two years after his V-2 rockets rained down on London, another of his rockets put American astronauts on the moon.

Field Marshal Erhard Milch was a fighter squadron commander in World War I, even though he didn't fly. In 1929, at age thirty-six, he became chairman of Deutsche Lufthansa, the newly developed commercial airline meant to cover Germany's rebuilding airpower. Milch met Adolf Hitler in 1930, and he was impressed by *der Führer's* grasp of aviation problems. Hitler decorated Milch with the coveted Gold Party Badge, even though Milch's father was a Jew.

By 1935, Milch was head of the Air Ministry and was the deputy state secretary for the Reich air ministry under Hermann Göring. For a while, Milch (through Lufthansa) deposited 1,000 reichmarks a month in Göring's personal bank account. Needless to say, Milch and Göring were good friends.

Although other top Nazis attacked Milch as a half Jew, Göring demanded that he alone be the one to "determine who in the Luftwaffe is a Jew and who is not." To get around the fact that Erhard's father definitely was a Jew, Göring had Milch's mother sign an affidavit claiming that her husband wasn't really the father, that she'd had an adulterous affair with a minor aristocrat, Baron Hermann von Bier. It was the baron who was Erhard's father and, therefore, Erhard Milch (or von Bier) was a pure-blood Aryan. With his background certified, Milch became one of Nazi Germany's most vocally anti-Jewish citizens. That let him carry on his work with Lufthansa/Luftwaffe.

Back in 1939, Milch began pushing the development of the Me262 fighter, the world's first operational jet fighter. Without doubt, it was the most advanced aircraft that Germany put in the air: twin jets that pushed the Me262 to speeds upward of 540 miles per hour. It had partially swept-back wings and heavy armament. Officially, the Germans called it the *Schwalbe*, or Swallow. Usually, its pilots called it the Turbo. About 1,400 Me262s were built; luckily for the Allies, only about 300 got into operation.

By the end of 1944, Field Marshal Milch was in trouble. Hitler wanted Germany's new jet plane to be a bomber, the *Sturmvogel*, or Stormbird. Milch, however, insisted it be built as a fighter. *Der Führer,* of course, won the argument, and he fired Milch. As in many other cases, if Hitler had gone ahead with the more sane of his aide's ideas, the outcome of the war might have been far different.

The theory of jet propulsion wasn't new. It had been around so long that the original patent had expired. An RAF officer, Frank Whittle, once held the patent on the jet engine, but he had to let it lapse when he couldn't afford the renewal fees.

The public knew very little about jets. Once jet planes were flying in 1944, *Life* magazine felt that it had to run a three-page story on jet fighters to explain how those strange planes flew without propellers.

Great Britain got its version, the Gloster Meteor into the air in early 1941. It was powered by twin Rolls-Royce turbojet engines, and went into limited operation in July 1944. About 300 Meteors were built, all late in the war. With a top speed of about 410 miles per hour, the Meteor was much slower than Germany's jet fighter. It was, however, fast enough that, in at least one instance, it downed a V-1. It happened on August 4, 1944, because the guns jammed on RAF Flying Officer T. D. Dean's jet fighter. Dean flew alongside the buzzing doodlebug, hooked a wing of his Meteor under the missile's fin, and sent the V-1 into a crash dive.

Early in 1945 the RAF began flying Meteors over Europe, hunting their German counterparts, but there never was a jet-versus-jet aerial dogfight. That came in the next war, the so-called Korean Police Action, when an American P-80 (renamed F-80) Shooting Star downed a Soviet-built MiG-15.

One of England's first operational Meteors was sent to the United States in exchange for the jet fighter that America was working on, the P-59A. The P-59A was a twin-turbojet, single-seat aircraft with a top speed about 100 miles per hour slower than many piston-engine fighters of the day. Like its British cousin, it was also much slower than the German Me262. None of the 20 P-59As or 36 P-59Bs delivered to the air force in the fall of 1944 ever saw combat in World War II.

While Germany was flying jet-powered planes and rockets, the Soviet Union continued flying the Po-2, a biplane first produced in

1928. The simple, cloth-covered plane was used primarily as a night bomber, but it was also used for reconnaissance and artillery spotting. Occasionally it was used to supply partisans and even to take injured soldiers to safety.

It had a top speed of about 90 miles per hour and a range of less than 300 miles and could carry a 600-pound bomb load. It required only 400 feet of runway to take off and less than 500 feet for landing.

About 35,000 Po-2 biplanes were built, almost as many as America's Douglas DC-3 and its many military designations. Most of the Po-2s were built during the war, but production continued into the 1950s. Some Po-2s are still flying in Russia today as crop dusters.

CHAPTER TWELVE

Weapons Stranger Than Fiction:
Is This a Gun I See Before Me?

Weapons are an important factor in war, but not the decisive one; it is man and not materials that count.

—Mao Tse-tung, lecture, 1938

Lack of weapons is no excuse for defeat.

—Lt. Gen. Renya Matuguchi, commanding general, Japanese Fifteenth Army

In the fifties and sixties, television actor Don Herbert became popular as Mr. Wizard, showing America's youth how there was more to a chemistry set than the ability to burn sulfur and clear out the house. He enlisted as a private in the army, then volunteered for flight school. He graduated and became a B-24 pilot, flying fifty-six missions with the Fifteenth Air Force. Herbert was awarded the Distinguished Flying Cross and the Air Medal with three Oak Leaf Clusters (small bronze devices attached to the original medal ribbon in lieu of a subsequent medal).

One of World War II's strangest weapons was the kind of thing you'd see in cartoons, a gun that shot around corners. But it was no cartoon; it actually worked. The idea grew out of house-to-house fighting in Stalingrad in 1943. As the Allies pushed into Germany, street fights grew more commonplace. Every time a German soldier stuck his head around a corner to fire a shot, someone shot at him instead, reasonable enough if you were on the other side. The solution was a device designed in armaments minister Albert Speer's technical office. The tricky part of the weapon, the part that actually curved around a corner, was called the *Krummer Lauf*. It was bolted onto a *Machinenpistole* MP43, the German rendition of the

113

Russian burp gun. The working model had a thirty-degree angle; designers had a forty-degree model under development but it never went into production. They even tested one bent at ninety degrees; with this last design, if you weren't careful, you might shoot your own troops.

The *Krummer Lauf* was about nineteen inches long and an inch thick. Add that to the *machinenpistole* itself and you had a long and heavy weapon, one decidedly unwieldy. At first, it had no sight, so although you could shoot around corners, you couldn't see what you were firing at. Later, designers attached a prismatic sight made by the famed Zeiss optical firm. You aligned the mirrors with the weapon's regular sight and fired away. Panzer crews particularly liked the around-the-corner weapon, because they could stay inside their tanks while fighting off would-be boarders.

Allied troops on both fronts captured the devices and quickly tested them. The U.S. Army Ordnance Corps tried the ninety-degree model, and it worked. There were, however, several drawbacks. You could fire only three shots in one burst; the bullets were torn into several pieces (meaning it was better for short-range fighting); and it had a powerful kickback, which made it tough to hold. Mounted on a tank, according to an ordnance corps report, the weapon was excellent. In fact, tests showed that it shot perfectly at distances up to 100 meters.

Invention of the weapon that shot around corners came too late for the Third Reich. About 10,000 of the devices were first ordered; then another 20,000 per month. Produced earlier, it might have cost thousands of Allied lives. As it was, it became merely another curiosity of the war.

The bazooka is an accepted weapon of war these days, but before 1942 it didn't exist, except, that is, for a 1940s musical device—*device* is the operative word here—played by Bob Burns, a popular comedian and musician.

The story goes that army captain Leslie A. Skinner and Lt. David E. Uhl came up with the design for the weapon. At first, recoil was a problem, but they solved that by removing the back end of the tube, allowing recoil-producing gases to vent. Skinner and Uhl had modified a British-made, hollow-point, high-explosive charge and put fins on it. A bent piece of wire added to the launch tube served as a crude sight. Their big day came at the Aberdeen Proving Grounds in Maryland, where army experts (which may be an oxymoron) were testing various weapons, hoping to find one that would knock out a tank.

None of the other would-be tank stoppers did the job, but when it came time for the Skinner and Uhl device, it took just one shot of this relatively small, hand-held rocket-launcher. Uhl pulled the trigger and pop! For good measure, Skinner reloaded the bazooka, and it was all over but the shouting; there was plenty of that. The next thing the captain and lieutenant knew, they were surrounded by generals wanting to have a go at it; this strange antitank (AT) weapon looked like fun.

A few days later, Army Chief of Staff George Marshall heard about the fun things going on at Aberdeen and ordered the new AT weapon into pilot production, 5,000 of them, right off the bat. You can't order a weapon that has no name, so somebody asked Captain Skinner what it was called. Thinking quickly, and remembering comedian Bob Burns, who called himself the "Old Arkansas Traveler," Skinner said, "It's a bazooka." The name stuck.

Bob Burns once claimed that he got the idea for his device after fooling around with a funnel-ended farming instrument used to plant a garden by hand. He'd rest the instrument on his shoulder and play what he claimed was music. Actually, it sounded something like a sick trombone.

Officially, the bazooka was called the Launcher, Rocket, Anti-Tank, M1, and the General Electric company was contracted to build the first order. Because it was so simple and seemed to work so well, General Marshall wanted them in the troops' hands in 30 days. All 5,000 of them. The project would take precedence over all other arms projects.

No designer, industrial or military, is ever satisfied with a product; make a change here, a variation there. Simple though it was, the bazooka was no exception. With an order in hand for 5,000 copies of the new weapon, GE decided to take it back to the drawing board. Design, test, redesign, and retest. When they got it down just right, GE had only a few days left to build them, which meant a lot of scurrying around and overtime and extemporaneous tactics. At one point, the factory had wooden gunstocks delivered in the trunks of siren-wailing police cars. Bazooka number 5,000 came off the factory line with just 89 minutes to spare.

The foot soldier now held in his hands the power of artillery. The tubelike device was 54 inches long, 2.36 inches in diameter, and fired a 3.5-pound projectile with a shaped charge. It was light, it could be folded in half, and it could be carried over the shoulder.

Normally, a two-man crew worked the bazooka—one man loading and the other aiming down the barrel and firing. In a pinch one man could do the job. Troops quickly learned not to fire the bazooka in an enclosed room or building; the concussion was too powerful. Writing after the war was over, one soldier remembered the bazooka's kickback:

> I picked up a bazooka and crawled among our dead men in the upper floor, looking for bazooka shells. Those shells weighed about four pounds each. . . . [When] I pulled the trigger . . . all the pressure came out of the back end of that tin pipe with a lot of red flame, and the house shook.

American troops first used bazookas in the North African campaign as an infantry weapon to counter German tanks. They didn't do much harm to a tank's heavy armor, but they worked well on the tank's tracks or even where the tank's armor was somewhat lighter. They were effective up to 400 yards, and more than 500,000 bazookas were manufactured during the war.

Almost as soon as America's bazooka hit the battlefield, it was captured by the enemy, and Germany developed its own version. Called the *panzerfaust* ("armor fist"), it weighed about the same as the American variety but had a longer range and was more accurate. The British also used a variant, calling theirs the PIAT. Toward the end of the war, the Soviet Union got into the bazooka business and began turning out its own particular (and peculiar) version. They tried to copy the German *panzerfaust,* but something must have gone wrong in the design translation. The Soviet bazooka lacked some of the German improvements, grew in size, and lost some of the *panzerfaust*'s newly gained range.

• • •

Germany's "Bouncing Betty" was one of the most hated weapons of World War II. It was the name that American GIs gave to the German *Schützenminen*, an antipersonnel land mine.

Land mines were invented during the Civil War by Confederate general Gabriel James Rains. He converted artillery shells, added hair-trigger percussion caps, buried them in the ground, and covered them with tin roofs for protection. Spread a bit of dirt and a few leaves over the bomb and wait.

The Bouncing Betty was a lot more and a lot worse. The mine contained a one-and-a-quarter-pound explosive charge and was filled with steel pellets. Prongs set in a triangular fashion ensured that the mine sat above the ground. A light covering of leaves served as camouflage. Sometimes trip wires were used for unwary feet to catch. If one of the prongs was disturbed, the mine exploded and shot upward three to six feet before it exploded. It showered steel pellets over a wide area, sometimes 300 feet in all directions.

The object of the Bouncing Betty was to injure, not to kill. The military realized that it required two or more men to carry a wounded soldier off the battlefield. A larger charge might kill one soldier while others continued the fight.

Another bouncing weapon was used, the upkeep bomb, a cylindrical device that was dropped from a plane and would bounce to the target. It was used only once, when the RAF wanted to destroy dams in Germany's Ruhr Valley. The aircrew set the bomb spinning backward at 500 revolutions per minute to extend its range. Flying at 220 miles per hour only 60 feet above the water behind the dam, the crew released the bomb so that it skipped across the water. It reached the dam, plunged over the edge, and exploded about 30 feet beneath the water's surface. The bomber crews became known as the "Dambusters."

CHAPTER THIRTEEN

Submarines:
More Than Just a Sandwich

Sighted sub, sank same.
    —Donald Francis Mason, U.S. Navy pilot, radio message, January 28, 1942

Light breaks where no sun shines;
Where no sea runs, the waters of the heart
Push in their tides.
    —Dylan Thomas, *Light Breaks Where No Sun Shines*

The first known submarine was called the *Turtle,* invented by Yale College graduate David Bushnell in 1775. It was built of heavy oak beams and looked like two turtle shells or a barrel, hence the name. Bushnell equipped the *Turtle* with pedal-powered screw propellers to drive it up and down, forward and backward; he added a hand-operated drill so that the operator could bore through an enemy ship's hull. The one-man crew-captain had a compass to determine correct direction but pretty much used the by-guess-and-by-God method of judging distances. A periscope would have come in handy, but the *Turtle* wasn't equipped with one.

David Bushnell's invention came close to sinking a British frigate in New York harbor during the American Revolution. On September 6, 1776, Sgt. Ezra Lee, of the Connecticut Line, pedaled the *Turtle* against HMS *Eagle,* planning to attach a waterproof time-charge bomb to the English warship's hull. Lee couldn't make the connection, however, and began pedaling back to shore. The British saw something strange muddying up the water and sent a boatload of troops after Lee and the *Turtle.* Trying to make his getaway, Lee dropped his load of explosives and, just as the British boat scooted nearby, the explosives detonated. Nobody on either side was hurt in the world's first submarine attack.

During America's Civil War, two other submarine-type crafts were built, both by the Confederacy. Each had its first (and only) moment of battle off Charleston, South Carolina. The *David* was more a semi-sub; it didn't completely submerge. It almost sank the USS *New Ironsides* in Charleston harbor, but the federal ship's officer of the deck spotted the little boat and sounded an alarm. *New Ironsides* rolled with the punch when the Rebel boat's torpedo exploded. The blast, however, swamped the sub's engine, and its crew went scampering overboard to save their lives. All but one man were captured, and he tried to give up. When no one noticed him, he reboarded the *David*, restarted the engine, and headed back to Charleston.

The *H. L. Hunley* was called a torpedo boat. Not only did it also operate off Charleston harbor, it's still there. It sank three times during trials. Each time a crew drowned, once taking its inventor, Horace Hunley. On February 17, 1864, it sank the USS *Housatonic*, but it sank itself (possibly from the blast of its own torpedo) before it could return to shore. In 1995, the *Hunley* was discovered on the harbor floor, and there's talk of refloating and restoring it.

German U-boats, or *Unterseeboots*, almost defeated Britain in World War I and were well on the way to victory during World War II. The Versailles Treaty at the end of the Great War forbade Germany from having submarines; of course, that didn't stop them, and by 1920 the Berlin government had begun a clandestine submarine design program in Holland, Finland, Spain, and Turkey, with the first boat launched in 1935. It was clandestine but well known. Winston Churchill called it a "brazen and fraudulent" violation of the treaty, which also didn't stop the Germans. Instead, the British admiralty proposed a bilateral treaty to allow the German navy to build up to 60 percent of British strength in submarines. By 1939, Germany had 57 U-boats. The United States had 114 commissioned submarines when war broke out, about half of them fleet boats operating out of Pearl Harbor or Manila Bay in the Philippines. Another 63 American submarines operated on the East and West Coasts. On December 7, 1941, there were 73 fleet submarines under construction in U.S. shipyards. By the end of the war, a total of 202 new U.S. submarines had been built.

Several American submarines already were at sea when the Japanese attacked Pearl Harbor. Immediately, the navy ordered their captains to attack any Japanese ship they found, military or merchant.

Early in World War II, U.S. submarine fleet admirals thought in terms of sheer tonnage, not in the *kind* of tonnage. In 1942, for example, American submarines sank 180 Japanese ships, a total of about 750,000 tons.

Those figures are good considering the major problem that U.S. submarines had at the time: faulty torpedoes. It took the navy until mid-1943 to come up with solutions. Two things were wrong with American torpedoes. First, they used drinkable, if nonvintage, alcohol as fuel to create steam propulsion. Thirsty sailors occasionally tippled on "torpedo juice," which when mixed with grapefruit juice became something called a pink lady. When the weapons, drained of their alcohol, were fired, they fizzled and flopped. The navy solved the problem by replacing the alcohol in the torpedoes (along with the alcohol in such items as compasses) with deadly carbon tetrachloride and attaching notices warning "Do Not Drink."

The second problem was the torpedoes' exploder. The U.S. Navy's top-of-the-line torpedo, the Mark-14, used a magnetic exploder. If it came near a steel-hulled ship, it was supposed to explode. The technique called for the submarine to fire the torpedo under the target; the exploder, the navy claimed, would be "triggered by the changes which a steel-hulled ship caused in the Earth's magnetic field." If the torpedo exploded beneath a ship's keel, the theory went, the vessel's back could be broken.

Mark-14s cost about $10,000 each in 1940s money, a far cry from today's million-dollar-a-missile armaments. But it was expensive for the times, so expensive that the navy originally failed to test live warheads. As a result, the Mark-14 usually ran deeper than set for, so it often passed harmlessly under the target ship.

Now, bureaucracies being bureauracracies, the govenment's Bureau of Ordnance ignored field reports showing what was wrong. Holding to their ways, they refused to run further tests until pressured into it. Finally, they did, and the new tests confirmed reports from frustrated submariners. Which did not mean the problem was solved. Since magnetic exploders, in effect, worked with the Earth's magnetic field, the mechanism reacted differently according to where the ship was. A Mark-14 fired in the South Pacific, for instance, reacted differently from one tested off New England, where the torpedo had been developed. It wasn't until mid-1943 that the navy corrected the problem and submarines began doing consistent damage to German and Japanese shipping.

American torpedoes in World War II were inferior to Japanese models in everything that counts—speed, range, and warhead power. The United States built 64,000 torpedoes during the war, and the U.S. Navy fired approximately 14,750 of them at 3,184 ships. American torpedoes sank 1,314 ships totaling 5.3 million tons.

The first successful U.S. submarine attack of World War II came barely a week after Pearl Harbor, on December 15, 1941. The *Swordfish* sank the *Atsutasan Maru,* a Japanese merchant ship, off the coast of Indochina. *Swordfish* later was used to evacuate Philippine president Manuel Quezon and his family from the island of Corregidor.

World War II U.S. submarines operated primarily in the Pacific Ocean, although they carried out at least 86 patrols along the U.S. East Coast and near the Panama Canal. One submarine, *SS-78,* reported making contact with a German U-boat off the coast of Bermuda in the spring of 1942. The American skipper says he fired four torpedoes at the German boat, and the U.S. Navy gave him credit (and a Navy Cross) for sinking a sub. A postwar check of German records turned up no mention of a U-boat being in the area at the time.

Early in the war, German U-boats took a devastating toll on Allied ships, sinking 2,742 for a total of more than 13 million gross tons. The turning point of the war in the Atlantic came, as it did in the Pacific, in 1943, with the Allies' development of radar and sonar Huff-Duff (high-frequency direction finding), along with escort carriers and their sub-hunting planes. Allied ships and aircraft outgunned the German boats.

World War II submarines were equipped with both diesel engines and electric motors, the batteries recharged by the diesels. That had to be done on the surface, however, which made submarines highly vulnerable to being spotted from the air. Generally, submarine captains tried to run on the surface at night and stay submerged during the day.

As early as 1897, navies around the world tinkered with devices that would allow them to run submerged on something other than battery power. In the 1930s, a Dutch submariner named J. J. Wichers developed an efficient means of getting the job done. The British referred to it as a "snort," and British subs using the device were said to be snorting. To the Germans, it was a *schnorchel.* American sailors called it a snorkel. In whatever version, whatever language, it had two valves which, when raised a few feet above the water's surface, allowed fresh air into the sub and kept water out. When Germany invaded Holland in 1940, several Dutch snorkel-equipped submarines were captured. It wasn't until 1943, however, when the Allies began winning the undersea war, that the German navy began experimenting with snorkels. After an initial test proved satisfactory, all German U-boats were equipped with the device.

It wasn't a perfect system. Submarines had to cut down their speed to keep from breaking off the snorkel tube. If a wave closed the snorkel's valve, the boat's diesel engine sucked air from the sub itself, and that quickly changed the air pressure within the boat, often resulting in damaged eardrums for U-boat crews.

With a snorkel, it took about three hours running at reduced speed to recharge the boat's batteries. That was fine unless a sharp-eyed airplane pilot or crewman noticed the wake left in the water by the snorkel.

Germany was working on another method for submarines to run longer and faster underwater. Engineer Helmuth Walter proposed a closed-cycle turbine engine that used energy produced by the decomposition of hydrogen peroxide. It could power a submerged submarine at sustained high speeds.

German admiral Karl Dönitz liked the idea, and two prototypes were built that ran submerged for five and a half hours at the then unheard of speed of 20 knots. In bursts, they reached 25 knots, this at a time when the normal run-of-the-ocean submarine's speed when submerged was more like 10 knots. Dönitz ordered 100 submarines built with closed-cycle engines, but thanks to bureaucratic bungling, none was completed before the war ended in 1945.

In 1941, Germany had an average of 30 U-boats at sea at any one time. By the end of 1943, the average was up to 100. The U-boat fleet was at its peak in May 1943, when an average of 118 German submarines were on duty. After that, the numbers fell rapidly.

Germany continued U-boat construction up to the moment of surrender. During the war, the Third Reich lost 784 submarines out of about 1,153 built. Another 154 surrendered, and 218 were scuttled by their crews. About 830 U-boats actually were commissioned. They conducted about 3,000 war patrols and sank more than 3,500 enemy ships totaling 18.3 million tons.

Serving on board a German submarine was deadly work. Of the more than 40,000 men who served on German U-boats, about 28,000 of them died in the war—a 70 percent death rate. Another 5,000 were taken prisoner. Germany's undersea service was voluntary and, despite the high death toll, there were always those willing to take a chance.

American servicemen, always with a way for words, called German submarines hearses. Which, of course, meant that U-boat crew members were pallbearers.

On June 4, 1944, Capt. Daniel V. Gallery, commanding officer of the carrier *Guadalcanal,* issued an order unheard from an American ship's captain since the War of 1812: "Away all boarders!" For the first time in more than 130 years, American seamen were about to capture and board an enemy vessel on the high seas.

It came off the coast of French West Africa. *Guadalcanal's* hunter-killer group had located the German submarine *U-505.* Just over four years old, it was one of Germany's largest long-range boats—250 feet long and displacing 1,232 tons when fully loaded. *U-505* was designed to operate on the surface most of the time and to dive only when she was about to attack or be attacked. She carried a crew of four officers and 56 men and was armed, at the time of the event, with 22 torpedoes and antiaircraft weapons.

A bit of the boat's history. In July 1942, *U-505* was at her peak, running submerged on routine patrol. A lookout spotted an unusual sight, "a three-masted schooner flying no flag [and] making violent zigzags back and forth." Hans Goebeler was a crewman on board the *U-505*. He says it was "not the kind of zigzags a sailing ship makes to move across the wind, but the kind a ship makes to avoid torpedoes." And that, Goebeler adds, "made us suspicious." The sub surfaced and her captain ordered a shot fired over the schooner's bow. They made a mistake, however, and instead of a warning shot, the *U-505*'s deck gun blew off the schooner's mainmast, "and that ship wasn't a sailing ship anymore." The sub's captain felt that he couldn't leave evidence floating around, so he fired another shot to sink the schooner.

It turned out, however, not to be just any old sailing ship. It belonged to a Colombian diplomat, and sinking it led to Colombia's declaring war on Germany.

Over the next two years, the *U-505* occasionally sustained minor damage and had to be repaired. She was sabotaged at least twice while undergoing repairs. Once, a workman packed ropes into welding seams to interfere with the hull's integrity, and *U-505* had to put back in to correct the damage. The second incident involved a pencil-sized hole punched in the fuel tank. As the submarine steamed out of port, she left "a trail of diesel oil, which could be spotted by Allied aircraft," Hans Goebeler remembers. Back to port for more repairs.

In the summer of 1944, *U-505* was patrolling off Freetown, West Africa, now the capital of Sierra Leone. Most commercial traffic had abandoned the area, but other ships—*Guadalcanal*'s hunter-killer task force—were there, all hounding *U-505*.

It was about 11 A.M. on June 4, *U-505* was quietly working her patrol when suddenly her sound detection equipment picked up faint propeller sounds. Instead of checking the area with his periscope, the captain decided to surface. When he did, he found himself right in the middle of the American task force. Three U.S. destroyers and several aircraft were rushing toward him. As fast as she could, *U-505* dived but not before one of the aircraft could mark her. Within minutes, the destroyers dumped hedgehogs (antisubmarine mortars) and depth charges on the German sub. One explosion damaged torpedoes stored in the sub's upper deck. Another jammed the boat's main rudder and diving planes. The German crew got off one torpedo shot, but it missed. Their boat badly damaged, the crew surfaced and abandoned ship.

It was up to the chief engineer to set demolition charges, but as soon as *U-505* surfaced, he jumped overboard to save himself. Air relief valves were stuck closed, and the crew couldn't open them to scuttle the submarine. All this time, as seaman Hans Goebeler remembers, American destroyers and aircraft "were giving us hell, firing antiaircraft, antipersonnel and high-explosive weapons at our boat."

Realizing there wasn't much they could do, the crew swam away from the damaged sub as fast as they could. Meanwhile, according to Goebeler, "The planes were shooting the water between us and the boat, chasing us away from *U-505* like a cat playing with mice. But none of us was crazy enough to want to go back to that boat because she was sinking fast!"

Aboard *Guadalcanal*, Captain Gallery had something else in mind. He was afraid that the German captain had managed to scuttle the submarine, but he hoped he could get there in time. So he gave the "Away all boarders!" order; take and board the enemy submarine. Lieutenant Junior Grade Albert David and eleven men jumped into a whaleboat from the destroyer *Pillsbury*. They were to take control of the German vessel and sail it to a port in the Caribbean.

Meanwhile, *U-505* continued steaming away, her rudder locked and making a continuous starboard turn. It didn't take long for Lieutenant David and his men to catch up with the submarine and board their prize. Now they had to secure it. The sub's stern was settling in the water, and the Americans were afraid that the boat's destruction devices might explode at any minute.

A quick search located an eight-inch stream of water pouring in. A machinist's mate quickly found a cover, jammed it in place, and secured it. Within minutes *Guadalcanal*'s chief engineer arrived and stopped the sub's engines. Good news and bad; *U-505* was no longer steaming away but she was no longer under way. She began to settle deeper in the water, a dangerous condition.

German submarines usually carried fourteen demolition charges. The American boarders hadn't located any of them, and no one knew if one or more might explode at any minute. Uncertain how much time they had, the American boarding crew proceeded uncertainly, pumping out their prize, putting the rudder amidships, and attaching towlines.

Earlier in the war Britain captured four other Axis submarines. *U-505* was America's first, and the navy worked hard at keeping it a secret from Germany. The longer it took Germany to discover that the United States had one of Adm. Karl Dönitz's submarines as well as Nazi code books and machines, the better for the Allies. As a destroyer towed the captured submarine to Bermuda, everyone in the escort group was sworn to secrecy.

Seaman Goebeler says that once he and his fellow crew members were plucked from the water, they were taken on board the carrier and locked up near the ship's engines, "in a cage just below the flight deck." It was so hot, he claims, during the trip to America that most of the men lost between twenty and thirty pounds each due to dehydration. Later, they were sent to a prisoner of war camp in Louisiana but weren't allowed to speak with representatives of the International Red Cross, because "The Americans didn't want . . . our navy [to] know that the U-boat had been captured." The German POWs worked on farms and in logging camps, then were transferred to Great Britain in 1945 until finally released in December 1947.

After the war, the U.S. Navy took *U-505* on a tour of U.S. ports, letting sailors who had feared her and her kind see just what it was they had been fighting.

Hans Goebeler came back to America. At age seventy-four, he lives in semiretirement in central Florida, selling coffee mugs with pictures of *U-505* on them. He makes a modest income.

As for *U-505*, there's nothing modest about her current existence. She's on display at Chicago's Museum of Science and Industry, just off the city's famed Lake Shore Drive. Every year, more than half a million tourists walk her decks. On sunny summer days, would-be submariners peer through *U-505*'s periscope, looking for targets of opportunity. Instead of the Atlantic Ocean and ships to be challenged, they see Lake Michigan and billowing sails of another generation taking to the water for a far different reason.

Submarines were used not only as attack weapons; some were used principally as minelayers, some for carrying cargo, some as oilers, and some as troop-carrying boats. Germany's type XIV submarine carried fuel and provisions needed by smaller submarines and earned the nickname Milch Cows. After the Allies broke Germany's codes, Milch Cows became prime targets.

Occasionally, submarines were used to land agents on islands to carry out reconnaissance. They ferried navy and marine frogmen, members of underwater demolition teams (UDT), just offshore, where the flipper-wearing divers were dropped off. Swimming underwater with breathing apparatus such as Jacques Cousteau's scuba gear, frogmen cleared obstructions and mines from beaches scheduled for assault.

Beginning in early 1943, frogmen were trained at Fort Pierce, Florida. They had to be able to swim at least two miles and were expected to be expert in hand-to-hand combat, flipper-to-flipper if they swam up against their Japanese counterparts. And they had to defuse bombs. Lieutenant Commander Draper Kauffman was the head of the Florida UDT school.

Before the war, Kauffman had been a civilian ambulance driver in Paris. He was captured and jailed by the Germans, but he escaped two months later and traveled through Spain before winding up in England. He served in the Royal Navy until Pearl Harbor, then joined the U.S. Navy, which rushed him to the scene at Pearl Harbor to recover unexploded Japanese bombs—one of them a 500-pounder—and to search for victims of the attack. He was awarded the Navy Cross. Kaufmann had learned bomb disposal with the Royal Navy in Britain during the Blitz, and now he taught it to America's first school of frogmen.

Before the war began, the United States gave Poland an old, outdated submarine as part of Lend-Lease. The Polish navy also had two new subs built in Holland. Together, the three were part of an effort to create a navy strong enough to defend Poland's ninety-mile-long northern coastline.

One boat, the *Orzel* (or Eagle), was Poland's most famous. When Hitler's army stormed across Poland's borders on September 1, 1939, *Orzel* escaped from the port of Danzig, only to be captured by a supposedly friendly nation, Estonia. At first, Estonian officials seemed to welcome *Orzel's* Polish crew to Tallinn, the capital city. Under pressure from both Germany and the Soviet Union, however, Estonian troops boarded the boat and put the submarine and her crew under armed guard. Within days, workmen began off-loading *Orzel's* torpedoes. Only six torpedoes remained when, around 3 A.M. on September 18, members of *Orzel's* crew took an ax to lines powering telephones and a nearby searchlight. Quickly, the crew locked up their onboard guards. Using her electric motors for silence, she slipped her mooring cables and moved away from the dock. Almost immediately, the high-bowed, 1,500-ton boat went aground on a mudbank. Her captain, Lt. Comdr. Jan Grudzinski, had no choice but to order the *Orzel's* diesel engine started to try to break free. Suddenly, all hell broke loose; *Orzel's* escape attempt was discovered. Sirens screamed, searchlights blazed, and gunfire erupted. Somehow, Grudzinski managed to get away and set the sub on the nearby sea bottom to wait out any vessel looking for her.

By now, Hitler's invasion force had completed its Polish blitzkrieg, and the *Orzel* no longer had a port to call home. The captain and crew headed for England, where they and their boat were assigned to the Royal Navy's 2d Submarine Flotilla. Six months later, on April 8, 1940, the *Orzel* became the first Polish warship to make a successful torpedo attack. Captain Grudzinski sent three torpedoes against a German merchant ship, the *Rio de Janeiro*. The ship originally was a passenger liner traveling between Europe and Latin America. This time, she carried troops as part of the invasion of Denmark. One of *Orzel's* torpedoes missed, but the other two broke the ship's back and the *Rio de Janeiro* sank.

A month later, on May 10, the Polish sub headed toward France. It was the last time she was heard from. Apparently, *Orzel* and her crew of six officers and forty-nine enlisted men fell victims to a German mine in Skagerrak Straits, between Denmark and Finland. She sank without a trace.

The Japanese navy apparently wasn't ready to deal with the number of submarines that the United States would eventually put in the Pacific Ocean. Before the war began, Japanese military officials believed they'd have no problem transporting food and equipment to conquered lands and fuel and raw materials to the home islands. They estimated they would lose about 800,000 tons of shipping in the first year of the war. After that, they felt certain, losses would drop off sharply as the fighting continued to go their way and their enemies were defeated. Giving them this false hope was the obvious failure of U.S. torpedoes and Japan's condescending belief that American submarines were inferior to their own. They failed to factor in rapid improvements that America would make to both submarines and torpedoes. All told, about half of Japan's merchant fleet was destroyed along with about two-thirds of its tanker fleet. By the end of 1944, oil from the East Indies no longer flowed into Japan, and bulk imports fell by 40 percent. The Land of the Rising Sun was sinking.

Japan entered World War II with 63 submarines. At the time, the United States had 73 fleet boats under construction.

Japanese subs outclassed those of many other nations. They were, however, crowded, noisy, and difficult to handle when submerged. Even submerging took far too long. Not until late in the war did the subs carry radar.

At the start of the war, the Japanese submarine fleet didn't do too well. At Pearl Harbor, for example, Japanese I-boats never even sighted an American warship much less sank one. Not long afterward, American planes from the carrier *Enterprise* sank one of the Japanese boats at Pearl Harbor, the *I-70.*

A fleet of three Japanese submarines returning to Tokyo from operations off California communicated so often by radio that the American sub *Gudgeon* was able to plot the enemy's course and wait for them to come along. Come along they did, and *Gudgeon* sank *I-173,* the first Japanese warship to be sunk by a U.S. submarine in World War II.

Japan continued to build its submarine fleet, including the I-400 class, the largest undersea craft built in World War II by any nation. Boats in the I-400 class were more than 400 feet long, displaced 6,500 tons, and needed a crew of 144 to keep them going. Tokyo hoped that these new supersubs would do the trick.

Initially, I-400-class submarines were built to carry and launch floatplane bombers against the United States. In addition to the floatplanes, these supersubs had eight 21-inch torpedo tubes, a 5.5-inch gun, and ten 25-mm antiaircraft weapons.

The first of their class, the *I-400* and *I-401*, were launched in May 1945. Along with smaller escort boats, they were to be submarine carriers and could launch a total of ten floatplanes. In trials, the submarines surfaced, prepared for launch, and sent floatplanes off in 45 minutes. The Japanese navy planned an attack on the Panama Canal, but the plan was changed; instead, the submarine carriers would attack American warships anchored off the Caroline Islands. The date was set for August 17, but the war ended before the boats and planes could attack.

When the surrender was announced, *I-400* and *I-401* surfaced, destroyed their aircraft, launched their torpedoes, and returned to Japan to surrender. The largest submarines of the war never fired a shot in anger.

Tokyo had planned to launch 18 supersubs, but only one other, the *I-402*, was completed and it never sailed on a mission. All three I-400-class submarines were studied by the U.S. Navy. The first two were scuttled off Pearl Harbor and the third was used for target practice before it was scuttled in 1946.

Traditionally, one difference between a ship and a boat is its size. A boat can be lifted out of the water for repairs; a ship is so large that it has to be sent to a dry dock. Because submarines were for years small enough, at least on paper, to be lifted onto a dock, they were called boats, not that anybody ever seriously considered lifting a 250-foot World War II submarine out of the water. Still, even today, the term *boat* usually is used in referring to a submarine. The tradition of ships being referred to as "she" or "her" also continues today. Never mind that a vessel bears a masculine name, tradition lingers on.

By today's standards, World War II fleet submarines were small. Midget submarines, however, were even smaller. Britain, Italy, Germany, and Japan all built midget subs.

Britain's were called X-craft, and work on their design began in the 1930s. The X-3 was delivered to the submarine force in 1942, a fifty-foot boat with all the features of her larger sisters. Unlike those sisters, the X-3 could be lifted out of the water. She carried two two-ton explosive charges attached to the hull, and she had a small floodable chamber to accommodate divers swimming in and out.

Battle tactics would have the midget sub's three- to four-man crew maneuver beneath an anchored enemy ship. Divers would slip out of the flooded chamber, detach the explosive charges from the sub's hull, and attach them to the enemy vessel. The charges would be detonated by a timer. If all went well, the divers would be able to return to the midget, and then would scamper out of range before time ran out.

Five of the original X-3 midget subs were built, along with twenty-five others that were slightly larger. Most of them were used in the Pacific.

The most famous operation by Britain's midgets came on September 22, 1943, against the German battleship *Tirpitz.* Allied forces had tried just about every way possible to attack *Tirpitz,* but they were unsuccessful. Finally, the British navy towed three X-craft midget subs into the area of Alten Fjord in Norway. Two of the midget subs managed to attach explosives beneath the German battleship. When the charges exploded, they did considerable damage to *Tirpitz.*

Not enough however, and the ship was repaired and ready for action again in the summer of 1944. It took a series of 12,000-pound, 21-foot-long Tallboy bombs, each almost half the size of a midget sub, to sink the *Tirpitz.*

Other British X-craft were used in Norway. On D day, a pair of the midget subs was stationed off the Normandy coast to serve as beacons for troops assaulting the beaches. In 1945, larger British midgets, the XE-craft, were sent to the Pacific and towed into Singapore harbor. A diver from *XE-3* managed to attach six mines to the hull of the Japanese heavy cruiser *Takao. XE-1* was unable to reach the target but dropped her mines nearby. The mines exploded, and

Takao sank. Seven British X-craft were lost during the war, including one that sank after colliding with her towing submarine.

The Italian navy built twenty-six midget submarines, models CA and CB, and planned others. Designated *Costiero,* or coastal, they ranged up to twenty-five tons in the larger CB class. They carried two torpedoes and crews of two or four. Mussolini's government hoped to take one of the CB-class midgets to America and to attack U.S. harbors, but he never carried out the plan.

Italy sent six CB subs to Romania by rail in 1942 and hoped to use them against the Soviet Union in the Black Sea. One of them may have accounted for the only known success of an Italian midget sub. According to German and Italian records, *CB-2* sank a Soviet submarine; however, the alleged sinking was never confirmed.

The German navy got into the midget submarine act in the fall of 1943, at about the time the Nazis' undersea effort began to flounder against heavy Allied pressure. Germany built 324 six-and-a-quarter-ton midgets of the *Biber,* or beaver, class. The *Biber* had a one-man crew and carried two 21-inch torpedoes. Later, larger *Molche* (salamander) type of midget subs were built. These were 10¾-ton vessels, whose underwater performance was greatly improved over the smaller version.

Still larger were the 11¾-ton *Hecht* (pike) and 15-ton midgets called *Seehund,* or seal, were built. By 1944, the *Seehunds* were efficient enough to remain at sea for a week or more. Germany's midget submarine program probably did about 100,000 tons of damage to Allied shipping from January to May 1945.

While the Japanese navy had the largest submarines in the war, it also had the smallest; they built 440 midget subs from 1934 to 1945. They operated against the British off Madagascar (where two of them sank a tanker and damaged the British battleship *Ramillies*), dove into Sydney harbor in Australia, and operated off Guadalcanal and in the Aleutians off Alaska. The Japanese sent five midget subs to torpedo U.S. ships during the Pearl Harbor attack. Only one got inside the harbor, however, and it did no damage. All five of Japan's little subs at Pearl Harbor were captured. One midget sub crewman was captured, the first Japanese prisoner taken by American troops.

None of Japan's midget subs at Pearl Harbor did any damage, but one may have done some good. The U.S. Navy shipped it back to the States and sent it on a tour of the country. Posters announced the display: "Coming Soon! Captured 2-Man Jap Sub. See your newspapers and listen to your radio for local details." Seeing what the enemy sent against the United States sold a lot of War Bonds.

Japan also had the *Kaiten,* which wasn't exactly a midget submarine. It was more a human torpedo, an undersea kamikaze craft. The Japanese navy took its 24-inch diameter, 48-foot-long, type-93 torpedo, cut it in half, and put a cockpit section in the middle with room enough for a suicide-minded pilot and a control panel. *Kaiten*s were carried on top of regular submarines to where enemy ships were located. With a pilot on board and driven by an oxygen-fueled engine, a *Kaiten* could reach speeds up to 40 knots. It carried 3,200 pounds of explosives. The Japanese navy's General Staff insisted there be provisions for the pilot to eject 150 feet from the target. There's no record of any *Kaiten* pilot taking that option—they were all volunteers, and only one was married. Only nine *Kaiten* missions were carried out.

One *Kaiten*-carrying Japanese submarine almost launched its suicide torpedoes against the cruiser *Indianapolis.* It was just after midnight on July 30, 1945, four days after the former flagship of the Pacific Fleet dropped off components of the atomic bomb at Tinian Island. *Indianapolis* was running at twelve knots when Lt. Comdr. Mochitsura Hashimoto targeted the ship in the periscope of the submarine *I-58. Kaiten* pilots onboard the sub begged Hashimoto to let them attack the cruiser, but the captain decided against it, believing *Indianapolis* was such an easy target that there was no need to waste a life—a Japanese life, that is.

Two torpedoes struck the thirteen-year-old heavy cruiser. No SOS was sent before she sank, and it was almost four days before any survivors were located by a PBY flying a routine patrol. By then, only 318 of *Indianapolis'* crew were found. Scores of those who died were killed by sharks.

About 50,000 men served in the U.S. submarine service during World War II, on boats and on shore. About 16,000 men actually served in submarines during war patrol. About 3,500 men lost their lives in the submarine service. The death ratio of submariners—those sailors who served in submarines—was the highest of all U.S. military groups, 22 percent, far less than the percentage of "pallbearers" who died in German "hearses."

CHAPTER FOURTEEN

Remembering Pearl Harbor:
A World Without Peace

The war no longer bears the characteristics of former inter-European conflicts. It is one of those elemental conflicts which usher in a new millennium and which shake the world once in a thousand years.

—Adolf Hitler, speech to the Reichstag, April 26, 1942

I hear the Eagle bird
Pulling the blanket back
Off from the eastern sky.

—Anonymous, *Invitation Song,* Iroquois

On December 9, 1941, the Portland *Oregonian* commented on "the reactions of the American citizens of the Pacific coast to the opening of war with Japan." They are no "different from those of fellow citizens in another part of the country. . . ." The headline was a phrase apparently used for the first time: "Remember Pearl Harbor!" It became the by-word of the war and a well-remembered song:

Let's Remember Pearl Harbor as we go to meet the foe.
Let's Remember Pearl Harbor as we did the Alamo.*

By 1940, U.S. cryptanalysts were able to read even the most secure Japanese diplomatic code—Code Purple, Americans called it. The Japanese continued using it, never fully realizing that their messages no longer were secret. By reading their decoded diplomatic messages, it was fairly obvious that there was little hope of an agreement with Japan to prevent war with the United States and Great Britain.

*Lyrics by Don Reid, music by Don Reid and Sammy Kaye, copyright 1941.

Ever since American commodore Matthew Perry's "black ships" opened the self-isolated island empire to American trade in 1853, a group of militant and nationalistic young samurai had been calling for an industrial and political revolution in Japan. In doing so, they hoped to put Japan's business in competition with that of the West. Big business, a big army, and a big navy.

Tradition and law allowed Japanese army and navy leaders to determine who controlled the government. Ministers of the army and navy were chosen from active duty officers and if the services refused to name a minister, the officer corps could force the dissolution of an existing government. At the same time, the military claimed the "right of supreme command," under which the chiefs of the army and navy general staffs were independent of the civilian government; they were responsible only to the emperor and claimed a special relationship with him.

By the thirties, Japan's officer corps was made up of the sons of petty landowners and small shopkeepers, firmly lower middle class. They were far less sure of themselves than the aristocrats who had dominated the Japanese military command prior to World War I.

A network of para- and promilitary organizations worked within rural Japanese society: the Imperial Military Reserve Association, the Youth Association, and the National Defense Women's Association, the last alone having more than 4,000 branches. These groups were, by and large, conservative and blamed any setback in life on modern western books, music, and social customs. When Wall Street went bust in 1929 in the United States, so did Japan's financial system; this strengthened the rural conservative belief that all things bad came from the West.

One thing good, they thought for a while, was modern technology—industry, electrical power, and communications—all driven by oil. Not unlike America in the 1970s and its relationship with the Near East, Japan in the 1930s became dependent upon the United States for oil. Japan, then, was dependent upon the very culture that its most conservative groups despised.

The education of Japan's new officer corps stressed a mission, which (along with the love-hate relationship with America) led the military in its first step, not toward the United States but toward

Manchuria and China. The Mukden Incident of 1931 was followed in 1937 by the "Rape of Nanking" .

It took two years for the League of Nations to condemn Japan's fake attack on China and the puppet government of Manchukuo set up in Manchuria. When the Mukden Incident was brought up for discussion, Japan quit the league. Once again, the League of Nations dithered, hedged, and wavered until the issue was moot.

It all gave rival army factions in Japan grist for their feuding mills. In 1936, one group revolted, seizing government buildings and the prime minister's home. Group members assassinated several high officials and published a manifesto calling for a new government. The rebellion lasted less than a week, and the leaders were quietly tried, convicted, and executed. Although it didn't amount to much, it gives a good idea of the ferment of bellicosity within Japan's military.

The Japanese army taught its cadets that "offense was the best tactic under any circumstances without regard to cost." Loyalty, faith in victory, aggressiveness—these were the attributes instilled in the new Japanese officer. It would be these young troops who would guide the Imperial Japanese Army in the Pacific war.

A longtime practice of the military around the world was to send young officers to observe the way that other armies and navies operated. Prior to World War II, however, Japan sent its bright, young, would-be generals and admirals to Germany and the Soviet Union; they almost never sent visiting officers to Great Britain or America. When an American suggested that a Japanese officer visit the United States, the officer (who later became an adviser to Japan's so-called "surrender cabinet") said, "The only occasion on which I plan to visit the United States is when I arrive there as chief of the Japanese forces of occupation."

Some historians, politicians, critics, and conspiratorial theorists claim President Roosevelt, along with a small group of advisers, knew in advance about the Japanese attack on Pearl Harbor. Their reasoning is that Roosevelt wanted a war in order to drag the country out of the Great Depression; President Roosevelt, they claim, "knew that the attack was coming, but refrained from warning his army and navy commanders in Hawaii." British prime minister Churchill, these conspiracy believers claim, also knew about the coming attack. They maintain that Churchill prevented warnings of the Japanese attack from going out to Pearl Harbor because he wanted America to join in the fight against Hitler. An attack such as at Pearl Harbor certainly would pull America into the war, not only with Japan but with Nazi Germany as well.

There is evidence that American officials believed the Japanese would attack, even that they would attack Pearl Harbor. The American ambassador to Japan had picked up rumors that the fleet would be attacked, but it was just one of many rumors circulating at the time regarding who might attack and where; they varied depending on who was doing the whispering. The rumors contradicted one another, and no one knew which, if any, rumor should be taken seriously.

On January 24, 1941, nearly a full year before Pearl Harbor, U.S. secretary of the navy Frank Knox wrote his counterpart, Secretary of War Henry Stimson, with something more than just a rumor: "If war eventuates with Japan, it is believed easily possible that hostilities would be initiated by a surprise attack upon the fleet or the naval base at Pearl Harbor. The dangers envisaged, in order of their importance and probability, are considered to be (1) air bombing attack, (2) air torpedo plane attack, (3) sabotage, (4) submarine attack . . . ."

Warnings did come, but how accurate were they? Between January 1 and December 7, 1941, American radio intercept stations picked up a total of 1,280 messages between Tokyo and its diplomats in Washington. Only about 600 of them were decrypted.

On December 4, 1941, an American ship picked up a message from Tokyo. Decoded, it seemed to indicate that a force of Japanese aircraft carriers was headed eastward toward Hawaii. It is questionable, however, whether shipboard technology in late 1941 could have determined where such a force was, much less where it was headed.

On December 5, an intercept station monitored a coded Japanese military broadcast. Experts said it indicated relations between the United States and Japan were in danger of breaking apart: "Contact Commander Rochefort immediately thru Commandant Fourteen Naval District regarding broadcasts from Toyko reference weather."

On that same day, during a White House cabinet meeting, Secretary of War Stimson announced: "The Philippines are indefensible. We have always known it. Every Army officer in the United States above the rank of lieutenant is familiar with the plan for the handling of the Philippines in case of war."

Plan Orange, as the strategy was known, was developed before World War I, one of several "color" plans, with each hypothetical enemy assigned a color. For instance, Great Britain was Red; Germany was Black; Mexico was Green. Even the United States (as a belligerent) was assigned a color—Blue. Japan was Orange. Under Plan Orange, the Philippines were not only indefensible, they were expendable. After all, Manila is 7,000 miles from California, almost 5,000 miles from Hawaii.

For years, officers at the Naval War College debated and tested Plan Orange, moving model ships around tabletops to simulate war. They sent miniature American battleships and cruisers across a wooden Pacific Ocean to do battle with miniature Japanese ships. They believed they knew what Japan would do, were equally certain they could defeat the enemy. Moving model ships around a wooden table was easy and painless; a real war, they realized, would be "sharp, bloody and confused."

Realizing the horrors of war, however, isn't the same as suffering them.

In May, army chief of staff Marshall told President Roosevelt that American forces at Pearl Harbor were "the strongest in the world." Should an attack be launched against the base,

> . . . Enemy carriers, naval escorts and transports will begin to come under air attack at a distance of approximately 750 miles. This attack will increase in intensity until, within 200 miles of the objective, the enemy forces will be subject to all types of bombardment closely supported by our most modern pursuit. . . . An invader would face more than 35,000 troops backed by coast defense guns and antiaircraft artillery.

Since June 1940, Hawaii had had three air-raid alerts and numerous drills against submarine attacks. The military believed it was ready.

On December 7, 1941, all of the battleships in the U.S. Pacific Fleet were at Pearl Harbor except for *Colorado,* and that was in a West Coast dry dock. On airfields near Pearl Harbor, nearly 400 navy and Marine Corps planes were parked wing tip to wing tip as a precaution against sabotage.

On December 2, a message went out from Tokyo to the Japanese fleet: *Niitaka Yama Nobore,* "Climb Mount Niitaka," a mountain in Formosa, then part of Japan. They were the code words to launch the attack.

On the morning of December 7, the Japanese fleet was 230 miles north of Oahu, in the Hawaiian Islands. Officers and pilots on the carriers listened to their commanders' instructions, then bowed in prayer before the Shinto shrines aboard the ships. The first wave of 183 planes took off.

It was Sunday. At Pearl Harbor, the American fleet was in, returned from weekday exercises, its men and defenses relaxed. On ships around the harbor, men slept late, did laundry, played cards; some attended church services.

In Washington, American and Japanese diplomats were preparing to meet again. Japanese ambassador Kichisaburo Nomura and special emissary Suburo Kurusu would meet with U.S. secretary of state Cordell Hull at the White House. Hull was an idealist who at first refused to negotiate with the Japanese until they removed their troops from China and Southeast Asia. That gave the impression the United States was intransigent in its dealings with the Japanese. By this time, many Americans believed there was no way to avoid war; the Japanese were certain of it.

At Griffith Stadium, the summer home of baseball's Washington Senators and fall home to the Redskins, a crowd of about 27,000 sat in the green grandstands and bleachers. The 'Skins were taking on the Philadelphia Eagles.

At 6:53 A.M. in Hawaii, U.S. Navy lieutenant Harold Kaminski received a message from the destroyer *Ward;* the ship had attacked a submarine off Hawaii in an area where no submarine was known to be and where none had any business being. Kaminski telephoned his chief of staff, who requested confirmation from *Ward.* After all, no one else had seen anything.

At 7:02 A.M., Privates George E. Elliot and Joseph L. Lockard of the U.S. Army Signal Corps were putting in some free time on their new radar tracking system in a shack at Opana, near Kahuku Point, 137 miles north of Oahu. They saw something "completely out of the ordinary"—blips about 130 miles away, three degrees north. Apparently, it was a flight of airplanes headed for Hawaii. It was, as Lockard described the blips, "an unusually large flight—in fact, the largest I have ever seen on the equipment." Lockard talked with the watch officer, Lt. Kermit A. Tyler, a fighter pilot in the 78th Pursuit Squadron. The blips Elliot and Lockard were seeing, Tyler said, were a flight of B-17 bombers arriving from California. "Don't worry about it," Tyler told the men.

At 7:15 A.M., Japanese captain Mitsuo Fuchida flew over Oahu; he had homed in on a Honolulu commercial radio station. "I had seen all the German warships assembled in Kiel harbor," he recalled later; "I had also seen the French battleships in Brest. And finally, I had seen our own warships assembled in the deepest peace, anchored at a distance less than 500 to 1,000 yards from each other. . . . This picture down there was hard to comprehend." Fuchida keyed his telegraph, sending back clusters that spelled out *Tora, Tora, Tora*—Tiger, Tiger, Tiger—the code indicating the attack was a surprise. Fuchida swept through the haze over Diamond Head. Civilians on an incoming American passenger ship looked up in surprise, pleased to see what they believed was a very realistic military exercise.

(Mitsuo Fuchida had gained combat experience during Japan's China campaign in the 1930s. After Pearl Harbor he led air attacks on the Dutch East Indies and against British ships and bases in the Indian Ocean. He was injured during the air attack at the Battle of Midway but recovered. After the war he became a rice farmer and a nondenominational preacher. In 1960, in perhaps one of the greatest ironies of the century, the man who had led the Japanese sneak air attack on Pearl Harbor became an American citizen. He died in 1976.)

Hearing the code words, pilot Inichi Goto released a torpedo. It hit the battleship *Oklahoma*.

At 7:58 A.M., Rear Adm. Patrick N. L. Bellinger, naval air commander at the base, broadcast the alert: "Air raid, Pearl Harbor. This is no drill." The message worked its way to watch officer Lt. William

L. Tagg, then to Rear Adm. Richmond K. Turner of the War Plans Division, then to Adm. Harold Stark, chief of naval operations, and on to Secretary of the Navy Knox. Knox read the message and said, "Those little yellow bastards!" He telephoned the president.

John Garcia was sixteen years old at the time, working for sixty-two cents an hour as a pipe-fitter apprentice at the Pearl Harbor Navy Yard.

> I was working on the USS *Shaw*. It was a floating dry dock. It was in flames. I started to go down into the pipe fitter's shop to get my toolbox when [a] wave of Japanese came in. I got under a set of concrete steps at the dry dock where the battleship *Pennsylvania* was.

An officer asked Garcia to go into the *Pennsylvania* to help put out fires started by the bombing. "I said, 'There ain't no way I'm gonna go down there.' It could blow up any minute." Garcia says now, "I was young and sixteen, not stupid."

Pennsylvania was hit by a bomb, which did minor damage. Because he refused to go down into the burning battleship, Garcia was to be called before a navy court a week later. Because he was not in the navy and only sixteen at the time, charges were dropped.

What had been a European war and a war to conquer China became World War II. Three hundred fifty-three Japanese bombers, torpedo bombers, and fighters knocked out half of the U.S. Navy.

In less than two hours, the Japanese crippled the American Pacific Fleet. They killed more than 2,400 Americans and wounded another 1,200. Most of the victims were on the battleship *Arizona*.

A 1,760-pound bomb (a 16-inch armor-piercing shell fitted with fins) hit *Arizona* near her number two turret. The bomb penetrated the forward magazine and exploded, killing 1,104 navy and marine officers and enlisted men, including Adm. Isaac C. Kidd, the commander of Battleship Division 1, and Capt. F. Van Valkenburgh, the *Arizona*'s commanding officer. Two torpedoes and several other bombs apparently also hit the ship. *Arizona* still is at the bottom of Pearl Harbor where she sank, now a memorial that occasionally leaks oil and memories into the harbor waters.

Utah was also destroyed, as was *California*. Eighteen ships were sunk and 188 planes were destroyed. The Japanese lost only 29 planes, a fleet submarine, and five midget submarines.

Fortunately for the United States, sadly for Japan's plans for conquest, the three American carriers stationed in the Pacific were not in port and were not attacked. They survived to become the nucleus of the Allied attack on Japan.

Just as the diplomats entered Secretary Hull's White House office, he received the flash that the Japanese had attacked Pearl Harbor. Kischisaburo Nomura handed Hull the final Japanese reply to an American formula for peace in the Pacific. It was a mixture of insults and misstatements. Hull looked at the reply, then turned on the Japanese diplomats. What he said was a verbal blasting without precedent in American diplomatic history.

> I must say that in all my conversations with you during the last nine months, I have never uttered one word of untruth. This is borne out absolutely by the record. In all my 50 years of public service I have never seen a document that was more crowded with infamous falsehoods and distortions—infamous falsehoods and distortions on a scale so huge that I never imagined that any government on this planet was capable of uttering them.

The Japanese diplomats left without a word. Hull never let on that because the United States had already cracked the Japanese code, he had read the message that Nomura gave him long before the diplomat walked through the White House doors. In fact, Hull likely read it before the Japanese diplomat himself did. Trying to retain secrecy, the Japanese foreign office in Tokyo had ordered that only Japanese might type up the message. Because it was a Sunday, only a lower grade functionary was in the embassy, and he couldn't type well, so it took longer to decode and type the fourteen-page message. American cryptologists were way ahead of them. The Japanese timing was way off. They expected their diplomats to hand over the document before the bombing began. The slow-typing lower functionary, who was also hung over from a before–Pearl Harbor party, threw them behind.

At Washington's Griffith Stadium, sportswriters were told by the Associated Press to "keep it short"; the wires would be jammed with news from Pearl Harbor. Stadium officials, however, refused to use the public address system to announce the attack, saying, "We don't want to contribute to any hysteria."

The stadium announcer began a series of squeaking calls and one after another, military personnel stood up and left the stands. A woman sent a telegram to her husband watching the game: "War with Japan! Get to office!" Ambassadors left. Military personnel left. Radio and newspaper reporters ran off to their offices.

Washington won that final game of the NFL season, beating Philadelphia 20 to 14. Only after the game ended did the few fans left in the stands learn about the attack on Pearl Harbor. One can only wonder what they felt when everyone else ran off.

William Pefley worked at the Norfolk Naval Shipyard in Portsmouth, Virginia. He heard the news about Pearl Harbor on the office radio, went out to the shop, and told the rest of the crew.

> [There] was a complete change in attitude. We weren't just helping England anymore; we were helping ourselves. Now it was our war. So everybody decided, "No matter what the hours may be, let's get the ships out. Whatever we can do to help this effort, we are going to do it." And from that point on, we started working ten, twelve, sixteen hours at a stretch.

They wouldn't have to work long, according to radio commentator H. V. (Hans van) Kaltenborn. Known by some as the "voice of doom," Kaltenborn, who went on to do a bit of commenting and reporting himself, reported the attack and offered his analysis, which was "based on no information whatsoever," according to David Brinkley. Brinkley later wrote that Kaltenborn "speculated about how many days and hours, depending on the winds and current, it would take the U.S. Navy to sail across the Pacific and devastate the home islands of Japan." Kaltenborn said it would be a very short war.

That night President Roosevelt met with his cabinet. He would speak to Congress and the nation on Monday. What did the cabinet members think? Even those who had opposed war now felt it could not be avoided. Yes, the president said, a declaration of war, but what else? Direct the nation's rage toward the Japanese; that was all. The speech would say little else. It would be delivered at noon.

The next morning, fearing the sneak attack on Pearl Harbor might lead to an equally sneaky attack on the president, the White House Secret Service detail began looking for a bulletproof car to take Roosevelt to the Capitol. The agent would have bought one if he could, but federal regulations prohibited buying any car, even for the president, that cost more than $750. There was, however, a huge armored limousine over at the Treasury Department; federal agents had seized it as part of their tax evasion case against Alphonse "Scarface Al" Capone. When told where the limo came from, Roosevelt said, "I hope Mr. Capone won't mind." Mr. Roosevelt used the car until the Ford Motor Company offered to build an armored vehicle and lease it to the White House for $500 a year.

Sunday, December 7, 1941, President Roosevelt told Congress, was "a date which will live in infamy." A New York City radio station set up a sound truck, and thousands of people listed to the president: "The United States was suddenly and deliberately attacked by naval and air forces of the Empire of Japan." RCA Victor recorded the speech and quickly began selling copies to Americans who wanted to hear it over and over again: "I ask that Congress declare that since the unprovoked and dastardly attack by Japan, December 7, a state of war has existed between the United States and the Japanese Empire."

A resolution to declare war on Japan, Germany, and Italy passed with only one "no" vote. That vote came from Jeanette Rankin, the first woman elected a U.S. representative. In 1917, she had also voted against the United States entering World War I.

December 7 in Pearl Harbor was December 8 west of the international date line. Within hours after the attack on Pearl Harbor, other Japanese forces hit Wake, Guam, Hong Kong, Malaya, and the Philippines.

Not only were Americans surprised by the Japanese attack on Pearl Harbor, so was Adolf Hitler. He wanted the third member of the Tripartite Pact to join the fight, but Tokyo's military leadership didn't bother contacting Hitler until after the bombs started falling.

It was near midnight when Adolf Hitler learned of the Japanese attack. "Now it is impossible," he said, "for us to lose the war. Now we have an ally who has never been vanquished in three thousand years." Hitler's top military advisers were more than just surprised; they had no idea where Pearl Harbor was and hurried to globes and maps to find out.

Once he got over his surprise, Hitler was so pleased at the Japanese action that four days later, over the objections of some of his top aides, he declared war on the United States. He made all the Japanese "honorary Aryans." So honorary Aryan, Hideki Tojo—who was not-so-blond-haired and not-so-blue-eyed—joined a self-proclaimed Aryan, Adolf Hitler—who also was not-so-blond-haired and not-so-blue-eyed—in the world's largest war.

CHAPTER FIFTEEN

Censorship:
Fighting the War in Black and White

Loose lips sink ships.
—Government slogan, World War II

Assassination is the extreme form of censorship.
—George Bernard Shaw, *The Rejected Statement*

During America's nineteen-month venture into World War I, the government didn't take any chances; it prohibited publication of any photographs showing American dead. For the first year and a half of World War II, pictures showing American dead were also prohibited. *Life* magazine, for instance, showed plenty of pictures of starving Russians and Poles, of dead Jews from the Warsaw ghetto. What they didn't show was dead Americans.

We knew about the deaths at Pearl Harbor; we knew about the deaths at Wake Island; we even knew about the Battle of the Philippines. We saw pictures of ships burning in Hawaii, and we saw Jimmy Doolittle set out from the carrier *Hornet,* heading for his "thirty seconds over Tokyo." What we did not see were pictures of the thousands who died at Pearl Harbor, pictures of the victims of the Corregidor Death March, or photographs of the execution of one of Doolittle's men whose plane was shot down over Japan. American dead might be shown, but only if they were background, surrounded by other, living Americans charging the enemy.

In the July 5, 1943, issue *Life* told a story about Red Oak, Iowa. Twenty-three of the town's sons were missing in action while on active duty with the Iowa National Guard. The magazine "showed where every one of them lived." Many of the missing, "later turned up as POWs," *Life* would later report. But what of those Red Oak, Iowa, boys who by this time were dead? *Life* showed them as they lived, not as they died.

Not until the battle for Buna Beach in New Guinea, when America retook the island in September 1943, did the U.S. government censors release pictures of dead or dying GIs.

Life magazine later on said it intended to show "the truth . . . the good and the bad," not to show only those pictures that would "please the eye and soothe the nerves." It wasn't that the editors were against showing death in general on glossy pages, just American war death. *Life* readily showed photos of the war's victims from other nations, even showed pictures of blacks lynched in the United States, but it didn't show the lifeless forms of American boys. *Life,* as did other magazines, gave us a sanitized version of war and death. A censored version.

During World War II, the American government used photographs of pain and death as what can only be called a public relations ploy, as propaganda. The word *propaganda* comes from the Latin *Congregatio de propagandi fide,* a Roman Catholic organization for spreading the faith. Propaganda, World War II style, was more than spreading the faith; often it meant spreading lies. The U.S. government used pictures of dead Americans only when it thought they would do the most good. The government also forbade their use when it believed that showing American dead might hurt the Allies' cause.

Even before the United States entered the war, the Joint Army and Navy Public Relations Committee proposed a $50 million system for the "complete censorship of publications, radio, and motion pictures within the U.S.A." Roosevelt rejected the idea, calling it "fishy" and a "wild scheme." The committee, he said, "obviously. . . knows nothing about what the American public—let alone the American Press— would say to a thing like this."

Actually, he gave the press more credit for journalistic ethics than they deserved. Take prize-winning *Life* magazine photographer Margaret Bourke-White. She admitted she shot photos of the action during the Italian campaign of 1943, then sent the unprinted negatives directly to the Pentagon. Either army signal corps or *Life* technicians working with the army looking over their shoulders (censorship number one) printed the pictures and then passed them on to military censors (censorship number two). When the photographs were joined with their captions, they were censored again (censorship number three). Only then did *Life* get to publish them and the American public get to see them. It's not exactly what we'd now think of as freedom of the press.

In general, the military didn't care what pictures photographers *took*, just what pictures newspapers, magazines, and newsreels *showed*.

Eleven days after the attack on Pearl Harbor, Congress established the War Powers Act, and President Roosevelt went about setting up the Office of Censorship, a civilian agency. The military, however, didn't like the idea of civilians controlling what the American public could see and hear in time of war. They wanted to do it themselves.

Under civilian authority, U.S. censorship was relatively mild. When the military got hold of it, things became a lot tighter. For the most part, they didn't even want enlisted personnel doing the job; you had to be an officer and a gentleman. Only later were a few enlisted men recruited to handle the growing volume of mail in the Pacific.

Twenty-year Associated Press veteran and executive news director Byron Price was named director of censorship with authority to restrict and withhold news from the public. Price chose to make censorship voluntary by members of the news media, at least in the continental United States. Most journalists respected Price, so they complied with his request. There was nothing voluntary about censorship in combat zones.

The media generally cooperated, and for a while newspapers and radio stations even stopped carrying weather forecasts, believing it might help potential enemy invaders if they knew what the weather was like in Chicago or San Francisco or Minneapolis. Nobody had developed a plane or missile capable of reaching either coast from Japan or Germany, much less the Midwest, but never mind that.

A couple of problems made the public sit up and listen and read. The Radio Priest, Father Charles E. Coughlin, first on Detroit radio station WXYZ, then on a nationwide network, preached anti-Semitism, anti-Rooseveltism, and pro-Nazism. When he began, although the Roman Catholic hierarchy didn't like it, it allowed Father Coughlin to continue his radio broadcasts and his *Social Justice* publication. Finally, Father Coughlin's bishop ordered him to cease broadcasting, to shut down his newspaper, and in general to put a lid on the rhetoric. Well into the 1970s, the bishop's order stood; Coughlin was forced to decline all invitations to speak on radio or television, even to be interviewed.

Another publication that ran into a bit of trouble was the now relatively sedate *Esquire* magazine. The U.S. Post Office tried to ban *Esquire* from the mails, claiming that the magazine was lewd, lascivious, wanton, lustful, and obscene.

In those pre-*Playboy* days, *Esquire*'s pinups were paintings, not photographs, of scantily clothed, voluptuous young ladies. Young ladies, American men fighting abroad might believe, constituted a good reason to keep the enemy on the opposite side of any and all oceans.

Despite the efforts of the post office—and they pushed it all the way through to 1946—*Esquire* continued sending to servicemen overseas special editions of its magazine, printed on lightweight paper to make shipping cheaper and easier. Such special editions were marked, "compliments of *Esquire* for the exclusive use of the armed forces." *Life* also sent complimentary, ad-free magazines to U.S. servicemen, lest servicemen around the world be deprived of "Big Red," as its fans called the magazine.

The post office ignored *Esquire*'s articles by some of America's best authors. It was the painted pinups that they objected to. Their own censors carefully examined every page of the 1943 *Esquire* output. They marked in pink every drawing, every slightly naughty line of prose or poetry, every somewhat off-color cartoon. The court said there wasn't enough there to bother about. Failing to get the magazine on obscenity charges, the post office finally claimed that *Esquire* didn't contribute enough to the war effort to warrant second-class postage privileges.

A year after the war was over, the U.S. Supreme Court ruled against the post office. Deliver the mail, the post office was told; don't try to censor it. The court called such actions abhorrent to American traditions.

• • •

In mid-1942, well-known radio commentator Elmer Davis took over as director of the Office of War Information. The OWI controlled the dissemination of official news on every continent except Latin America, which was left to the coordinator of inter-American affairs, Nelson A. Rockefeller. Davis's deputies included educator Milton Eisenhower (who also served as director of the War Relocation Authority, the federal agency responsible for the removal of Japanese Americans from the West Coast to isolated internment camps) and writers Robert E. Sherwood and Leo Rosten. At one point, the OWI employed 5,693 workers. In 1943, Congress ordered a cutback.

Both Byron Price and Elmer Davis tried to keep the government out of the business of writing, photographing, and presenting what America saw and heard of the war. For the most part they were successful, even though, for the Normandy invasion, OWI sent 440 of its own employees to report, apparently not trusting the regular media to do the job the way the government wanted it done. On the last day of World War II, Price said, "Those of us in the censorship business have consistently abhorred it just as all American citizens do." He added, "It has been one of the grim necessities of war, and we are happy to have it stop with the end of the shooting."

Which is not to say that some military men were happy with the way Davis and Price ran things, or with the way some of their own reacted. Bill Mauldin was an army sergeant whose cartoon strip "Up Front" featured a couple of lovable if totally disheveled and footsore soldiers, Willie and Joe. Mauldin loved dogfaces, and dogfaces loved him. One cartoon showed Willie or Joe (some of us were never too sure which was which) about to be awarded the Purple Heart for being wounded. "Just gimme a coupla asprin," the caption said. "I already got a Purple Heart."

Bill Mauldin was, just as his cartoon said, up front with the troops, drawing and commenting for the army newspaper *Stars and Stripes*. After the war, he wrote,

I'm convinced that the infantry is the group in the army which gives more and gets less than anybody else. I draw pictures for and about the dogfaces because I know what their life is like and I understand their gripes. They don't get fancy pay, they know their food is the worst in the army because you can't whip up lemon pies or even hot soup at the front, and they know how much of a burden they bear.

General George S. Patton, however, for reasons best known to him and Mauldin, once threatened to shoot the cartoonist on sight. At the time, General Eisenhower pretty much shared Mauldin's views on GIs, and he stepped between the cartoonist and the tank commander. Mauldin went on to win a Pulitzer Prize and continued covering wars as a satirical cartoonist through Korea and Vietnam. After fighting postwar wars as an editorial cartoonist for the Chicago *Sun-Times*, Mauldin finally retired to Arizona.

Mail from servicemen overseas usually was censored to one degree or another. Folks at home often received photostats of letters with words and whole lines blacked out. The military had finally gotten into the act. Not all mail was censored, of course. If you knew the right person—say, someone working in the army or navy's censorship department—you might get uncensored mail. Obviously, it was up to those uncensored individuals not to write about what unit they were with, where they were, what was happening, where they were going, what the weather was like, and even whether they were being censored.

Folks at home usually received V-mail, something on the order of the *Readers' Digest* of letters. Ostensibly to save space and weight, letters were photographed and the film was shipped to distribution points where it was printed on 4- by 5½-inch postcards. Specially designed 8½- by 11-inch stationery was sold at post offices. "Very small writing," troops were warned, "is not suitable," so "write plainly." Troops got only about 150 words per letter-turned-photographic film-turned-postcard. The government called it speed mail and claimed that mail weighing 2,575 pounds could be reduced to a mere 45 pounds when processed as V-mail. More than a billion V-mail letters were sent during World War II. After the war, the process became the modern microfilm technique. Still, not everyone accepted V-mail. Many believed it was too impersonal and, although it contained an entire if brief letter, it left recipients feeling as though they'd received nothing more than a postcard.

CHAPTER SIXTEEN

A Big Mac Attack:
When an Old Soldier Was Young

I shall return.

> —Gen. Douglas MacArthur, March 30, 1942,
> arriving in Australia from the Philippines

I have returned. By the grace of Almighty God, our forces stand again on Philippine soil.

> —Gen. Douglas MacArthur, October 20, 1944,
> on landing on Leyte, the Philippines

On November 25, 1863, during the Civil War's Battle of Chattanooga, Union troops charged up Missionary Ridge. Troops of the 24th Wisconsin pushed forward, but their flag bearer was shot and fell. The unit's eighteen-year-old first lieutenant, who'd been promoted from sergeant only three months before, picked up the flag and carried it to the top. His name was Arthur MacArthur, and for his bravery he was awarded the Congressional Medal of Honor.

In 1912, while addressing the fiftieth reunion of his Civil War regiment, recalling the days of the Battle of Chattanooga and Missionary Ridge, Arthur MacArthur fell dead of a stroke. Quickly, his adjutant wrapped MacArthur in the regimental flag. As he did, the adjutant himself dropped dead of a stroke.

In 1880, Arthur MacArthur and Mary Pinkney Hardy MacArthur had their third child, their second son. They had hoped that the child would be born at Mary's antebellum family home, Riveridge, in Norfolk, Virginia. The child, however, had other thoughts and entered the world early, at Little Rock, Arkansas, where Arthur MacArthur was serving. The *Norfolk Virginian-Pilot*, on January 27, 1880, ran a notice about his birth: "Douglas MacArthur was born on January 26, while his parents were away."

Douglas hoped to attend the U.S. Military Academy at West Point, but he couldn't get a political appointment. Instead, he competed for a presidential appointment, which entailed much work and study. He remembered, "I never worked harder in my life." The competition, MacArthur said, "was a lesson I never forgot. Preparedness is the key to success and victory."

A classmate and competitor at the Academy was Ulysses S. Grant III. Their mothers were in competition as much as the two cadets were, each hoping her son would win top honors. The ladies moved to a small, grubby hotel near the West Point parade ground, Chaney's Hotel, where they cheered on their sons. In 1903, Douglas MacArthur graduated first in his class of ninety-seven, winning virtually every possible award at the Academy. The only graduate of the Academy whose average exceeded Douglas MacArthur's was Robert E. Lee, and that was seventy-four years earlier.

Apparently, both Douglas and his mother, Mary, won. In that class of 1903, Ulysses S. Grant III was ranked sixth.

From the start, Lieutenant MacArthur's military career seemed charmed. He was commissioned in the corps of engineers, a choice assignment. He served briefly in the Philippines, was shipped back to San Francisco, then joined his father in the Far East as aide de camp (ADC) to President Theodore Roosevelt. By 1914, he'd served as a military observer in Mexico, been recommended (but rejected) for the Medal of Honor, and appointed a junior officer of the War Department General Staff. During World War I, Col. Douglas MacArthur commanded the 42d Division, the Rainbow Division, formed at MacArthur's suggestion of troops from several state National Guard units. Quickly, MacArthur became known as The Fighting Dude, Beau Brummell of the 42d, and d'Artagnan of the Western Front. (D'Artagnan you'll remember from *The Three Musketeers*.)

In 1918, MacArthur earned his first star, becoming at age thirty-six the youngest general in the Allied Expeditionary Forces in France, the AEF. Once again, his mother had been cheering him on. Mary Pinkney Hardy MacArthur had sent AEF leader Gen. John J. "Black Jack" Pershing a letter.* "My dear General Pershing," she be-

---

*Pershing apparently was given the nickname "Black Jack" while commanding black troops before the war.

gan, then went on to suggest that her son be promoted to brigadier general. She signed the letter, "Faithfully, your friend—Mary P. MacArthur." How much weight Mrs. MacArthur's recommendation pulled isn't known; nor is it known if General Pershing paid her any more attention than he would the mother of any other officer. It is known that General Pershing personally disliked the young officer although he held a "begrudging professional admiration."

By the end of the Great War, MacArthur had been awarded two Distinguished Service Crosses, a Distinguished Service Medal, and six Silver Stars, not to mention two wound stripes (later honored by Purple Heart medals). He was about to be promoted to major general when the armistice intervened.

With the War to End All Wars at an end, Douglas MacArthur became the youngest superintendent in the 117-year history of the U.S. Military Academy. Quickly, he dominated the Academy, doubling the size of the school, modernizing its curriculum, and reversing the wartime trend of shortened classes. The system had virtually destroyed the Academy during the wartime emergency.

In 1922, Douglas MacArthur, as he put it in his *Reminiscences*, "entered into matrimony." She was the beautiful and wealthy New York socialite Henrietta Louise Cromwell Brooks. Louise had been married before to a rich Baltimore contractor, Walter Brooks, and in Paris during the Great War had met General Pershing. Following a divorce from the contractor, Louise became Pershing's official hostess while "Black Jack" was the army's chief of staff.

Seven months after his wedding, Douglas MacArthur, along with his new wife and her two children, sailed for the general's new post in the Philippines. By this time, Douglas was a major general, having received the second star he'd missed out on when World War I ended too soon. Once again, it seems, his mother had stepped in. Once again, Mary Pinkney Hardy MacArthur had written General Pershing suggesting that her son be promoted.

Douglas and Louise MacArthur were not an average married couple. Apparently, they were not happy at *being* a couple. In what may have been a last-ditch effort to save their marriage, they moved to Louise's estate, called Rainbow Hill, near Baltimore. The last ditch didn't work; in 1929, in the best tradition of soap operas and grade B movies, Louise briefly took up residence in Reno, Nevada. She sued MacArthur for divorce on grounds of "failure to provide."

The marriage was a painful episode for MacArthur. In his memoirs, he wrote very little about his life with Louise Brooks, only that it "was not successful, and ended in divorce." The official biography issued by the MacArthur Memorial in Norfolk, Virginia, puts it even more tersely: "During the twenties, MacArthur was married to and divorced from Louise Cromwell Brooks." They'd been together only seven years. It would be several years before he tried marriage again.

The year of his divorce, MacArthur was ordered back to the Philippines as commander of U.S. troops there. It was his second visit to the Philippines, and he would return again and again. A year later, in 1930, President Herbert Hoover appointed him army chief of staff, making MacArthur one of the youngest ever to hold the position. President Roosevelt would retain him there.

It was as chief of staff that, in 1932, MacArthur led U.S. troops in one of his most publicized, if unsavory, actions. It's still not totally clear who did what, and whether MacArthur wound up with dirty hands.

During World War I, troops were promised a bonus, to be paid at a later date. With the Great Depression all around them, veterans tried get the bonus early. The government was also having financial problems and refused. Thousands of veterans and their families huddled together in what were called, after the president, "Hoovervilles." As many as 17,000 members of a so-called "Bonus Army" marched on Washington, where they picketed Congress and the president. Still, the answer was "no." By late July, all but 2,000 to 3,000 had been appeased enough to go home. When the last holdouts refused to leave, the Metropolitan Washington police moved in; in a wild confrontation, two policemen and two veterans were killed. That didn't settle the situation, and Hoover put Secretary of War Patrick Hurley in charge.

Hurley had been a lieutenant colonel of artillery in the war and, later, had grown wealthy on real estate and oil holdings. He called out the army, about 600 infantry and cavalry troops under Gen. Perry L. Miles. Hoover asked General MacArthur, as army chief of staff, to go along, and he took with him his aides, Majors Dwight Eisenhower and George Patton. In his memoirs, MacArthur claimed that the hard core of the Bonus Army was made up, not of veterans, but of Communist Party members—"outside agitators," they might be called thirty years later during anti–Vietnam War demonstrations.

MacArthur's backers say that he ended the Bonus March without firing a shot. However, there are still pictures and newsreel films of the general, hands on hips, standing in the midst of tear gas, with armed soldiers on horseback, and tanks churning up the scene. The press claimed then, and some sources claim now, that Douglas MacArthur was right in the thick of it. The general, however, denied this in his memoirs. "When I challenged this distortion," he wrote, "they were merely shrugged off with the expression, 'It was only politics.'" Whatever happened, and whoever did it, the Bonus March ended right there.

In 1934, ten years younger than the mandatory age, MacArthur retired. He remained military adviser to the new Philippine Commonwealth and in 1935 he sailed for Manila. He took Major Eisenhower with him. He also took along his letter-writing mother, the widow Mary Pinkney Hardy MacArthur.

On board the ship *President Hoover,* MacArthur met thirty-seven-year-old, Tennessee-born Jean Marie Faircloth on her way to visit friends in Shanghai. She was described as a feisty, poised, and cultured brunette; in April 1937, she and MacArthur were married. Ten months later, in February 1938, Jean gave birth to the couple's only son, Arthur MacArthur IV.

To help with baby Arthur, the general hired a Chinese wet nurse, an *amah* named Loh Chiu. In one of his few known instances of humor, Douglas MacArthur referred to Loh Chiu as "Ah Chew."

Japan invaded China in 1937; three years later it joined Germany and Italy in the Tripartite Pact. That turned an informal alliance into a formal one in which the three nations (the Axis) agreed on mutual aid if attacked by any country not involved in Europe or China. It was worded so that the United States was included, but not the Soviet Union, which pleased Josef Stalin, who didn't want any part of a possible two-front war.

The Philippines had enacted universal military training, hoping to build a 10,000-man army along with a 250-plane air force and a navy with 100 patrol boats circling the islands. When Douglas MacArthur returned to Manila, he called for, in addition to the regular Philippine army, 12,000 Filipino scouts, enlisted men to serve under American officers. The regular Philippine army, MacArthur believed, should consist not of 10,000 men but of 100,000. From Washington, General Marshall wrote MacArthur, "I have directed that United States Army Forces in the Philippines be placed in the highest priority for equipment, including authorized defense reserves for fifty thousand men." By October 1941, some in the War Department believed "American air and ground units now available or scheduled for dispatch to the Philippine Islands in the near future have changed the entire picture in the Asiatic area."

It was obvious to most, however, that, should war come, the Philippine Islands would be prime targets. In planning their defense, MacArthur relied heavily on his dreamed-of 100,000-man Filipino army with the 12,000 Filipino scouts under U.S. command. MacArthur believed that war would come; however, in November 1941 he assured Washington that fighting would not break out before April 1942, and by then he expected that his preparations to defend the Philippines would be complete.

In the event of a massive enemy invasion, the army's official U.S. War Plan Orange-3 (WPO-3) called for American and Philippine troops to retreat into the rugged jungles of the Bataan Peninsula at the entrance to Manila Bay; the rear would be guarded by Corregidor, an island fortress. There, surviving troops would await American reinforcements. Douglas MacArthur, however, wanted to halt the Japanese on the beaches.

Within hours of the raid on Hawaii, other Japanese forces assaulted Wake, Guam, Hong Kong, Malaya, and the Philippines. Back in Washington, the so-called military experts were astounded. They couldn't believe those "little yellow bastards," as the Japanese often were called, could mount more than one major offensive at a time.

Quickly, Japanese air and sea forces attacked the Philippines, and the following day, they landed unopposed. Despite warnings of the attack, MacArthur did not disperse his air force and nearly half of his aircraft were destroyed on the ground. He was familiar with the Philippine troops—he had, after all, been their commander—but failed to take into account their lack of training and readiness. MacArthur's official biography says, "Although built up considerably prior to the outbreak of war, especially in their air strength, the U.S.-Philippine units were no match for the combined naval-air-ground assault of the Japanese." The Japanese move in and the American-Philippine forces move out became known as MacArthur's Disaster. His troops began calling him Dugout Doug, claiming he spent most of his time in bombproof shelters.

By December 20, Japan controlled the air over the Philippines. American and Philippine troops were driven out of the cities and up the Bataan Peninsula. Without consulting the U.S. Navy, MacArthur declared Manila an "open city" beginning December 26, meaning that the city was undefended and free of military activity; the enemy was expected to spare an open city. Japan disregarded the declaration and bombed Manila into submission.

MacArthur convinced himself he could defeat the Japanese, but clearly the U.S. forces in the Philippines were no match for the enemy's combined naval-air-ground assault. On Christmas Eve, MacArthur fell back on the Bataan Peninsula and the islands blocking Manila Bay. By then, it was all over but the hurting.

MacArthur, however, left the hurting to others. Under orders from President Roosevelt, he turned command over to Maj. Gen. Jonathan M. "Skinny" Wainwright.

On March 11, Douglas A. MacArthur, his wife, and their young son, Arthur (along with the boy's Chinese wet nurse and several of the general's aides), stood on Corregidor Island's weathered wooden dock, preparing to follow his commander in chief's orders to leave the Philippines.

The strain of the three-month Japanese attack, along with his ordered evacuation, showed on the 62-year-old veteran soldier. The disappointment clearly revealed itself; he was having to abandon his combined American-Filipino army, nearly 80,000 troops, leaving them to certain death or capture and torture. MacArthur was 25 pounds lighter than he had been three months earlier when the Japanese attack began; his face was pale and he had "a sudden, convulsive twitch beneath his eyes" as he looked back at the island. He removed his gold-encrusted khaki hat ("scrambled eggs," some called the gold braid on his hat's bill) and raised it in a final salute to the island fortress. Then he stepped aboard the 77-foot patrol–torpedo boat that would be his means of escape.

"You may cast off, Buck, when you are ready," MacArthur said, and Lt. John D. Bulkeley's *PT-41* joined up with four others to began threading their way through 35 miles of defensive minefields, heading for the Mindoro Strait, where enemy ships were known to prowl.

When MacArthur arrived in Australia, he delivered perhaps the most famous three-word speech in military history: "I shall return." It would be two and a half years before he could live up to those words.

MacArthur continued directing the Philippines campaign by radio. He split his command among four officers, with Wainwright holding the largest portion. MacArthur, however, hadn't informed the War Department of his plans, and the arrangement was unworkable, not to mention more than a bit bizarre. After two weeks of confusion, General Marshall promoted Wainwright to lieutenant general and gave him command of all Allied forces in the Philippines. With no PX in the neighborhood, someone cut up a tin can and made stars out of it for the new two-star general.

Japanese planes pounded away night and day at the Bataan garrison. In January, U.S. and Filipino troops went on half rations, then they killed and ate the cavalry horses, including Wainwright's prize jumper. They ate monkeys, deer, iguana, and snakes. By the end of March, even those were gone. On April 3, the Japanese launched a new offensive. An American and Filipino counterattack netted heavy Allied losses.

From Australia, MacArthur ordered Wainwright to attack again, spelling out how to do it. Allied troops were to break Japanese positions wide open, allowing the Americans and Filipinos to plunder enemy supplies. Thus refreshed and victorious, they would head for the mountains of Luzon, where they were to wage guerrilla warfare against the Japanese. That would put them right where War Plan Orange-3 had intended them to be four months earlier.

Obviously, MacArthur's ordered counterattack could not work; Allied troops were too few and too weakened by hunger to mount any major offensive. General Wainwright, however, felt duty bound to follow the spirit, if not the letter, of the order. On April 9, he told Maj. Gen. Edward L. King, Jr., to carry out MacArthur's instructions. King sent only two men forward, and one of them carried a white flag. Bataan had fallen.

With that, General Wainwright led about 2,000 men and a few nurses to Corregidor, a fortified island about 3,500 yards off the tip of Bataan at the entrance to Manila Bay. An American war correspondent, however, chose to fly to safety, and as he left the island, he told General Wainwright that he should get out. The general replied, "I have been one of the 'battling bastards of Bataan,' and I'll play the same role on The Rock as long as it is humanly possible."

April 29 was Emperor Hirohito's birthday, and the shelling increased as a gift to him. It was a preinvasion barrage.

For twenty-seven days and nights, Japanese bombs and shells rained down on the Americans and Filipinos on Corregidor. All during the barrage, U.S. Army Signal Corps radio operators kept a continuous signal going to the outside world. They told of the bombing, the hardships, and the conditions under which those in the rock-hewn Malinta Tunnel lived.

On the night of May 5, Japanese landing barges came ashore. American troops raked them with devastating fire, and for a while it looked as if the landing could be turned back. Then, thousands more Japanese troops came ashore. While the defenders fired back with pistols and rifles, the Japanese brought in tanks and artillery.

Finally, on May 6, 1942, starving, demoralized, and dejected— General Wainwright surrendered. He and 11,500 Americans and Filipinos became prisoners of war. Very soon, however, they discovered that their captors did not consider them to be prisoners of war; instead, they were treated as some low form of life.

Wainwright's men were part of the 76,000 military personnel and civilians taken prisoner by the Japanese in the Philippines. Some were immediately executed.

The conquering Japanese put the defeated Americans on show, humiliating them whenever possible. After all, the Japanese army had ordered its own troops to fight to the death or to commit suicide and felt that American troops should have done the same.

Japanese troops assembled their American and Filipino captives. They ransacked officers' bags; Parker fountain pens were especially prized in Tokyo, and Japanese soldiers hoped to take one home. They collected wristwatches in five-gallon jugs, saying that anyone who refused to give up his watch would have his throat slit. They demanded that officers hand over their gold West Point rings; if a man refused, the conquerors cut off his finger and took the ring anyway. Because one man had a few bills of Japanese money in his wallet, they chopped off his head.

In groups of 500 to 1,000, the prisoners were herded off—no food or water. One American who escaped to tell about it said, "A Japanese soldier took my canteen, gave the water to a horse, and threw the canteen away." Under often barbaric conditions, the prisoners were marched the 65 miles from Mariveles to San Fernando. On the third day of what came to be known as the Bataan Death March, Japanese guards took a large number of Filipino troops from the 91st Division and tied their wrists together with telephone wire, then tied them man to man. The guards herded them toward a ravine. Then, with Japanese officers beginning at one end and enlisted men starting at the other, they began executing the Filipinos—beheading them, stabbing them with bayonets, killing the bound prisoners from behind. They killed between 300 and 400 men. The executions took more than two hours, and dying men screamed through the night.

The commander of the Japanese guards during the march was Nara Akira, a brigade commander who had been a student at Amherst College in Massachusetts.

The Bataan Death March largely remained a secret until Allied forces recaptured the Philippines. The War Department estimated that as many as 5,200 Americans died on the march. Many others died in prison camps, where the death rate was as high as 550 men a day.

After the war, a five-member military commission—all five were army generals, none was trained legally—tried Gen. Tomoyuki Yamashita, the "Tiger of Malaya," in connection with the Bataan Death March and other Japanese atrocities.

The trial raised several civil rights questions. Yamashita's chief defense counsel, Col. Harry Clarke, proved to the commission that the general was in Manchuria, nowhere near the Philippines, when the acts occurred. Then he said,

> The Accused is not charged with having done something or having failed to do something, but solely with having been something [commander of enemy troops who committed atrocities]. American Jurisprudence recognizes no such principle so far as its own military personnel are concerned. . . . No one would even suggest that the Commanding General of an American occupational force becomes a criminal every time an American soldier violates the law. . . . One man is not held to answer for the crime of another.

The prosecution claimed the atrocities committed by Japanese troops were so widespread that General Yamashita must have known about them. If not, "it was simply because he took affirmative action not to know."

The news media apparently wanted to get on with a hanging, calling the trial a "third-string road company of the Nuremberg show." A message to the commission from General MacArthur's office advised members that the Pacific theater commander was "disturbed by reports of [a] possible recess" in the trial, doubting the "need of Defense for more time." The message added that MacArthur "desires [the] proceedings completed [at the] earliest possible date."

The trial took nearly six weeks. The commission's findings were delayed two days so as to be announced on the fourth anniversary of Pearl Harbor. Yamashita was condemned to be hanged. The question arose, however, whether a U.S. military commission had authority to try General Yamashita, because Philippine civil courts were open and operating in the area. The Philippine Supreme Court declined to act on an appeal, and the U.S. Supreme Court ruled six to two that it could not interfere with General MacArthur's handling of the case. When President Truman announced that he would not grant clemency, Yamashita's fate was sealed. He was hanged on February 23, 1946.

CHAPTER SEVENTEEN

POWs:
Prisoner Mine, Prisoner Yours

This is depressing and it stinks, and I am a miserable human being and I'm going to die. But I am trying to live.

—Houston Tom "Slug" Wright, prisoner of war

*I never saw a man who looked
With such a wistful eye
Upon that little tent of blue
Which prisoners call the sky.*

—Oscar Wilde, *The Ballad of Reading Gaol*

Military intelligence officials in Hawaii during the thirties drew up secret lists of suspected spies in the large Japanese community. Their ties to Japan, officials claimed, might make them traitors to the United States. After Pearl Harbor, California newspapers reported alleged incidents of Japanese subversion. Sensationalist stories told of sightings of enemy planes and ships. A headline in the *Los Angeles Times* on February 25, 1942, read: "L.A. Area Raided! Jap Planes Peril Santa Monica, Seal Beach, El Segundo, Redondo, Long Beach, Hermosa, Signal Hill."

More than 1,400 rounds of antiaircraft ammunition were fired at supposed enemy aircraft. There'd been unidentified blips on radar screens, but no Japanese planes were sighted. Meanwhile, fragments of spent antiaircraft shells dropped out of the sky, scared hell out of everybody, and trigger-happy troops fired more shells at . . . whatever. No one ever figured out what caused the confusion.

On December 8, 1941, some people began demanding all Japanese Americans be jailed. Within three months nearly 120,000 Japanese Americans were removed from a 150-mile strip along the West Coast and sent to internment camps in Colorado, Utah, Arkansas, California, Idaho, and Wyoming, ostensibly to prevent any sabotage or espionage. For most internees, all they had done was to be born of Japanese parents, to have nonwhite skin and almond-shaped eyes. Congressman John Rankin of Mississippi was quoted as saying, "Once a Jap, always a Jap. You can't any more regenerate a Jap than you can reverse the laws of nature."

Racism, nativism, and religious bigotry were marks of America hurting from Pearl Harbor.

Residents of Hawaii accused old friends and old neighbors of being spies when, on calmer reflection, they remembered that their friends were farmers who had lived in Hawaii for years. It didn't help, of course, when a Honolulu newspaper claimed that Japanese American farmers were planting tomatoes in such a way that they pointed to airfields around Pearl Harbor. For years Hawaiians had relied on Japanese American fishermen to catch the staple of many local diets. Now they accused these same fishermen of equipping their boats with powerful radios to send spy reports to Tokyo.

On February 19, 1942, President Roosevelt issued Executive Order 9066 identifying certain military areas from which German, Italian, and Japanese aliens were to be barred. The order stripped thousands of Japanese Americans of their freedom and constitutional rights. California attorney general Earl Warren, who later became chief justice of the U.S. Supreme Court, claimed the lack of acts of sabotage proved nothing, that Japanese Americans were holding back "until the zero hour arrives."

> Unfortunately [many individuals] are of the opinion that because we have had no sabotage and no fifth column activities in this state . . . that means none have been planned for us. But I take the view that this is the most ominous sign in our whole situation. . . .
>
> I believe that we are just being lulled into a false sense of security and that the only reason we haven't had disaster in California is because it has been timed for a different date. . . . Our day of reckoning is bound to come in that regard.

Warren added:

> It seems strange to us that airplane manufacturing plants should be entirely surrounded by Japanese land occupancies.

It seems to us that it is more than circumstance that after certain Government air bases were established Japanese undertook farming operations in close proximity to them. You can hardly grow a jackrabbit in some of the places where they presume to be carrying on farming operations close to an Army bombing base. . . . So we believe, gentlemen, that it would be wise for the military to take every protective measure that it believes is necessary to protect this State and this Nation against possible activities of these people.

Liberal newspaper columnist Walter Lippman joined the call for quick action, and quick action was taken. On March 18, the government established the War Relocation Authority (WRA) as part of the Office of Emergency Management. Milton Eisenhower, brother of the general who would be president, was placed in charge. In a report to President Roosevelt in June, Milton Eisenhower said the federal government would "take all people of Japanese descent into custody, surround them with troops, prevent them from buying land, and return them to their former homes at the close of war."

A month later, the Western Defense Command and Fourth Army Wartime Civil Control Administration issued an order:

Instructions to all persons of Japanese ancestry living in the following area: All of that portion of the City and County of San Francisco, State of California. . . .

All Japanese persons, both alien and non-alien, will be evacuated from the above designated area by 12 o'clock noon Tuesday April 7, 1942.

No Japanese person will be permitted to enter or leave the above described area after 8 A.M., Thursday, April 2, 1942, without obtaining special permission from the Provost Marshal at the Civil Control Station.

Another notice advised Japanese Americans to take the following items for each member of the family: bedding and linens (no mattress); toilet articles; extra clothing; sufficient knives, forks, spoons, plates, bowls, and cups; and "essential personal effects." They were not, however, allowed to have razors, scissors, or radios. The size and number of packages they could take with them to wherever they were going would be limited "to that which can be carried by the individual or family group." The U.S. government would provide storage for large household goods, but storing family articles was "at the sole risk of the owner."

Henry Sugimoto was interned and remembers:

> My wife's parents had owned house; they built it. So we put all the stuff in the house, and I thought I might lock it up. But I asked a high school classmate, "You keep our house? If you want to rent to someone, rent it free, it's just that we want to keep our house, you know." So this classmate, he had own house, so he let other poor people, without house, move in our house. But these people all take my things away. My [art] material, lumber and everything, even trunks—you know we lock up trunks—all open and my wife's beautiful kimono from our wedding, they all took them away.

All Japanese Americans were interned, including nisei (that is, American-born, second-generation individuals—constitutionally American citizens), issei (first-generation Japanese immigrants, who were Japanese citizens at the time), *kibei* (native American citizens of Japanese immigrant parents, but who had for the most part been educated in Japan), and *nikkei* (the ethnic Japanese community).

Along the West Coast, signs sprouted up on stores: "Closing Out. Evacuation Sale." On a window at the Asahi Dye Works in Portland, Oregon, the owner wrote: "Closing. We won't take it to Owens Valley for you."

Manzanar, in the Owens Valley of California, was the largest U.S. concentration camp for Japanese Americans. Spread out over 5,000 acres were long, one-story, barrackslike buildings, often made of uncured wood backed by tar paper. Each family was allowed a 20- by 25-foot space. Privacy was almost nonexistent. Young children would knock knotholes out of the nearly green wood of the walls and peek into the next room. For a bit of privacy from both their own children and neighbors, internees hung blankets around bunks. Toilets and dining facilities were communal. Diarrhea from contaminated water was epidemic.

Relocation camps might have had highly evocative names—Topaz, Utah; Rivers, Arizona; Heart Mountain, Wyoming—but they were in arid, and above all, desolate, unpopulated areas that were demoralizing and degrading. Barbed wire surrounded the camps, and armed guards patrolled perimeters. The camps were crowded and living conditions were uncomfortable.

Henry Sugimoto and his family had lived in Hanford, California, but were sent to an internment camp at Jerome, Arkansas. Three, four people, had to share one room. He later he wrote

> We go in and there was nothing. Just a bed and mattress already filled and a blanket and a big stove for wintertime to make warm, you know. But we made ourselves furniture. I made a small table and bench. All families made it because mountain of scrap lumber outside the barrack. People pick up outside, make what they want to make. We shared the tools.
>
> Japanese mostly rice eaters. So that's why WRA everyday cook rice—lot of rice—that help us. Mess hall's not like restaurant; if you refuse [to eat], you have to go hungry.

Another internee complained about the camp food.

> It got so we couldn't stand looking at the women's magazines with all the jellos and cakes. We wanted to go home and bake a cake or something. Oh, yes, we just got so tired of camp food. They just handed you a tin plate all mixed up in one. And we missed the Japanese tea. We got orange pekoe type. Did you know toward the end, we all got accustomed to that? When we got out, Japanese tea tasted bitter.

Canada took similar action. A state of near panic erupted along Canada's West Coast when the Japanese bombed Pearl Harbor. Vancouver was as vulnerable to enemy attack as San Francisco or Los Angeles. Property was seized (supposedly held in trust for the duration) and the people were shipped off to holding camps. The Japanese

Canadians suffered in the same ways as Japanese Americans. As historian and broadcast journalist Bill McNeil puts it, "To the police and the politicians it was enough that [Japanese Canadians] looked Japanese. They had and deserved no rights."

Helen Sakon was a first-generation Canadian, born in Vancouver and married to a man who worked in the woods for a lumber company. She remembers how they considered themselves ordinary working-class Canadians.

> Anti-Japanese propaganda filled the newspaper, and the average west coast Canadian was being educated to fear "the enemy in their midst." As far as they were concerned, I suppose, every Japanese they saw was out to murder them. It was so bad that any Oriental was afraid to venture out on the streets.

Within a week of Pearl Harbor, the Canadian government ordered the Sakons to leave their home on Vancouver Island and go to the mainland. At the time, the Sakons had a three-month-old baby.

> The authorities just came to our door and told us to take everything we owned and get onto the boat to the mainland. This was an order which applied to all Japanese families, so there was a great deal of confusion and crying as we all hurried to pack and get things down to the dock.

They were taken to a camp called Lemon Creek, given a number—"mine was 02371," Helen Sakon remembers, and housed with an older couple and the couple's daughter.

> It was only one big room and a wall down the middle, with us on one side and them on the other. There was an outhouse in the yard, and there was a pump where we all went for our water. Often there would be a quarter-inch of ice on the floor in the morning, as the wood stove we had would go out while we slept. We lived there from 1942 to 1946.

Helen's husband, who'd been born in Japan but "considered himself Canadian," was sent to New Denver in the Rockies, "where he was put to work building places for Japanese families." The Canadian government sold Helen's mother's house for only "a fraction of its worth," with the Custodian of Alien Property holding the proceeds of the sale.

After the war, the Sakons had the choice of going to Japan or staying in Canada, but it had to be east of the Rockies. "They wouldn't permit us to go back to the West Coast," Helen Sakon remembers, because, "the people there didn't want us." Then stories began to circulate that the people of eastern Canada didn't want them, either.

Life in internment camps was especially hard for young people. First, the traditional Japanese courtship system with parental arrangement was disrupted, then teens could find no place to be alone with a new boy- or girlfriend. Lili Sasaki remembers, "The young kids [hated] to live with their parents in such close quarters. No place to go, except to the grandstand with their girlfriend. . . . "

One Japanese American who refused to relocate fought all the way to the U.S. Supreme Court. Gordon Hirabayashi claimed that the army had violated his rights as an American citizen. The court ruled that the threat of invasion gave the military the right to restrict the constitutional rights of Japanese Americans.

Beginning in 1943, Japanese Americans were allowed to join the U.S. Army. Eventually, more than 17,000 served in the all-nisei 442d Regimental Combat Team, the most decorated military unit in U.S. history. Their motto: "Go For Broke."

Together, they won 4,000 Bronze Stars, 560 Silver Stars, and 52 Distinguished Service Crosses. Sadao Munemori of the 442d was posthumously awarded the Congressional Medal of Honor. His mother, however, was refused permission to leave the internment center to receive her son's award. When some nisei soldiers returned from the war, the only home they had to return to was a relocation camp.

Most of the 120,000 Japanese American internees were held for the entire war, from 1942 through 1945. Of the 5,000 Americans of German and Italian ancestry who were relocated, many were released within a year.

In 1990, the United States formally apologized and began making reparations to the 60,000 Japanese American survivors of internment camps. They paid each of them $20,000.

• • •

Ten days after Pearl Harbor, a spokesman for the U.S. State Department made arrangements to incarcerate Axis diplomats and their families who remained at embassies in Washington, D.C. Some were sent to famous resorts—The Homestead in Hot Springs, Virginia; The Greenbrier in White Sulphur Springs, West Virginia; and the Grove Park Inn in Asheville, North Carolina. All three locations were relatively isolated, and all offered luxury accommodations. The FBI had investigated each employee of the hotels, giving special attention to foreign-born workers.

On December 19, a Washington newspaper described the group as they waited for buses to take them to the D.C. train station. They were a "well-dressed throng, abounding in fur coats and smart hairdos, with dozens and dozens of bags, boxes and bundles, piled picnic-style into their special buses."

From Washington, 159 Germans and Hungarians went by an 11-car Pullman train to The Greenbrier. By the end of March, more than 800 "guests" were housed at the resort at the expense of the American government. Included with the diplomats were bankers, newspaper correspondents, military attachés, servants, and their families. Most were prominent individuals "from the highest strata of society in their homelands."

Unlike American POWs abroad, these "guests" were treated well. The resort's golf courses and riding trails were off limits, but many spent their time playing tennis or swimming; they played chess, backgammon, and ping-pong. They were allowed one newspaper, the *New York Times*. Cottages were converted to classrooms for schoolchildren. Three weddings were performed and six babies were born, including one set of twins. On Hitler's birthday, members of the German legation staged a boisterous beer party in the main dining room. It was, a waiter commented, "a hell of a hall of heils."

On April 1, Italians, Hungarians, and Bulgarians were transferred from The Greenbrier to the Grove Park Inn, in North Carolina. The space vacated at The Greenbrier was filled by Japanese diplomats and their families. Repatriations began in May. For American wives of foreign diplomats, it was a time of increased apprehension, not knowing how they'd be received in Berlin or Tokyo.

By the end of July, the last of the diplomats and their families were gone, by train to New York and then onto ocean liners for home. As they left the luxury resort, the well-to-do, government-imposed guests thanked their resort hosts. At The Greenbrier, they handed out more than $65,000 in tips to bellmen, maids, waiters, and porters.

All told, the Allies and Axis held prisoner more than 12 million individuals—American, British, German, French, Italian, Japanese, and Soviet. Many died; many were never heard from again. When they were freed, many were scorned by their own countrymen. The Japanese often transferred prisoners without international supervision and, as a result, in one six-week period, American submarines sank Japanese ships carrying as many as 4,000 U.S. prisoners.

Neither side was totally innocent. An American sub sank a Japanese passenger and cargo ship even though the Japanese ship sailed under a guarantee of safe conduct and carried Red Cross relief supplies to American prisoners of war.

Yes, there was a Stalag-17, but it was nothing like the *Stalag-17* of Broadway and Hollywood, even less like *Hogan's Heroes* of television. *Stalag* was short for *Stammlager*, meaning permanent camp. There were more than fifty-five major, permanent prisoner of war camps in Germany.

Germany claimed it followed the Geneva Convention—technically, the Geneva Convention Relating to the Treatment of Prisoners of War—in its treatment of POWs. As agreed to in 1928 by representatives of forty-eight nations, the ninety-seven articles governed all aspects of military captivity. Observers from neutral nations would inspect prison camps or prisons. POWs were to be served food equal to that served to troops of the detaining country. POWs would not be kept in solitary confinement. The Geneva Convention recognized the privileges of rank and class, calling for the segregation of "different races or nationalities" as well as separate compounds for officers, noncommissioned officers, and enlisted men. Officers received pay comparable to that of officers of the detaining army, and they usually enjoyed better food, better recreational facilities, and better health care than did enlisted men. High-ranking POWs were allowed the service of orderlies and/or aides-de-camp, "who were expected to make the officers' beds, wash their clothes, and perform necessary duties around the camp, including cleaning the officers' latrines." POWs could be required to work, but the work could not be connected to the war effort. If questioned, a prisoner was required to give only "his true name and rank or his regimental number." Prisoners would not be pressured to give information regarding "their armed forces or their country." And prisoners who refused to answer questions would "not be threatened, insulted, or exposed to unpleasantness or disadvantages of any kind whatsoever." There were frequent lapses in the agreement.

China, France, Germany, England, and the United States ratified the agreement. Japanese representatives signed the document, but their government never ratified it, and Japan virtually ignored the convention when dealing with POWs. The Soviet Union never attended the convention meetings, and Josef Stalin refused to sign the convention. Stalin said that the Soviets would hold to the earlier (1907) Hague Convention, which, though basically the same, did not require neutral nation inspections.

Approximately 95,523 Americans were held captive by Germany. This is the U.S. Veterans Administration's 1980 figure, and other counts are different. On April 13, 1945, three weeks before Germany's formal surrender, the *New York Times* estimated there were 85,000 Americans in German hands. On November 1, 1945, the War Department put the total at 95,965.

About one-third of all American POWs in German camps were army air forces personnel—32,730 shot down in air raids over enemy or enemy-held territory. Hundreds of aircraft flew thousands of missions over Germany, doing untold damage to the Third Reich in death and destruction. Those same raids cost thousands of American lives and saw additional thousands captured and held for nearly two years.

Sergeant Daniel S. Abeles of Philadelphia, a B-17 radio operator and gunner, was shot down on his nineteenth mission and wound up in Stalag-17, at Krems, Austria. Two of his fellow prisoners at Stalag-17, Donald Bevan and Edmund Trzinski, wrote the play and film about the camp. Abeles was Jewish but says, while he feared for his life, he was not expressly mistreated because of his religion.

After the war people would ask me how many parachute jumps I made. I'd always tell them, "Two. My first and my last."

At Stalag-17 they took pictures of us and shaved our heads. On my POW card they put a big red "J" for *Jude.* Later I asked our American chaplain, "Father Kane, I'm very anxious. I know what happened to Jews in Germany after *Kristallnacht.** What should I expect?" He said, "It all depends how the war goes. If you were a Gentile and you escaped and were caught, you would be brought back. But [as a Jew] if you escaped, nobody would ever hear from you again." There was no segregation of Jews in the Stalag-17, but it was scary.

More than 50 years after World War II ended, the exact number of American POWs who died in Germany isn't certain. Estimates run as low as 1,121, but that doesn't take into account the number of American POWs who died during the final months of the war. Thousands of GIs were force-marched away from their camps when the Allies made their final big push eastward.

To get a true picture of the number of American POW deaths, the number of MIAs (missing in action) must be considered. Whenever and wherever there has been a war, there have been MIAs. There still are MIAs listed from the American Revolution, the War of 1812, and the Civil War. Some just took off before, during, or after a battle. Some were held in prison by the enemy long after the fighting ended; this reportedly is the case for some World War II, Korean War, and Vietnam War prisoners, used and abused for whatever purpose the enemy desired. Some who are listed as MIAs should be termed KIA (killed in action), because they died at or near a battle site but their bodies were never recovered. As late as July 1997, a soldier from America's Civil War—unknown as to

*See the chapter on the Holocaust.

name, unit, or even on which side he fought—was reinterred at Gettysburg National Cemetery; his body was only recently found buried on the battlefield where he'd fought 134 years earlier. If there had been a MIA list at the time of the Battle of Gettysburg, this unknown soldier would have been on it.

MIAs became a rallying point after the Vietnam War, when the U.S. government and Vietnam veterans groups used widely different figures. For instance, one figure gives the number as 2,273. American MIAs after World War II totaled 78,773. Some may have chosen to remain abroad, but surely not that many. Many died or were murdered during those times when Germany did not maintain a precise count.

Leslie Caplan was a prisoner on a forced march at the end of the war. Now a psychiatrist, he says, "We left a trail of slime and blood across Germany, so horrible that conditions cannot be evaluated by customary medical criteria."

Phil Miller was drafted into the army just 40 days after Pearl Harbor. After washing out of pilot training (he says he watched the clouds, not the instruments), he became a bombardier on a B-24. He was shot down over Ludwigshafen, Germany, on April 1, 1944, and spent most of his 405 days in prison in Stalag Luft 1.

There were constant escape attempts in our camp, but none was ever successful. A few guys got out but were quickly recaptured. Everybody considered building a tunnel. One barracks had so much dirt dug away on the side toward the fence that it leaned over in that direction. Every night the guards crawled around under the buildings looking for new tunnels. One night some men poured water on one of these tunnel hunters. He took out his pistol and began shooting up through the floor. The men went charging over to the [prison commandant] the next day to protest that the guard had violated their rights under the Geneva Convention.

Card games and chess matches went on constantly. When the men didn't have playing cards, they made them. Miller says their best food "came in their ten-pound Red Cross packages." Camp-provided food varied over time. It began with three meals a day but dropped to two when things got tough for Germany. From a standard two loaves of bread for each room per meal (fourteen men per room), during the Battle of the Bulge it dropped to one loaf per room twice a day. Says Miller, it was "baked with sawdust as a partial filling, and wood chips were sometimes found in the loaves." Still, he claims, "It was absolutely delicious and many of us agreed we'd never had such bread before."

Whenever they had bread pudding made with prunes or raisins, they picked out the fruit, soaked it in barrels, "and put the juice into kegs to ferment." There always "seemed to be an adequate supply of fermented juice for the kitchen staff and some of the higher ranking officers."

In April 1945, the prisoners heard Soviet artillery closing in. Miller remembers:

> One day we got up, and there were no guards in the towers. The officers had departed, leaving instructions for the enlisted men to stay on duty. They stayed just long enough for the camp to get good and dark, and then they left. We were now in charge.

They tuned the camp public address (PA) system to the BBC, the British Broadcasting system. The song being played was "Don't Fence Me In."

A few days later, the Soviet army arrived, driving a herd of 150 cattle before them. It was their gift to the Americans and was the "first fresh meat we had since arriving in Germany, and those cattle disappeared in one day."

The American Eighth Air Force arranged to move out the entire camp. As the men marched out, the PA system blared out the song "You Gotta Accentuate the Positive." B-17s came in one minute apart, loaded fifty men at a time, and took off again for Rheims, France.

Woody Floody of Toronto, Canada, joined the Royal Canadian Air Force (RCAF) in 1940; it wasn't long before he was flying Spitfires in Europe. He was shot down over northern France in the fall of 1941 but was able to bail out before his aircraft crashed.

• • •

I landed in a little village in front of a small house and, in a way, it was kind of humorous. Here was this strange man dropping out of the sky, and you'd expect the people to be frightened or even hysterical, but that's not what happened at all.

A little old lady opened the door of her small home and came out with a bottle of cognac in one hand and a glass in the other, and poured me a welcoming drink. By this time, I knew I'd had it anyway because I could see the German soldiers all over the place, and before I had properly swallowed the cognac they were closing in on me. I handed the glass back to the lady and thanked her in my high school French.

Floody was taken to Stalag Luft 3, in what is now part of Poland, where most of the other POWs were British airmen. Before the war, he'd been a miner in the northern part of the province of Ontario. "These Brits," he says, "laboured under the impression that anyone who is a miner must therefore be an engineer." They put Floody in charge of building an escape tunnel. They dug three tunnels, codenamed Tom, Dick, and Harry, believing that if the Germans found two, there'd still be one remaining to use for an escape. The men dug through the sandy soil, then spread around the camp the sand they'd removed. They made plans to get passports, papers, uniforms, civilian clothes, and compasses, all of course under tight security. Floody describes the process:

Everything down to the smallest detail was planned by a committee of the best brains in the camp, and it still amazes me how well those plans progressed. . . . The date for the mass escape of 200 men was set for the night of March 25, 1944.

As it turned out, there were only 76 men who actually made their way through the tunnel to the outside that night. . . . The ironic part of all this is that I wasn't even there the night of the escape, because the German guards had discovered and destroyed one of my tunnels a few weeks previously, and about 20 of us who were suspected of being involved were transferred immediately out to another prison camp a few miles away.

• • •

Of the seventy-six men who crawled through the tunnel, most were recaptured. Fifty were executed, Floody says, and just three made it back to England. Woody Floody "spent four years in those dreary camps." It was an exhilarating experience, however, and he says that after serving time as a POW,

> I knew that nothing in my life could ever be any worse. I felt that everything was going to be upwards and onwards from then on. In my opinion it has been.

Woody Floody died in 1989 at the age of seventy-one.

More than fifty years after being released from camp, former POW Phil Miller still attends therapy sessions at a nearby Veterans Administration hospital. In 1980, a new term—*PTSD*, post-traumatic stress disorder—appeared in psychiatric journals. Many World War II POWs likely suffered this and didn't even know it.

Former prisoners of war received long furloughs before being discharged. Theoretically it allowed them to be reunited with their families while still being monitored by military officials. It didn't always work. "There was no kind of care after we returned to the States," former POW John Pavkov remembers.

> No one told us what to expect. The army simply sent me home on a seventy-two-day furlough after which I ended up broke and alcoholic. The first two days I was just tickled pink to be home. . . . Then I started going out drinking. . . . [For] two years it was really bad.
>
> According to psychiatrist Leslie Caplan, at the time of liberation virtually every POW suffered some degree of malnutrition, gastritis, respiratory and skin disease, as well as frostbite and nervous disorders.

On December 17, 1944, Nazi SS troops herded captured American soldiers into a field at a road junction near the Belgian town of Malmédy. The Americans mostly were from Battery B, 285th Field Artillery Observation Battalion. According to a report later written for the Supreme Headquarters Allied Expeditionary Force (SHAEF):

• • •

[The Americans were] rounded up on a cleared field, being lined up six ranks deep. [They were searched for cigarettes] and other valuables. [Suddenly] for no apparent reason, shots were fired into this group of defenseless prisoners by the German guard. Immediately following this outbreak, two. . .German tanks began spraying the Americans with machine-gun fire from a distance of about 75 to 120 feet. Killed and wounded prisoners fell to the ground, as well as some who were not hit. But it is thought that these latter men were killed later when machine-gunners continued spraying the men on the ground.

As the tanks prepared to depart from the fields, they drove past the fallen prisoners, their machine guns pouring additional bullets into those already killed and men who were wounded. As a parting gesture, German infantrymen on top of the tanks fired their small arms into the helpless mass.

Finally, the German soldiers walked through, deliberately shooting those who still showed signs of life. Approximately twenty or twenty-five soldiers, the majority wounded, decided to make a run for it. Guards immediately opened fire as the men broke into a run. Only about fifteen eventually managed to gain their freedom.

It is known as the Malmédy Massacre. One account says 129 GIs were murdered, although the number is often questioned and may be as low as 94. The number varies because men from other units may have been mixed in with Battery B.

The U.S. State Department sent a formal diplomatic note to Berlin through the neutral Swiss government, voicing America's "strongest possible protest" against the shooting of unarmed American POWs who were complying with the rules of surrender. It would be a while before the public learned of the Malmédy Massacre, because SHAEF imposed a news blackout, claiming "a need for security."

It was the start of the Battle of the Bulge, the last major offensive of the Germans in World War II, and SHAEF kept a lid on information about the battle. German tanks and infantry had punched holes in the front along the Ardennes Forest in eastern Belgium. GIs were beaten back and overrun in many sections.

The Battle of the Bulge began on December 16, 1944, as warming weather combined with snow from the mountains turned into a dense mist that covered the hilly, fifty-mile front. The fog helped hide German columns that were jamming the roads and kept American aircraft from attacking them. Isolated U.S. units began falling back in disorderly retreat. General Omar Bradley at first believed that it was a "spoiling attack" aimed at slowing the Allies' drive for the Rhine River. The British military, however, remembered the Ardennes breakthrough in 1940 and believed Germany was beginning a daring attempt to retake Liège and Antwerp, split Allied forces, and disrupt their supply lines.

By December 17, intelligence had identified twenty-four German divisions in the Ardennes Forest, surprising the Allies who believed that Hitler was almost through. General Bradley asked, "Where in hell has this son of a bitch gotten all his strength?" Apparently, it came in great part from teenagers. Checking grave markers of those killed in the battle, historian Stephen Ambrose found that an overwhelming number of German troops in the Bulge were just fifteen to sixteen years old.

Meanwhile, English-speaking German soldiers under Waffen-SS officer Otto Skorzeny launched Operation *Grief* (Snatch), the infiltration of American lines to create havoc among U.S. troops, some of which were new to battle. Wearing American uniforms and driving stolen U.S. vehicles, the Germans filtered through the area, cut telephone wires, changed road signs, and gave confusing information to anyone who'd listen. They spread rumors (including one plot to kill Eisenhower) and confused GIs to the point troops could not trust anybody in an American uniform.

United States military police began questioning anyone and everyone, including General Bradley, who was stopped at least three times and asked trivial questions that supposedly he or any other red-blooded American boy would know: What is the capital of Illinois? (Springfield.) Where is a guard on a football scrimmage line? (Between the center and tackle.) Who is Betty Grable's husband? (Harry James, at the time.) Bradley got the Illinois and football questions right but missed the Grable–Harry James connection. They let him go anyway.

One of the American units defending the Bulge was the green 106th Infantry Division. More than 8,000 men surrendered, the second-largest surrender of American troops ever made, exceeded only by the surrender of Bataan in the Philippines.

Strong German forces cut off and attacked small American units. Cooks, bakers, and clerks who hadn't seen a rifle since basic training picked up weapons, shot at the enemy, and in general fought gallantly if awkwardly. Eisenhower sent both the 101st and the 82d Airborne Divisions to the area. To pull more men from the front, Ike would have had to demand that British field marshal Bernard Montgomery give him control of the Ardennes area, something the SHAEF leader didn't want to do. Politics, and all that.

The weather was unrelentingly bad. From warm mists and fog, it turned to subzero cold and snow. Air support was out of the question. Eisenhower asked Gen. George Patton how long it would take him to turn his quarter-million troops and armor around ninety degrees to relieve Bastogne, the Belgian town and road junction that became the focus of the battle. Patton's answer: forty-eight hours.

The 101st Airborne was under temporary command of Brig. Gen. Anthony C. McAuliffe. On December 19, he made military history and became a legend in one word. Using a captured American typewriter, the commanders of German panzer units attacking the paratroopers sent an ultimatum. McAuliffe's reply, "Nuts."

On December 22, the weather cleared, allowing U.S. planes to bomb and strafe German positions and to drop food and supplies to cut-off American troops. On the day after Christmas, Patton's troops were able to raise the siege.

General Montgomery, meanwhile, took time to "tidy up the lines," as he put it, stalling before he counterattacked German troops. On January 3, his tidying completed, Monty moved to flatten the Bulge and to take credit for "straightening out" the American problem. He claimed that he'd fought "possibly one of the most interesting and tricky battles I have ever handled." American GIs, he added, fought well enough as long as they had good leadership. His statement infuriated Winston Churchill, and the British prime minister lavishly praised his U.S. Allies for the "greatest American battle of the war."

By January 7, the Battle of the Bulge was over. Much of what had taken place in the first part of the battle, including the Malmédy Massacre, was only rumored at the time. SHAEF's press blackout had held.

In 1946, the German officers responsible for the Malmédy Massacre were tried for war crimes. A U.S. military tribunal sentenced forty-three of the SS officers to death and twenty-three others to life imprisonment. One of those given a life sentence was SS general Josef "Sepp" Dietrich, an ardent Nazi who'd been known as "Butcher Boy" since his early days with Adolf Hitler in Munich.

Back in the United States, Sen. Joseph McCarthy, a former member of the Marine Corps nicknamed "Tail Gunner Joe" by his fellow air crewmen, questioned the sentence. McCarthy claimed that U.S. interrogators had mistreated the SS officers in order to gain their confidence. In 1948, the court commuted all but six of the death sentences. In 1951, with McCarthy at the height of his Red-baiting power, the last of the death sentences were commuted. On October 25, 1955, the *New York Times* ran an article:

> Bonn, Germany, October 24—Sepp Dietrich, former commander of Hitler's elite guard, was released from the United States–governed prison at Landsberg, Bavaria, last Saturday.
>
> The former general was sentenced by an Allied court in 1946 for a number of war crimes including the massacre of American prisoners at Malmédy, Belgium, during the Battle of the Bulge.

American veterans spokesman Rudolph Pesata called "this release of General Sepp Dietrich . . . a gross miscarriage of justice." Another veteran, Timothy J. Murphy, said, "It is a tragedy that, in the short span of ten years, United States authorities have forgotten the violent deeds of one of Hitler's most vicious killers." Not long afterward, all of the SS officers still being held were released.

While Sepp Dietrich was still in prison, his wife appealed to U.S. military authorities to have her husband's life sentence reduced.

Three times she appealed to the U.S. commander in Germany. Three times the commander rejected her pleas. The commander was Gen. Anthony McAuliffe. Once again he said, "Nuts!" This time a different enemy won.

American POWs in Germany saved raisins and plums (and probably anything else that would ferment) in order to make home brew, but German prisoners of war at Camp Carson, Colorado, recreated an authentic beer garden to use during their off-hours. It was complete with chairs, tables, and decorations all made in the camp's woodcraft shop. Camp Carson's commander, Lt. Col. Eugene N. Frakes, told the *New York Times* on November 7, 1943, "Morale in the camp is unbelievably high."

In Camp Grant in Illinois, prisoners painted oil figures of such German notables as Frederick the Great and Field Marshal Rommel; local townspeople vied with guards to purchase the paintings. On rare occasions, German prisoners were allowed to wander outside of camp; in one exceptional case, five submarine officers were allowed to travel on their own to Camp Blanding in Florida. They spent several days on a train, during which time they dressed in American uniforms and wore Nazi pins in their lapels. The submariners spoke amiably with fellow passengers, who apparently had little idea of who the men were.

Some high-ranking German POWs were allowed to tour military shipyards and major ordnance depots in America, and were escorted on tours that included universities, religious institutions, George Washington's colonial home at Mount Vernon, and the restored colonial town of Williamsburg, Virginia. These POWs were so high in German society that the U.S. State Department believed that they could use their influence to bring about a peace settlement, forget the fact that the generals were in America, in custody, more or less. Forget the fact that Hitler wasn't too happy with any German who surrendered, much less high-ranking officers, and wasn't likely to do anything that these captured German officers might ask.

You go to war, you hope to win. You go to battle, you expect to kill, capture, or maim your enemy. It's that blunt. In so-called civilized warfare, you either turn the enemy dead over to their country, heal the troops you have just recently injured, or humanely house those you capture. The United States did the first two superbly. With the third, however, we may have gone a bit overboard. What to do about prisoners of war was a question the United States never fully solved during World War II. What we did do, however, was far and away more than either Germany or Japan did.

More than 135,000 German prisoners were shipped to the United States after the North Africa campaign. Another 142,000 arrived after the D-day invasion; 40,000 from northern France and 60,000 from Italy. From 1942 to 1946, a total of approximately 676,000 POWs were held in the United States. The highest number of POWs held at any given time was upward of 425,000, mostly Germans, housed in more than 155 POW camps and 500 branch camps. Of the then 48 states in the Union, there was at least one camp in every state except Montana.

Two-thirds of the main POW camps were built in the South and Southwest. Together, they housed approximately three-fourths of all the prisoners.

Regulations called for camps to be placed no closer than 170 miles from the coast, no less than 150 miles from either the Canadian or Mexican borders. They could not be placed near shipyards, munitions plants, or vital industries. So much for regulations; Camp Peary (now a CIA enclave) and Fort Eustis in Virginia are both near vital shipyards, as well as less than 100 miles from the Atlantic Ocean. There were several POW camps located near Detroit's automotive works, near the Canadian border. The Rock Island Arsenal was less than 100 miles from Camp Grant in Illinois. Camp Charleston, South Carolina, was located near both a navy yard and a munitions facility and was right on the ocean.

When the demand for camps grew (that is to say, when large numbers of prisoners were captured), new camps were opened, often using existing military establishments if there was extra space. When the first rush of POWs came over in 1942, the War Department clearly wasn't ready. They turned the gymnasium at Eureka College in Illinois—Ronald Reagan's alma mater—into a holding area, with bunks on the gym floor where the future president had played basketball. California's Santa Anita racetrack became a tent city.

To comply strictly with the Geneva Convention, when regular facilities were under construction but not yet available, and the prisoners had to live in tents, the guards had to live in tents as well, even if it meant that the guards' empty new barracks sat waiting. Many POW camps were converted Civilian Conservation Corps (CCC) camps, which later were transformed into modern state parks.

Generally, there were sufficient food, medicine, clothing, and shelter for POWs at U.S. camps. In fact, Axis POWs were treated so well that some members of the American press along with several politicians claimed we were coddling enemy prisoners, especially when it was learned how American POWs were faring.

Most of the POWs held in U.S. camps ended up working in private industry, everything from logging to food processing, agriculture to mining. They even sewed uniforms for American servicemen, which, because it contributed to the war effort, might have been classified as going against the Geneva Convention.

Many Germans held prisoner in the United States attended classes, often to learn basic English but at other times for college credit. When World War II ended and German prisoners returned home, some of them could list on their résumés their graduation from the University of Wisconsin or Michigan State University.

The military routinely censored prisoners' letters home to Germany, and the information gained indicates that most POWs were content. One prisoner wrote: "I have never as a soldier been as well off as I am here; we are being treated very decently—much better than we were by our own officers."

Another prisoner wrote:

> There is room for approximately 2000 men here. The wooden barracks are all equipped with electric lights and individual cots and quilts. The wash-room and showers may be used at any hour. The food is excellent and plentiful. Particular attention is given to the state of our health. . . . After everything we went through it is just like a rest-cure to be here.

A guard officer at the prisoner of war camp at Fort Lee, Virginia, was asked about POW escapees. So far, Col. Philip K. Moisan explained to the *Washington Post*, there had been none. "Hell," Moisan said, "you couldn't drive some of these fellows out!" Some did try and some succeeded by merely walking out the front gate.

The first escape occurred on November 5, 1942. Two German prisoners jumped from a train carrying them to a camp in Tennessee; they were caught two days later. As the number of German prisoners increased, the number of attempted escapes grew right along with them. From the middle of 1944 to the middle of 1945, more than a hundred German prisoners per month escaped, about three per day.

They cut wire fences, passed through camp gates in phony American uniforms, and smuggled themselves out in delivery trucks. At a camp in Texas, a group broke out by building dummies to stand in the back of lines while their comrades answered for them at role call so that guards didn't know they were gone. A POW who took part in that escape said, "It worked fine until one of the dummies fell over." In 1944 on Christmas Eve, 25 German prisoners, mainly submarine officers, escaped through a 200-foot tunnel they bored through rocky soil, apparently using nothing but a coal shovel. They were caught.

Still, less than 1 percent of all the German prisoners held in U.S. camps escaped. During the same period, a higher percentage of U.S. citizens escaped from federal prisons than POWs who ran off from camp.

The most famous, certainly most unusual, examples of escaped prisoners were Kurt Rossmeisl and Georg Gaertner. Rossmeisl was a former officer in Rommel's 10th Panzer Division. On August 9, 1945, when he was on a wood-gathering detail outside Camp Butner, North Carolina, Rossmeisl pushed a wheelbarrow past several guards, made his way to town, then caught a train for Chicago. He spent the next fourteen years living under the name Frank Ellis. He was so much a part of the community that he even joined the local Moose Lodge. On May 10, 1959, the fifty-two-year-old Rossmeisl walked into an FBI office and gave himself up. He was lonely and tired of running, he said.

Georg Gaertner escaped from Camp Deming in New Mexico on September 21, 1945. He'd been a camp translator who, when he learned that the United States was about to repatriate all German POWs, didn't want to go; his hometown was Schweidnitz, in soon-to-be East Germany. Gaertner rolled under the barbed wire fence at Camp Deming, caught the first freight train he saw, and landed in California.

He worked as a dishwasher, a migrant farm laborer, and a ski instructor. He even played tennis with some Hollywood movie stars. One, Robert Stack, strangely enough, would become the host of a television show dealing with escaped prisoners and such. In 1985, Gaertner discovered Dr. Arnold Krammer's book, *Nazi Prisoners of War in America.*

At the time, Gaertner went by the name Dennis Whiles. He called Krammer, complimented him on his book, and admitted to being the last fugitive Nazi prisoner in America. On September 12, 1985, he turned himself in to Krammer. It was almost forty years to the date since he'd escaped. Krammer and Gaertner (or Whiles) co-authored a book published in Germany as *Einer blieb da* (One Remained There). In the United States, it became known as *Hitler's Last Soldier in America.*

Some German POWs thought that the way they were being treated was a sign of American weakness. They'd been transported in Pullman cars, not cattle cars; fed better than when they were still fighting—American white bread, which they called "cake," instead of the black bread and pumpernickel from the German army—and even were given English lessons. Others believed that "When Germany wins the war, this will make at least one good point in your favor." The majority, however, saw their treatment as a sign of the true American nature.

POWs held in the United States were paid at least 80¢ a day. With incentives, a hard-working prisoner could earn as much as $1.50 a day, payable in canteen coupons. One reason they weren't paid in U.S. currency was to protect against their escaping and being able to pay their way onto trains, buses, or trolleys. Prisoners got around this by trading with guards their coupons and any foreign currency they still had, of course, for souvenirs to show the folks back home in Düsseldorf.

With prisoners working in foundries, quarries, and meatpacking plants, objections from American labor were inevitable; POWs, after all, were taking jobs away from Americans. The first objection came in December 1943, when Local 56 of the Amalgamated Meat Cutters and Butcher Workmen (AFL) demanded 25¢ a week be deducted from the POWs' wages at Seabrook Farms in New Jersey. The meatpackers passed on the objection, saying said it was an issue between the army and the union. To avoid an out-and-out war with the union, the War Department recruited farmworkers, women, high school students, even soldiers on leave to take jobs in meatpacking plants. With enough non-POW employees in place, the POWs were replaced and the question of dues became a nonissue.

The War Department battled the railroad unions when the army tried to use POWs on railroads. "My God," President George Harrison of the Brotherhood of Railway Clerks cried in the *New York Times* on October 15, 1943:

> [Do they] not know that Railroading is a most delicate operation. . . . We carry on night and day in split second schedules. I have not been able to get a reason for turning loose Nazi soldiers skilled in demolition practices, so that they may run amuck on the railroads.

When the railroad unions challenged the War Department in court, government lawyers convinced judges to dismiss claims that POWs might sabotage America's rail system. Once again, to avoid the issue, the army pulled POWs off railroading projects.

How many German troops were held prisoner in the United States is not certain. There may have been as many non-Nazis as there were "true believers." The United States made only a superficial division of Nazis and anti-Nazis; this was a time, of course, when most Americans conceived of only one breed of Germans, and that was the most violent—the Nazis. Besides, officials hoped to instill "democratic reeducation" into prison camps; once German troops were away from the superrace propaganda, they would realize how wrong they had been. In some cases, this worked. In many others it didn't.

German prisoners were allowed to wear their uniforms, often with their Nazi and SS insignia intact (although guards frequently stole medals and insignia as souvenirs). Prisoners were even allowed to hang pictures of Hitler on the wall if they wanted to. The War Department informed all POW camps even it had "no objection to the display by prisoners, adjacent to their bunks or on lockers, of small pictures of their national leaders, national flags or emblems."

German prisoners were even allowed to retain what might be called the Hitler salute. Arm straight out at an angle: *Sieg Heil!* The Geneva Convention required all prisoners to be allowed to salute in the manner accepted by their own army. Until late in the war, a German soldier saluted the same way as soldiers of most other nations, including the United States. If the individual was wearing a hat, cap, or helmet, he smartly snapped his hand to his head at kind of a forty-five-degree angle. Only members of the Nazi Party used what might be called the Hitler salute. On July 20, 1944 it all changed. On that day an attempt was made to assassinate Adolf Hitler. From then on, members of the German Army swore allegiance, not to the state, but to Adolf Hitler. They saluted, not Germany, but *der Führer,* Adolf Hitler. Clearly, the Hitler salute was a blatant political gesture, but the War Department accepted it from German prisoners from the moment they arrived in America.

There was anti-Nazi sentiment from the first, much of it from within the ranks of prisoners themselves. Occasionally, hardened fanatical Nazis attacked, beat, and even murdered those opposed to Adolf Hitler and his regime. In March 1944, four German prisoners asked the camp commander to move them to another facility for safety. At an Omaha, Nebraska, conference of camp commanders, an unnamed commander related the following incident:

> I was advised that four prisoners were asking to be transferred to another camp. A secret tribunal had judged them traitors to the Nazi regime. . . . The four . . . were veterans of the campaign in France, Russia, and North Africa, and while they denied being traitors to Germany, they did admit to having criticized Hitler. Now they were desperately afraid of reprisals against their families. . . . One of them told me that he was sure

he would be hanged the very minute he set foot on German soil. . . .

There are prisoners in the camps who are, in their hearts, violently anti-Nazi, but who are desperately afraid that their comrades will discover their true convictions. . . .

At Camp Grant, Illinois, a group of fanatical Nazis tried to kill 42 other POWs they believed were anti-Nazis. They locked them in their barracks and set the building on fire. At Camp Tonkawa, Oklahoma, Cpl. Johann Kunze unwittingly attended a secret meeting of about 200 die-hard Nazis at the camp mess hall. With the doors barred, witnesses spoke out about a man they believed was a traitor, someone who was not a fervent Nazi. They claimed that the man had revealed to Americans knowledge about secret installations in Germany, information that could be useful in future Allied bombing raids. To his shock, Kunze learned he was the suspect, and a tribunal of his fellow POWs convicted him of treason. By popular acclaim, he was ordered executed and his fellow POWs beat him to death with clubs and broken milk bottles. After a State Department investigation, five German prisoners were executed, the first foreign prisoners of war to be executed in American history.

In late 1943, Cpl. Hugo Krauss, who was born in Germany but had lived for several years with his parents in the United States before returning to Germany, was beaten to death at Camp Hearne, Texas. He had served as an interpreter for the camp commander, and apparently his fluency in English was enough to seal his fate. According to a newspaper report:

After the lights were put out at 9 P.M. on December 17, 1943, from six to ten men entered the compound through a hole they had cut in a wire fence . . . and invaded Krauss' barracks. He screamed for help but no one came to his aid. His barracks mates looked on while his skull was fractured, both arms were broken and his body was battered from head to foot.

Six days later Krauss died in the camp hospital. His killer or killers were never discovered.

• • •

Among the first prisoners taken in World War II were more than 694,000 Polish troops captured by Germany during the September 1939 blitzkrieg. The fate of most is not known; they simply vanished, as far as official records are concerned.

When the Soviet Union moved into Poland to take its perceived share of land, it captured another 217,000 Polish troops, and once again it's unknown what happened to many of them. Partial details of one appalling incident, however, are known. In 1940, Soviet troops slaughtered upwards of 15,000 Polish army officers. Ironically, it was the Germans who brought this to the world's attention. On April 12, 1943, German radio announced its troops had found the bodies of 4,150 Polish officers; all had their hands tied and had been shot in the back of the head. They were found in eight communal graves in the Katyn Forest near Smolensk in the Soviet Union. The group was part of a large number of Polish officers who disappeared after surrendering to the Soviets four years earlier.

Because it was the Germans who first announced the grim discovery, the Soviets blamed them, denying all charges that they themselves had murdered the captive Poles. When the Polish government-in-exile asked the International Red Cross to investigate the incident, the Soviet Union broke off diplomatic relations with the Poles.

The Germans allowed an International Medical Commission team to investigate and to perform autopsies. Eight bodies were dissected; however, one coroner abstained from giving an opinion, saying the examination indicated the bodies were not decayed enough, therefore the victims had not been dead long enough for the incident to have occurred when it was supposed to have.

Charges flew back and forth, and there were several versions why the men were murdered. At the Nuremberg trials, the Soviet Union continued to claim Germans murdered the Polish officers. In 1952, a U.S. House committee claimed that the Soviet Union's NKVD murdered the Poles in an attempt to rid Poland of all intellectual leadership. The NKVD was the People's Commissariat for Internal Affairs, the combined internal and foreign intelligence agency; in 1943, the KGB split off and became the sole agency for the Soviet Union's internal state security.

In 1989, the time of the falling of the Berlin Wall and the disappearance of Communist governments in Eastern Europe, the former Soviet Union admitted its culpability. Members of the new Russian government (now claiming to be non-Communist) agreed with the 1952 U.S. House committee report. The Poles had been murdered by the Soviet secret police, the good-old NKVD, in the spring of 1940. It was also suggested that Soviet premier Josef Stalin had ordered the murders because of his innate hatred of Poles.

A researcher in 1990 claimed the NKVD had been emptying its prisons to make room for deportees from what came to be known as the Captive Nations—Estonia, Latvia, and Lithuania—when, rather than evacuate the Polish prisoners, the Soviets murdered them. Finally, in 1994, former KGB general Paval Sudoplatov claimed NKVD head Lavrentiy Pavlovich Beria had written Stalin, recommending the execution of some "25,700 Polish prisoners taken during and after the Russian occupation of eastern Poland in 1939."

Some die-hard Communists still deny the Soviet Union had anything to do with the Katyn Forest massacre, which brings up an old story. Thirty-five years ago in Vienna, President John Kennedy asked Soviet leader Nikita Khrushchev, "Do you ever admit a mistake?" Khrushchev replied, "Certainly. In a speech before the Twentieth Party Congress, I admitted all of Stalin's mistakes."

German propaganda minister Joseph Goebbels insisted, "The Russians are not people, but a conglomeration of animals." Adolf Hitler claimed that the Soviet army was made up of "Mongol half-wits and said "his enemy consists not of soldiers but to a large extent only of beasts." On top of this, Josef Stalin scorned and rejected his own soldiers who had been captured. While the Germans were winning, captured Soviet troops didn't have a chance.

The German army took an estimated 5,250,000 to 5,750,000 Soviets prisoner during its invasion of the Soviet Union. However, because Hitler considered captured Soviet troops to be "beasts," and because the Soviet Union had not signed the Geneva Convention, Soviet troops were not classified by Berlin as POWs. Consequently, they were not treated in the manner that such status generally requires.

A secret memo drafted in September 1941 claimed captured members of the Soviet military were criminals and should not be segregated from civilian prisoners but housed together in huge camps in Ukraine and Belorussia; those already held in Polish camps should be transferred. This meant German-held Soviet POWs suffered the same racism and the same extermination as millions of private citizens in the Slavic countries. After all, according to Hitler, war in the East was not a conventional war but a war of extermination.

The German army murdered many Soviet prisoners. It starved to death many others, as remarked upon by none other than Nazi Reichsmarshal Hermann Göring:

> In the camp for Russian prisoners they have begun to eat each other. This year between twenty and thirty million persons will die of hunger in Russia. Perhaps it is well that it should be so, for certain nations must be decimated.

German records admit that 1,981,000 Soviet prisoners died in camps; 1,308,000 are listed under "Death and Disappearances in Transit," "Not Accounted For," or simply "Exterminations." SS chief Heinrich Himmler said that in 1941, "Prisoners died in the tens and hundreds of thousands of exhaustion and hunger." The starvation of Soviet prisoners by the Germans was intentional, and it continued until the Germans needed more slave laborers to sustain Berlin's war effort. Execution by starvation resumed when the worker-prisoners could no longer perform as their Nazi masters insisted.

About 40 percent of Germany's prisoners—an estimated 7.5 million—were employed in munitions plants during the final full year of the war. About 30,000 of them were even forced to man antiaircraft guns to protect the munitions plants where they and their friends and loved ones were enslaved.

There was a tragic and bitter afternote for German-held Soviet prisoners. Many who survived Adolf Hitler's camps returned home only to face Josef Stalin's wrath. Stalin claimed that any Soviet soldier who fell into enemy hands was a traitor, because the soldiers had been ordered to fight to the death or to commit suicide. Those who disobeyed Stalin's orders and somehow managed to survive Hitler's death camps were intensely questioned, then sent off to concentration camps in the Siberian gulag.

By one count, more than 40 percent of Americans held prisoner by the Japanese died at their captors' hands. Of the roughly 25,900 Americans held prisoner by the Japanese, 10,600 died in captivity. Their deaths were due in part to poor food and living conditions but, in great measure, to the deliberate mistreatment by guards and prison officials. Despite claims that it would abide by the Geneva Convention regarding treatment of prisoners of war, Japan never did; POWs were persistently maltreated. Japanese prison camps were charnel houses. Japanese prison guards starved, beat, tortured, shot, and beheaded POWs.

Much like Germany's infamous Dr. Joseph Mengele, Japanese doctors used prisoners to test new surgical procedures, usually without anesthesia, because such medicines were always in short supply. Prisoners who survived surgery were murdered anyway, because the Japanese felt no need to practice postoperative skills.

In one instance, professors at the Kyushu Imperial University took eight B-29 crewmen, cut them up while they were still alive, drained their blood, and replaced it with seawater. Japanese doctors removed lungs, livers, and stomachs. They stopped the flow of blood to the heart just to see how long it would take a man to die. They dug holes in one man's skull and stuck a knife in his still-living brain, just to see what would happen.

Almost all Americans held prisoner by the Japanese were captured in the first months of the war, which meant those who survived spent years in prison camps living under horrendous conditions. Although the Japanese did not herd prisoners into gas chambers or burn their corpses in ovens as did the Germans, they killed them in just about every other way. Author Gavin Davis says the Japanese drove prisoners toward mass death.

> They beat them until they fell, then beat them for falling, beat them until they bled, then beat them for bleeding. They denied them medical treatment. They starved them. . . . They sacrificed prisoners in medical experiments. They watched them die by the tens of thousands from diseases or malnutri-

tion like beriberi, pellagra, and scurvy, and from epidemic tropical diseases: malaria, dysentery, tropical ulcers, cholera. Those
who survived [such cruelties] could only look ahead to being
worked to death. If the war had lasted another year, there would
not have been a POW left alive.

Early in the war, Japan began beheading prisoners to show how
little respect they had for enemies who surrendered.

It should be noted that none of the stories of Japanese atrocities
were taught in Japanese schools. Many Japanese students even today
believe that Caucasians, specifically Americans, caused World War
II. The war began and ended, they learn, with the United States dropping atomic bombs on Hiroshima and Nagasaki. Pearl Harbor, they
say, was forced upon them. Japanese textbooks, however, do not tell
how Japanese troops forced Asian and Allied prisoners by the hundreds of thousands to hand-build a 265-mile military railway from
Siam (now Thailand) to Burma, murdering those who could not
stand the day-to-day, month-to-month starvation and beating. Part
of that railway was a bridge over the River Kwae Noi. It became famous, not because the Japanese acknowledged its atrocities, but from
the book and movie *Bridge Over the River Kwai*. Years after the war,
the area around the bridge became the site of a summer camp for
children of foreign diplomats.

In World War II, as it does today, Japanese culture preached its superiority over the Caucasian race. Because all races other than its own
were inferior, the Japanese showed no hesitancy in abusing and
killing those individuals unlucky enough to fall into their hands. Mass
punishment by the Japanese at POW camps was not unusual, even
for simple infringement of their rules. Guards would force whole sections of prison camps to stand at attention in the heat of the sun with
no food or water. For hours. All day, all night, and again all the following day. Guards often made prisoners pair off and hit each other;
if the Japanese thought the POWs were faking their punches, guards
would take over and beat both prisoners, using iron bars or baseball
bats. They would tie a prisoner with signal wire or barbed wire, pretend to offer the bound man a cigarette, then "shove it down his
throat, or stick it in his nose or his ear, or grind it out on him." Be-

cause Japanese soldiers often were shorter than their American prisoners, guards would stand on boxes to look their victims in the eye, or they'd make the prisoner dig a ditch and then stand in it.

Eric Lomax was a member of Britain's Royal Corps of Signals. After the fall of Singapore in February 1942, Lomax was taken prisoner by the Japanese and put to work on the Burma-Siam railway. He was held at a camp in Kanchanaburi in Siam. He remembers when he and four other POWs were forced to stand in the middle of their camp for twelve hours, the whole time expecting to feel an enemy bayonet "thrust between my shoulder-blades." Finally, one prisoner was called to stand with his arms over his head. "A hefty Japanese sergeant moved into position," Lomax writes, "lifted his pick-handle, and delivered a blow across [the prisoner's] back that would have laid out a bull. Then, he writes, "the thugs . . . set to in earnest." Soon, it was Lomax's turn.

> They stood facing me, breathing heavily. There was a pause. It seemed to drag on for minutes. Then I went down with a blow that shook every bone. . . . I could identify the periodic stamping of boots on the back of my head, crunching my face into the gravel; the crack of bones snapping; my teeth breaking; and my own involuntary attempts to respond to deep vicious kicks and to regain an upright position, only to be thrown to the ground once more.

> At one point I realized that my hips were damaged and I remember looking up and seeing the pick-helves coming down towards my hips, and putting my arms in the way to deflect the blows. I remember the actual blow that broke my wrist.

When Red Cross packages arrived in POW camps, Japanese guards routinely stole whatever they wanted—canned milk, canned butter, fruit, chocolate, and coffee. They even stole the SPAM. The only thing the guards didn't steal was cheese, because its aroma offended the sensitive Japanese nose. In some areas, the only thing that saved POWs from starvation was a strange new vegetable, one that Asians had depended upon for years but was virtually unknown to Americans: soybeans.

During the Battle of Midway, three American flyers whose aircraft crashed were picked out of the water by Japanese sailors. Two were weighted down and thrown back overboard. The third was beheaded with a fire ax.

In Batavia, four American flyers were captured, held for months, then taken outside, forced to stand in their own grave and shot to death.

At the Outram Road jail in Singapore, Japanese airmen took over from the regular guards, paraded captured B-29 crewmen through the streets, and chopped off their heads. Eric Lomax was a prisoner at Outram Road jail, and remembers, "In the past some men in our [cell] block had become so ill that they had died quietly in their cells, from a combination of disease, brutality and starvation. It was a place in which the living were turned into ghosts, starved, diseased creatures wasted down to their skeletal outlines."

Civilians in the Japanese home islands were told that any white man parachuting to safety after his plane was hit by antiaircraft fire deserved to be killed. When one pilot landed in a river, local fishermen beat him to death. In Tokyo, an American POW was interrogated for sixty-seven days straight, then moved to a zoo where he was locked naked in the monkey cage to be stared at.

In some camps Japanese guards killed POWs and ate their victims' hearts. In others, they forced living prisoners to eat the bodies of their dead comrades.

Rita Tobiason was one of a kind. She was the only U.S. Army nurse held prisoner by the Germans in World War II. She was heading for her assignment at the Ninth Army Air Force when she was shot down near Aachen, Germany. It was September 27, 1944, and she was sent to Stalag Luft 9. The camp had no facilities for female prisoners, and she was placed in a solitary cell. She was exchanged about five months later and was awarded the Air Medal and the Purple Heart.

Years after the war ended, some POWs still suffer. They were tortured, abused, starved, and beaten. All the while, the world went on without them. In the years just after the war the death rate among Japanese-held POWs was higher by far than that of civilians of their age, and considerably higher than for war veterans who had not been POWs.

Beatings and abuse left former POWs psychologically impaired and physically torn. They showed high rates of anxiety, depression, and insomnia. They suffered cardiovascular, gastrointestinal, urogenital, ophthalmic, and spinal problems. It all could be traced back to prison camp.

"Prisoners-of-war," Eric Lomax says, "don't find it easy to settle" into nonprison life. Today, "fifty years after the end of the war, I know of a man about my age, who was also a prisoner in the Far East." Each morning the man leaves his house "and goes walking, walking, walking until it is dark. He cannot sit and relax." Nightmares are a real part of many former POWs' lives. Each night they relive the starvation, the beating, the suffering.

To top it off, when some POWs finally returned home, people who had never gone anywhere during World War II, who had never faced any danger, considered former prisoners cowards because they had not fought to the death.

Just the way Japan considered its POWs.

Just the way the Germans and the Soviet Union considered theirs.

CHAPTER EIGHTEEN

Reporters, Writers, and Photographers: Don't Shoot the Messenger

The gallery in which the reporters sit has become a fourth estate of the realm.
—Thomas Babington, Lord Macaulay,
On Hallam's Constitutional History

What lies behind us and what lies before us are tiny matters to what lies within us.
—Ralph Waldo Emerson

Douglas MacArthur lived up to his promise to return to the Philippines. There are different versions of his return, just as there are different versions of many other events in MacArthur's life.

On October 20, 1944, U.S. forces invaded Leyte Island in the Philippines. A few hours later MacArthur waded ashore and delivered his famous "I have returned" speech. A controversy lies in the pictures taken of MacArthur wading ashore. An army signal corps photographer, Maj. Gaetano Faillace, photographed the general in a sideways view along with three other men: MacArthur's aide, Brig. Gen. Richard Sutherland; Gen. Carlos Romulo, of the Philippine army (also a reporter for the *Philippines Herald;* he won the 1942 Pulitzer Prize for General Correspondence); and even a CBS Radio reporter, Bill Dunn.

Two questions arose: was this the first photo taken of MacArthur wading ashore in the Philippines and was it rehearsed. For years, a rumor floated around that the general began his walk to shore, but the photographer wasn't ready. "How about going back and doing it again?" Major Faillace, or someone else, allegedly asked General MacArthur, and the rumor goes that the publicity-conscious general agreed; then Faillace took the picture. Good story, and it may be true.

Life magazine photographer Carl Mydans, however, claims the rehearsal rumor just wasn't so. His was an even more famous photo of

MacArthur wading ashore in the Philippines. His photograph was taken several months after Faillace's, on January 9, 1945, and that may be where the rumor and controversy got their start. Mydans says he was with MacArthur when the group stepped ashore in January about a hundred miles north of Manila. According to Mydans, a landing craft (LC) with the general on board pulled up to a shore ramp laid by the Seabees. Mydans jumped off but the landing craft pulled away, reversed engines, and began running parallel to the beach. Mydans had been with MacArthur before, and says he knew the general's LC would run down the beach for a bit, would stop, and without using a ramp, MacArthur would wade ashore. It would make a better picture. "I ran to shore and kept running parallel to the LC. . . . When it turned in, I was ready." Mydans took a nearly perfect head-on shot of the general and company calf-deep in water. It shows Brigadier General Sutherland, Col. Lloyd Lehrbas, MacArthur, and an unidentified staff sergeant. The photographer denies that General MacArthur posed for the picture or agreed to wade back out and back in again. It was only the one time, he claims.

So, we have two pictures: a side view taken by Maj. Gaetano Faillace on October 20, 1944, and a head-on view taken by Carl Mydans on January 9, 1945. Or maybe we have a third. The full frame of Mydans's 35mm picture shows another photographer off to the left side. If this other photographer took a picture the same day as Mydans did, it's not widely seen. Perhaps that, along with the earlier photograph, is what started the rumor.

Americans got their first look at World War II in newsreels, those short film clips shown between movie features. Before Clark Gable faced Charles Laughton in *Mutiny on the Bounty*, audiences saw flickering films of Mussolini invading Ethiopia. Before Charlie Chaplin and Paulette Goddard showed us *Modern Times*, we saw Hitler test his blitzkrieg in the Spanish Civil War. And before Snow White watched Dopey, Doc, Sneezy, et al. "hi-ho" their way to work, American newsreel audiences saw British prime minister Neville Chamberlain declare that there would be "peace for our time."

Newsreels were the evening news before television. They showed massed swastika flags waving in Berlin and panzer columns rumbling through Prague. Movie audiences saw the beginning of the Blitz and the Battle of Britain. Newsreels brought the war home, somewhat censored, but nonetheless Americans saw the face of war.

Americans also heard about the war on the radio, thanks to a new breed of war correspondents: William Shirer, Walter Cronkite, Eric Sevareid, and Edward R. (the R for Roscoe) Murrow, among the best.

Murrow was unforgettable. "This," and he would pause, "is London." His deep, resonant voice would continue:

> Three red buses drawn up in a line waiting to take the homeless away, men with white scarfs around their necks instead of collars and ties, leading dull-eyed, empty-faced women across to the buses. Most of them carried little cheap cardboard suitcases and sometimes bulging paper shopping bags. That was all they had.

Poet Archibald MacLeish wrote of Edward R. Murrow, "You burned the city of London in our houses and we felt the flames that burned it. You laid the dead of London at our doors and we knew that the dead were our dead."

Other war correspondents approached the war differently. John Hersey, a correspondent for *Time* magazine, later admitted that it bothered him that during the war he'd referred to "Japs" as "a swarm of intelligent little animals." He later wrote *A Bell for Adano,* about an American officer's efforts to help rebuild a small Italian town. The novel won a Pulitzer Prize in 1945. While in the South Pacific, Hersey heard talk about a harrowing story involving a small navy boat that was rammed and sunk while barreling up The Slot in the Solomon Islands. He tried selling the story to *Life* magazine, but they turned him down. *The New Yorker* liked it and bought the story of *PT-109* and its captain, navy lieutenant John F. Kennedy.

In 1942, years after he wrote *Grapes of Wrath,* author John Steinbeck wrote the novel *The Moon Is Down,* a melodramatic tale of an unnamed nation occupying an equally unnamed (but Scandinavian) country. It wasn't too difficult to see that Steinbeck had fictionalized the German conquest of Denmark and Norway. Later, Steinbeck was a correspondent for the New York *Herald Tribune.* After the war was over, he admitted:

• • •

> We were all part of the war effort. We went along with it, and not only that, we abetted it. . . . Yes, we wrote only a part of the war but at that time we believed, fervently believed, that it was the best thing to do.

Another afterthought of World War II came from correspondent Fletcher Pratt: "The official censors pretty well succeeded in putting over the legend that the war was won without a single mistake by a command consisting of geniuses."

Some, however, didn't have the chance to change their minds after the war ended. Of about 800 correspondents who served and wrote, 38 were killed and another 36 were wounded. In fact, war correspondents suffered a 22 percent casualty rate compared to the 5 percent rate for combat servicemen.

In 1942, photographer Margaret Bourke-White was on board the SS *Strathallam* off the coast of North Africa when it was torpedoed by a German submarine. Also on board was General Eisenhower's secretary-chauffeur (and possibly mistress) WAC Capt. Kay Summersby. Neither was injured.

Margaret Bourke-White was the first woman accredited to be a correspondent-photographer with the U.S. Army Air Forces. Working with *Life* magazine, she was one of only twenty-four women accredited by the Allies to cover the war. In 1944, she excerpted from the magazine some of her words and pictures for her book, *They Called It "Purple Heart Valley," A Combat Chronicle of the War in Italy*.

> We made our way up the steep crags in the darkness, pulling ourselves up sometimes by our hands and knees, and then staggering on without even the aid of the usual red-lensed blackout flashlight. Even this feeble beam, it seemed, might draw fire.
>
> We had to follow a white tape just faintly visible in the dark. The mountain had been so newly captured that our sappers had had a chance only to clear mines out of a slender pathway. The white tape was the characteristic marking indicating mine clearance. . . .

Right beneath my feet, at the foot of the cliff, was a row of howitzers sending out sporadic darts of flame. Since I was so high up and so far forward, most of our heavies were in back of me, and I could look over the hills from which we had come and see the muzzle flashes of friendly guns, looking as if people were lighting cigarettes all over the landscape.

The whole valley was clanging with fire.

Ernie Pyle was known as the GI's reporter. His hometown of Dana, Indiana, was small when Pyle was born in 1900, and it's small now. For miles all around these days, signs point to the Ernie Pyle State Historic Site. The town is proud of the sharecropper's son. Pyle was in the naval reserves in the first World War, but in the second World War he became a hero, a noncombatant one. He studied journalism at Indiana University but quit just short of getting his degree. The girl he was dating dumped him, so instead of sticking around for graduation, Pyle quit to become a cub reporter for the LaPorte, Indiana, *Herald*. LaPorte is larger than Dana, Indiana, but not by much.

Three months later Pyle moved to the Washington, D.C., *Daily News*, owned by the Scripps-Howard Syndicate. Four years after joining the *Daily News*, the newspaper promoted Pyle to managing editor, but that tied him to a desk and he didn't like that. He talked Scripps-Howard into letting him rove the country, writing whatever he wanted, a dream for just about any writer. His column ran in the company's newspapers as "The Hoosier Vagabond," telling homespun, chatty, offbeat, and unusual stories about everyday people.

He was in England in December 1940 and watched from a balcony as the Luftwaffe bombed London. Forty-one years old when World War II started, he was too old to be drafted, so he drafted himself. As a war correspondent, he continued writing the kind of stories he'd written before the war. Writing for the United Features Syndicate, after London he took his typewriter to North Africa where American troops were slogging through the desert sands looking for Rommel. "Recently," he wrote while in Tunis, "I have been living with a front-line outfit." He used simple, declarative sentences telling of the reality of war.

Pyle was with the infantry during the invasion of Sicily. On January 10, 1944, he wrote about war in the mountains of Italy, near San Pietro. It's believed to be the most repeated of all his war stories. It is terse. It is blunt. It is emotionally draining to read but well worth that drain.

> I was at the foot of the mule trail when they brought Capt. [Henry T.] Waskow's body down. The moon was nearly full at the time, and you could see far up the trail, and even part way across the valley below. Soldiers made shadows in the moonlight as they walked.
>
> Dead men had been coming down the mountain all evening, lashed onto the backs of mules. They came lying belly-down across the wooden pack-saddles, their heads hanging down on the left side of the mule, their stiffened legs sticking out awkwardly from the other side, bobbing up and down as the mules walked. . . .
>
> The first one came early in the morning. They slid him down from the mule and stood him on his feet for a moment while they got a new grip. In the half light he might have been merely a sick man standing there, leaning on the others. Then they laid him on the ground in the shadow of the low stone wall alongside the road.
>
> I don't know who that first one was. You feel small in the presence of dead men, and ashamed at being alive, and you don't ask silly questions. . . .
>
> One soldier came and looked down, and he said out loud, "God damn it." That's all he said, and then he walked away. Another one came. He said, "God damn it to hell anyway." He looked down for a few moments, and then he turned and left.
>
> Another man came; I think he was an officer. It was hard to tell officers from men in the half light, for all were bearded and grimy dirty. The man looked down into the dead captain's face, and then he spoke directly to him, as though he were alive. He said: "I'm sorry, old man."
>
> [He] squatted down, and he reached down and took the dead hand, and he sat there for a full five minutes, holding the

dead hand in his own and looking intently into the dead face, and he never uttered a sound all the time he sat there.

And finally he put the hand down, and he reached up and gently straightened the points of the captain's shirt collar, and then he sort of rearranged the tattered edges of his uniform around the wound. And then he got up and walked away down the road in the moonlight, all alone.

Six times a week, Pyle's columns were published in more than 300 newspapers around the United States; more than 13 million readers awaited his tales. The censors disapproved, but Erie Pyle often used real troops in his columns, with real names and real hometowns. He wrote that GIs "lived like men of prehistoric times, and a club would have become them more than a machine gun."

With the war in Europe winding down, Pyle headed for the Pacific, admitting, "I feel that I've used up all my chances."

He waded ashore at Iwo Jima and was with the 1st Marine Division on D day at Okinawa, April 4, 1945. Two weeks later, on the island of Ie Shima, his prophecy came true; he'd used up all his chances. Japanese snipers opened fire on a jeep Ernie Pyle was riding in, and he dove into a ditch. The firing stopped, and he looked up to see what was happening. The snipers were still there, and they shot Pyle in the left temple.

Ernie Pyle was forty-five years old. He died twenty days before Germany surrendered in Europe, four months before Japan surrendered in the Pacific. They first buried Ernie Pyle on the island of Ie Shima near where he'd been killed. Chaplain Nathaniel B. Saucier of the 305th Infantry, 77th Division, recovered Pyle's body and conducted the burial service:

We placed him on a litter and returned along the same hazardous way by which we reached him. We left the sunglasses and camouflage helmet just as we found he had been wearing them. We expected orders to ship the body back to the States, but none came. During this time many soldiers passed by and looked on him with sad faces.

At 11 A.M., 20 April, 1945, we laid the body of Ernie Pyle to rest in the presence of about 200 servicemen including all ranks, all arms of the service and various nationalities. It seemed that all nature called a halt and with bowed head paid respect to a noble man now departed. With the exception of an occasional blast of distant guns and the murmuring of the waves not far away, all was quiet.

On Pyle's body when he was killed was the draft of a column he'd written about the Allies' victory in Europe and the war and coming victory in the Pacific:

And so it is over. The catastrophe on one side of the world has run its course. The day that so long seemed would never come has come at last.

It has been seven months since I heard my last shot in the European war. Now I am as far away from it as it is possible to get on this globe.

To me the European war is old, and the Pacific war is new.

[T]here are many. . . who have had burned into their brains forever the unnatural sight of cold dead men scattered over the hillsides and in the ditches along the high rows of hedge throughout the world.

Dead men by mass production—in one country after another—month after month and year after year. Dead men in winter and dead men in summer.

Dead men in such familiar promiscuity that they become monotonous.

Dead men in such monstrous infinity that you come almost to hate them.

These are the things that you at home need not even try to understand. To you at home they are columns of figures, or he is near one who went away and just didn't come back. You didn't see him lying so grotesque and pasty beside the gravel road in France.

We saw him by the multiple thousands.

For a while, a simple wooden marker stood over his grave, the inscription painted with a cotton-wrapped stick dipped in ink:

AT THIS SPOT
The 77th Infantry Division
Lost A Buddy
ERNIE PYLE
18 April 1945

On July 19, 1949, the body of Ernie Pyle was reburied in the Punchbowl Memorial Cemetery in Hawaii. He lies alongside thousands of other victims of the war.

For a while in the sixties, kids in Ernie Pyle's hometown of Dana, Indiana, regularly vandalized the home he'd been born in. In 1974, some of his boyhood friends raised money to buy the house (Ernie's sharecropper parents hadn't owned their home) and move it across the railroad tracks, where they turned it into a museum. Over the years it's been filled with memorabilia, not just of Ernie Pyle but of the war. Much of it is in storage, some in a basement that gets musty and mildewed when it rains. Now they've built two World War II–style Quonset huts; all the memorabilia will be displayed there, along with a 1943 army jeep.

Ernie Pyle wasn't a great man. He may not have been a great writer. But he was a man and a writer who understood what the common soldier was all about. He wrote simple, understanding stories about those common soldiers. No pretention to his writing, like the man himself.

CHAPTER NINETEEN

I Spy, You Spy:
The Few, The Proud, The Secret Agents

All's fair in love and war.
> —Francis Edward Smedley, *Frank Farlegh,* chapter 50

I would like a medium vodka dry Martini—with a slice of lemon peel. Shaken and not stirred.
> —Ian Fleming, *Dr. No,* 1958

Six months before the United States entered World War II, President Roosevelt appointed Col. William Joseph "Wild Bill" Donovan as Coordinator of Information (COI). It was the cover name for America's fledgling attempt at spying.

Donovan was an oddity, an Irish Catholic Republican. His heritage might have made him a lifelong Democrat, but Donovan's life was almost a textbook of how to succeed in a wealthy Republican society. He earned the nickname "Wild Bill" playing football at Columbia University. Law school completed, Donovan married the daughter of one of the oldest and wealthiest families in Buffalo, New York. When World War I broke out, he organized a cavalry troop and fought with the 42d Infantry Division, receiving the Congressional Medal of Honor, the Distinguished Service Cross, and the Distinguished Service Medal.

After the war, Donovan traveled to China and Siberia and was a special counsel in Europe. In Poland, Donovan met Herbert Hoover while Hoover worked with the Rockefeller Institute's food mission. Donovan later became the future president's adviser and speechwriter.

In 1922, Donovan founded a New York law firm, quickly became a millionaire, and was active in state Republican politics. He ran for lieutenant governor and lost; he also ran for governor, a race which he also lost. For a while Donovan was an assistant attorney general during Calvin Coolidge's presidency. He visited Ethiopia, where he witnessed Italy's ouster of Emperor Haile Selassie in 1935, and went to Spain in time for the 1936 Civil War.

Although he opposed Franklin Roosevelt's domestic programs, Donovan agreed with FDR's plans for military preparedness to protect American neutrality. Donovan was an unofficial observer in Great Britain for fellow Republican Frank Knox, Roosevelt's secretary of the navy. Knox was pleased with his reports and, at the secretary's suggestion, Donovan toured southeast Europe and the Middle East to observe resistance movements. When he returned to the United States in July 1941, Roosevelt named Donovan Coordinator of Information (COI).

His was a quasi-intelligence organization, ostensibly a private firm, but in reality funding came from the U.S. Treasury. (Well into the 1960s, CIA employees were technically listed as treasury employees.) As COI, Donovan got in a bit of so-called "black" propaganda, operating a fake German radio station in Britain, broadcasting messages from and to nonexisting anti-Nazi groups. Six months after Pearl Harbor, Donovan's COI became the Office of Strategic Services (OSS), which later became the Central Intelligence Agency (CIA). Wild Bill Donovan was a fan of Britain's MI6 Secret Service and patterned the OSS after it, often coordinating with British and Canadian espionage operations.

The OSS offices were in Temporary Building Q in Washington, D.C., along the Mall, next to the reflecting pool between the Lincoln Memorial and the Washington Monument. The organization had uniforms made by Brooks Brothers, and many of its supplies came from Abercrombie &Fitch—sleeping bags, air mattresses, and foul weather gear. Not your usual sort.

Donovan gathered around him what historian R. Harris Smith calls "a chaotic organization of left wing activists and intellectuals, right wing corporate attorneys, and people from America's wealthiest families." Among this disparate group were historian Arthur M. Schlesinger, Jr. (who wrote, among other things, a biography of FDR and his times), writer Gene Fodor (who went on to author the Fodor

Guide series for tourists), Arthur Goldberg (who went on to the U.S. Supreme Court), and Julia Child (who went on to make pastries and tarts on TV). It was Child who once claimed OSS meant "Oh! So Secret!" Many in the group were so famous, however, that the letters took on another meaning: "Oh, So Social." Social, perhaps; experienced in spying, no. Donovan's OSS eventually recruited upward of 16,000 people and sent many of them behind enemy lines.

At first, the OSS centered its operations in North Africa, from which it launched many of its European operations. Working with Britain's Special Operations Executive (SOE) and the Free French, the OSS launched teams referred to as "Jedburgh agents." The name "Jedburgh" was derived from the twelfth century border wars between the Scots and the British invaders in the Jedburgh area of Scotland where a local Scottish group conducted guerrilla warfare. William Colby, who later became head of the CIA, was a Jedburgh agent during the war.

Jedburgh squads were made up of agents from each of the three cooperating nations. Wearing uniforms to avoid execution as spies if they were caught, Jedburgh agents parachuted into France following the D-day landing at Normandy. They worked with French Resistance forces to divert German troops from the invasion site.

Other OSS agents operated with British troops in the China-Burma-India theater. Operatives worked in Lisbon, Madrid, and Berne, Switzerland, where Allen W. Dulles was head of OSS operations, coordinating with anti-Hitler elements to arrange the surrender of German troops in Italy. By the end of World War II, the OSS had placed nearly 200 agents in Germany, disrupting Berlin's war effort and sending back information on the results of Allied air raids. General MacArthur, however, refused to allow the agents to operate within his command in the Southwest Pacific.

President Truman abolished the OSS on September 20, 1945, its functions transferred to the State and War Departments. Two years later, Truman used some former OSS personnel as cadre in forming the Central Intelligence Group, later changing the word *group* to *agency*.

Donovan returned to his law practice for a while, then served as the U.S. ambassador to Thailand from 1953 to 1954. Perhaps not unexpectedly, this was about the same time American intelligence operations began to expand in Southeast Asia.

To a great degree, Britain's MI6 handled Ultra, the code name given to much of the intelligence derived from deciphering Germany's machine-encoded radio messages. In 1939, Britain set up its Code and Cipher School in an ugly Victorian mansion about forty miles north of London—Bletchley Park in Buckinghamshire. It was there the code breakers went to work on Enigma-generated codes.

Enigma was Germany's typewriter-like machine used to encode and decode messages; it had been around since 1923. The German navy began using Enigma machines in 1926, and the army followed in 1928. The machines were so reliable that the Luftwaffe began using them in 1933. At one point, there were some 20,000 Enigma machines of different types and vintages in use. Making it worse for the Allies, in 1934 Japan began using Enigma machines.

The Enigma had a typewriter-like keyboard, a battery, a series of lights, three removable rotors, and a stationary wheel (called the *Umkehrwalze*) about the same size as the rotors. The battery tied keys to rotors to tiny flashlight-sized bulbs. They were all joined by a maze of wires and plugs.

To encode a message, a clerk hit a key; the current flowed (via the wires and pins and contacts) through the three rotors to the wheel, which reflected it back through the movable rotors. Lights were lit, messages were sent and received, and the Allies were confounded. Those who know claim "the number of possibly different wired rotors was equivalent to factorial 26," something like 403,291,461,126,605,635,684,000,000. And that doesn't even take into account the number of possible different *Umkehrwalze* permutations.

The rotors, wheel, and plug-in connections on the encoding machine had to match exactly those on the decoding machine. Later in the war, the three-wheel system gave way to four- and five-rotor models. The interchangeable rotors and plug connections afforded up to 200 quintillion permutations. To make it more difficult, the rotor settings would be changed several times a day.

Much of the decrypting work was a British show; however, three detachments of Americans were assigned to the program. Secrecy was so strict, many of those in the American detachments didn't know of the others' existence.

What really helped break the code was the capture of a large Polish machine called the "bombe," a high-speed electromechanical marvel (something like an early card-carrying computer) that according to one expert "could rapidly move through rotor permutations to find a key within a reasonable amount of time." Later, an Enigma machine was salvaged from a sunken German submarine. Even knowing that the Allies had Enigma machines didn't faze the German high command, who believed there were so many possible settings as to make Ultra messages indecipherable. Both Great Britain and the United States put a lot of time and effort into cracking the code, and, thanks to the early work done by Polish scientists, by the end of the war the Allies were regularly reading Ultra-encrypted messages.

Meanwhile, on the other side of the war, the U.S. Navy had broken Japan's diplomatic and military codes. Actually, they'd cracked Tokyo's highest code, Purple, two years before the war even started.

Knowing exactly what the enemy is going to do can be hazardous to your mental health. What if you learn, through a secretly decoded message, that the enemy plans to bomb a major city. If you evacuate everybody, that lets the enemy know that you've broken the code.

On the night of November 14–15, 1940, a flight of 449 German bombers dropped 150,000 incendiary bombs along with 503 tons of high explosives on the city of Coventry, England, (the alleged site of Lady Godiva's fabled if unlikely nude horseback ride). Hitler had expressly ordered Coventry bombed in retaliation for Britain's bombing of Munich on November 8, an attack that coincided with the anniversary of *der Führer*'s Munich Beer Hall Putsch seventeen years earlier. Coventry was one of Britain's most industrially important and historically appealing cities. The story has circulated since the war that Winston Churchill had advance warning of the attack—thanks to Ultra intercepts—but chose not to inform Coventry officials or call for an evacuation, because it would have tipped the Germans that England had cracked their codes.

Churchill regularly received decoded Ultra intercepts, referring to them as "my eggs," the nickname indicated perhaps that he considered them the eggs from the golden goose of Bletchley Park. MI6 called it "Boniface;" by whatever name, it was the "sole form of intelligence, or indeed of spying, in which Churchill was interested." MI6, however, had other ways of determining British targets.

German agents in England would set up two widely separate narrow-beam radio signals as a sort of pathway for Luftwaffe bombers. The two signals would intersect at the target location. By midafternoon on November 14, the RAF had triangulated the beams and determined that either Coventry or the London vicinity would be the night's target.

About the same time, a German prisoner of war told a barracks stool pigeon about the coming bombing raid; both the POW and the stoolie were disregarded. Intelligence professionals don't like amateurs telling them their game.

So, *did* Winston Churchill know about the coming bombing of Coventry and choose not to warn the city in order to protect the breaking of the code? Several self-proclaimed experts now say he did not know, claiming that the word *Coventry* never appeared in any Ultra intercepts. Others say that, since the Luftwaffe aircraft would home in on the radio beams, all they had to do was jam the radios. The RAF apparently tried that but jammed the wrong signal. The raid went off as planned, and Coventry was nearly destroyed: 550 people were killed and 1,000 more were injured; 50,749 houses were destroyed or damaged. Coventry's famed 1,000-year-old St. Michael's Cathedral was also destroyed. Its bombed-out shell remains as a monument beside a new, magnificent cathedral. The rest of the city was rebuilt also, but as one tourist guidebook puts it, Coventry "contains some of the worst postwar rebuilding to be seen in Britain, and the less said the better."

That the Ultra code was broken remained a secret until 1974, when RAF group captain F. W. Winterbotham published an account titled *The Ultra Secret*. According to Winterbotham, cracking Ultra was the next best thing to . . . well, the next best thing to inventing Ultra. Winterbotham claimed that knowing the German code was "crucial in routing the U-boats and winning the Battle of the North Atlantic, had reversed British fortunes against [General Erwin] Rommel in North Africa and had turned the German airborne invasion of Crete into a ghastly Pyrrhic victory."

• • •

An American code the enemy never completely broke wasn't just a code; it was a different language. During World War II, Native Americans from the Navajo tribe served as "code talkers." Their language in itself is complex; mixing it with short military code words, completely confused the Japanese.

In April 1942, marine recruiters enlisted volunteers from New Mexico and Arizona reservation agency schools. All were fluent in both Navajo and English. They reported to the San Diego Marine Corps Recruit Depot and initially were designated as the 382d Platoon; quickly, they became known as "The Navajo School." In addition to their regular duties, they helped devise a new Marine Corps military code. They used short, easy to learn and quick to recall words and devised a two-part code. Part one was a 26-letter phonetic alphabet using Navajo names for animals or birds; in addition, they used several different words for letters—*ice* for *I, nut* for *N, quiver* for *Q,* and so on to *zinc* for *Z.* Part two was a 211-word Navajo vocabulary and the English equivalents. One code talker, a boarding school student before joining the marines, remembers how "the U.S. government told us not to speak Navajo but during the war the government wanted us to speak it."

Some white officers admitted that they didn't understand how the system worked, but because it did, any initial distrust that the top brass at the Pentagon may have felt soon was erased. By August 1943, nearly 200 Navajo tribesmen had been trained, and more would follow. Eventually, there would be 421 code talkers.

Second-generation Japanese Americans who volunteered for the military served in the all-nisei 442d Regimental Combat Team in Europe. The Navajo marines, however, went to the Pacific, which sometimes meant trouble for them. White Americans often confused Navajos with Japanese, and some code talkers were captured and interrogated as Japanese. Others were almost killed by their fellow troops.

Navajo code talkers served with all six marine divisions in the Pacific as well as with Raider and parachute units. By all accounts, the Navajo code was a deciding factor in many engagements. According to Maj. Howard Conner of the 5th Marine Division, the marines' entire landing operation at Iwo Jima was "directed by Navajo code."

Conners adds that, "during the two days that followed the initial landings I had six Navajo radio nets working around the clock. . . .They sent and received over 800 messages without an error. Were it not for the Navajo code talkers, the Marines never would have taken Iwo Jima."

When the Navajo code talkers returned after the war, they were greeted by family reunions where purification rites, traditional dances, and curing ceremonies were held. The ceremonies were an ages-old tradition meant to counter any harmful or toxic influences the tribesmen might have encountered while off the reservation.

Back home, they encountered many of the same problems that other veterans did: jobs were scarce, especially on the reservation; readjusting to nonmilitary life was difficult. Add to that the problems between Native Americans and whites; before the war they'd often been abused and scorned, and the same abuse and scorn returned after the war.

The last code talker to leave the Marine Corps finally retired in 1972. For more than twenty years after the war, the Navajos' code was a highly classified military secret. It was declassified in 1968, and the following year the code talkers were honored at the 4th Marine Division's annual reunion in Chicago. Twenty veteran code talkers attended the reunion and marched in a parade with the other veterans down Michigan Avenue. While others wore tired, old uniforms, often faded and tight across the stomach, the Navajos wore their best tribal regalia. They were honored by a presidential certificate of appreciation.

Perhaps the highest honor for the code talkers came from a Japanese general who in the war assigned his most skilled cryptographers to decipher the marines' messages. The Japanese never succeeded. The Navajo code talkers beat the best the enemy could put against them.

Amy Elizabeth Thorpe's friends called her Betty, but her code name was Cynthia. She was one of the Allies' best spies during World War II. Her father was a U.S. Marine Corps officer who took his family to posts around the world. He resigned his commission to study law, and that brought them back home. When Betty was just eleven years old, she used pictures and information on postcards from what the song called "far away places with strange sounding names" to write a romantic novel titled *Fioretta*. An Italian naval attaché much older than Betty met her at a diplomatic picnic and fell in love with her novel (not to mention Betty herself). The two began an apparently platonic relationship. The attaché, Alberto Lais, called Betty his "golden girl."

By the time she was eighteen, Betty Thorpe was described as beautiful, well bred, and graceful. Now a young woman, she ended her platonic relationship with the Italian naval officer and began a full-blown affair with a British embassy official. Arthur Pack was nineteen years Betty's senior, and their relationship led to marriage at Washington's Church of the Epiphany, to dual citizenship for her, and to a son born five months after the wedding. Even with all that, Betty seemed bored with Arthur. For reasons not fully understood, she turned the boy over to foster parents.

When Pack was transferred to Spain on the eve of that nation's civil war, Betty took up undercover operations—smuggling nationalists out to safety and smuggling medical supplies in to Franco's Fascist forces. By 1937, Amy Elizabeth Thorpe Pack was a full-fledged member of His Britannic Majesty's Secret Service, working under MI6's wealthy Canadian-born director, William "Little Bill" Stephenson. It was Stephenson who gave her the code name Cynthia.

It was her husband, Arthur, however, who gave her another child, this time a girl. Betty, Arthur, their new daughter, and a nanny went off to Warsaw, where Arthur was stationed at the British embassy.

Their marriage, which may have had a tough go all along, floundered seriously when Arthur informed Betty that he was in love with another woman. While Arthur was busy with his new love, Betty got busy working elsewhere—at the game of espionage. Bill Stephenson provided funds for Betty to use in cultivating Polish sources.

Stephenson's nominal title was British passport control officer, and he was sent to New York to train America's Bill Donovan. It was there Stephenson became known as the man called Intrepid, the channel for intelligence between Winston Churchill and Franklin Roosevelt.

With the war under way in Europe, Amy Elizabeth Thorpe Pack left her husband and joined Stephenson in America. As Cynthia, she set up shop in Washington, D.C., posing as a journalist in order to obtain information about the Italian navy's code system. Her old platonic friend Alberto Lais—now Admiral Lais, was sixty years old, apparently still infatuated with Betty, and ready to resume their relationship.

Alberto was back in the States on a special mission. Mussolini was "convinced that the United States would soon join the war," and wanted something done about the more than two-dozen Italian merchant ships being held in American ports.

Betty telephoned Alberto, saying "It's your golden girl. Can we meet?" He couldn't say no. Within hours, Alberto Lais allegedly threw off the thoughts of his wife, threw off his country, and especially he threw off his clothes. Their earlier platonic relationship changed drastically, although Betty herself later hedged a bit about the affair, claiming that their friendship was "sentimental and even sensual, rather than sexual." Whatever she thought, he obviously thought it involved a whole lot more, especially while the two lay in bed with the admiral whispering sweet nothings in Betty's ear. He apparently also whispered his navy's plans to sabotage those twenty-seven Italian merchant ships. When the bombs exploded, he bragged, the ships would be so heavily damaged that they'd be useless if the United States tried to seize them.

Getting rid of Alberto as quickly as she could, Betty phoned the U.S. Office of Naval Intelligence, but it was too late; most of the bombs had already exploded. A few ships were saved and, just as Mussolini had feared, the United States seized them. Secretary of State Cordell Hull immediately ordered Admiral Lais out of the country. As Alberto prepared to leave, according to Betty, he had one final gift for his golden girl: the Italian navy's code and cipher books.*

Her Italian lover gone, Betty moved on to other conquests: the Vichy French embassy. Back in her pose as an American journalist,

*In 1967, Alberto Lais's relatives read accounts of how the admiral had betrayed military secrets. They sued in an Italian court and won. In 1988, when David Brinkley's book *Washington Goes to War* was first released, Lais's sons protested. They claimed their father had never had a sexual relationship with Betty Pack and persuaded the Italian defense ministry to publish ads in three leading East Coast American newspapers, denying the allegations.

she contacted the embassy in May 1941. Almost immediately, press
attaché Charles Brousse fell for her, and by June he was handing over
to her embassy cables, letters, and files. To make the exchange of information easier, Betty moved into the hotel where Brousse and his
wife lived.

With the aid of the two Bills—Stevenson and Donovan—she
hired a thief nicknamed "Georgia Cracker" to break into the French
embassy's safe. Brousse convinced the embassy's watchman to give
him a room for a liaison with a lady friend, and the French being
the French, the watchman looked the other way. Just to make certain that they would not be interrupted, they slipped phenobarbital
into the watchman's food. The Georgia Cracker opened the safe, but
it took so long that Betty couldn't copy down the codes. They'd have
to try again another night.

The second time, Betty had the combination to the safe (thanks
to that good-ol'-boy Cracker) and, voilà, it was open! Suddenly, Betty
sensed a problem. Quickly she stripped off her clothes, told Brousse
to do the same, and as they stood naked a guard walked through the
door. His flashlight on Betty as she stood resplendent in necklace
and high heels, the guard muttered, "I beg your pardon a thousand
times," and closed the door. Getting dressed she passed the code
books out the window, waited while another agent copied them,
then—all fingerprints wiped from the books—returned them to the
safe.

When the time came for the Allied landings in North Africa, the
Allies put to good use the codes Betty had stolen. It's not known, of
course, how many lives were saved because the Allies could read the
coded messages, but estimates run into the thousands.

In 1945, Betty's husband, Arthur Pack, committed suicide. French
press aide Charles Brousse was divorced by his wife, and Charles and
Betty married. She and her new husband moved to the south of
France and settled in a medieval castle on a mountaintop. When
asked whether she was sorry for all the sex-for-secrets acts she had
performed during the war, Betty answered:

> Ashamed? Not in the least. My superiors told me that the re-
> sults of my work saved thousands of British and American

lives. . . . It involved me in situations from which "respectable" women draw back—but mine was total commitment. Wars are not won by respectable methods.

Besides, she added, she considered herself a patriot. Patriotism cannot prevent tragedy. Betty died in 1963, the victim of mouth cancer. Her husband lived another ten years until he was accidentally electrocuted by an apparently faulty electric blanket. The fairy-tale castle where Charles and the spy called Cynthia lived their last years was destroyed in the ensuing fire.

James Bond was a fictional spy, but his creator, Ian Fleming, was a real one, and sometimes the deeds of the literary spy mocked the human one. As an aide to the chief of British naval intelligence, Fleming took the code name 17F, not nearly so cool as Bond's code-name, 007. Fleming and the chief, Sir John Godfrey, were in Lisbon, Portugal, headed for the United States when the writer-spy recognized a group of German agents playing cards. In a scene that sounds much like the spy he later created, Fleming decided to try to cripple the German agents' ability to move around the world by gambling with them and winning all their money. The author wasn't up to his character's ability, however, and instead of taking the Germans for all they were worth, Ian Fleming lost all the money he had on him.

Fleming later was ordered to go ashore in the 1942 raid at the French port of Dieppe. The raid failed, apparently because of inadequate preparations by the British and quick intervention by the Luftwaffe. The Allies lost more than 1,200 men killed and about 2,200 taken prisoner. Mostly, the losses were to Canadian units. The Dieppe raid is still a sore point with the Canadians, who believe it was a British publicity stunt more than a real invasion effort. In any event, Ian Fleming wasn't able carry out his mission to collect German code books at Dieppe.

The spymaker-to-be also commanded an assault unit during the invasion of Normandy. Once again, his mission was to capture enemy code books, but once again he apparently failed.

Fleming's master spy, James Bond (the character almost was called James Gunn), may have liked vodka martinis, but author Ian

Fleming preferred gin. Medium dry-martinis, English gin and American vermouth. He preferred them to excess, and by the end of the war he was drinking a quart of gin a day along with about three and a half packs of cigarettes a day; understandably he died at the age of fifty-six. By then he considered himself a very old man, writing about the adventurous deeds of someone far younger.

Although Fleming may have partially modeled his fictional character after himself, apparently he took a lot of James Bond's character—Bond, James Bond—from Dusko Popov, a high-living playboy from Yugoslavia who was a double agent code-named Tricycle. Four months prior to the attack on Pearl Harbor, Tricycle's German masters asked him to gather information about the Hawaiian base's defenses. Instead, Popov warned American FBI director J. Edger Hoover of the Axis' interests. Hoover denounced Popov as nothing more than a Balkan playboy son of a millionaire and ignored the information, which would never have happened to James Bond. Maybe even to Ian Fleming.

CHAPTER TWENTY

Frozen in Time:
A Little Bit of This, A Little Bit of That

The V sign is the symbol of the unconquerable will of the occupied territories, and a portent of the fate awaiting the Nazi tyranny.
—Winston Churchill, speech to the London
County Council, July 14, 1941

Never before have we had so little time in which to do so much.
—Franklin Roosevelt, Fireside Chat, February 23, 1942

The American military went to the dogs in World War II. The army's K-9 Corps—an abbreviation for canine—was formed in 1941. The guard dogs would be used to patrol military facilities and occasionally perform hazardous jobs. European armies had used dogs in World War I, but it wasn't until World War II that the United States used them.

Originally, dog handlers were picked from some 5,000 GI volunteers. Several thousand dogs were also employed, but they didn't have much say whether or not they'd volunteer.

Many K-9 Corps dogs were donated by civilian owners through a program called Dogs for Defense. While German shepherds are the breed generally shown in photographs, no particular breed was used, just as long as the dogs were large, strong, and healthy. Just like human draftees and recruits, the dogs were given physical examinations. If they passed, they were trained alongside their new masters. Some were trained to patrol and attack, some to carry backpacks, and some were messengers, with canisters carried around their necks. Despite what the movies show, you can't just tell a dog, "Take this message to headquarters, boy." The army had to have a human trainer on either end of the message line. Since the dog had to know two men, both trained him, one for each end of the message.

It wasn't an easy life for many in the K-9 Corps. After all, they were trained to obey, often at the cost of their lives. There were stories of dogs saving their masters and of masters saving their dogs; how many of these stories are true, it's impossible to say. Neither is it possible to say how true are the stories of dogs receiving military honors. One of the most widely known is about Chips, a mongrel member of the K-9 Corps, who reportedly went ashore with his handler, Pvt. John R. Powell, when the 3d Infantry Division landed on Sicily. The story has it that Chips single-handedly (perhaps single-pawedly) captured an Italian machine-gun position. He supposedly was awarded the Silver Star for bravery and the Purple Heart, when he was wounded, or was it the Distinguished Service Cross? The story isn't clear.

Another canine, George, landed with the marines at Iwo Jima. It was his third amphibious landing of the war. And an unnamed dog of unknown origin went along with British paratroopers on the Normandy invasion. The dog, perhaps sensibly, didn't want to jump. The man who took him along chased the dog all over the aircraft until he finally caught the pooch, attached the dog's parachute (yes, he had one) to the static line, and threw the poor, scared animal after the paratroopers. The canine paratrooper survived.

Those dogs who lived through the war generally were given honorable discharges. Before being returned to civilian life, they had to be retrained. After the war, some military masters retained their dogs.

Another "George" wasn't a dog. It was the nickname given to the automatic pilot used in U.S. bombers in World War II. It may have given rise to the phrase, "Let George do it."

For two nights beginning on February 13, 1945, the British Bomber Command and the American Eighth Air Force dumped thousands of incendiary bombs and 1,232 tons of high-explosive bombs on Dresden, Germany. A briefing at England's Bomber Command told members of the RAF about to raid the city:

> Dresden, the seventh largest city in Germany and not much smaller than Manchester [England], is also by far the largest

unbombed built-up area the enemy has got. In the midst of winter with refugees pouring westward and troops to be rested,
roofs are at a premium, not only to give shelter to workers,
refugees and troops alike, but to house the administrative services displaced from other cities. [Dresden] has developed into
an industrial city of first-class importance, and . . . is of major
value for controlling the defence of the [western] front.

Dresden was noted for its eighteenth-century architecture and culture, a city well known to many of England's gentry who earlier had
taken the Grand Tour of Europe, a city the British intelligentsia had
studied, and a city to which the British middle class looked for fine
porcelain.

An Associated Press dispatch from SHAEF reported that "Allied
air chiefs [had embarked on] deliberate terror bombing of German
population centers as a ruthless expedient to hasten doom." Civilians huddling in bomb shelters were baked alive in temperatures of
more than 1,000°F that were generated by the firestorm resulting
from the incendiaries. The death toll was 135,000.

Novelist Kurt Vonnegut, Jr., was a prisoner of war in Dresden during the bombing. In his book *Slaughterhouse Five* (the title comes from
the cellar under a cattle slaughterhouse where Vonnegut was held
prisoner), Vonnegut writes: "There were sounds like giant footsteps
above. Those were sticks of high-explosive bombs. The giants walked
and walked."

German minister of propaganda Joseph Goebbels wrote in his diary one month after the Dresden attack: "The morale of the German
people, both at home and at the front, is sinking ever lower."

Goebbels was called "Little Joe," because he was only five feet
tall. He claimed his right foot was crippled during World War I, but
he lied. It was a birth defect, and since congenital birth defects
would have disqualified him for office (pure Aryans had to be perfect in everything), he couldn't have a birth defect, so he told everyone it was an old war wound. Goebbels had "a puny body, an out-
size head, jug ears, loose lips, and a bad limp after having a bone
operation at the age of seven." His soul, if he had one, likely was
also defective.

• • •

Hitler and the German armed forces were defeated by the Allies, but it wasn't until a quarter of a century later that the German soldier, generically speaking, was beaten. For years, fiction pictured the German soldier just as Hitler hoped the world would—as a superior being. Undoubtedly, this in part was due to American filmmakers who always showed German troops clean shaven (GIs could have week-old beards) with clean uniforms (GIs often were shown truly dirty), with every button buttoned and every crease sharp. A lot of this incorrect image also came from German filmmakers before the war. Hitler's favorite filmmaker was Leni Riefenstahl, a former dancer in a Russian ballet company and an actress turned director and producer. She drew Hitler's attention, which caused the instant jealousy of Little Joe Goebbels.

Riefenstahl has been called "the most innovative documentary film director of the Nazi era—indeed in the history of the cinema," which may or may not be true, depending on the definition of *documentary*. Her most famous film was *Triumph of the Will*, a 1935 spectacular built around the 1933 Nazi Party congress and rally at Nuremberg. Actually, Riefenstahl directed the rally as well as the film. She admitted, in *Leni Riefenstahl: A Memoir*:

> Preparations for the congress were fixed in conjunction with preliminary work on the film—that is to say, the event was organized in the manner of a theatrical performance, not only as a popular rally, but also to provide the material for a propaganda film. . . .

Everything, she said, "was decided by reference to the camera." Speer and Riefenstahl scripted many of the congress's events to fit the camera, adding Wagnerian music to innovative photographic techniques. The film's name came from Hitler, but Riefenstahl refused to allow him to make any changes, a dangerous move she apparently got away with—until, that is, Goebbels's persistent animosity won out; then Riefenstahl fell out of *der Führer*'s favor.

Leni Riefenstahl vehemently denied she was either a Nazi or Hitler's mistress. There are, however, persistent rumors. During her

1936 documentary about the Berlin Olympic Games, she appears nude, shown only from the rear. Viewing the film at a private showing, Adolf Hitler took one look at the nude and cried out, "Leni!"

After the war, Leni Riefenstahl also fell out of favor with her fellow film directors. She eventually moved to Africa, where she developed a new career as a still photographer specializing in underwater cinematography.

During the war, about 15 percent of America's population—an estimated 20 million people—left their homes to find employment. They traveled from New England's mill towns and Appalachia's hollows, from the backwoods of Mississippi and the plains of Oklahoma. They headed for auto plants in Detroit, stockyards in Chicago, aircraft plants in Washington, and steel mills in Indiana; they found jobs in defense plants in almost all 48 states in the union. When they got wherever it was they were going, they often had trouble finding a place to live. If someone complained, someone else just as bad off offered the universal answer: "Don't you know there's a war going on?"

Life became a headache for both military and civilian personnel; however, some people made a career out of it. One such person was Bill Levitt, who, all things considered, made a name for himself and used his name to earn a fortune.

Thousands of military and civilian workers poured into towns which previously had been small, often sleepy, communities. Take the Tidewater area of Virginia, with several army and navy bases as well as one of the nation's oldest navy yards. At one point in mid-1940, the naval shipyard in Portsmouth, Virginia, hired new workers at the rate of 1,000 per month. When these new workers came into the area, they and their families had to have a place to call home. For a while, the government housed them and their families in trailers, set row after row in nearby camps. Trailers were only a temporary measure, and that's where Bill Levitt came in.

He and his brother Alfred contracted with the navy to build 2,350 war workers' homes. As author David Halberstam put it, "It was a disaster; everything went wrong." The apartments at Riverdale, as the project was called, rented for $33 a month, but even dropping the rent to $29 a month couldn't fill the buildings. They were built in remote locations at a time when gasoline was rationed and cars were wearing out. And, too, there were innovations the public may not have been ready for. Concrete bathtubs, for instance. Finally, Bill Levitt gave up and took a navy commission with the newly formed SeaBees, the Construction Battalions. After the war, he turned his talents to other, even larger projects. Adapting Henry Ford's mass production techniques, he built Levittown on New York's Long Island, and the nation's suburbs took off.

In 1943, the United States found itself short of a lot of things, including trained nurses. To remedy the shortage, the federal government established the Victory Nurse Corps to grant scholarships and stipends to women who attended nursing school. Representative Frances Payne Bolton of Ohio and Senator Josiah W. Bailey of North Carolina introduced the Nurse Training Act. The Bolton Act, as it became known, had a first-year appropriation of $65 million. The program continued past the end of World War II, and 124,065 nurses graduated from the Cadet Nursing Corps, as it later was called.

In America's Civil War, one out of every 65 soldiers died in battle; they stood a far greater chance of dying of disease. Troops in World War II had a one in 14 chance of being killed or seriously wounded, a far less chance than had their grandfathers.

In World War I, about four out of every hundred wounded men could expect to recover. By the time World War II rolled around, the chances were much better: about 50 percent of the wounded lived. If a soldier received treatment within an hour of being wounded, the odds increased to 90 percent; if it was more than eight hours later, only 25 percent survived.

Overall, in World War II, 1.9 percent of all American men and women who served Uncle Sam were killed in action. Another 0.7 percent died from accidents and disease. Still another 4.1 percent were wounded in combat and survived. More than half of all who served were injured or suffered some disease, or other. Most of the "or other" disease category was either the inconvenient gonorrhea or the potentially fatal syphilis.

During the war, troops heading on furlough or liberty received prophylaxis kits (prokits) consisting of a condom and an anti-VD ointment. These items weren't always put to good use. One soldier reported that he couldn't swallow the whole tube of ointment. Some troops claimed that the condoms reduced their virility. Others found an immediate use for them; during amphibious landings, they placed the condoms over their rifle barrels to keep out moisture as they waded ashore. (In the Gulf War of the 1990s, GIs used condoms to keep sand out of the barrels of their weapons.)

A lot of things contributed to a World War II soldier's enhanced chances of survival. Surgical techniques improved, and the military devised the system of triage. Those most likely to survive—not those most badly wounded—received aid first. The greatest saviors of the greatest number of World War II wounded were the "miracle" drugs—sulfa, penicillin, and streptomycin. Penicillin controlled syphilis so well that even men who had the disease were accepted into the army.

Most Civil War deaths came to soldiers who were poorly treated by surgeons using septic instruments, septic hands, and septic hospital care. In World War II, men carried into combat packets of the antibiotic powders, sulfanilamide and sulfathiazole. The men sprinkled some of the antibiotic powders over any wounds. It didn't heal the wounds but helped stave off infection until further treatment came along.

Daily doses of Atabrine, a substitute for quinine, were issued to troops in areas with a high incidence of malaria. Quinine was always in short supply, because most of the raw product came from tropical countries held by Japan. Like quinine, Atabrine didn't cure malaria, but it suppressed the symptoms and allowed the infected individual to function.

By mid-1944, about 35 percent of the German army's troops had been wounded at least once, 11 percent wounded twice, and 6 percent three times. Not just the German foot soldier, either. Over the course of the war, the average officer slot had to be refilled 9.2 times.

The most ubiquitous character of World War II was the mythical, yet omnipresent, Kilroy. "Kilroy was here" was written in pencil, ink, chalk, in just about everything and on just about everything. Half a face with a long nose draped over a fence, his hands holding on, Kilroy showed up wherever American military personnel did. Where Kilroy began is less certain. One story traces him to an inspector at the Fall River Shipyard in Quincy, Massachusetts. The widow of James J. Kilroy claimed Jimmy had counted the holes filled by riveters working on a per-rivet basis, preventing them from being paid twice for the same job. Sort of an "Inspector No. 10" of World War II.

Another story has it that the face and slogan came from Sgt. Francis J. Kilroy, who wrote his name everywhere he went as something of an inside joke. The joke, this version of the Kilroy story claims, was picked up and carried on by others around the world.

Recruits often worried about their girls and wives back home. They wrote home, and the words of an Andrews Sisters popular song, told their story. One of the sisters, Maxene, told author Studs Terkel of a time in Seattle, "when a whole shipload of troops went out." Patty, Maxene, and Laverne stood there on the deck "all those young men up there waving and yelling and screaming. As we sang 'Don't Sit Under the Apple Tree,' all the mothers and sisters and sweethearts sang with us as the ship went off. It was wonderful."

Vaughn Monroe sang about "When the Lights Go On Again All Over the World." Jo Stafford told about the time "Long Ago and Far Away." Helen Forrest and Dick Haymes (who was 4-F because of hypertension) promised "I'll Buy That Dream." Kay Kyser looked up at that "Old Buttermilk Sky," and the Andrews Sisters promised "I'll Be With You in Apple Blossom Time." Sammy Kaye (whose orchestra invited you to "Sing and Sway") told how "I Left My Heart at the Stage Door Canteen," a New York club for servicemen operated by theater and movie personalities who passed out doughnuts and coffee and jitterbugged with GIs and sailors on leave.

Duke Ellington gave the country the classic-to-be "Take the A Train"; Hal McIntyre took a "Sentimental Journey." "Sunrise Serenade" by Glenn Miller and Dinah Shore's "I'll Walk Alone" were big wartime hits, as was Tommy Dorsey's "I'll Be Seeing You." Vera Lynn had one of the most poignant wartime songs: (There'll Be Bluebirds Over) "The White Cliffs of Dover."

Frank Sinatra was 4-F but promised "I'll Never Smile Again." Johnny Mercer had "G.I. Jive," and Cab Calloway wanted to "Take the Long Way Home." When U.S. Navy and Marine Corps pilots took off from aircraft carriers, traditionally, if somewhat weirdly, they were sent off with the playing of "The Sheik of Araby," by Spike Jones and the City Slickers. When U.S. submarines came home, port officials played "Roll Out the Barrel."

Composer Carl Sigmund wrote the 82d Airborne's marching song, "The All-American Soldier." Sigmund served with the 82d, receiving six combat stars and a Bronze Star.

On the day Japan bombed Pearl Harbor, composers Charles Tobias and Cliff Friend wrote "We Did It Before" (And We Will Do It Again). During World War I, composer Irving Berlin wrote the hit Broadway show *Yip! Yip! Yaphank!* Berlin pulled one song he'd written for the show and later used it in his new show, *This Is the Army.* The song? "God Bless America." With Kate Smith belting it out, records of it are still being sold. Not as patriotic or reverent was a song composed by Fred J. Coats early in the war that became a popular jukebox favorite: "Goodbye, Mama. I'm Off To Yokohama."

At Pearl Harbor, a legend arose about Chaplain (they generally were known as sky pilots) William A. McGuire, who helped out gunners firing at the Japanese. It, too, became a popular song.

> Down went the gunner, a bullet was his fate,
> Down went the gunner, and then the gunner's mate.
> Up jumped the sky pilot, gave the boys a look
> And manned the gun himself as he laid aside the Book,
> Shouting: "Praise the Lord and pass the ammunition!"*

Chaplain McGuire later denied saying it.

Dance band leader Glenn Miller was at the height of his career when in late 1942 when he gave up a lucrative contract with CBS Radio and became Maj. Glenn Miller in the U.S. Army Air Forces. The Miller band recorded "Bugle Call Rag." It is still a favorite. For

---

* Music and lyrics copyright Frank Loesser, 1942.

the next two years, Glenn Miller and the Army Air Forces Orchestra entertained millions of troops through more than 500 radio shows and 300 concerts. On December 15, 1944, Glenn Miller took off by plane for Paris to make arrangements for the orchestra's next scheduled appearance in the newly liberated city. It was a small plane, and Miller ignored warnings of foul weather. Eleven days later the public was informed that he was missing, presumed dead. His plane may have gone down in either the North Sea or the English Channel. Although it's assumed that his plane crashed because of the weather, there have always been rumors that it may have been shot down. One such rumor has it that Miller was lost to friendly fire; he was headed eastward when U.S. bombers were headed westward after a run on Germany. The rumor has it someone mistook Miller's small plane for an enemy aircraft going back to Germany, and shot it down.

When American bombers began flying daylight missions over enemy territory and started taking incredible losses, they came to be called "Flying Targets" by the British and "Flying Coffins" by German fighters. Songwriters began writing about bullet-ridden bombers limping home. One of the best and most popular with pilots told about the crew of one torn-up plane:

> One of our planes was missing, two hours overdue.
> One of our planes was missing, with all its gallant crew.
>
> The radio sets were humming, they waited for a word;
> Then a voice broke through the humming and this is what they heard:
>
> Comin' in on a wing and a Pray'r,
> Comin' in on a wing and a Pray'r.
>
> Tho' there's one motor gone, we can still carry on,
> Comin' in on a wing and a Pray'r.*

*Lyrics by Harold Adamson, music by Jimmy McHugh, copyright 1943.

Here is another song popular with pilots:

> Off we go, into the wild blue yonder,
> Climbing high into the sun.
> Here they come, zooming to meet our thunder.
> At 'em boys, Give 'er the gun!
> Down we dive, spouting our flame from under,
> Off with one helluva roar!
> We live in fame or go down in flame.
> Nothing'll stop the Army Air Corps.*

The line "Off with one helluva roar!" carried a proviso: "For radio use, substitute 'terrible' for 'helluva.'"

We learned a lot of new words and phrases from World War II. Blitzkrieg (two German words meaning lightning and war) wasn't really German at all and was first written as Blitz-Krieg in the October 7, 1939, issue of *The War Illustrated 1939*. We learned Gestapo (an acronym for *Geheime Staatspolizei*, or secret state police), and we picked up snafu (situation normal, all fucked up, which in polite conversation translated as all fouled up) and tarfu (things are really fucked up). According to longtime journalist and critic H. L. Mencken, snafu was "one of the few really good coinages of the war." Marines in the Philippines took the Tagalog word *bundok*, meaning mountain, and turned it into boondock, any isolated area. You've heard of bawdy houses? Well, GIs turned the word "bawd" into "broad," a word certainly more popular in World War II than in the 1990s' world of feminism. GI probably came from the term general issue, or GI-this, GI-that. Pretty soon it was GI Joe. There were GI Jills, too, the name given to WACs. The term was inspired by actress Carole Landis, who spent much of her time and not a little of her money on USO tours, then wrote a book about it, *Four Jills and a Jeep*.

---

*Words and music copyright by Robert Crawford, 1942. From the film, *Men With Wings*, starring Ray Milland, Fred MacMurray, and Louise Campbell.

Radar came from radio detection and ranging. Americans, British, French, and Germans developed radar simultaneously in the 1930s. Experiments in the fall of 1922 at the U.S. Naval Aircraft Radio Laboratory in Washington, D.C., showed that this reflection of radio waves would work, but no one did anything more about it for almost a decade.

V-Homes was the term given to families that carried out certain duties to aid the war effort and for which they received V-Home certificates. Secretary of Agriculture Claude R. Wickard called on Americans to plant vegetables in victory gardens because farmers were too busy producing for the military. It's estimated that more than 20 million victory gardens produced at least one-third of all the vegetables grown in the United States during the war. The gardens took over backyards, corner lots, parks, and city rooftops. Workers used a horse-drawn plow to dig up Boston's historic Common.

From the army we learned "armored cow" was canned milk and an "army banjo" was a shovel. "Army strawberries" were prunes, and "baby food" was any type of breakfast cereal. Army coffee was "battery acid"; the navy took theirs "blond and sweet," with cream and sugar. Eggs were "cackle jelly"; food itself was "chow," which might include "dog fat," known as butter to civilians. Too often you pulled KP, kitchen police duty, peeling potatoes in back of the "mess hall," the dining facility also known as "ptomaine domain." After that you went on a "crumb hunt," cleaning up the kitchen. The "Molotov bread-basket" wasn't located in the mess hall; it was a box of incendiary bombs. And a "Molotov cocktail" didn't come from a bar; it was a gasoline-filled glass with a rag stuck in the top. Set on fire and thrown at an enemy tank, it was the "partisan's pineapple," a grenade.

"Grandma" was low gear on a truck, and "Rachel" was high gear. An officer was a "brass hat." The jail was a "brig" in the navy, the stockade in the army. You kept your valuables in a "didie" bag; "jack" was money, which you received on payday, or the "day the eagle shits," which might give you the wherewithal to go on "skirt patrol" looking for "quiff"—available young women, maybe a "Geechie," a native girl in the South Pacific. If you were unlucky, you wound up with a "scupper," a cheap prostitute, and should see the "pecker checker" or "pill roller," physicians who'd check you for venereal disease. If things were really serious, they took you in the "meat wagon" (an ambulance) to see the "sawbone" (a surgeon, who might send you to sick bay, the shipboard hospital, or he might just order you to the sack (bed) for a blanket drill (sleep).

A marine "boot" was a new recruit who wore boondockers (heavy shoes). A "gunny" (gunnery sergeant) was a fellow "Gyrene" (GI marine). Cattle cars (tractor-trailers used to transport people) transported marines to cattle boats (naval transports). After hitting the beachhead (enemy shore), you watched out for bogies (Japanese aircraft). "Hey, Jackson," one marine might say to another, "let's pull a 48 [two-day leave] and dig up a couple of Fifis [girlfriends]."

You needed a dictionary to translate everyday life.

CHAPTER TWENTY-ONE

Building the Atomic Bomb:
Trinity and Bathtub Row

We are in God's hands now.
— William Shakespeare, *King Henry V*, Act III, vi 164

Nothing could have been more obvious to the people of the early twentieth century than the rapidity with which war was becoming impossible. And as certainly they did not see it. They did not see it until the atomic bombs burst in their fumbling hands.
— Herbert George Wells, *The World Set Free*, 1914

Roughly 1.4 million years ago, a huge volcanic eruption created the mountains, valleys, mesas, and riverbeds of what is now New Mexico. Into this area came the Anasazi, which means the "Old Ones." For more than a thousand years, from A.D. 1 to 1300, the Anasazi lived in the area we now know as northern New Mexico, eastern Arizona, Colorado, and Utah.

It is estimated that the Anasazi numbered at least twice the total population now living in the same area. Amazing, yet they abandoned the area so fast they sometimes left food in bowls, hides hanging in the middle of the tanning process, and tools waiting for hands. They abandoned a culture modern in many ways, including four- and five-story condominium-like homes. Archaeologists and anthropologists still haven't unraveled the riddle of the Anasazi. This mystery, of course, is one reason that the area is interesting to today's tourists.

When the Anasazi left, others (now referred to as Pueblo Indians) moved in, bringing more times of peaceful farming and herding of animals. The term *Pueblo,* incidentally, refers not to a single tribe but to a group of people who share a common culture and, often, follow a similar way of life. Today, the word takes the Spanish meaning of "townsmen."

The culture that gave the Pueblos their name arrived in about 1540. Spanish soldier-adventurer Francisco Vásquez de Coronado began a two-year search for the Seven Cities of Cíbola, the fabled Seven Cities of Gold. What he found was flat, sandy hills with a few bush-like trees that from a distance looked like the stubble of some scraggly beard. Here and there were cities built of mud and straw. At sunset, and from a distance, that straw apparently reflected light and changed reality to dream. The hoped-for Seven Cities of Gold were actually the seven cities of mud.

When the Spanish arrived in the middle of the sixteenth century, approximately 40,000 to 50,000 Native Americans lived in New Mexico's pueblos. European diseases, drought-caused famine, attacks by Apache raiders, and murder by Spanish conquerors reduced the Pueblo population to not more than 14,000. The number of villages declined by more than half.

One of the few remaining villages sat peacefully at the top of a mountain, the Tewa area of the Pajarito Plateau. Because the trees there were the most predominant, the village was known as The Poplars, in Spanish *Los Alamos*.

In 1934, German scientists discovered nuclear fission, the splitting of uranium into two elements of approximately equal weight. It wasn't long after Adolf Hitler and his brown-shirted Nazis had taken over the German government. Millions of substances and discoveries, not to mention weapons, danced in the scientists' heads. By 1939, however, guessing what lay ahead for Jews in the European scientific community, Albert Einstein, Enrico Fermi, Edward Teller, Eugene Wigner, and Leo Szilard among others had sought refuge in the United States.

On August 2, 1939, Einstein wrote President Franklin D. Roosevelt a letter. Einstein was urged on, and more than just a little assisted in his letter writing, by Hungarian refugees Teller, Szilard, and Wigner.

> Some recent work by E. Fermi and L. Szilard, which has been communicated to me in manuscript, leads me to believe that the element uranium may be turned into a new and important source of energy in the immediate future.

Einstein—the charming, cuddly, fuzzy-haired, mustachioed, sweat-shirt-wearing, wife-ignoring, mistress-taking, bicycle-riding, address-forgetting genius that he was—started it all for the American government with his letter to the president "this new phenomenon," not only could

> . . . set up nuclear chain reaction in a large mass of uranium, by which vast amounts of power and large quantities of new radium-like elements would be generated [but it] would also lead to the construction of . . . extremely powerful bombs of a new type.

A single such bomb, Einstein declared, "carried by boat and exploded in a port, might very well destroy the whole port together with some of the surrounding territory."

Right you were, Albert. The trouble was, neither you, nor Enrico Fermi, nor Szilard, nor anyone else knew how much "surrounding territory" might be destroyed. All things considered, as far as power of the then theoretical explosion, you were flying blind and playing with our future. Teller, for instance, believed that an atomic bomb might "ignite the atmosphere."

Given that thought, you wonder about the effort to build and test such a weapon. Wonder, of course, is just what led to the atomic bomb, to the Cold War, and to the world almost blasting itself back into tiny particles.

Born in Ulm, Germany, in 1879, Einstein quickly developed an aversion to all things German. When he was only fifteen years old he renounced his German citizenship to live in Switzerland. While still employed as a patent officer in Berne, he began work on his theory of relativity. At the age of forty-two, he was awarded the Nobel Prize in physics. Meanwhile, he antagonized right-wing Germans with his well-publicized support of the League of Nations, pacifism, and Zionism. He was a visiting professor at the California Institute of Technology in 1933 when Hitler came to power in Germany. A few months later, when book burning became the politically correct way of life in Nazi Germany, Einstein's works were prominent among those publicly piled up and put to the torch. Being both Jewish and not known for any degree of stupidity, Einstein realized there was no place for him in a Germany led by Hitler. He remained in the

United States. The Nazis seized his property and declared Einstein a traitor. The man who may have been the smartest mathematician of them all joined Princeton University's Institute of Advanced Studies and became a U.S. citizen in 1940.

The letter to President Roosevelt kicking off America's push for the bomb was written under his name, but Einstein himself didn't do much work on either the missive or the missile, the bomb. Einstein-the-scientist consulted on the project and occasionally visited the test labs, but Einstein-the-man opposed the use of atomic power in weapons of war.

Leo Szilard was born in Hungary in 1889, received his Ph.D. from the University of Berlin in 1922, and worked alongside Einstein for the next decade. He was a guest lecturer at Columbia University in September 1939 at the time that Nazi Germany invaded Poland. Quickly, Szilard realized that he wanted nothing to do with Adolf and his bunch. He also realized the possible military applications of nuclear power, so he opted to stay in America.

The Italian-born Enrico Fermi earned his doctorate at the University of Pisa in 1924, spent some time in Germany, then taught at the University of Rome. He left Fascist-controlled Italy in 1938, stopped off briefly in Stockholm to collect his Nobel Prize in physics, then moved on to Columbia University, where he began experimenting with a chain-pile reactor. Fermi's wife was Jewish, so to avoid persecution they chose not to return to Benito Mussolini's Italy.

To these three men, it was obvious that a weapon as powerful as the atomic bomb would be dangerous beyond imagination in the hands of Nazi Germany, which is why Einstein wrote Roosevelt. On October 19, 1939, Roosevelt wrote back: "My dear Professor: Please accept my sincere thanks." In the best tradition of governments everywhere, Roosevelt promised Einstein he would convene a board "to thoroughly investigate the possibilities of your suggestion."

Nearly everyone—Einstein, Szilard, and Fermi included—believed Nazi Germany was far ahead of the rest of the world in the search for atomic power. In truth, they weren't nearly so far along the road to the big bomb as we believed. Often it is belief, not reality, that fuels research, and it did so in the forties.

Less than a year after Pearl Harbor, on December 2, 1942, in an abandoned squash court beneath the University of Chicago's Stagg Field, Enrico Fermi and his group at the Metallurgical Laboratory performed a miracle of sorts. They achieved an experimental demonstration of a self-sustaining nuclear chain reaction. It put them halfway along the road to making an atomic bomb. It not only proved the principle of the atomic bomb, it showed that a chain-reacting pile could be used to produce plutonium. Because plutonium was an ingredient in America's recipe for an atomic bomb, the Fermi demonstration was key.

Fermi's arch antagonist back in the old country was German physicist Werner Heisenberg, who favored the use of so-called heavy water, or deuterium, to moderate a chain reaction; Fermi and his Chicago gang chose graphite to slow down the neutrons produced in the fission of uranium-235. Heisenberg claimed that the graphite method was inadequate. Working with another physicist, Walter Bothe, at the University of Berlin, Heisenberg used Bothe's test results to prove that graphite wouldn't work. The trouble was, Bothe's results and Heisenberg's belief were based on mistaken calculations. Fermi was right, Heisenberg was wrong, and America won the race to atomic power.

Shortly after the Japanese raid on Pearl Harbor, the Office of Scientific Research and Development (OSRD) stepped up America's atomic research. Early on, the navy had done the serious research on atomic weapons, but when Roosevelt ordered increased study into building a bomb, he turned it over to the army, reasoning that such a weapon would be dropped from an army air forces bomber. Then, too, the army had more experience constructing training camps and such. They needed places to work.

America's nuclear program was a many-headed, unruly animal. Plutonium was produced (in minute quantities) at Site W in Richland, Washington. Scientists at Site X in Oak Ridge, Tennessee, worked with enriched uranium. Other programs ran off in all directions at the same time—at Harvard University, the University of Chicago, the University of California, and Columbia University, and in Texas, Minnesota, Wisconsin, Indiana, and Washington, D.C.

Said physicist John Manley of Chicago, "It was really a very discouraging sort of physics. . . . [You could not] run a railroad in this fashion." The answer was obvious. The various parts of the program had to be brought together.

Colonel Leslie Richard Groves (nicknamed "Goo Goo" for some reason) was the army corps of engineers' deputy chief of construction. During the 1930s, he built his reputation on Works Projects Administration (WPA) jobs. A brusque manner added to his notoriety as a human bulldozer. As he wrapped up another project—a huge, five-sided building near Washington to be known as the Pentagon—he was named weapons director of the effort to build the atomic bomb. He'd hoped if he did a good job building the Pentagon, he'd be sent overseas to a combat command. Instead, in the best military tradition, he got a job he didn't want, supervising production of a bomb that he didn't believe would work. Groves referred to the proposed bomb as "that thing." His supervisors told him, "Do a good job [with that thing] and it will win the war." To mollify him, they replaced the silver eagle on his shoulder with a Silver Star. There's nothing quite like promoting a colonel to brigadier general to give him incentive.

On August 16, 1942, General Groves took command of the project and gave it the code name Manhattan Engineer District, or MED, which became known simply as the Manhattan Project. The location would be known as Site Y; accordingly, the Manhattan District work would be Project Y. Groves and MED were in charge of production plants, but no one had made provision for a bomb design laboratory.

General Groves wanted someone prestigious to run his lab, preferably someone with a Nobel Prize gathering dust in a hall closet. Ernest Lawrence of the University of California-Berkeley Radiation Laboratory would have fit the bill; after all, he had developed the only method of large-scale production of uranium-235. He was busy on another project, however, and other Nobel laureates were also tied up. Groves continued to look around.

In the spring of 1942, Dr. Julius Robert Oppenheimer, a theoretical physicist, was teaching at both the California Institute of Technology and the University of California. He was also busy working on the feasibility of a nuclear weapon. That summer, he gathered together a group to develop a preliminary design for a bomb. He was only thirty-nine years old and had not won a Nobel Prize. Otherwise, he was just what Groves was looking for, so he was made the director of the new laboratory.

Ernest Lawrence, the man whom Groves originally wanted for the job, protested. Among other things, Lawrence claimed Oppenheimer was incapable of doing the job. Primarily, however, Lawrence objected to Oppenheimer's politics. Like many other academics in the 1930s, Robert Oppenheimer held some left-wing views and had some left-wing friends. FBI director J. Edgar Hoover became incensed and demanded that Groves fire Oppenheimer. Groves told both Lawrence and Hoover to back off. "We were not going to find a better man," Groves later wrote, adding, "I felt his potential value outweighed any security risk."

The project became a joint operation. Groves ran the military side of it, and Oppenheimer rode herd on the scientists. Without either man, it's doubtful the project would have been completed, certainly not as fast as it was.

Groves and Oppenheimer went looking for a laboratory site. For security, Groves wanted it located at least 200 miles from a coastline or an international border. Oppenheimer wanted year-round good weather for testing. The area should be sparsely populated yet big enough to accommodate a large number of scientists. All of this had to be shrouded in secrecy, of course.

In the fall of 1942, they sent army major John Dudley to hunt for a location where scientists could do more than tinker with the idea of an atomic bomb. Dudley covered in excess of a thousand miles, driving "on two-lane roads, one lane for the left wheels and one lane for the right." He searched California, Nevada, Utah, Arizona, and New Mexico. "When the going got tough," he remarked, "I switched to a jeep, and when it got even tougher, I rode a horse." Dudley found a "delightful little oasis in south central Utah," good water supply, a railroad only sixteen miles away, and an airport nearby. The only problem was, it would require moving several dozen families and taking over a large amount of farm acreage. That might attract the kind of attention that nobody wanted.

A bit farther south, Dudley discovered the little town of Jemez Springs, New Mexico. It had a small hot springs and a resort hotel, not much more; there still isn't much at Jemez Springs except a monastery, a nunnery, and a restaurant specializing in chicken-fried steak. The area also had an abundance of trees and mountains to hide what MED hoped to build. Best of all, Jemez Springs had very few people who might be injured if an accident occurred. "If the place blew up," Dudley said, "only the six scientists would be involved."

Oppenheimer wasn't satisfied with the Jemez Springs location, but he knew of an even better site not far away, one he'd visited while staying at his family's summer home in northern New Mexico. It was the mountaintop town called Los Alamos. In mid-November 1942, General Groves visited Los Alamos and agreed with Oppenheimer. It would be their secret city on a hill, upon which they would build a bomb that might destroy humanity.

All that was wrong with Los Alamos was that it was more or less occupied by a few natives and the New Mexico Ranch School for Boys. The natives would be no problem, they felt. Neither would the school.

Two educators, Ashley Pond and Edward Fuller, had started the school in 1918. Their idea was to take physically weak or sickly boys, educate them, and turn them into healthy young citizens. It was the type of education that many adventurous American boys then and now might take to. But they had to be wealthy.

The Ranch School was small and very exclusive. By the early 1940s, Pond and Fuller were charging the near-astronomical tuition of $2,400 a year; at the time the average annual salary in the United States was $1,299. The students paid for their own uniforms (Smoky the Bear hats, Boy Scout–style kerchiefs, and short pants) and provided their own transportation to the isolated mesa. The New Mexico Ranch School obviously attracted only the rich in those pre- and early-war times. Over the years, Arthur Wood (former president of Sears, Roebuck, Inc.) was a proud Ranch School student; so were Roy Chapin, Jr. (president of American Motors) and Antonio J. Stuart (future president Lyndon B. Johnson's brother-in-law). Author Eugene "Gore" Vidal was a graduate, as were baseball team owner Bill Veeck and Col. Whitney Ashbridge, comanager of the Manhattan Project. Ashbridge would be right at home.

In the school at the top of Pajarito Plateau, the boys slept year-round on an unheated outside porch. They rode horses in the nearby woods. In summer they went skinny dipping in the nearby pond named after school headmaster Ashley Pond, which made it "Ashley Pond Pond." In winter they played hockey on the frozen pond. When it came time for dances, young ladies from a girls' school at the foot of the mountain were bused up; the girls wore formal gowns and the Ranch School boys danced in their uniform shorts. It was quite a sight.

Nine days after Oppenheimer and Groves looked over Los Alamos, the War Department approved its acquisition. The school wasn't allowed either to approve or disapprove. "Dear Sir," Secretary of War Stimson wrote to school president A. J. Connell on December 1, 1942, "You are advised that it has been determined necessary to the interests of the United States in the prosecution of the War that the property of the Los Alamos Ranch School be acquired for military purposes." The notice of condemnation reached the school exactly one year after the Japanese attack on Pearl Harbor.

The government gave the school two months, until February 8, 1943, to get its business in order, to graduate its last class, and to vacate the premises. And don't bother telling anyone why you're closing, down either: "You are further advised that all records pertaining to the aforesaid condemnation proceeding will be sealed, by order of the [United States District] Court, and public inspection of such records will be prohibited." The letter from Stimson continued: "Accordingly, it is requested that you refrain from making the reasons for the closing of the school known to the public at large." The last class of the Los Alamos Ranch School for Boys consisted of four students; they stood smiling in the cold, bright sunshine, still decked out in their uniform shorts as they received their diplomas.

Wealthy students out; not-so-wealthy (but perhaps eccentric) scientists in. With them came their often flustered wives and bewildered children. Their bewilderment and perplexity were just beginning.

Oak Ridge, Tennessee, was the largest of three cities dedicated to constructing an atomic bomb. It had a population of 75,000, along with 13 supermarkets, nine drugstores, and seven movie theaters. Richland Village, Washington, housed about 17,000 men, women, and children on the then remote banks of the Columbia River. Oak Ridge and Richland Village built parts for the bomb; Los Alamos put them together.

Los Alamos was perhaps the most important of the three atomic cities. Sitting in secure isolation on top of a mesa in New Mexico, it certainly was the least accessible and, perhaps for that reason, it's the site that draws the greatest interest.

The project maintained an iron-barred office in downtown Santa Fe. There was no sign on the door saying something on the order of "secret atom bomb project"; no sign of any kind. Today, with the Cold War behind us, and the millennium just ahead, it all seems a bit much. At the time, such secrecy was accepted; "Loose lips sink ships," and all that. The secrecy, however, saw scientists and their families emotionally rewriting the lyrics to a popular song of the era: they were bemused, burdened, and befuddled.

Take Nick Metropolis's introduction to the program. The young physicist from Chicago was hired by the project and ordered to report to the unmarked office building in downtown Santa Fe. Once there, an unseen voice, coming from behind a door, told him his next assignment, should he chose to accept it, was to report somewhere else, to 109 East Palace Avenue. Almost immediately, Metropolis got lost. He wandered around the town plaza, looking for the mysterious address to which the mysterious voice had cryptically directed him. Walking behind Metropolis was another man; every time Metropolis looked back, he glimpsed the other man ducking into a doorway. Aha! A spy! Had to be. This being wartime, and everyone knew that spies skulked behind every bush and tree, Metropolis thought he'd found one, right there, lurking behind him. This time, however, it wasn't a spy, just Rene Prestwood, another new employee also searching for 109 East Palace Avenue. Prestwood had seen Metropolis and thought that *he* was the spy.

To maintain secrecy, all mail to residents of Los Alamos was addressed to Box 1663, Santa Fe, New Mexico. Children born on the project site had birth certificates listing their hometown as Box 1663, Santa Fe. For residents of Los Alamos who drove, their New Mexico drivers' license listed numbers instead of names. We're reminded of a 1960s television show about a secret agent, the theme song telling us how they took away his name and gave him a number.

"We know you will want to have as clear a picture as possible before coming to Los Alamos," a memorandum on the Los Alamos project proclaimed to newcomers. The setting was described further:

> An hour's drive takes you to Santa Fe for shopping purposes or an occasional dinner in town; a few minutes' walk or ride by horse takes you onto mountain trails in pine, aspen and spruce country.
>
> Winters produce snow and winter sports, but the weather is not too severe for comfort. Spring brings wind, and summer [sic]rain. It can be hot in the daytime, but nights are always comfortable because of the altitude.
>
> The country is a mixture of mountain country [sic] such as you have not [found] in other parts of the Rockies, and the adobe-housed, picturesque, southwest desert that you have seen in Western Movies.

The memorandum, since declassified, clearly stated it was a restricted document:

> Within the meaning of the Espionage Act, the contents of this document are not to be discussed with anyone unless he is known to you to be a member of this project. You may discuss them with your wife if she accepts those limitations in all strictness. We want to keep our work, organization and future plans from becoming known outside the project for as long as possible in order to reduce the probability of effective espionage.

Scientists and technical people hired at Project Y were young, generally in their twenties or thirties. They were well educated, healthy, middle class, almost invariably white, and—very important to them at the time—they were employed at something that didn't involve their being shot at. They all shared a similar fate, and it held them together. They were going someplace unknown, hired to perform an unknown job, didn't know how long it would take, and they couldn't tell anybody anything, even if they'd known, which usually they didn't.

The forties were, like it or not, a man's world, and that left the scientists' spouses often fending for themselves and their children. Bernice Brode's situation was fairly typical. Her husband, Robert B. Brode, of the University of California-Berkeley Physics Department, was already at Los Alamos when Bernice and her two children arrived in Santa Fe, uncertain what was ahead of them. Sitting outside 109 East Palace Avenue was an army bus being loaded by armed soldiers—household articles, boxes and bags, potted plants, mops, and kiddie cars. It would become a familiar, if not always welcome, sight. The bus from Santa Fe to Los Alamos was on its regular run packed with day-trippers from the project who had come to town to purchase supplies they couldn't find at what, in effect, was a company store, the army PX.

Residents made the winding, thirty-five-mile trip up the mountain to Los Alamos either by military bus or, in only a few instances due to gas rationing, by private car. Today, it's a well-maintained two-lane highway, often listed among the nation's most scenic routes. In 1943, it was an unpaved dirt road with no guardrail to hamper the view or to save you from going over the edge. What now are panoramic overlooks must have been panic-causing dropoffs into space.

In writing about the times, Jane Wilson tells how, on her initial trip to Los Alamos, she had to show her identification to the military driver just to get on the bus; then she sat through the bumpy ride as the vehicle wound its way up the narrow road to the 7,300-foot-high peak. It almost seemed the driver was selected for his social skills, not any ability to handle the bus. It was "disconcerting to have the driver swivel around for a little chat with a passenger" while piloting the rickety bus over ever heightening curves.

Eleanor Jette, who drove her family on its first trip up the narrow road, says that a couple of times she almost skidded into the Rio Grande. Reaching the top, she stopped her car at the gate; quickly, her car sank up to its hubcaps in mud. The town, she remembers, "looked like hell."

Once at the project site, everyone had to stop at the main gate, where armed guards checked names against lists, checked lists against ID cards. Los Alamos and the Manhattan Project were among America's most carefully guarded secrets. General Groves later wrote:

> From the standpoint of security, Los Alamos was quite sat- isfactory. It was far removed from any large center of popula- tion, and was reasonably inaccessible from the outside. . . . Also, the geographically enforced isolation of the people working there lessened the ever-present danger of their inad- vertently diffusing secret information among social or profes- sional friends outside.

Everywhere there was either choking dust or wheel-clogging mud. In 1943, Los Alamos still was pretty much as it had been when it was home to the Ranch School and a handful of nomads herding sheep on the high desert mesa. Now, it's a well-ordered society. Then, it was row after row of unnamed, unpaved, rutted streets with dirt paths and only an occasional wooden sidewalk. Everything and everyone was liberally dusted with soot from the soft New Mexico coal burned in furnaces to keep workers and their families warm on cold mountain nights. The U.S. Army and the Forest Service pur- chased about 54,000 acres, and up alongside the old school build- ings went laboratories, Quonset huts, trailers, prefab dormitories, and buildings made with wood so green that no one knew how long they'd last.

A letter introducing new residents to Los Alamos claimed the army-built homes weren't "luxurious [but] are more than adequate and quite comfortable." Adequacy and comfort apparently were sometime things.

Los Alamos was the only stateside army post that permanently housed civilians; it even had a civilian-run town council. The coun- cil looked into everything from inadequate restaurant facilities in the communal dining hall to overcrowded public laundries; washers were thirty cents an hour and irons (actually mangles) rented for forty cents.

Once Project Y took over the area, the army surrounded everything with barbed wire fences and set gun-toting, horse-riding guards patrolling outside. Inside was a competition and social caste system that depended upon where one (or one's spouse) stood in technical ratings. Even though it was an army camp, a junior officer's family often ranked above that of a senior, depending on who was higher up the scientific ladder. It was a system with which military personnel and their families, used to a tradition of rank having its privileges, never felt comfortable.

Like the outside world, residents of Los Alamos faced rationing, but those living on the mesa had it worse; nearly everything they had, had to be delivered to them up the mountain. And that included water. Don't flush toilet bowls unless absolutely necessary, they were told; lather up with soap before turning on the shower water, instructions insisted. This ignored the likelihood that the would-be shower-taker would stand waiting, literally all in a lather, with no water dripping out of the showerhead.

Everyone was subject to the military's famed system of hurry up and wait, then substitute. Even the simplest request had to be put in writing and was subject to military misplacing. When project coordinator Robert Oppenheimer wanted someplace to hang his famous porkpie hat, B. E. Brazier, an administrator recruited to head construction operations at Los Alamos, had to requisition a nail to be hammered into the wall. When Oppenheimer didn't get what he wanted, Brazier again wrote the powers that be: "While you sent him a very nice coat and hat rack this morning he would still like a nail for his hat. Please put one up in his office."

On October 18, 1943, Brazier asked:

Will you please build a table for Mr. Oppenheimer, [room] A-209, [size] 26" wide x 27" high x 30" long. Will you please build a nice table, sand it and varnish it. Since it is for Mr. Oppenheimer's office I would like a nice table; he wants this for his telephone.

The telephone book, which eventually sat alongside Oppenheimer's telephone once he got a table, was highly restricted. It carried names and phone numbers but no street addresses. Like a lot of other things in the secret world of atomic design, addresses were on a need-to-know basis.

Besides, those who had telephones considered themselves lucky. Physicist Enrico Fermi's wife, Laura, said that, because of the lack of telephones, "we had to run around a lot." In 1943, the forest service installed one outside telephone line to serve the community; in 1945, only three existed.

Residents occasionally gave large parties, Mrs. Fermi remembers, "cooking on rudimentary appliances."—coal- and wood-burning stoves (nicknamed "Black Beauties"), which often did more belching of smoke and burning of food than they did cooking of meals. Laura Fermi says, "We rushed to Santa Fe for anything that was not food or the little else that the Army could sell."

As well as parties, the scientists and their families occasionally threw dances. Jean Bacher, whose husband, Robert, had been a physicist at Cornell University prior to joining the project, remembers how, on Saturday nights, "the mesa rocked". "Fenced in," she said, "our social life was a pipeline through which we let off steam." A soldier at the compound said Laura Fermi's husband Enrico, winner of the 1938 Nobel Prize for physics, did "one of the best jitterbugs I have ever seen."

Letters written to friends and loved ones off the Project Y reservation had to be left unsealed. Censors (usually the military, but often civilian personal friends) read the letters for any telltale points of interest. If the letter writer said too much, the letter would be returned to the sender with a note to make whatever changes were necessary if he or she wanted it delivered. Unlike military mail, there would be no blacking out of words or sentences; to do so would hint to those at home that the individual was engaged in some censorable activity. In fact, residents of Los Alamos couldn't even use the word *censor* in writing home. They also couldn't use the word *physicist* and weren't allowed to talk about going to Los Alamos; they went to "The Hill."

They lived in poorly constructed, army-built homes and had used government furniture. Many residents had to get along with showers that often didn't work. They had modern electric refrigerators, but the power frequently went out, which made it especially tough on individuals who cooked on electric hot plates instead of government-supplied woodstoves. The ugliness of the housing was matched by the inadequacy, not to mention danger, of the heating systems—oversized furnaces that glowed cherry red in the middle of cold winter nights.

The project used the Ranch School's Big House, where those long-gone students had slept on a screened porch, for a commissary, and residents bought groceries for cost plus 10 percent. The Big House also housed the new town's library and its own army-operated radio station, KRS. For a while, some of the first scientists brought in for the Project lived in the Big House. It had one thing going for it: a single bathroom shared by all.

The group of buildings originally built for Ranch School faculty became homes to a select few atomic scientists, plush compared to the army-built apartments. Outside of the Big House, these buildings were the only housing with bathtubs, and the street quickly became known as "Bathtub Row."

By early 1943, 1,500 workers lived atop the Los Alamos mesa. A year later, the population was 3,500; by 1945 it was 5,700. With residents ranging in their twenties and thirties, and extracurricular activities being somewhat limited, babies came along at a frequent rate. In the first year of Project Y, 80 babies were born and by 1945, Los Alamos had 330 new infants on hand. One of the babies was born to Dr. and Mrs. Oppenheimer.

The need for housing quickly outgrew the supply, and officials gave thought to hiring only single individuals, which of course in the nineties would not have necessarily cut down on births. In the family-oriented 1940s, it might have stopped cold such new growth. Instead, schools were built for those children already in place and old enough to attend. The original Central School opened in 1943, but it was so expensive that General Groves, holder of the project's purse strings, objected to its cost. He had intended only cheap, temporary structures be built to last through the war; he hadn't planned on anyone staying long enough to raise a family.

For parents who wanted to check out the latest movie, take the long ride to Santa Fe, or dance away the night at a community-sponsored event, finding baby-sitters was a problem. Those living on Bathtub Row had an advantage; they could and did use the bathtubs as an inducement to accept a baby-sitting job.

The Ranch School Big House, Bathtub Row, Fuller Lodge, and the main gate and guardhouse were within yards of the Tewa area of the Pajarito Plateau, where remained the prehistoric ruins left by the Anasazi. Ironically the modern atomic age began so close to something so ancient.

The compound had two movie theaters, one operating nightly and the other three nights a week. Among the movies shown were *Hitler: Beast of Berlin*, with Ronald Drew and Alan Ladd. Another featured movie, strangely enough, was *Uncensored*, which they certainly weren't. On Sundays, the second theater doubled as a chapel; before the preacher preached, the congregation swept up popcorn and other litter from the previous night's movie.

As often as not, Sundays saw both scientists and technicians take part in some amateur activity or other—amateur sports, amateur painting, or amateur theatrics. Amateur photographers had to be careful what their snapshots showed; they couldn't photograph anyone other than their own family and couldn't picture anything in the background that might give away their location.

Say you wanted to take that thirty-five-mile mountain drive into town for a quick burger. Security was so tight that you weren't allowed personal contact with relatives, and you couldn't go more than 100 miles from Los Alamos without permission. If you did go for that Santa Fe burger(southwestern style, green chilies on the side), and you met a friend from outside the project, you had to report to officials every detail of the meeting. "I couldn't go to Santa Fe without being aware of hidden eyes upon me," an early resident remembered, "watching, waiting to pounce on that inevitable step. It wasn't a pleasant feeling."

General Groves was concerned about his scientific counterpart's safety. He wrote Dr. Oppenheimer that "in view of the nature of the work in which you are engaged . . . it seems necessary to ask you to take certain special precautions with respect to your personal safety." On July 29, 1943, the general made the following request of the scientist:

(a) You refrain from flying in airplanes of any description; the time saved is not worth the risk. (If emergency demands their use, my prior consent should be requested.)

(b) You refrain from driving an automobile for any appreciable distance (above a few miles) and from being without suitable protection on any lonely road, such as the road from Los Alamos to Santa Fe. On such trips you should be accompanied by a competent, able bodied, armed guard. There is no objection to the guard serving as chauffeur.

(c) Your cars be driven with due regard to safety and that in driving about town a guard of some kind should be used, particularly during hours of darkness.

No telling what might happen, or who might be lurking about—after dark on a lonely mountain fenced in by barbed wire and patrolled by armed guards.

The inducement for young scientists was that they were right in the middle of what was happening at the time. If you were an atomic scientist in the mid-1940s, you couldn't get a more important job. Los Alamos, General Groves said, "stood for the same sort of thing that Hollywood represents to an aspiring starlet. Most of the great men of physics and chemistry were there at one time or another."

They were there, of course, to build bigger and better bombs. The theoretical basis for these weapons was well known to most of the world's superclass scientists. What wasn't known, however, was whether they would work, or whether they would blow up the world with them. In theory, when scientists set off the first test, it could have meant either the end of World War II or the end of the world.

Scientists at Los Alamos gambled with our lives, no doubt about it. But, then, that's what they were paid to do, we suppose, worry on our behalf. The theory apparently was: better our side to gamble and lose than for the other side to gamble and win. In reality, if the worst imagined theory (cracking the earth's surface) had occurred, we'd all have lost.

In 1913, not even dreaming of this, a German immigrant named Franz Schmidt built a ranch in the area now known as the White

Sands Missile Range. By the 1930s, the ranch had passed on to one George McDonald, who built an addition onto the house. It's a one-story, 1,750-square-foot, adobe-plastered building. In 1942, the ranch lay abandoned and was taken over by the Alamogordo Bombing and Gunnery Range to use in training bombing crews.

For three years, the ranch house sat empty, but early in 1945, personnel from the Manhattan Project arrived to prepare for tests. They named the site Trinity, either after the Christian Holy Trinity (the Father, the Son, and the Holy Ghost) or after a sonnet by John Donne, Dr. Robert Oppenheimer's favored version of the name:

> Batter my heart, three-person'd God; for, You
> As yet but knock, breathe, shine, and seek to mend.

In February, General Groves ordered a freeze on the bomb design in order to make the deadline. If he hadn't, scientists might have continued changing the "gadget," as they called it, not wanting to use the word *bomb*.

The word *gadget* apparently came to the United States in 1884, along with the Statue of Liberty. It took years of convincing Americans that this gift from Paris was worth the cost of putting it in place. When it was completed, however, the statue was an instant favorite, not only in New York, but nationwide in miniature. The French firm that built the statue was Gaget and Gauthier, who also built miniatures of the statue, with the company's name prominently engraved. Americans took the name Gaget to mean anything strange and interesting. Out of it, apparently, we concocted the word *gadget*. Gaget and Gauthier are out of business now, their former location noted only by a bronze plaque. Where the firm once stood is a free clinic for the poor, fitting perhaps for both the Statue of Liberty and the atomic bomb.

Originally they set the first test for July 4, 1945, but that date slowly slipped away. Groves hoped to have the results before the coming Potsdam Conference, in which President Harry Truman and Prime Minister Winston Churchill would face Soviet leader Josef Stalin to map out the concluding days of the war with Japan and to decide the fate of Europe.

Meanwhile, back at the ranch, work was progressing rapidly at the old Schmidt-McDonald place. To prevent dust from damaging the instruments, windows and doors in the ranch house were covered with plastic. Cracks were sealed with tape. During the hot summer of 1945, scientists and technicians used the ranch's water storage tank as a swimming pool.

In early July, the mechanical portion of the Manhattan Project's test device was driven down the mountain by truck. The active material, plutonium (P-239), was loaded in the backseat of an army car. George Kistiakowsky, a Ukrainian refugee, and Al van Vessem, one of the lead test scientists, had only two hours' sleep the night before delivering the plutonium to the test site. They drove the plutonium down the winding road from Los Alamos and across the desert to the test site. Once at the ranch house, they demanded that Groves's assistant, Brig. Gen. Thomas F. Farrell, sign for the delivery of this rare and very expensive material. Farrell then turned the incomplete device over to the pit assembly crew, known as G-1. G for gadget.

While project scientists assembled the bomb inside the Schmidt-McDonald house, they kept a jeep outside in case something went wrong and they needed to make a quick getaway, apparently never questioning whether they could get far enough away fast enough. They joined together the two hemispheres of plutonium and positioned an initiator. The core created its own heat and was warm to the touch. The gadget, complete except for its detonators, was driven to ground zero, where it would be placed in the bomb assembly. Robert Oppenheimer, still wearing his trademark porkpie hat, supervised the preparations. By late afternoon on Saturday, July 14, the final wiring was completed. Slowly, the assembled bomb was hoisted to the top of a 100-foot wood tower. The firing unit was wired.

Sunday was declared a day off, the bomb's builders told "to look for rabbits' feet and four-leaved clovers." Detonation was set for 4 A.M. on Monday, July 16, but shortly after midnight the test site was hit by a thunderstorm. Lightning flickered around the tower and its contents.

Back at Los Alamos, other scientists continued to run other tests. One experiment seemed to indicate that the bomb would not work.

Some questioned whether the Trinity test should be postponed. Robert W. Seidel, later the administrator of the Bradbury Science Museum in Los Alamos, said yet another indication was that detectors used in the Los Alamos test likely could not distinguish between success or failure. The test was go at Trinity.

More or less. Because of the storm, however, the test was postponed for ninety minutes to avoid a rain-out of fission products from the bomb's expected cloud. The guessing continued. Scientists had no real understanding of the bomb's potential radiation effects. Some believed that radiation strong enough to cause death would be limited to a radius of 1,000 yards from ground zero. Some at the test sight believed that all radioactivity would disperse within 24 hours of an explosion.

"[Robert] Teller bet that [the test yield] might exceed 40 kilotons," according to Seidel, whereas "Fermi was heard taking side-bets that the bomb would incinerate New Mexico. [General] Groves called the governor of New Mexico to alert him that an evacuation of the state might be required." The governor might have to declare martial law. The countdown continued.

Two A.M., and meteorologists predicted the weather would clear by morning. "You'd better be right on this," Groves told the forecasters, "or I will hang you."

Everyone not needed at the test site was ordered out. The final countdown began at 5:10 A.M. Groves would remember, "As we approached the final minutes, the quiet grew more intense." Recounted the *New York Times* of August 7, 1945:

> Scientists waited in tense expectancy. Minutes lengthened seemingly to hours. Lying face downward, with their feet toward the steel tower, the watchers waited, nearly breathless. They were "reaching into the unknown" and did not know what would happen.

At fifteen seconds before 5:30 on the morning of July 16, 1945, the sky over the New Mexico desert blazed suddenly in shades of purple and red and violet. The light was so glaringly bright that it competed with the sun, and it won the competition, recasting the hills and ravines in tones of gold and gray and blue. A story would circulate of a young girl more than a hundred miles away who, blind since birth, accidentally faced the sudden brilliance and saw light for the first and only time in her life.

According to General Groves, "There was a lighting effect within a radius of 20 miles equal to several suns in midday; a huge ball of fire was formed which lasted for several seconds. This ball mushroomed and rose to a height of over 10,000 feet before it dimmed."

Five miles from the heart of this brilliance, two soldiers hid below in a concrete bunker. They stood up and the blast immediately knocked them back down.

Then came a roar such as had never been heard before, never even imagined. Early-morning risers more than 150 miles away in Gallup heard the sound. A strong, sustained roar that "warned of doomsday," General Farrell remembers, "[making] us feel we puny things were blasphemous to dare tamper with the forces heretofore reserved for the almighty."

General Groves remembers: "I was on the ground between [Vannevar] Bush and [James Bryant] Conant. As I lay there in the final seconds, I thought only what I would do if the countdown got to zero and nothing happened."

From Edward Teller: "We were told to lie down on the sand, turn our faces away from the blast, and bury our heads in our arms. No one complied. We were determined to look the beast in the eye." The firing circuit closed at 05:29:45. Research scientist Kenneth Griesen put it plainly: "My God, it worked!"

Enrico Fermi used a simple method of dropping a bit of paper and measuring its displacement "while the blast was passing." The drift, he says "was about 2½ meters, which, at the time, I estimated to correspond to the blast that would be produced by ten thousand tons of T.N.T." He wasn't half right. He had his face protected by a large board in which a piece of dark welding glass had been inserted.

My first impression of the explosion was the very intense flash of light, and a sensation of heat on the parts of my body that were exposed. Although I did not look directly towards the object, I had the impression that suddenly the countryside became brighter than in full daylight. I subsequently looked in the direction of the explosion through the dark glass and could see something that looked like a conglomeration of flames that promptly started rising. After a few seconds the rising flames lost their brightness and appeared as a huge pillar of smoke with an expanded head like a gigantic mushroom.

Trinity was the first atomic explosion this side of the sun. When the gadget detonated, the tower on which it stood evaporated. A second tower, anchored in concrete, built to resemble a structure needed to support a fifteen- to twenty-story building and constructed a half mile from ground zero, was torn from its foundation, leaving a twisted and rippled mess.

Heat from the blast fused sand at ground zero. The green, glasslike substance found in the area of ground zero is called Trinitite; it is still too radioactive to touch.

Kenneth T. Bainbridge, of Harvard University's Cyclotron Laboratory, was the scientist in charge of the Trinity test. In the midst of the jubilant celebration over the test's results, Bainbridge told Robert Oppenheimer, "Now we are all sons of bitches."

"We knew the world would not be the same," Oppenheimer remembers. "A few people laughed, a few people cried. Most people were silent. I remembered the line from the Hindu scripture the *Bhagavad Gita*: 'I am become Death, the destroyer of worlds. . . .'"

Bhagavad Gita translates from Sanskrit as "the Lord's song." There's another line in it that reads: "If the radiance of a thousand suns were to burst forth at once in the sky, that would be like the splendor of the Mighty One."

Scientists had a pool, betting who could come closest to guessing the power of the test. Dr. I. I. Rabi, of the Massachusetts Institute of Technology Radiation Laboratory, won with a guess of 21,000 tons of TNT. He took home $102 in prize money.

A coded message about the bomb test went out from White House special assistant George L. Harrison to President Truman and Secretary of War Stimson, who were attending the Big Three Potsdam Conference in Germany:

TOPSEC Secretary of War from [George] Harrison.
Doctor has just returned most enthusiastic and confident
that the little boy is as husky as his big brother. The light in his
eyes is discernible from here to Highhold and I could have
heard his screams from here to my farm.

The flash was visible for 250 miles, the distance from Washington
to Stimson's Long Island estate called Highhold; the sound carried
50 miles, the distance from Washington to George Harrison's farm
in Virginia. The test went off at 5:29 A.M. in New Mexico, 1:29 P.M. at
the conference in Berlin.

President Truman informed Prime Minister Churchill, who remarked, "This is the Second Coming, in wrath." With the British
leader's consent, President Truman approached Soviet premier
Stalin and told him of this "great new fact." Truman did not give
Stalin any of the particulars, and either the Soviet leader wasn't impressed by the news or he didn't fully understand its significance. He
seemed to slough it off.

It took two years, three months, and sixteen days from the time
work began at Los Alamos until the Trinity test. Seeing the explosion, Gen. Thomas Farrell, for one, believed that the "war was over."

"Yes," said General Groves, "just as soon as we drop one or two of
these things on Japan."

He was correct. It took two of "those things," less than a month
later, at Hiroshima and Nagasaki.

CHAPTER TWENTY-TWO

Uncle Sam Wants You, Maybe:
Don't Ask, Don't Tell, Don't Want to Know

America, the land of unlimited possibilities.
—Ludwig Max Goldberg, *Observations on Economic Life in the United States*, 1903

I became one of the stately homos of England.
—Quinton Crisp, *The Naked Civil Servant*

In 1942, in America, you could get a haircut for half a buck. A man's Harris tweed coat cost about twenty-seven dollars and a woman's washable rayon dress was four dollars. The unemployment rate was 4.7 percent. America was fighting back.

That same year, Paramount released its first major motion picture about World War II, *Wake Island,* with Brian Donlevy and William Bendix. Early in the movie, the hard-bitten (but lovable) marine played by Bendix is seen shaving. Beside his mirror is a picture that would become more famous than the movie, more famous than Bendix, perhaps more famous even than the battle for the island itself. It is the swimsuit picture of blonde and beautiful Betty Grable looking shyly back at us over her shoulder.

From that moment on, most American men knew what they were fighting for—Betty and Lana and Rita. Real men, the unspoken message was, go for pinups. The government walked a fine line here, the post office on one hand trying to censure *Esquire,* and the military on the other trying to let the GIs know why they were fighting. The British, of course, knew why American servicemen were "over there," and frequently they didn't like it. "Overpaid, oversexed, and over here," the Brits moaned.

By the end of the war, more than a million black men and women had served in America's armed forces. On the eve of World War II, however, there were fewer than 4,000 blacks in the American armed services; that was fewer than at the turn of the century.

Gone were the days of the "buffalo soldier," blacks who, more likely than not, had served in the Union army during the Civil War and went on to make up a large portion of the postwar cavalry out West. Despite an outstanding history of service during the Civil War, military consensus held that blacks made only mediocre soldiers, could perform well only when led by whites, and took longer to train than whites. Blacks serving at the beginning of World War II were, in most cases, no longer assigned to fighting roles. Members of the army's predominantly black 9th and 10th Cavalry, for example, truly were "service" personnel; they were truck drivers, orderlies, cooks, and grooms for horses. In 1940, there were only twelve black officers in the army, including Col. Benjamin O. Davis, the grandson of a slave who had purchased his freedom in 1800. Davis was a veteran of the Spanish-American War.

In October 1940, Congress created nearly a hundred new brigadier general slots, mainly because army chief of staff George Marshall wanted to promote into command position bright and shining young colonels such as Mark Clark and Omar Bradley.

Benjamin Davis was sixty-three years old and ready to retire on his next birthday. Normally, he would not have been considered among the "bright and shining young colonels" set for promotion. While an ROTC instructor at Tuskegee Institute, Davis once stood in full uniform to confront a KKK march. When his son, Benjamin Oliver Davis, Jr., graduated from the Military Academy in 1936 (thirty-fifth in a class of 276), together they became the only black line officers in the U.S. Army.

General Marshall wanted to create a joint black and white cavalry regiment, with Ben Davis as its commander. Because Davis was a former horse soldier, that seemed appropriate to Marshall. Not everyone agreed, especially former Judge William O. Hastie. He was also former dean of law at Howard University and now Secretary Stimson's civilian aide for Negro affairs. Hastie wanted President Roosevelt to integrate black soldiers into white companies.

General Lesley James McNair, one of the army's so-called "big four," objected. He said, "The introduction of Negroes throughout our fighting units would tend to leave a commander with no outstanding units."

President Roosevelt ordered Davis promoted to general. It was just one week before the 1940 election. It was a well-publicized event, Davis got his star, and Roosevelt overwhelmingly got the black vote and another term in the White House.

In July 1941, just as he'd planned and just as the law then required, Davis retired from the army. The next day, Marshall had him returned to duty and assigned to the inspector general's office as the expert on black troop issues. Davis-the-elder retired for the second time in 1948 after fifty years of military service.

When Davis-the-younger graduated from West Point as only the third black in fifty years, he joined the segregated 24th Infantry Regiment at Fort Benning, Georgia. As a captain in the spring of 1941, he was accepted for pilot training at Tuskegee; he won his wings the following March. As lieutenant colonel, Ben Davis, Jr., helped raise the 99th Pursuit Squadron and took it to North Africa and Sicily. In 1954, he too won his star, and before he retired in 1970 he had three of them as lieutenant general.

Blacks joined the paratroopers, but the army kept them in the United States fighting forest fires instead of fighting Japanese or Germans. Initially, there were no black marines. Ninety percent of blacks in the navy were mess boys or stewards. There were exceptions, of course, all to the military's benefit. If a black mess boy on board ship was serving coffee to an admiral when general quarters were sounded, the mess boy put down his serving tray, picked up a helmet, and turned out for duty manning a gun alongside his white shipmates. After the battle, he'd return to his apron and serving tray.

To most of the military brass, blacks were virtually as strange as monks or nuns. The few they saw were hotel and railroad porters, maids, laundresses, servants, and waiters. The military took it as an article of faith that blacks couldn't and wouldn't fight; they were shiftless and worthless, mysterious and sex driven, unskilled, unhealthy, undisciplined. They were good only at stealing and stabbing.

At the same time, they were cheerful, dark-skinned children who had to be led by their betters, that is, whites. A self-proclaimed authority on blacks claimed:

> There is always one top Negro who is the boss. . . . We got one from the Hampton Institute [then an all-Negro college in southeastern Virginia] who is a great big six-foot six-inch fellow. . . . This head man was advised to caution his men when they arrived to be quiet and modest, not to be too forward, not put themselves out in front and not to be conspicuous. . . . They were told not to get in any arguments with white people or talk back since it was accepted as a basic fact that no trouble could start without words being first passed.

The first soldiers to be drafted for World War II were white. It would be a while before "colored men" were called up. Few Negroes (1940s term) served on draft boards, virtually none in the South, and until 1943 eligible blacks (1960s term) were passed over, despite the fact that African Americans (1990s term) represented more than 10.5 percent of America's population during World War II. When the law was changed to induct nonwhites, boards tried to induct a percentage equal to the population as a whole—that 10.5 percent. They never reached that number, and it wasn't until late in the war that white losses forced the army to use black soldiers in combat. When they did serve, the official policy was to keep black and white servicemen and servicewomen in separate units, although there was some mixing of races in hard-hit sections late in the fighting.

In November 1941, the army air forces gave in to a threatened lawsuit and set up a pilot training center for blacks at Tuskegee Institute in Alabama. It was the only school that would do the job (university president Frederick Patterson was a personal friend of George Marshall), and those who trained there proudly called themselves the Tuskegee Airmen. They were also known unofficially as the Black Eagles, but officially they were the 99th Fighter Squadron. A member of the 99th later recalled, "We fought two wars: one with the enemy and the other back home in the United States of America— Hitler and Jim Crow." About 1,000 black airmen trained at Tuskegee.

The first class graduated on March 7, 1942, but the top brass didn't know what to do with them, so the army kept them at Tuskegee. Finally, they were sent to North Africa, where their commanding officer was Lt. Col. Benjamin Davis, Jr.

Three other all-black squadrons were added to the 99th Fighter Squadron, and they became the 332d Fighter Group of the Fifteenth Air Force. They flew ground support over the beaches of Anzio and escorted bombers on missions over Italy. Together, the Black Eagles shot down more than a hundred enemy planes.

Almost as soon as the military began drafting blacks, there was racial trouble. The world of the forties was replete with racism, and sending large numbers of blacks from Chicago and Detroit and New York to rural areas of Mississippi and Alabama and South Carolina practically ensured clashes with the local population and police. Actually, the army felt that it knew what it was doing. Southerners, the Pentagon believed, had some unique knowledge and understanding of blacks, so the army often sent urban black recruits to southern bases, putting them under farm-born white southern officers.

Primarily, these white officers had wanted to serve in white units, commanding white troops. It's not using a stereotype to say that such whites didn't like blacks and didn't want to risk their lives with them. Black troops, still without endangering any stereotypes, held little trust or respect for white officers.

An Alabama state policeman shot and killed a black soldier, apparently for no reason at all. In London, military officials worried how American black officers—usually well educated, well fed, and well paid—would be perceived in British possessions. At the same time, when London civilians treated America's black soldiers as equals, U.S. troops nearly rioted. In Australia, girls who dared to attend dances at the black Booker T. Washington Leave Center sometimes were beaten by their white neighbors when they left the center.

When black troops were assigned to Fiji, management at the *Fiji Times and Herald* criticized the move. An editorial claimed the local "natives" would be spoiled by the high wages black soldiers would pay them as laundry workers. The American consul general apparently agreed and, on February 3, 1943, sent the editorial back to the State Department in Washington:

> [Custom] rather than ordinances govern the relationship between European and native races here, and if these [Negro] troops were accorded European privileges, dissatisfaction would result. The colony's racial situation, already complicated with Fijians, Indians, Chinese, and half-castes, if aggravated might well become a major problem.

American blacks in the military faced discrimination from Americans as well. In May 1942, the Australian army minister, the Honorable F. M. Forde, wrote General MacArthur telling of an incident involving black and white U.S. troops. Black GIs, the letter claimed, were riding in a truck when a gang of white GIs stopped them and forced them to get out of the vehicle. Jeers and name calling developed into a fight; the black troops were then confined to camp, and black military police were disarmed. When the black troops were allowed back into town, dance halls in Sydney were declared off-limits. On May 21, 1942, the Australian Labor Party general secretary passed on the letter to the Allied command and called on MacArthur to "eliminate this unjust discrimination before it leads to serious clashes."

On May 28, 1941, MacArthur replied:

> There is absolutely no discrimination against colored troops. Without knowing anything of the circumstances, I will venture the opinion that any friction that may have arisen was based not upon racial lines but upon individual deportment and incidents of conduct. Even if the incident you speak of occurred exactly as you have surmised, it would still represent merely an isolated case of inefficiency and officiousness on the part of some subordinate commander which will be promptly corrected. You may rest completely assured that so far as I am concerned, there is no differentiation whatsoever in the treatment of soldiers.

• • •

Blacks drove nearly every truck in the European Red Ball Express. They piloted every vessel that ferried ammunition and gasoline from ships to invasion beaches. It wasn't enough, however, to do the grunt work. Although black troops constituted only about 8 percent of military personnel, about 22 percent of all troops brought before court-martial were black. Blacks were given the majority of death sentences handed down by such courts for various capital crimes. Of all American military forces tried by court-martial, blacks were four times more likely than whites actually to be executed.

Individuals whose religious beliefs prevented their serving were eliminated from the draft and listed as conscientious objectors (COs). During the war, a total of 42,793 COs were listed, but there may have been more; the numbers aren't clear. COs were offered noncombatant jobs in either the armed forces or in unpaid service camps set up by churches such as the Quakers or in Civilian Public Service Camps (CPSCs). If you got into a CPSC you wouldn't have to fight the war but would not be exempt from work. The camps were *noted* for hard work, long hours, no pay, and—it might not be in a combat zone, but that doesn't mean there was not danger—they often involved hazardous labor. Not only that, but some CPSC men were kept until 1948, long after the shooting war was over.

Only about 5,000 men were imprisoned during the war for failing to register for the draft or for refusing to serve in some sense. Most of these were members of the Jehovah's Witnesses. Jehovah's Witnesses in Germany and Poland were sent to concentration camps with other "undesirables," so it seems that they couldn't win, no matter which side they were not on.

There was said to be one surefire plan to avoid the draft. All you had to do was carry a bag of Oxydol laundry soap in your armpit for a day or so before undergoing your physical; it supposedly caused incorrect high blood pressure readings and you would be rejected. No data are available on the results, and it's difficult to imagine how you would carry around a bag of laundry soap in your armpit in the first place. A variation of this saw draft evaders trying to eat Oxydol.

It might have been better to have just given up and gone in, probably even less dangerous.

After all was said and done, perhaps the only sure way to avoid the draft was to claim to be homosexual. All that any reluctant draftee had to do was say he was gay, as the 1990s term has it. The 1940s terms weren't quite so politically correct.

It could, of course, be worked to the opposite effect. Many homosexuals who wanted to serve denied their sexual preference.

In the preinduction examination, psychologists sometimes bluntly asked, "Do you like girls?" If that didn't work, they simply excluded any man, homosexual or not, who appeared "so effeminate in appearance and manner that he is inevitably destined to be the butt of all the jokes in the company."

A 1990 study of homosexuals during World War II claims that once homosexuals got into the service—depending upon circumstances and individuals involved—they might be "hospitalized, diagnosed as sexual psychopaths, and discharged from the service with the label of homosexuality appearing on their military records." About 5,000 men, the same number who served prison time for not registering for the draft, were discharged for being gay.

Gays who remained in the service might be put into areas of the military in which, at least according to the classification officers, their lifestyles would be better suited. The 1990 study says:

> Medical officers began to generalize about what special talents they believed gay male soldiers possessed and what classifications typically included them. . . . Effeminate gay men, butch lesbians, and others assigned to cross-gendered jobs did not represent the majority of gay male and lesbian GIs—they were merely the more visible.

The U.S. Articles of War declared acts of sodomy as criminal. A military court might be lenient, in which case a soldier or sailor convicted of sodomy might receive an involuntary discharge. Those courts not so lenient could sentence an individual to from five years for army officers or enlisted men to ten years for an enlisted seaman and twelve years for a naval officer. Those convicted were sent to the "queer stockade." If a man or woman had only tested the waters of homosexuality, "through intoxication or curiosity," efforts would be made toward "rehabilitation." But this rehabilitation may not have worked. In 1945, a study contacted 183 homosexual servicemen, everyone from a navy gunnery officer to an air combat intelligence specialist. They'd all been given "blue" discharges, the same discharge given to drug addicts and compulsive thieves.

British playwright, composer, singer, and author Noel Coward was, as a biographer puts it, a homosexual of "impeccable dignity . . . untainted by pretense." Coward was also a good friend of Britain's Lord Mountbatten, and he wrote a movie, *In Which We Serve,* based in great part on the activities of Mountbatten's destroyer *Kelly.* Not only did Coward write and produce the movie, he played the Mountbatten character.

In 1944, Coward inveigled his friend the lord to provide him with air transportation so that he could entertain U.S. troops at Ledo, India. General Joseph W. "Vinegar Joe" Stillwell was in charge of the area, and he was having enough trouble getting transportation to build a road through the area, much less bring in piano-playing entertainment for the troops. When Stillwell refused to provide air transportation for Coward, the entertainer appealed to Mountbatten. Lord Mountbatten was the general's senior commander, and Stillwell was forced to give in. The general, however, got the last word. When Coward's performance fell flat, Stillwell was openly delighted. He wired his deputy, "If any more piano players start up this way, you know what you can do with the piano."

CHAPTER TWENTY-THREE

The Crown Jewels of War:
To Rise Up and Fight Again

People of Western Europe: A landing was made this morning on the coast of France by troops of the Allied Expeditionary Force....
—Gen. Dwight David Eisenhower, broadcast, June 6, 1944

I'm glad I'm here. I'd hate to miss what is probably the biggest battle that will ever happen to us.

—Anonymous Allied soldier

America's youngest combatant in World War II was Calvin Graham, of Fort Worth, Texas. He was born in 1930 and enlisted in the navy early in 1942 when he was only twelve years old. Obviously, he lied about his age, and just as obviously he was big for twelve.

Calvin served on the battleship *South Dakota* during the Guadalcanal campaign of August 1942. He was wounded and awarded the Bronze Star and Purple Heart, and that's when the military discovered just how young Calvin was. When *South Dakota* returned to base, the navy sent him back to his recruiting station. The recruiters didn't know what to do with Calvin, so they sent him home. Because he wasn't on board ship, the navy classified him a deserter. They arrested him and put him in jail. Yes, it was the same navy that had sent him home in the first place.

Rather than sit in the brig, Calvin admitted his age. He was all of thirteen by then, which didn't please the navy, so they gave him a dishonorable discharge, took away his medals, and declared that, despite his wounds, he was ineligible for disability benefits, all because he'd given recruiters false information when he enlisted.

Well, you can't keep a good man (or boy) down, so when Calvin really was old enough to enlist, he rejoined the navy. It took special congressional legislation, however, to restore his pay and lost benefits from his underage enlistment. Known as the "Baby Vet," Calvin Graham finally received an honorable discharge in 1978, thirty-six years after he'd answered his country's call and enlisted.

Calvin Graham wasn't the country's only underage soldier or sailor. It's believed that several hundred boys under the legal age of seventeen used forged birth certificates or similar documents to join up.

The opening shots of America's two deadliest wars were fired in what real estate agents would call "choice waterfront locations"— World War II at Pearl Harbor, Hawaii, and the Civil War at Fort Sumter, South Carolina.

When World War II came, Fort Sumter was reactivated, with searchlight towers and 90mm howitzers in the parade ground and a whole new set of problems to deal with. It became part of the Fort Moultrie defenses outside Charleston. Manning the garrison this time were members of the South Carolina National Guard, southern troops activated as the 263d Coast Artillery to take charge of the old Union fort once bombarded into submission by the South.

The sixty to one hundred men stationed at Fort Sumter in World War II were ordered to watch for enemy airplanes (there were none) and submarines (they really couldn't do much about it if they spotted one). The closest the Fort Sumter garrison came to action in World War II were the few times German U-boats surfaced in the night to lay mines across Charleston harbor. The coast artillery sounded an alarm and waited for the channel to be cleared for vessels sailing into or out of the navy yard.

Other than that, Fort Sumter was good duty, offshore in the summer sun, which was good for getting a tan and making the girls at nearby Folly Beach swoon when the troops were on leave. No one attacked Charleston in World War II, and by 1948 Fort Sumter once more was allowed to rest silently, this time as a national monument.

Lieutenant Colonel James H. "Jimmie" Doolittle was a flight instructor in World War I's army air service but resigned his commission to become an aviation experimental engineer and pilot. He became the only nonregular officer to command a major combat air force. When it became apparent the United States would be going to war again, the army recalled Doolittle to active duty. It was 1940, and his job was to help turn peacetime automotive manufacturing into wartime aircraft construction. In early 1942, he took command of thirty-one other army air forces pilots and forty-eight air crewmen; their mission was to bomb Tokyo. It looked as if Doolittle had little chance of succeeding, but he and his men did just that, with a combination of good luck for the Americans, bad luck for the Japanese, and proof that Murphy's Law works: "If anything can go wrong, it will."

President Roosevelt liked the idea of bombing Tokyo. Britain's air chief had even suggested such a plan for a carrier raid to Gen. Hap Arnold, who thought it impractical. Carrier planes couldn't fly far enough. Captain Francis S. Low, aide to chief of naval operations Ernest J. King, however, suggested an alternative method: don't use conventional navy carrier planes. Instead, use army air forces aircraft; with their greater fuel capacity, they could launch from outside the range of Japanese land-based fighters. General Arnold was already thinking about flying air force bombers off carriers in a projected invasion of North Africa, and he agreed to the Tokyo raid.

That made it a combined navy–air force operation: the navy would supply a carrier to get the air force and its planes close enough to Tokyo to launch the attack but far enough away that Japanese aircraft couldn't attack the carrier. Jimmy Doolittle was picked to lead the mission, and he chose the equipment: B-25B Mitchell medium bombers. He would lead a flight of sixteen Mitchells off the carrier *Hornet.*

The Mitchell was a twin-engine, midwing aircraft with a distinctive twin-tail configuration. It could carry up to 3,200 pounds of bombs. It normally needed from 1,200 to 1,500 feet of runway, but for the carrier flight it would have only 450 feet. Because of the plane's size, they would not be able to return to the *Hornet* and land after the raid. The aircraft would fly to friendly air bases in China. It would take good weather, good flying, and good communications. They got one out of the three—good flying.

What they were about to do had never been done before, but finding men to fly the mission was no problem. Just weeks after the Japanese raid on Pearl Harbor, aircrews were pumped with adrenaline; their feeling of patriotism was high. Doolittle didn't explain what the project was, because he couldn't; it was too secret. He asked for volunteers and he got them, target unknown. The standard B-25 crew was six men, but Doolittle would use only five per plane, eighty men in all.

Doolittle and his small band of men and planes from the 17th Bombardment Group began a month-long cram course in the fine art of taking off from an aircraft carrier. To practice, they used land-based mockups at Eglin Field near Pensacola, Florida, stripes painted on the concrete to simulate a 450-foot carrier deck. None of the pilots ever flew off a carrier until the actual raid. Doolittle's men trained so hard at taking off from a carrier that they never got around to learning how to bail out from a bomber, and only a few of the men who took part in Doolittle's raid had ever parachuted from a plane. It was something that might come in handy, but they'd have to learn it through on-the-job training, so to speak.

When the army was satisfied that the men could take off from a carrier-sized strip of concrete without ending up in the ocean, Doolittle's group flew from Florida to San Francisco. At the Alameda Naval Base, the aircraft were loaded by cranes onto the *Hornet*. It was April 1. The *Hornet* steamed out to join Vice Adm. William F. "Bull" Halsey on board the carrier *Enterprise*.

Halsey, incidentally, was nicknamed Bull not by his friends but by the press, and that was a mistake, a typographical error in an early newspaper report. The mistake persisted because (a) no one caught the typo until it was too late and (b) because Bull made a much more interesting nickname than Bill. Despite the press, Halsey's friends continued to call him just plain Bill.

Hornet left port on almost the same day the Japanese government began planning a full-dress air-raid drill for Tokyo. The date set for the drill was the same as that set for Doolittle's raid: April 18, 1942.

Task Force Mike, as Halsey's group was called, included the carriers *Hornet* and *Enterprise,* three heavy cruisers, one light cruiser, eight destroyers, and two oilers. Almost from the beginning, the weather was foul, just about as foul as communications seemed to be.

Because the B-25s were to land in China after the raid, there had to be good communication with the Chinese, letting them know when, where, and how many planes would be coming. That never really happened, and Chinese partisans never were certain when and where the American airmen hoped to land. As it turned out, it didn't much matter.

The navy, of course, couldn't come right out and broadcast detailed plans. Instead, it tried to work around it. In one bit of double-talk, they told Chinese generalissimo Chiang Kai-shek they were shipping him forty to fifty bombers from India. That pleased Chiang, until he found out what really was happening; he wasn't getting any aircraft but was expected to welcome American planes and personnel who had just bombed Tokyo, keeping them out of the hands of Japanese troops then traipsing around China. Chiang wasn't pleased at that, but he agreed.

Timing, they say, is everything, and Task Force Mike's timing was off. Going east to west, Halsey's group crossed the international date line. The navy planners, however, apparently hadn't taken the date change into consideration, and Halsey and his ships were a full twenty-four hours behind schedule.

The Doolittle raid on Tokyo came on the 167th anniversary of another famous American event, the midnight ride of Paul Revere. Revere had been captured by the British before completing his ride; Doolittle hoped to be luckier.

The plan was to launch the bombers when *Hornet* was 500 miles east of Tokyo. Doolittle would take off with a load of incendiary bombs and light up Tokyo's sky as a marker. The remaining 15 aircraft would take off from *Hornet* 30 minutes later. The plans had to be changed, however, when radar on board *Enterprise* picked up two enemy ships only 11 miles away. It was 3:10 A.M. on the morning of April 18, and the task force was still 650 miles east of Tokyo.

To avoid making further contact, Halsey turned north, then back west. A patrol plane returned with word that an enemy ship had been sighted 42 miles directly ahead. Suddenly, another radar sighting occurred. Halsey realized he was coping with enemy picket boats on the perimeter of a force larger than he wanted to meet.

A Japanese picket boat sent out radio word that it had made contact with an American force. How large, it wasn't certain; its purpose, it didn't know. The U.S. cruiser *Nashville* immediately turned aside and sank the enemy patrol, but it was too late to stop the radio message. The Japanese high command received the report but believed that the American ships had to come closer if they planned to launch an attack; they assumed that planes on board *Hornet* and *Enterprise* were conventional carrier aircraft, with no more chance of reaching Japan from that distance than Japanese land-based aircraft would have of reaching them.

Taking off earlier than planned had several consequences. The raid originally was designed as a night attack; now it would be in the middle of the day. Forced to fly 150 miles farther to reach Tokyo, Doolittle's B-25s had no chance of landing at Chinese airfields. They would all have to crash-land.

The *Hornet* turned into the wind to launch the bombers. The ship rolled violently, and green seas broke over the bow as Colonel Doolittle's heavily loaded B-25 rolled down the carrier's deck. It was 8:18 A.M. (7:18 A.M. Tokyo time) on board *Hornet* as Doolittle took off into a 42-knot wind. He circled the carrier twice to get his exact heading and to check his compass, then aimed for Tokyo. Speed: 150 to 166 miles per hour, not the B-25's maximum speed but its most economical; they had a long way to go. Almost as soon as Doolittle took off, the second aircraft followed, with Lt. Travis Hoover piloting. Instead of 30 minutes in front of the pack, Doolittle was only three minutes ahead.

The flight plan had them crossing the Japanese coastline at Cape Inubo, then flying at treetop level until they reached their targets. It wasn't just Tokyo, either. Kawasaki, Yokohama, Osaka, and Kobe were all in a row, and they too would be bombed. By 8:10 A.M. Tokyo time, the flight was well on its way.

Except for plane number 8. As soon as Capt. Edward York took off, he realized that his aircraft was eating gas so fast he'd never be able to drop his bombs and get beyond the Japanese islands. He immediately headed for Vladivostok, in the Soviet Union, where he hoped to be welcomed. York and his crew were interned by the Russians for several months before being freed.

Doolittle's flight was down to 15 aircraft.

About 600 miles out, Doolittle's plane was fired on by a Japanese freighter, but the freighter missed, and Doolittle flew on. Later, he passed over a Japanese cruiser, but for some reason the ship ignored him. Doolittle made landfall on the Honshu coast at 11:55 A.M., but he was 50 miles north of Cape Inubo after edging into the teeth of a 40-knot wind. Doolittle wasn't the only one off course. Faulty instruments, faulty navigation, bad weather, human error—they all played their part in scattering the remaining 14 aircraft headed for Tokyo. Only two planes crossed the Japanese coastline where they'd planned. Which meant that the flight came in from several points of the compass. Which itself meant that the Japanese would be totally confused; they'd have no idea where the attack originated. As the planes passed over the Japanese countryside, civilians beneath them waved them on their way, thinking that they were friendly aircraft, never imagining that they were the enemy.

When Doolittle's aircraft reached Tokyo, there was no enemy opposition in the air. Murphy's Law was working for them. The air-raid drill planned more than a month earlier was just coming to an end; barrage balloons, launched to impede simulated enemy aircraft, were being hauled down at the mouth of the Tama River; traffic was resuming its flow, and pedestrians gawked at what they thought were Japanese fighter planes overhead. The city had been alerted for the drill, but that was over. No rules covered what they should do now, how officials could realert the population, so nothing was done.

Doolittle's plane was right above the Imperial Palace, but he pulled out without dropping his bomb load on the building. At 1,200 feet, he released his load of incendiary clusters, aiming at the Tokyo armory. The bombs missed and hit the city's largest hospital, burning it to the ground. Doolittle's crews had been instructed to avoid the Imperial Palace, and they did. Still, the Japanese considered bombing close to the palace an obscenity.

Behind Doolittle, Lieutenant Hoover turned west at the Sumida River across the northern part of the city, then released his three 500-pound demolition explosives. Bombs from the two planes fell at the same time. It was 12:15 P.M.

A Japanese antiaircraft crew opened fire, but they were uncertain whether the planes and bombs were part of the drill. They stopped firing without hitting either Doolittle's or Hoover's aircraft. Finally, Japanese attack planes were sent after the two American bombers.

The U.S. ambassador to Tokyo, Joseph Grew, had not yet been repatriated to America, and he was having lunch with the Swiss ambassador. "Sounds like the real thing," the Swiss ambassador said. "Must be your fellows."

"Impossible," Grew assured him. "Just the air show."

"Bet you a hundred dollars," the Swiss said.

"Taken," Grew answered.

As Doolittle and Hoover flew off, the Japanese military and civilian populations reeled. The military had boasted that the country, not to mention its capital city, could never be hit by enemy bombs. Civilian and military personnel both looked around at what the two American planes had done and were shocked.

Twenty minutes later, more of the squadron arrived. Then others. There was a little antiaircraft flak and a handful of Japanese fighter planes made runs at them, but nothing much happened.

In plane number 4, Lt. Everett W. Holstrom was having trouble. His right engine had been acting up ever since he'd launched; now, he was leaking gas from his left tank. The crew flew on, not knowing that they were partially defenseless; a repairman had accidentally left unconnected the electrical lead to the gun turret. With Japanese pursuit planes coming toward him, Holstrom jettisoned his bombs in the ocean and headed west to what he hoped would be safety.

Captain David M. Jones in plane number 5 and Lt. Dean E. Hallmark in plane number 6 made landfall about 30 miles above Cape Inubo, then turned south until they reached the mouth of Tokyo Bay. Hallmark dropped his load of bombs; then, apparently hit by enemy fire, he crashed into the sea. Jones bombed a nest of oil tanks along the city's southwestern bay shore.

The last aircraft to arrive on target, Lt. Harold F. Watson in plane number 9 and Lt. Richard O. Joyce in plane number 10, were the only two who had hit landfall where they'd planned. It was close to

1 P.M. when they arrived over Tokyo, and by then the raid had been under way for close to 45 minutes. Japanese defenses were alert now, and all the way from the coastline Watson and Joyce had been under heavy attack. Watson headed right for his target, across the Imperial Palace and toward Kawasaki. He aimed his bombs at the Kawasaki Truck and Tank plant but instead hit the Tokyo Gas and Electric Engineering Company.

Lieutenant Joyce looked for his target, the Japanese Special Steel Company. His first two bombs hit right on target. By then, antiaircraft fire had zeroed in on him, and a large section of Joyce's plane broke off and fell into a crowd watching below.

While trying to avoid pursuing enemy fighters, Capt. Charles R. Greening dropped his bombs on what he thought was a thatched village. It turned out to be a camouflaged tank farm, and all four of his incendiaries hit. Seconds later, the tank farm erupted in a blast of burning fuel.

It was 1:41 P.M., and the first U.S. raid on Tokyo was over. Of the sixteen B-25 bombers aimed at Japan, fifteen actually bombed the enemy.

The carrier *Hornet*'s role in Doolittle's raid was kept quiet for a long time. In Washington, someone asked where the bombers came from. In a lofty and whimsical manner, President Roosevelt replied, "Shangri-La," referring to the mythical Asian kingdom in James Hilton's novel *Lost Horizon*.

Almost immediately, the U.S. Navy christened an aircraft carrier under construction the *Shangri-La*.

When Doolittle's fourteen remaining aircraft managed to reach China, their fuel was exhausted. The crews had to crash-land or bail out. Japan sent 100,000 troops into the province of Chekiang, where most of the bombers had crashed. For three months, the Japanese ravaged the area looking for the American airmen. They burned out whole villages, destroyed towns, and killed about a quarter of a million Chinese, an atrocity on the scale of the Rape of Nanking.

One pilot, Lt. Ted W. Lawson, of plane number 7, ditched his plane, the prophetically named *Ruptured Duck*—it had a picture of Walt Disney's Donald Duck on crutches—about a mile offshore. Lawson's leg was injured in the crash landing and had to be amputated. His Chinese rescuers carried Lawson to safety. Later, he wrote about the Doolittle raid in his book *Thirty Seconds Over Tokyo*, and served as adviser when Hollywood made the book into a movie.

From the time of the Doolittle raid onward, the Japanese referred to American flyers they took prisoner as war criminals, not as prisoners of war protected by the Geneva Convention. Of the eighty men who carried out the Doolittle raid, one died while bailing out. Five were held for months by their allies, the Soviets.

Eight others were captured by the Japanese and held prisoner. They were tortured almost constantly during their forty months of captivity. Sometimes they'd be sentenced to death, only to be returned to their cells and tortured again. Lieutenant Dean Hallmark, whose plane crashed into the sea near Tokyo, was among those captured. His crew was charged with war crimes and imprisoned; Lieutenant Hallmark was beheaded almost immediately.

After the war, the U.S. Naval War College studied the Doolittle raid and could find "no serious strategical reason" why it had been launched. The key word here is *strategical*. The raid really was a big boost to U.S. morale, both military and civilian. Besides, although it didn't inflict much physical harm on Japan, it caused a lot of psychological damage to the Japanese people. The Japanese army and navy had failed to protect the people and, more importantly, endangered the emperor's life. The Tokyo press clamored for protection, and squadrons of Zeros were brought back from the battlefront to soothe public fears. The Doolittle raid also forced the Japanese to push forward their planned assault on Midway atoll. The speedup prevented two Japanese carriers from joining the strike force at Midway. And that gave the American navy better odds in the coming battle.

Japan's plan to control the Pacific was a simple one: destroy all Allied forces in the region, seize all Allied colonies and possessions, and then quickly sue for peace on favorable grounds. In the beginning, the destruction and seizure parts worked.

The two sides started out about equal in naval forces. The Japanese navy, however, had ten aircraft carriers, while the U.S. Navy had seven under commission. In one of the few military miscalculations made by Japan at Pearl Harbor, no American carrier was in port. Two of the three American carriers in the Pacific when war broke out—*Lexington* and *Enterprise*—were out to sea delivering Marine Corps aircraft to outlying islands. *Saratoga* was off the coast of California. The three carriers had been prime targets for the sneak attack. The fact that they weren't destroyed made all the difference in Japan's simple plan.

Japanese air and land forces had a vast numerical superiority. On Wake Island, for example, more civilian contractors were at work building up the small outpost than there were marines there to defend it. Pan American Airways used Wake as a refueling point between San Francisco and Manila and kept a staff on the island.

When the Japanese attacked Wake Island on Monday, December 8, a Pan Am Clipper was at the base, loaded with more than 200 tires for P-40 Warhawks of the Flying Tigers in China and Burma. As soon as the first wave of Japanese attack planes departed, the Pan Am crew unloaded the tires, set them on fire to keep them out of Japanese hands, and flew the Clipper to safety. By January 12, 1942, it was all over for Wake Island. The small marine garrison, with civilians fighting alongside, couldn't stop the Japanese. Four days after the invasion, the Japanese loaded more than 1,200 U.S. civilian and military prisoners onto a converted passenger liner and shipped them off to POW camps in China. During the twelve-day voyage, for no apparent reason, Japanese guards beheaded five American prisoners of war. No, they were not abiding by the Geneva Convention rules or by any other rules except those of barbarity.

Admiral Chester Nimitz, America's senior naval officer in the Pacific, guessed what Japanese admiral Isoroku Yamamoto was up to. The problem was, he had a much smaller fleet than did Yamamoto.

In early May, American and Japanese naval forces fought the Battle of the Coral Sea (which really took place in the Solomon Sea), an area between Queensland, Australia, on the west and New Hebrides and New Caledonia on the east. There were several "firsts" about the Battle of the Coral Sea: the first naval battle in which participating warships did not fire on one another, the first naval battle to be fought entirely by carrier aircraft, and Japan's first defeat of World War II.

The Japanese force included two large aircraft carriers, one small carrier, cruisers, destroyers, and troop-carrying transports. Facing them was the U.S. Navy's Task Force 17 under Rear Adm. Frank Fletcher with a small fleet of destroyers and cruisers, along with the carriers *Lexington* and *Yorktown*. The latter had arrived from the Atlantic fleet and was Fletcher's flagship.

On May 3, the Japanese landed troops at Tulagi, off Guadalcanal in the Solomon Islands. Overhead, spotter aircraft from *Yorktown* saw only a few minor ships off Tulagi. They continued looking, and by May 7 the two fleets had found each other, more or less.

An American spotter plane reported sighting a Japanese fleet of two carriers and two heavy cruisers. It really was two cruisers and two destroyers.

Japanese spotters also goofed in their report, claiming to have seen a cruiser and an aircraft carrier. When Japanese aircraft arrived, however, the American "cruiser" turned out to be a destroyer, and the "carrier" really was a tanker.

Fighters from opposing aircraft carriers went on the attack. American planes sank the light carrier *Shoho*, and as the Japanese ship went down, Lt. Comdr. Robert Dixon, on board *Lexington*, radioed back, "Scratch one flattop!" From then on, the term *flattop* became synonymous with aircraft carriers.

On the morning of May 8, spotters from each side sighted the opposing fleets, and the battle began all over again. Bombers from *Lexington* and *Yorktown* blasted the Japanese carrier *Shokaku*. Japanese torpedo bombers found *Lexington* and attacked. At one point, the wakes of eleven torpedoes were spotted headed for the "Lady Lex." Explosions rocked the ship on both sides. "In the deepening twilight," a war correspondent on board *Yorktown* reported, the burning *Lexington* "was a sight of awful majesty. The leaping, towering flames . . . hid all feebler light from the skies." About five hours after *Lexington* was attacked, orders were given to abandon ship; her 2,735 officers and men were evacuated. Admiral Fletcher ordered a U.S. destroyer to sink the burning hulk to keep her out of enemy hands.

Nightfall, and things were so confusing, at one point, pilots from a Japanese carrier stumbled onto *Yorktown, and* believed that it was one of their own, prepared to land. They escaped just in time, a hail of antiaircraft fire chasing after them.

Even though *Lexington* was lost, the Battle of the Coral Sea was a technical draw and a strategical victory for the Allies. They forced the Japanese to cancel plans to capture Port Moresby on the south coast of New Guinea.

Yorktown was damaged in the Battle of the Coral Sea, but in something of a miracle she was quickly repaired. The carrier limped back into Pearl Harbor's dry dock, which the Japanese hadn't touched on December 7. With 1,400 workmen swarming over *Yorktown,* repairs were completed in just three days. Patched up, refueled, and her stores replenished, *Yorktown* steamed back to sea with an air group formed with planes from three other carriers.

Japanese admiral Yamamoto, commander in chief of the Combined Fleet, realized he faced a formidable opponent in the U.S. Navy. He knew he had to annihilate the American fleet in 1942 or lose the war. To do this, Yamamoto assembled a fleet of 165 warships, then split it into several task forces. Part of the fleet steamed north to attack the Aleutian Islands off Alaska and the remainder sped toward Midway. It was just short of a month after the Japanese setback at the Coral Sea.

Admiral William Halsey was commander of Task Force 16, but he was hospitalized in Honolulu with a serious skin rash. For the two months that Halsey was out of action, he named Raymond Spruance to take over. It was a controversial decision. Spruance had been in relatively subordinate positions prior to being pushed ahead by Halsey. More important, he was not an aviator, and aviation and air carriers more and more were being recognized as the keys to victory in the Pacific.

The Japanese fleet wanted Midway Island to use as an unsinkable aircraft carrier. Because America had broken Japan's Purple Code, the U.S. Navy knew Yamamoto's plans and had all three of its available Pacific carriers standing off Midway Island.

Defensively, Midway Island was a hard nut to crack. Yamamoto knew that he had to soften it up with a bombardment before cracking it open with an amphibious invasion.

The U.S. Navy knew what the Japanese were up to, but the Japanese navy wasn't even aware that American aircraft carriers were anywhere nearby. That, along with a mistake by the Japanese, made the difference. On June 4, Admiral Yamamoto sent carrier aircraft to attack Midway Island's defenses and to wipe out American aircraft based there.

Admiral Chuichi Nagumo was the commander of the Japanese carrier force, aristocratic in attitude, short in stature, and, according to historian Samuel Eliot Morison, "extremely hot tempered." At the Battle of Midway, a combination of bad luck and tactical errors cost Nagumo four of Japan's six first-line carriers. It became a turning point in the Pacific theater.

When Japanese planes returned to their home carriers after bombing Midway island, Admiral Nagumo had them reload with bombs for another run. With the aircraft fully loaded for one kind of battle, a reconnaissance pilot informed Nagumo that American carriers were approaching Midway, and meant that the Japanese bombers needed not bombs but torpedoes. Nagumo ordered them to reload. While Japanese crews were busy changing their bomb loads, American planes struck.

It was just then that Adm. Raymond Spruance sent his torpedo dive-bombers after the Japanese fleet. The distance was 200 miles, beyond the normal attack radius of U.S. carrier planes; it was too far to fly, attack, and then make it back safely. They flew anyway; torpedo dive-bombers from the carrier *Hornet* went on the attack.

Torpedo planes flew in at wave-top level, aiming toward their target. Weapons on board the Japanese aircraft opened up, and Nagumo's fighter planes were drawn down from where they'd been flying air cover. Meanwhile, dive-bombers from the carrier *Enterprise* arrived and were virtually unopposed.

Bombs were stacked on the Japanese carriers' decks; planes were loaded with highly volatile fuel. As the first Zero plane started down the carrier *Akagi*'s flight deck, bombs from American planes exploded. One by one, the sixty-odd planes on board the Japanese carrier exploded.

Mitsuo Fuchida, the man who had led the Japanese attack on Pearl Harbor, was on board *Akagi*.

• • •

The terrifying scream of the dive bombers reached me first, followed by the crashing explosion of a direct hit. There was a blinding flash and then a second explosion, much louder than the first. I was shaken by a weird blast of warm air. There was still another shock, but less severe, apparently a near miss. Then followed a startling quiet as the barking of guns suddenly ceased. I got up and looked at the sky. The enemy planes were already gone from sight. Looking about, I was horrified at the destruction that had been wrought in a matter of seconds.

As the captain of *Akagi* later remarked, "We were unable to avoid the dive bombers because we were so occupied in avoiding the torpedoes."

Meanwhile, four bombs hit the carrier *Kaga*, touching off a raging inferno among her fueled and armed aircraft.

Seventeen dive-bombers from *Yorktown* aimed at the carrier *Soryu*. Three bombs hit. Fuel and bombs on board the Japanese carrier exploded. With no place to land, the Japanese carrier planes one by one dropped into the sea.

The fourth Japanese carrier, *Hiryu*, fought back, sending its planes on a strike against the American carriers, surprising *Yorktown* with two torpedoes. It was less than a month after *Yorktown* was damaged in the Coral Sea. "She seemed to leap out of the water," a witness reported, "then she sank back, all life gone." The paint was hardly dry on her patched-up flight deck, and now the order came to abandon ship. Her crew was picked up by nearby destroyers and cruisers. With their ship abandoned and apparently sinking, *Yorktown*'s dive-bomber pilots were forced to land on *Enterprise*. Not all were able to make it. Before *Enterprise* could take them aboard, two of the seventeen bombers ran dry and their pilots had to ditch. When a *Yorktown* fighter pilot who'd been badly wounded crash-landed on the *Hornet*, he forgot to cut his gun switches. His six .50-caliber machine guns, jarred by a rough landing, fired a burst that killed five men and wounded twenty.

Yorktown was down, but was not yet out. Repair crews made a belated effort to save her. But a Japanese submarine spotted the badly damaged ship, took aim, and sent a torpedo into her while the destroyer *Hammann* had her in tow. Too many watertight doors had been sprung, too many bulkheads had been weakened by the attack for her to survive.

A work party on board *Yorktown* was ordered to abandon ship, but a few men were blocked by wreckage and couldn't make their way out. An officer tried to contact all of those left below and finally reached someone on the fourth deck. "Do you know," the officer asked, "what kind of fix you're in?"

"Sure," he was told, "but we've got a hell of a good acey-deucy game down here." The voice paused, then, "One thing, though. . . ."

"Yes?"

"When you scuttle her, aim the torpedoes right where we are. We want it to be quick."

Scuttling wasn't necessary. Early the next morning, *Yorktown* turned over on her port side and sank in 2,000 fathoms of water, with all her flags flying. The torpedo that doomed *Yorktown* also sank the destroyer *Hammann* lashed to it.

Bombers from *Enterprise* avenged *Yorktown*'s loss and put down the final Japanese carrier. Among the bombers who destroyed *Hiryu* were pilots from *Yorktown* who no longer had their own carrier to call home.

The Battle of Midway marked the end of America's defensive war in the Pacific and the beginning of its counteroffensive. From then on, it was a matter of time, as well as death and destruction, before the Rising Sun would set. Admiral Yamamoto lost his four best carriers; they and their air groups were wiped out. Japan scrapped its plans to capture New Caledonia, the Fijis, and Samoa. The Stars and Stripes still flew over Midway Island.

South of the Arctic Circle, the great trade routes of the Atlantic Ocean are shrouded in winter storms and summer gales. Numbing cold and an unbroken horizon were the lot of those who sailed into the area. The North Atlantic winter is more bitter, more hostile, than most men or their ships can endure. Yet, it was here that the longest and perhaps most complex battle of World War II took place, the Battle of the Atlantic.

At first, the German navy with its wolf packs of submarines ruled the waves. Germany began the war with 57 U-boats in commission, about half of them large enough to range though the Atlantic

Ocean and the North Sea. In the first month of the war, U-boats sank 41 merchant ships. The following month it was worse.

When the United States entered the war, its ships became equal targets with the British, and U-boats began attacking ships all along America's eastern seaboard. By mid-1942, U-boats had almost severed Great Britain from the United States. In June alone, 173 Allied ships were lost to German submarines, and new U-boats were being delivered at the rate of 30 each month.

By March 1943, there were 400 U-boats in service. In that same month, German subs sank 82 ships in the North Atlantic alone; they sank another 38 in other areas of the world.

From the American continent to Britain and Europe, ships lined up in convoys to avoid German U-boats. Radar and sonar searches became more successful. Lighter-than-air blimps and PBY floatplanes made their appearances in the skies over the American and European coasts. Allied planes began outgunning German submarines. By the end of 1943, the Battle of the Atlantic was over. German U-boats sank 2,452 merchant ships in the Battle of the Atlantic, a total of 12.8 million tons. Another 175 naval warships were lost along with tens of thousands of British and American seamen.

According to Winston Churchill, "The only thing that ever really frightened me during the war was the U-boat peril." He was more anxious about it than about "the glorious air fight called the Battle of Britain."

There was never any doubt that the Allies had to take the war to Europe. The air war of both nighttime and daylight bombing, with carpet bombing sweeping German industry underground, had not succeeded either in stopping Hitler's war machine or in turning the public against *der Führer*. Only an invasion of what Hitler called "Fortress Europe" would suffice. Josef Stalin had long asked for a second front in the west to divert German attention and troops from him.

In July 1943, Allied troops invaded Italy in Operation Husky, aimed, according to Prime Minister Churchill, at "Axis-held Europe's soft underbelly along the Mediterranean." The plan was for American troops to sail from North Africa and land on the south central coast of Sicily; they'd take care of the western half of the island before moving along the northern coast. British troops would join them at Mount Etna after landing on the southeast coast and pushing around the eastern region. The Combined Chiefs of Staff named Gen. Dwight Eisenhower as Allied supreme commander, as he had been in Operation Torch (the Allied invasion of North Africa in late 1942); however, as in Torch, British officers were chosen as senior commanders of ground, sea, and air forces.

In a gambit that smacked of Hollywood (and, indeed, Hollywood later made a movie about it), British espionage forces left a dead body to float onto a Spanish beach. It was an effort to fool the Germans into believing the coming invasion would take place somewhere else, such as the Balkans. An unknown corpse was chosen and given the name "Maj. William Martin," Royal Marines, serial number 09560. He became, as the book and movie title have it, "The Man Who Never Was." Taking to the idea at hand, a small interservice, interdepartment group gave Major Martin a past complete with a girlfriend named "Pam." They bought shirts that they thought were appropriate to one of his background (which they also supplied), left used theater tickets in his pocket, and gave him a letter from his girlfriend (". . . all my love, Pam") along with another letter about a bank overdraft (£79.19s.2d.). They shackled a briefcase to his wrist. Inside were phony papers about a phony Allied invasion nowhere near where troops really would be going ashore. To an extent, the plan worked, and German defenses in the Balkans were beefed up.

Fifty-seven days after the Allies had defeated German troops in Tunisia, Eisenhower began Operation Husky; it was July 10, 1943. Three thousand ships carried 160,000 men, 1,800 artillery pieces, and 600 tanks from Africa to Sicily. The Allies hoped to entrap Axis forces in the northeastern corner of Sicily, preventing them from escaping to the mainland of Italy through the Strait of Messina. American troops landed at night in the area of Gela. The British landed on the eastern end of the island near Syracuse. American forces under Gen. George Patton succeeded in dominating the region. British forces under Gen. Bernard Montgomery didn't do as well and were stopped by savage German resistance. George Patton pushed on, driving to Palermo in the northwestern area, then turning toward Messina.

Allied troops took the island, but 100,000 enemy troops and 10,000 vehicles escaped across the Strait of Messina. In 38 days Operation Husky was complete; the island of Sicily was secured for Allied troops, and the Allies took more than 100,000 troops prisoner.

On September 3, even as Italian army officials secretly were negotiating a surrender, Allied troops went ashore on the mainland across the Strait of Messina. Five days later, as American forces prepared to invade Salerno, southeast of Naples (Operation Avalanche), General Eisenhower announced Italy's unconditional surrender. The Germans, however, still held on to the Italian boot.

Initially, U.S. troops at Salerno met little resistance, but German troops quickly moved in and just as quickly pinned down the GIs on the beachhead. When German troops threatened to push the Allies back into the sea, Gen. Mark Clark of the U.S. Fifth Army sent in paratroops. Using both day and night drops, the U.S. 82d Airborne dropped a total of 4,000 men behind enemy lines. On September 15, troops from the British Eighth Army drove northwest from its own amphibious landing and made contact with U.S. troops. On the eighteenth, the Salerno beachhead was finally secured and Allied troops could begin to move inland. The battle for Italy wasn't over yet, but it was clear that it wouldn't last much longer.

Most of Italy's demoralized 1,090,000 troops were easily disarmed by the 400,000 Germans operating under Gen. Albert Kesselring. The general, however, was badly injured in an accident involving his car and a mobile gun coming out of a side road. He was hospitalized for three months, and that may have changed the German army's performance; Kesselring had earlier proved himself to be a master of defense and delay in ground operations.

American troops arriving in Naples were shocked at the sight of the malnourished residents, who were dressed in rags and who picked over scraps of garbage left by the arriving troops.

American troops were also shocked at something else: the large number of prostitutes crowding around them, girls and young women driven to offer sex for food or money. Not much money, either, only 25¢. In April 1944, the British Bureau of Psychological Warfare estimated that some 42,000 women in Naples were practicing prostitution.

As the U.S. Army pushed through Italy, the venereal disease rate began to soar among both local and American troops, assuming a major importance for the first time in the European campaign. In a two-week period in August, more than 4,000 Neapolitans showed up at a U.S. military hospital in Naples asking to be treated for VD.

Six days after the Allied invasion of Sicily, Italian authorities took dictator Benito Mussolini into custody. The new anti-German government of Italy moved him from hiding place to hiding place. On September 12, three days after the landing at Salerno, German operatives working with Capt. Otto Skorzeny rescued *Il Duce.*

Mussolini was being held in a heavily guarded resort hotel on a 6,000-foot-high plateau in the Gran Sasso mountains. Landing a glider on a 3,000-foot meadow next to the hotel, Skorzeny intimidated Mussolini's guards, found *Il Duce,* and told the former Italian leader that Hitler had sent him. "You are free!" Skorzeny said, and shoved Mussolini into a light plane that had just landed. With barely enough room in the meadow to take off, the Fi-156 Storch delivered Mussolini from the mountains to Vienna that night. From there, Mussolini went on to Munich and a meeting with Hitler at the German leader's retreat, Wolf's Lair, in Rastenburg. With Hitler backing him, Mussolini claimed to rule the "Salo Republic," which didn't exist except for the small village of Gargagno on the western shore of Lake Garda. Mussolini had with him his longtime mistress, Clara Petacci.

In April 1945, Mussolini visited his wife, Rachele, in Milan, trying to persuade her to flee the Allied army already sweeping their way. She refused, and Mussolini (wearing a German infantryman's greatcoat and helmet) took Mistress Clara and headed northward, where he hoped to take refuge in the Tyrol. Italian partisans, however, found him when they stopped his convoy near Lake Como. They drove *Il Duce* and Clara about a mile away, and on April 24 they machine-gunned to death Mussolini, his mistress, and twelve captured Fascist leaders. The next day, the bodies of Mussolini and Clara, along with four others, were taken to a gas station under construction in Milan's Piazelle Loreto. It was the site of the execution eight months earlier of more than a dozen partisans.

The bodies of Mussolini and Clara Petacci were hung by their heels and displayed to the public. Allied officials ordered the bodies cut down. Mussolini's body was buried in a cemetery in Milan, but in 1946 it was stolen by a band of neo-Fascists, who hid it in a monastery at Patvia. Italian officials found the body and secretly reburied it northwest of Milan. Finally, in 1957, the body was interred near that of Mussolini's son Bruno, a fighter pilot who died in a 1941 air crash, in the home cemetery of San Cassiano in Predappio, Italy. Being buried there was a request Mussolini had made in his final letter to his wife, Rachele. Clara Petacci lies buried in Rome.

After the war, Benito Mussolini's son Romano married Maria, the sister of actress Sophia Loren; the wedding was held in a church that Mussolini built in 1934. Romano and Maria Mussolini's daughter Allesandra (*Il Duce*'s granddaughter), like her Aunt Sophia, is an actress.

On June 4, 1944, the U.S. Fifth Army under Gen. Mark Clark took the city of Rome. There was little opposition. Clark staged a celebration, then continued on with the war in northern Italy.

Two days after the taking of Rome, Allied troops landed at Normandy, the largest invasion of the war, and the most vital.

Eisenhower's orders from the Combined Chiefs of Staff were simple and direct. They came to him on February 12. "You will enter the Continent of Europe and, in conjunction with the other United Nations, undertake operations aimed at the heart of Germany and the destruction of her Armed Forces." Simple orders, but carrying them out wouldn't be so easy.

It was the second front of the war in Europe, the "Far Shore," as Allied leaders in England referred to the area. Operation Overlord involved the greatest allied technical feat of the war. It could not have occurred at any other point in history. Never before could an armed force so large be gathered and moved so great a distance. Never again would so large a force be *able* to gather without a technically advanced enemy knowing exactly where, when, and how the invasion would come.

"It looks," German field marshal Erwin Rommel wrote his wife on April 27, 1944,

> . . . as though the British and Americans are going to do us a favor of keeping away for a bit. This will be of immense value for our coastal defenses, for we are now growing stronger every day—at least on the ground, though the same is not true for the air. . . . Every day, every week . . . we get stronger. . . . I am looking forward to the battle with confidence.

American military authorities favored a quick and, they thought, easy attack across the English Channel. Once on the Far Shore, they would drive deep into the heart of industrial Germany, bringing a quick end to World War II in Europe. The British, however, had memories of Dunkirk and Dieppe, both failures on that Far Shore.

The Normandy invasion demanded the safe disembarkation of hundreds of thousands of men and weapons on a heavily fortified coast, an area where Germany for four years had been preparing a reception. The Normandy invasion succeeded because of good planning by the Allies, bad planning by the Germans, and luck on both sides—good luck for the Allies, bad luck for Germany. As it turned out also, the Allies may have won because they made fewer mistakes.

Four months after the concerted bombing began on German rail and road targets, Allied forces prepared to land in France. They would gather a total invasion force of 1,527,000 troops, around 150,000 landing on D day. Getting them there would take the largest armada ever assembled—4,400 ships and landing craft. In addition, 1,500 tanks would be ferried over while 11,000 fighters, bombers, transports, and gliders flew overhead for protection, support, and, later, supplies.

There were no port facilities large enough and near enough in France to sustain the invasion, so the Allies would take with them their own port, two huge floating docks called mulberry harbors. They'd be towed into position off the Normandy coast.

More than 60 percent (by weight) of battle supplies consisted of oil and gasoline. To supply this fuel, the Allies would build PLUTO (pipeline under the ocean) beneath the English Channel. It would deliver 1 million gallons of fuel a day.

Even without the spy satellites of the 1990s, there was always a danger that Germany would learn when and where the invasion would come. To prevent that, security forces kept as much information as possible about the invasion away from the troops. "We were put into a field," British bombardier Richard "Dickie" Thomas remembers, "marched into a field . . . which was completely surrounded by barbed wire, to make sure we couldn't get out. We didn't have the foggiest idea what was going on. It was a good 8 foot of barbed wire."

Of the forty-seven Allied divisions used in the invasion, twenty-one were American. The rest included British and Canadian divisions, along with units from France, Poland, Italy, Belgium, and Czechoslovakia—representatives of nations whose lands were held by Hitler's Nazis.

By mid-April 1944, all military leave was canceled for Allied troops. Everywhere there were "Snowdrops," as the British called the American military police who wore white pistol belts, white gloves, and white helmets. British MPs were "Red Caps." Signs posted near military encampments warned: "Do Not Loiter. Civilians Must Not Talk to Military Personnel." Narrow English roads were choked with trucks, tanks, field guns, and jeeps. The buildup was equally large and imposing in English ports.

To fool the Germans, complicated deception measures—codenamed Operation Fortitude—were taken. The Allies repeatedly bombed Pas-de-Calais to make the German staff believe that it was the intended target. Much to his initial disgust, Gen. George Patton commanded a dummy army, the First U.S. Army Group (FUSAG) that marched up and down England. With the help of *National Geographic* magazine, which published pictures of shoulder insignia, the U.S. Army spread word of a special, nonexistent Fourteenth Army, with two fictional corps and nineteen nonexistent divisions.

Despite all the planning, an incident occurred during training that could have blown the whole thing. It was a major foulup, but full details weren't learned until reports were cleared in 1974. Early on the morning of April 28, 1944, a convoy of LSTs (landing ship, tank) were off Slapton Sands on Lyme Bay in southern England; that part of the Devon coast was similar to the Normandy area where the troops would go ashore on D day. Apparently, both the army and navy were more interested in the training than in watching out for the enemy, and only one ship guarded the practice. It wasn't even on the same radio frequency as the LSTs. Nine German E-boats (similar to American PT boats) picked up heavy radio traffic in the area. Making a quick run for Lyme Bay, they saw the LSTs and attacked, sinking two of the larger ships and damaging several others.

The Allied command kept it quiet to prevent Germany from knowing the full extent of the disaster and, through that, learning more about the coming invasion. Still, although the official death toll was 749, the unofficial toll was said to be closer to 1,000. Many who died at Slapton Sands were from the 4th Infantry Division. In the actual Normandy invasion, the division lost only one-fourth as many men as it did during the rehearsal.

Meanwhile, as invasion plans continued and troops prepared to fight, the weather grew questionable. Donald Burgett, of the U.S. 101st Airborne, remembers:

> On June 3d they issued each of us an escape kit, consisting of a small compass, an unmarked map, and seven dollars in French money. We were also issued a metal cricket apiece, one click being the challenge to anyone we met in combat and two the password to keep from getting one's head blown off.
>
> That night we sat sharpening knives, cleaning weapons and sorting through personal things we figured we could or would need after the heavy fighting was over. . . .
>
> It was raining that night, and all the canvas and blankets were wet, but we didn't mind.

SHAEF planners had chosen June 5, 6, and 7 as the best dates for the invasion, weather permitting. Each date promised a late-rising moon followed by a low tide at dawn. If the invasion wasn't held then, the next time for favorable tide conditions wouldn't be until June 18 through 20. The next favorable moon conditions wouldn't be for another month.

Monday, June 5, was set for the invasion. The ships were loaded; the men were primed. But the high seas and overcast skies jeopardized the planned attack. The Allied command had no choice. "A large portion of the 4,000 ships already were at sea," Eisenhower's aide, Capt. H. C. Butcher, remembered; they had to be called back.

On the night of June 4, Eisenhower met with his staff in the library of Southwick House. The big question was the weather on the Calvados coast of Normandy. It was storming when they met, and one group of meteorologists forecast continued rain. A second group said that it likely would clear in time for the invasion. Eisenhower believed the second set.

Or wanted to believe them. He knew a second delay would demoralize the troops, and returning them to their camps could destroy months of tight security. "I am quite positive we must give the order," Eisenhower said. "I don't like it, but there it is. . . . I don't see how we can do anything else." At another meeting six hours later, with the weather clearing just as Eisenhower hoped it would. He said, "OK, we'll go."

On the other side of the English Channel, Ike's opposite number, Erwin Rommel, believed his own set of meteorologists, and they said the foul weather would continue, so he left the coast. June 6 was his wife's birthday and he was going back to Germany to celebrate with her. He would be twenty-four hours late getting back to the front.

German troops manning the defenses along the Atlantic Wall were lulled by the weather. The navy canceled patrols; the seas were too high, the winds were too strong, and the visibility was too low for an invasion, they believed. Several of Rommel's senior staff officers were away from the coast, attending a map exercise in Rennes. In Berlin, Adolf Hitler slept, and his aides were afraid to awaken him.

"On that night of 5 June none of us expected the invasion anymore," a German private later wrote.

There was a strong wind, thick cloud cover, and the enemy aircraft had not bothered us more that day than usual. But then—in the night—the air was full of innumerable planes. We thought, What are they demolishing tonight? But then it started. I was at the wireless set myself. One message followed the other, "Parachutists approaching."

Some soldiers and sailors slept as their ships moved silently toward the French coast; others spent the night playing cards or throwing dice. Many wrote letters home, fearful that it might be the last time; for many it was. Some sat and thought about what was ahead.

On the German-held side of the Far Shore, the invasion came as a shock. "There were so many vessels," Sgt. Richard W. Herklotz, of Germany's 110th Field Artillery, remembers, "so many ships, that there was nowhere on the horizon that you could look and not see some type of vessel." Among the Allied vessels was USS *Nevada*, which had been at Pearl Harbor when the Japanese attacked, and HMS *Warspite*, a British battleship that had also been at the Battle of Jutland in 1916. Operation Overlord was under way. "Everywhere in the air," Herklotz says, "there were barrage balloons on cables from each ship. It seemed that they filled the sky."

American paratroopers wore jumpsuits, boots, gloves, and helmets, main chutes and reserve chutes, Mae Wests in case they landed in the sea. Each man carried a rifle, a .45 automatic pistol, a trench knife, a jump knife, and a hunting knife. Some even had machetes. In addition, each man had one cartridge belt, two bandoliers of ammunition, two cans of machine-gun ammunition, a Hawkins land mine, four blocks of TNT, blasting caps, first-aid kits, morphine needles, gas mask, canteen of water, three days' supply of K rations, two days' supply of D rations, one orange smoke and one red smoke grenade, one blanket, a raincoat, a change of socks and underwear. They carried black face cream, manufactured by cosmetic manufacturer Elizabeth Arden, camouflage for their faces. And the ever lovin', ever present army entrenching tool. They were as ready as they could get.

British paratroopers weren't quite so heavily laden. To save the Exchequer money (£20 sterling then, about $1,000 now), the British army didn't issue its men reserve parachutes. If British troopers were scared at the prospect of jumping without a reserve chute, they might have used another item the army did provide, greaseproof bags officially labeled "Bags, Vomit, for Use of."

Hours before other troops landed on the beaches, one British and two U.S. airborne divisions were dropped into the dark French countryside.

The U.S. Army had tried gliders for the first time in the 1943 assault on Sicily. Now, these unpowered, gliding aircraft were used in the massive assault behind German lines.

In the gray dawn, the landing craft doors were thrown open and men were thrown into water sometimes hip deep, sometimes over their heads. For many, it was their last step in life. The rest stormed onto five code-named beaches—the Americans at Utah and Omaha; the British and Canadians onto Gold, Juno, and Sword.

As Allied planes and ships continued their bombardment (sometimes too far behind enemy lines to do any good), German troops— nine infantry divisions and one panzer division—lay low in their bunkers.

As the Allied troops struggled ashore, duplex drive (DD) tanks— Sherman tanks especially equipped with propellers and canvas water dams—rolled off LSTs. DD tanks were supposed to "swim" to shore unassisted. Some didn't; rough seas played havoc with them, and their canvas dams, called "bloomers," collapsed or were destroyed by German shells. Sinking tanks took their crews to the bottom with them. Like sardines in a can, one soldier remembers; they didn't have a chance. Twenty-seven of the thirty-two DD tanks assigned to the 16th Infantry at Omaha Beach foundered on the run in. Almost the opposite at Utah Beach, twenty-eight DD tanks made it safely ashore.

By midnight on June 5, 822 C-47s were over the Channel, carrying the 82d and 101st Airborne Divisions—13,000 men. Skies were clear until they reached their drop zones. Antiaircraft flak was heavy, and it scattered the flight's tight formation. As a result, several sticks (eighteen paratroopers per stick) came down in flooded river bottoms in the Bay of the Seine, far behind enemy lines. Others had to fight through and around hedgerows (the French called them *bocages*) and marshes in the Ste.-Mère–Eglise area. Still, the paratroopers and those who'd flown in on gliders disrupted German efforts to reinforce their defenses behind Utah Beach. Disrupting German reinforcements was also the job of the French Resistance, who prevented panzers from racing to the front by replacing axle grease with glue.

The beaches of Normandy were fought over and won by enlisted men. Only one general officer, Brig. Gen. Theodore Roosevelt, Jr., went in with the first wave at Utah Beach. When the fifty-seven-year-old, severely arthritic general (he normally needed two walking sticks to get around) realized that his men had landed a mile south of their assigned beach, he decided to head inland, saying simply, "We're going to start the war from here." He was awarded the Congressional Medal of Honor; however, it came posthumously. He died of a heart attack on July 13, 1944.

Nearly 150,000 Allied troops—along with their vehicles, equipment, munitions, and provisions—were ashore on D day. The Allies had won their fingerhold on the European continent. General Omar Bradley called the assault on Utah Beach "a piece of cake." The landing there was the big success story of the Normandy invasion. There was no cake at Omaha Beach. The landing on "Bloody Omaha" almost ended in disaster. American troops suffered 6,603 casualties on D day, 1,465 killed and another 3,184 seriously wounded, by far the largest number of casualties. British casualties ran from 2,500 to 3,000, while Germany suffered from 4,000 to 6,000 casualties on D day. General Rommel reported that by the end of June his casualties totaled "28 generals, 354 commanders and approximately 250,000 men."

By late July, 2 million troops and 250,000 vehicles had landed in France. Now, Germany could be pincered from all sides.

CHAPTER TWENTY-FOUR

The Holocaust:
Victims of War in All Shapes, Sizes, and Religions

First, they came for the Communists, and I didn't speak out because I wasn't a Communist. Then they came for the Socialists, and I didn't speak out because I was not a Socialist. Then they came for the trade unionists, and I didn't speak out because I wasn't a trade unionist. Then they came for the Jews, and I didn't speak out because I wasn't a Jew. Then they came for the Catholics, and I didn't speak out because I wasn't a Catholic. Then they came for me, and by that time no one was left to speak out.
—Martin Neimoeller, pastor, German Confessing Church

SS Sergeant Abraham was a vulgar beast. He tortured, beat to death, and drowned many people in Buchenwald. He targeted the Jews in particular.
—Robert Siewart, Berlin, *The Buchenwald Report*

In 1935, propaganda chief Joseph Goebbels located a blond, blue-eyed, rosy-cheeked boy and had him photographed alongside German chancellor Adolf Hitler. The boy would be the Nazi Party's poster child, a fine example of the pure Aryan race, just what every good German man wished he were. Hundreds of thousands of copies of the picture were sold as postcards. Just as with Hitler's *Mein Kampf*, every Nazi household had to have a copy.

Only later did Goebbels learn that the boy was not Aryan, at least not according to the preachings of Hitler and the Nazi Party. The boy was Jewish, the grandson of a rabbi. Goebbels's underlings destroyed as many of the postcards as they could find. They may also have destroyed the boy.

Outside the Florida Holocaust Memorial Museum and Education Center stands a fifteen-ton World War II–vintage railroad boxcar. It is not very large, yet was the suffocation chamber for the hundred people or more who were squeezed inside, en route to German death camps. It is one of three such boxcars in the United States; one is in Dallas and the other is exhibited at the United States Holocaust Memorial Museum in Washington, D.C. They hauled Boxcar number 1130695-5 from Gdania (Gdansk), Poland, to Florida despite objections from the Polish government, which was afraid that it would become a symbol of the Holocaust. They were right, it is.

Shoah is the Hebrew word for holocaust, and has its origins in thirteenth-century Greek. *Holo Kaustus* is the burnt sacrificial offering dedicated exclusively to God. A more modern definition of holocaust is a sacrifice wholly consumed by fire; a whole burnt offering. Some modern authors use the word *extinguished* in writing of the Holocaust; that lacks emotion. It is more illustrative to say Hitler's Germany *murdered* more than 6 million Jews. Murdered. Killed. Gassed, shot, burned. "Remember . . ." a brochure for the Florida museum begins,

> We must never forget the Holocaust. The systematic destruction of six million Jews by the Nazis, and the murder of six million others whom they deemed unfit to live, constitute the most tragic unfathomable episode of modern times—the Holocaust.

There seems to be a distinction here; 6 million Jews were destroyed, but 6 million "others" were murdered. They all were murdered—at least 12 million, probably more; we'll never really know. Murdered. Killed. Gassed, shot, burned.

Beginning on October 28, 1938, Nazis launched an assault against thousands of German Jews who had lived in the Reich for years. Even by Nazi standards it was brutal, but other Germans watched passively, in their own anti-Semitism perhaps relishing what was happening to the Jews.

Hitler's henchmen snatched children off street corners without notifying their parents and jammed them into trucks and trains. Along with the aged and the infirm, these children were taken over the Polish border and dumped; they were allowed to take no more than ten marks (then about four dollars) and the clothes on their backs. The weather turned bitter cold, and they sought refuge in empty railroad cars, in abandoned buildings, and in the open no-man's-land between the frontiers.

Among the estimated 10,000 people who had been abducted, transported, and left to die was the Zindel Grynszpan family of Hannover, Germany. Their seventeen-year-old son, Herschel, had fled to Paris earlier. After his father wrote him describing the family's suffering at the hands of the Nazis, Herschel bought a pistol and went to the German embassy in Paris. He demanded to see Ambassador Johannes von Welczeck. Instead of the ambassador, a minor official named Ernst von Rath was delegated to deal with the apparently deranged visitor.

It was November 7, 1938, and Herschel Grynszpan shot Von Rath as he walked toward him. Immediately, Grynszpan was taken into custody by the French police. As Von Rath lay unconscious, the German press began fermenting a massive reprisal against all Jews. Under questioning by French authorities, Herschel Grynszpan said, "Being a Jew is not a crime. I am not a dog. I have a right to live and the Jewish people have a right to exist on the earth. Wherever I have been I have been chased like an animal."

Two days later, Von Rath died. At 2:00 A.M. the next day, a wave of arson, looting, murder, and arrest began.

There were three groups that attacked the Jews: the SA storm troopers (*Sturmabteilung*, or storm detachment; originally, they were a gymnastics and sports division of the NSDAP, the *Nationalsozialistische Deutsche Arbeitpartei*, the National Socialist German Workers' Party—they were the Brown Shirts), the SS (*Schutzstaffel*, or protection squadron), and the SD (*Sicherheitsdienst*, or security squadrons). Encouraged by pronouncements from Goebbels and his loyal press, the three groups took to the streets. They burned 195 synagogues and 800 shops, looting 7,500 others. Operating under "methodically drafted orders" from Reinhard Heydrich, Heinrich Himmler's commander of security, Nazi units killed more than 200 Jews and severely injured more than 600. It's believed that the total number of deaths in two days of killing, looting, and burning ran between 2,000 and 3,000. More than 30,000 men and boys were incarcerated in concentration camps, some for a short time, and then were released; hundreds of others died. A *New York Times* headline of November 11, 1938, read: "Nazis Smash, Loot and Burn Jewish Shops and Temples Until Goebbels Calls Halt."

Times reporter Otto D. Tolischus wrote:

> Beginning systematically in the early morning hours in almost every town and city in the country, the wrecking, looting

and burning continued all day. Huge but mostly silent crowds looked on and the police confined themselves to regulating traffic and making wholesale arrests of Jews "for their own protection."

Austrian Nazis followed suit, burning 21 synagogues in Vienna. In some Austrian communities, every male Jew was sent to a concentration camp.

Under Nazi pressure, insurance claims were paid, then the German government confiscated the money—approximately 1 billion marks.

Walther Funk, the Nazi president of the German Reichsbank and one of Hitler's most ardent followers, had drawn up laws excluding Jews from the nation's economic life. It was he who, in a somewhat lighthearted mood, is said to have coined the word *Kristallnacht,* "crystal night," alluding to the shattered plate glass shop windows that littered the streets of Germany. After the war, Funk was captured along with Japanese embassy personnel. Tried in Nuremberg, Funk was convicted of helping exploit occupied areas and of indirect involvement in slave labor operations. He served eleven years of a life sentence in Spandau Prison, then was released for ill health.

Ernst von Rath was the Third Secretary at the German embassy in Paris. At the time he was shot by Herschel Grynszpan, he was under Gestapo investigation because of his opposition to anti-Semitism.

Anti-Semitism is a corollary and inference of Christianity. The first Christians, including Jesus Christ himself and all his Apostles, were Jews. In the early years of the religion, as believers of Christ turned beyond their origins and looked to a wider congregation, Christians began preaching against Jews and Jewish beliefs. Within a few generations, practically speaking, there were no more Jewish Christians.

To mollify the world, modern theologians hold that it was the ancient Romans who crucified Jesus, not the Jews. It is an easy belief; after all, the ancient Romans are all dead, so we can blame them all we want. Jews still live, even though Adolf Hitler, et al. tried to murder them all. It fits very well, this modern theology.

In *Mein Kampf,* Hitler wrote, "I am now convinced that I am acting as an agent of our Creator by fighting off the Jews. I am doing the Lord's work." To fit his own beliefs, Hitler twisted Christian dogma, which holds that Mary, the mother of Jesus, conceived without physical intercourse, that Jesus' father was God, not Mary's husband, Joseph. Therefore, Hitler declared, Jesus was not Jewish, neatly forgetting that Mary very much was. To persuade the masses, however, the Nazi Party's official doctrine stated that Jesus was a *Mischlinge*, a nonpracticing half-Jew. With this nonpracticing half-Jew's blessing, Hitler claimed, he would rid the world of Jews.

At 2:10 P.M. on April 11, 1945, a contingent of General Patton's Third Army rolled past a camp in a wooded area located about four miles from the German city of Weimar. It was the first sign that the Americans were coming, and by ones and twos the SS prison guards abandoned their posts, ran into the woods, where they changed into civilian clothing, and emerged claiming to know nothing about any concentration camp a few feet away.

About two and a half hours after Patton's tanks passed by, an American civilian and a lieutenant assigned to Gen. Omar Bradley's Twelfth Army were in a jeep driving toward the camp, when they saw "thousands of ragged, hungry-looking men, marching in orderly formations," armed with rifles, rocket launchers, and "potato masher" hand grenades. "They laughed and waved wildly as they walked," civilian Egon Fleck and army 1st Lt. Edward Tenenbaum reported on April 12, 1945. "These were the inmates of Buchenwald, walking out to war." Fleck and Tenenbaum were met by a prisoners' militia, inmates who earlier had sneaked weapons into the camp and, once their Nazi guards ran off, took control. Fleck and Tenenbaum were the first Americans to willingly enter an occupied German concentration camp. Twenty-one thousand inmates remained at Buchenwald. When Fleck and Tenenbaum's jeep rolled into the camp, they were surrounded by thousands of dirty, malnourished former prisoners, many of them clearly close to death. They were so weakened that within a week, more than a thousand died. Only later did Fleck and Tenenbaum realize that perhaps half of the camp's population, another 20,000 or so, had only recently been murdered and cremated or removed to another camp for execution.

Weimar was the capital of the short-lived Weimar Republic after World War I. Buchenwald was built outside the city to serve a nearby munitions plant. Thousands of Jews, mentally ill patients, dissidents, and others were rounded up and taken to the camp, where their SS guards worked them until the prisoners could work no more, and then they murdered them. Often, while still alive, prisoners were hung from ceiling-mounted meat hooks and their heads were bashed in with large clubs. Their bodies were stripped of everything the Nazi regime believed useful—from gold teeth to glasses to hair—then their emaciated bodies were cremated.

Days after Buchenwald was liberated, photographer Margaret Bourke-White arrived, and her pictures that were published in *Life* magazine shocked the world. CBS correspondent Edward R. Murrow also came and told of walking into what originally had been a stable for eighty horses.

There were 1,200 men in it, five to a bunk. The stink was beyond all description. . . . I asked how many men had died in that building during the last month. . . . They totaled 242. . . . In another part of camp they showed me the children, hundreds of them. Some were only six. One rolled up his sleeves, showed me his number. It was tattooed on his arm . . . B-6030, it was.

Murrow closed his radio report by saying:

I pray you to believe what I have said about Buchenwald. I reported what I saw and heard, but only part of it. For most of it, I have no words.

There would be more. On April 15, just four days later, the British army stumbled into Bergen-Belsen, near the city of Hannover, and even more prisoners there, even more dying of typhus and typhoid. Two weeks later, on April 29, American forces discovered the camp at Dachau, near Munich, with fifty railroad cars full of terribly emaciated bodies piled up "like twisted branches of cut-down trees." General Patton's Third Army liberated Mauthausen on May 3, and one of Patton's subordinates wrote that "the smell, the odor . . . burn in the nostrils and memory. I will always smell Mauthausen."

Sachsenhausen and Ravensbrück and Theresienstadt were to come. Gradually, anyone who cared to look at the evidence saw the brutality and inhumanity of the Nazi regime.

As part of his *Lebensraum* program, Hitler had launched the largest and most systematic campaign ever of racial genocide. There are claims that the rest of the world knew nothing about his attempt to extinguish the Jewish people, but clearly this is not so. Anti-Semitic writings and laws came almost as soon as Hitler and the Nazi Party took power. By the 1920s, right-wing Germans had begun their campaign against Jews, scrawling on the walls and windows of Jewish-owned stores *Juda Verrecke!* (Death to Judaism). The German word *verrecke* previously had been used only in describing the killing of cattle.

In *Mein Kampf*, Adolf Hitler stated repeatedly his views on "racial purity." By the time he'd become chancellor in 1933, there was little doubt what he would do. It would come in four phases:

(1) Economic persecution,

(2) Enactment of laws removing Jews from Germany's mainstream of life,

(3) Rounding up Jews and forcing them to migrate to other countries, and

(4) Elimination of all Jews.

On April 1, 1933, phase one began, with Hitler repeating, "I believe that I act today in unison with the Almighty Creator's intention: by fighting Jews I do battle for the Lord." On that same day, propaganda minister Joseph Goebbels wrote in his diary:

The boycott against the international atrocity propaganda has burst forth in full force in Berlin and the whole Reich. I drive along the Tauentzien Street in order to observe the situation. All Jewish businesses are closed. SA men are posted outside their entrances. The public has everywhere proclaimed its solidarity. The discipline is exemplary.

Again, on April 2, Goebbels wrote:

> The effects of the boycott are already clearly noticeable. The world is gradually coming to its senses. It will learn to understand that it is not wise to let itself be informed on Germany by the Jewish emigrés. We will carry out a campaign of mental conquest in the world as effective as that which we have carried out in Germany itself.

Hitler removed Jews and all persons who were non-Aryans from the German civil service; within a year, he eliminated them from banks, the stock exchange, journalism, law, and medicine. There was very little hedging in the new German law: "Civil servants of non-Aryan descent must retire. . . . Officials who are retired or dismissed . . . are not granted a pension, if they have not completed a ten-year service." The only exceptions were for those Jews who had fought for Germany during World War I or those who had been in the civil service since 1914.

Next came the Law Against the Overcrowding of German Schools and Institutions of Higher Learning. It inaugurated a strict limitation of the number of Jewish students in secondary and higher education; again, children of veterans were exempted.

On September 15, 1935, at the annual Nazi Party rally in Nuremberg, the German parliament proclaimed two additional laws, which would become centerpieces of anti-Jewish legislation in the Reich:

> A subject of the state is a person who enjoys the protection of the German Reich. . . .
> A Reich citizen is a subject of the state who is of German and related blood. . . .

Once Hitler had restricted citizenship to persons of "German or kindred blood," he could dictate other matters:

> Marriages between Jews and subjects of German or kindred blood are forbidden. Marriages nevertheless concluded are invalid, even if concluded abroad to circumvent this law.

Extramarital intercourse between Jews and subjects of German or kindred blood is forbidden.

The new law stipulated that a man violating the law "will be punished either by imprisonment or penal servitude"; however, no specific punishment was listed for a woman. Another new law of September 15, 1935, dealt with other situations.

Jews must not employ in their households female subjects of German or kindred blood who are under forty-five years old.
Jews are forbidden to fly the Reich national flag and to display the Reich colors.

One important item was missing from these new laws: just who was a Jew or "German or kindred blood." Two months later, officials tried to fill in the missing piece: full-Jew (having three Jewish grandparents), and part-Jew (everyone else who had Jewish blood). Soon, the category of half-Jew took a new meaning: *Mischlinge* (or mongrel). Still working to revise the Nazi Party interpretation, the Reich came up with first-class *Mischlinge* (those descended from two Jewish grandparents, "but not practicing Judaism and not married to a Jewish spouse") and second-class *Mischlinge* (individuals with only one Jewish grandparent).

This led to a new occupation in Germany—licensed family researcher—as individuals raced to clarify (often to lie about) their heritage in order to survive.

In a speech to the German Reichstag on January 30, 1939, hinting broadly that Jews would precipitate a war, Adolf Hitler said, if this occurred, the result would be the *Venichtung*, the destruction of all Jews. Seven months later, Hitler precipitated a war: he invaded Poland.

On September 21, Gestapo chief Reinhard Heydrich issued a secret memo on the "Jewish Question in Occupied Territory." On principle, he said, "Jewish communities of less than five hundred persons are to be dissolved and transferred to the nearest concentration center." Further, certain areas of Poland would become *Judenrein,* that is, free of Jews, and "a few concentration centers are to be set up, so as to facilitate subsequent measures." All Jews in Poland would be clustered into small areas, called ghettos. In April 1940, the Jewish ghetto in Lodz was sealed. It had become, in a definition going back to medieval times, a pale, "a district within determined bounds, or subject to a particular jurisdiction." In fifteenth-century Ireland, The Pale was the area around Dublin controlled by the English; that is, the English kept the Irish outside The Pale. In twentieth-century Poland, it was exactly the opposite; Germany kept the Jews inside The Pale.

The largest ghetto was at Warsaw. German troops evacuated all non-Jews from a section of town and ordered a ten-foot-high brick wall built around it; they made the *Judenrat,* the Jewish Council, pay for the wall that held them in. In November 1940, with more than 360,000 people inside the ghetto, the Germans ordered it sealed off from the rest of Warsaw. Inside the ghetto, about 5,000 people a month died. Typhus reached epidemic intensity. Still, the population of the Warsaw ghetto remained the same because the German army continued to pack it with Jews from other areas of Poland.

Escapees from the death camp at Treblinka told those in the Warsaw ghetto about the gas chambers, and the Jews planned a revolt. On January 18, 1943, they fired at their SS guards, using weapons they'd hidden away. When snipers killed about forty guards, the Germans took reprisals; about a thousand Jews were killed.

When the guards backed off a bit, ghetto inmates turned it into a honeycomb of tunnels and passages. They divided themselves into about twenty groups, armed with guns slipped in by Christians outside the ghetto.

But on the dawn of Passover on April 19, 1943, about 2,000 men entered the ghetto, backed up with tanks. Defenders attacked one tank with Molotov cocktails. The tank didn't stop, but neither did the ghetto's defenders. The commander of the German force later wrote a report to Heinrich Himmler:

> Over and over again, new battle groups consisting of twenty to thirty or more Jewish fellows, eighteen to twenty-five years of age, accompanied by a corresponding number of women, kindled new resistance.

• • •

After five days, the commandant of the German guards decided "to destroy the entire Jewish area by setting every block on fire." On May 16, he declared the ghetto "no longer in existence." He had killed between 5,000 and 6,000 Jews, although many others escaped to revolt again.

On July 31, 1941, Hermann Göring ordered Reinhard Heydrich to prepare a plan "showing the measures for organization and action necessary to carry out the final solution of the Jewish question." The policy was euphemistically called "resettlement."

SS *Einsatzgruppen*, action groups, would round up Jews by the thousands, "driving them to pits and gullie and shooting them en masse." The *Einsatzgruppen* followed the German army into the Soviet Union. First, they rounded up and murdered any they said were "Bolsheviks." Later, it was "Asiatic inferiors," "Gypsies," and "useless eaters," this last meaning the mentally or terminally ill. One specific report mentions killing 6,400 Polish mental patients.

Shortly after the German army captured Kiev, the capital of Ukraine, the Soviet secret police fought back by blowing up several German-held buildings. In retaliation, the German army issued the following order:

Kikes of the city of Kiev and surroundings!
On Monday, September 29, you are to appear at 7:00 A.M. with your possessions, money, documents, valuables, and warm clothing. . . .
Failure to appear is punishable by death.

From near a Jewish cemetery where they gathered, the Jews were marched to a place called Babi Yar. Under armed guard, thirty to forty people at a time were ordered to strip. Their clothing and valuables were gathered up and taken away. And then in a ravine SS action groups murdered them. They murdered thousands of them.

In *Witness to the Holocaust,* historian Michael Bernbaum writes, "The bodies of old men rested on the bodies of children who lay on their dead mothers." In *Hitler's Willing Executioners,* Daniel Jonah

Goldhagen says, "More than thirty-three thousand Jews . . . men, women and babies, were . . . lined up and machine-gunned." In *Europe: A History*, Norman Davies sets the number murdered at Babi Yar far higher—as many as 70,000.

During the Nuremberg trials beginning in November 1945, Otto Ohlendorf, commander of *Einsatzgruppe* D, testified about the killing of thousands of people. Colonel John Harlan Amen (associate trial counsel for the United States) questioned Ohlendorf:

Colonel Amen: Did you personally supervise mass executions of these individuals?

Ohlendorf: I was present at two mass executions for purposes of inspection. . . . A local *Einsatzkommando* [action group section] attempted to collect all the Jews in its area by registering them. This registration was performed by the Jews themselves.

Colonel Amen: On what pretext, if any, were they rounded up?

Ohlendorf: On the pretext that they were to be resettled. . . .[They] were later transported to the place of execution, which was, as a rule, an antitank ditch or a natural excavation. The executions were carried out in a military manner, by firing squads. . . .

Colonel Amen: In what positions were the victims shot?

Ohlendorf: Standing or kneeling. . . .

Colonel Amen: Were all victims, including the men, women, and children, executed in the same manner?

Ohlendorf: Until the spring of 1942, yes. Then an order came from [SS head Heinrich] Himmler that in the future the women and children were to be killed only in gas vans. . . .

Colonel Amen: How were the victims induced to enter the vans?

Ohlendorf: They were told that they were to be transported to another locality. . . .

Colonel Amen: How long did it take to kill the victims ordinarily?

Ohlendorf: About ten to fifteen minutes; the victims were not conscious of what was happening to them.

Later, Ohlendorf was questioned by another member of the court. Why, he was asked, did SS action groups carry out these executions? Ohlendorf replied, "Because to me it is inconceivable that a subordinate leader should not carry out orders given by the leaders of the state." In other words, they were only carrying out orders.

In January 1942, SS chiefs held a one-day conference to coordinate technical arrangements for Hitler's "final solution." They talked about acceleration of experiments with Zyklon-B, a chemical used to produce lethal gas. The I. G. Farben Corporation originally marketed Zyklon-B for pest control. In murdering Jews, Zyklon-B was first used at Auschwitz, where the amethyst blue crystals were dropped into chambers disguised as shower baths.

At that final solution meeting, Nazi leaders decided to create a number of camps dedicated to death—Chelmno, Belzec, Sobibór, and Treblinka. They would also expand Nazi concentration camps in occupied Poland—Auschwitz and Birkenau. To dispose of dead bodies, they would consult one of Germany's best firms in the designing of crematoriums, Topf & Sons. And they would draw up routes and timetables for rail transportation. They referred to prisoners as "units," and the units to be murdered numbered from 7 million to 8 million.

The city of Auschwitz was founded in 1270. When Germany occupied Poland in 1939, it built a concentration camp outside the city. Until 1941, it held about 9,000 prisoners. When Germany invaded the Soviet Union, thousands of prisoners of war were sent to Auschwitz, and the camp had to be expanded. Of 12,000 Soviet prisoners sent to Auschwitz in December 1941, only 150 survived the winter. Another camp—Birkenau—was already in the area. When the Auschwitz camp needed to be enlarged, the facility at Birkenau was incorporated as a killing camp.

A former commandant of Auschwitz, Rudolf Höss, boasted that he ran "the greatest extermination center of all time." In less than two months—May 15 to July 7, 1944—Nazi Germany shipped 437,000 Jews to Auschwitz. Höss first used carbon monoxide to murder the victims, but that wasn't fast enough, so he changed to Zyklon-B gas and his death toll escalated. When the Topf & Sons ovens could not cope with the number of corpses, Höss ordered huge pits excavated and the bodies buried. Within a 46-day period, between 250,000 and 300,000 victims were gassed or shot. He bragged that it took "from three to fifteen minutes to kill the people in the death chamber. . . . We knew when the people were dead because their screaming stopped." When the bodies were removed, he admitted, "our special commandos took off the rings and extracted the gold from the teeth of the corpses." The record at Auschwitz was 34,000 people murdered and their bodies cremated or buried in 24 hours.

As new prisoners arrived at Auschwitz, they were met by the camp physician, Dr. Joseph Mengele. As Mengele called out "Right" or "Left," one group went to work squads and the other to the gas chambers. At times, an orchestra made up of pretty young inmate girls wearing navy blue skirts and white blouses played music. Dr. Mengele's favorite was said to be "The Merry Widow."

Those who were chosen for work detail, through whatever method of selection Mengele used, were sent to the I. G. Farben plants, where they often produced the Zyklon-B they had escaped. Their escape wasn't for long; if they missed the gas chamber, they likely as not starved to death.

Rudolf Höss was convicted of war crimes and hanged on April 7, 1945, at Auschwitz.

It was to Auschwitz that young Anne Frank and her family were taken in August 1944. They had been in hiding, in a secret annex above a Dutch family's warehouse in Amsterdam, since 1941. "Who has inflicted this upon us?" Anne wrote in her now famous diary.

It is God that has made us as we are, but it will be God, too, who will raise us up again. If we bear all this suffering and if there are still Jews left, when it is over, then Jews, instead of being doomed, will be held up as an example.

Anne's mother died at Auschwitz, but Anne and her older sister, Margot, were seemingly given a reprieve. In early spring of 1945 they were sent to Bergen-Belsen. In March, 20,000 prisoners at Bergen-

Belsen were murdered, including Anne and Margot. British forces liberated the camp a month later, on April 14, 1945.

Only Otto Frank, the girls' father, survived. After he was freed, he returned to Amsterdam and visited the warehouse where he and his family had spent so many months in hiding. On the floor, among the debris caused by Gestapo agents tearing up the secret annex, was Anne's book, the *Diary of a Young Girl*.

Treblinka was built in a pine forest sixty-two miles northwest of Warsaw, Poland. It was the fourth-largest death camp; Auschwitz, Buchenwald, and Dachau were bigger. More than 800,000 people were sent to Treblinka, although it was not meant to be a concentration camp to hold prisoners; it was designed to be a death camp. Prisoners built the camp; then, to keep it secret, the prisoners were executed. They were replaced by a permanent cadre, *Hofjuden*, the Court Jews, who maintained the camp and served the SS supervisors and Ukrainian guards.

Death camps were built near rail centers. As with other camps, a special spur line was run off the main rail line to take the prisoners to Treblinka. Signs at a building designed to look like a provincial railroad station read: "Tailors" and "Carpenters." Incoming prisoners were made to believe they had been sent to a work center.

Guards held men near the railroad tracks, the women and children were taken off to "showers." Later, it was the men's turn, except for the 200 or so chosen to survive long enough to help the guards. Some male Jews, the *Totenjuden* (Jews of Death, by the guards) removed the bodies from the gas chambers. Another group, known as the "dentists," were ordered to pull any gold-filled teeth from the victims and to remove any jewels that had been concealed. The *Totenjuden* then dumped the bodies into ditches. *Platzjuden* (Jews of the Square) searched the victims' clothing and other personal items piled up outside the shower-death chambers, then separated the items into various categories for disposal by the SS.

Other prisoners scorned the Jews of Death, but on August 3, 1943, the *Totenjuden* revolted. It began when a young *Totenjuden* saw his wife and child taken to the gas chamber. He pulled out a hidden knife and stabbed a guard to death. That set other prisoners to thinking.

A fifty-year-old doctor from Warsaw, Julian Chorazyski, gathered a small group of other *Totenjuden* and began plotting. Using a crude but effective key to the armory, they stole weapons.

When a group of prisoners from Warsaw arrived and told other inmates of the revolt in the ghetto, it spurred on the *Totenjuden*. They set a time—5 P.M. on August 2, 1943. They would ambush the guards who were the chief murderers, disarm them all, cut the telephone wires to the outside, and destroy the death showers and crematorium. They would burn the camp to the ground using stolen gasoline. Finally, as they fled the burning camp, they planned to free other Poles held nearby.

At first, 60 or 70 prisoners knew about the planned revolt, but when they put their plan into action, more than 700 joined them. They set fire to the gas chambers, shot a guard and his dog, and attacked other Germans with axes and shovels. They burned the barracks. The fire aroused guards, however, and SS and police arrived from a nearby airfield, quickly attacking rebel prisoners. Only about 150 inmates managed to escape from the camp and the others were rounded up and killed. Perhaps a dozen got away. Twenty German guards were killed in the revolt.

When Soviet liberation forces arrived at Treblinka a year later, only 40 of the former prisoners were still alive. They were the only known survivors of Treblinka. In the three years of Treblinka's existence, 840,000 prisoners were executed there. Nearly all of them were Jews.

Two months after the revolt at Treblinka, prisoners at Sobibór camp also revolted, overpowering the guards, seizing the camp armory, and running off. Nine SS died in the revolt along with two foreign guards; approximately 300 prisoners temporarily escaped. Most were rounded up and shot.

A year later, on July 24, 1944, prisoners revolted at the largest camp—Auschwitz. It was not long after the camp's record-setting day of death. Soviet troops were moving toward the camp, and it wouldn't be long before they got there. Uncertain whether they should destroy the evidence of the crematoriums, camp officials decided instead to speed up the rate of execution.

That was just what the Polish underground was afraid of, and they tried to get word to the outside world about what was happening. The resistance leaders couldn't convince anybody themselves, so they decided to sneak a prisoner out of the camp; a former prisoner might be able to convince people of the truth. It wasn't easy; the combined Auschwitz-Birkenau facility was encircled by electrified barbed wire, deep ditches, and high watchtowers, and a 40-kilometer area around the camp was declared off-limits to civilians. Of the 230 attempted escapes during the camp's existence, only 80 or so individuals made it out; five of these were aided by the underground in the closing weeks of the war. Those five gave detailed eyewitness testimonials, suggesting the Allies should bomb Auschwitz. For all the good it did.

The Allied command declined, saying that bombers could not be spared. The U.S. assistant secretary of war, John J. McCloy, said that even if bombing the camp were practicable, it "might provoke even more vindictive [acts] by the Germans." With no outside help, the prisoners tried to destroy Auschwitz themselves.

Twenty-three-year-old Rosa Robota, who worked in the camp clothing section, had friends who worked in the Krupp's explosives plant at Auschwitz. The underground asked Rosa if she would get her friends to steal bomb-making material. Rosa hated the Germans and jumped at the chance. Soon, she had 20 young women smuggling dynamite and explosive charges out of the Krupp plant and into the camp, hiding the material in their bras. Inside the camp, a Russian prisoner packed the explosive materials into empty sardine cans. One bomb was located near the crematoriums by an inmate being forced to work there.

The guards' system was to use a group of prisoners to work the crematoriums, then gas those prisoners, and have a new set of prisoners load in the previous workers' bodies. Shortly before the revolt could begin, however, the man who had hidden the bombs near the crematorium learned that he was about to be executed. Instead of waiting for the August 2 target date, he blew up one of the crematoriums. About 600 prisoners escaped in the melee, but the Nazi guards chased them down and killed them all.

Through an informant, guards traced the explosives to Rosa Robota, and she was locked up. A friend managed to see her and said he could hardly recognize Rosa because she had been so badly beaten. Rosa said she'd taken the blame herself; as he left, she repeated the Hebrew greeting of the Hashomer Hatzair: "*Khazak v' hamatz*"—Be strong and live.

Over the years, there have been attempts to deny the Holocaust, saying that no one, no group could or would commit such a crime. It is, however, a simple matter of looking at the numbers. When World War II ended, there were from 5 million to 7 million fewer Jews in Europe than there were before. They were murdered by Nazi Germany. As high as 72 percent of prewar Jews were murdered from 1939 to 1945.

Which leads us to the question: How much did the outside world know, and when did it know it? Clearly, President Franklin D. Roosevelt knew about the treatment Jews were receiving in Germany and the rest of Europe. Yet, just as clearly, the knowledge that Hitler was out to rid the world of Jews and anyone else he disliked—Russians, Poles, and the mentally retarded—was not regarded as critical in the fighting of World War II.

When did Roosevelt and the rest of the world learn the Holocaust was under way? On October 30, 1939, the *New York Times* predicted, "Complete elimination of Jews from European life now appears to be fixed German policy." Freight car loads of Germans, it said, were heading eastward—"freight cars, but they are full of people."

There was worldwide newspaper and radio coverage of what Adolf Hitler proclaimed in *Mein Kampf* and what he and his Nazi cohorts did, beginning almost as soon as he took office.

In 1940, Adolf Eichmann of the Reich Security Main Office (the German initials are RSHA) was asked to develop a plan to deport 4 million Jews to the Vichy-controlled island of Madagascar. On January 20, 1942, he attended the Wannsee Conference, at which plans for the "final solution" were set in motion.

When the Japanese bombed Pearl Harbor and the United States declared war on Germany, Italy, and Japan, American newspaper reporters left Germany. This was before the Wannsee Conference and before the first use of Zyklon-B gas in August, so many of the details of the Holocaust weren't known until after the war. Much of what was going on in Nazi Germany, however, was already common knowledge, and more was learned from neutral government sources. On

June 30, 1942, the *New York Times* ran an article entitled "A Vast Slaughterhouse," which recounted: "1,000,000 Jews Slain By Nazis." Two days later the *Times* reported that the Polish government in London had urged the execution of Nazis in retaliation for the mass slaying. And on July 17, 1942, Berlin radio itself announced the arrest of 20,000 Jews in Paris; those arrested would be deported to Eastern Europe. Five days later, Germany began the "resettlement" of the remaining 380,000 Polish Jews to the Warsaw ghetto. The reports were not idle speculation; they were widely confirmed. Did London or Washington know about this, and if so, what would happen to these 400,000 people?

What did FDR believe would happen to them? In a letter read to a rally of 20,000 in New York City's Madison Square Garden, President Roosevelt said:

> The Nazis will not succeed in exterminating their victims any more than they will succeed in enslaving mankind. The American people not only sympathize with all victims of Nazi crimes but will hold the perpetrators of these crimes to strict accountability in a day of reckoning which will surely come.

Former Auschwitz commandant Rudolf Höss wrote in a death-cell autobiography:

> I had to watch coldly as mothers with laughing or crying children went to the gas-chambers. I had to stand for hours on end in the ghastly stench. I had to look through the peepholes . . . and watch the process of death itself. My family, for sure, were well provided for at Auschwitz. When I saw my children playing happily, or observed my wife's delight in our youngest, the thought would often come over me, how long will our happiness last.

Höss knew and watched as thousands upon thousands died. Germany knew, and turned its head. The world knew, and we were all shamed.

EPILOGUE

Peace as a Personal Thought:
What Will Happen if Tomorrow Comes?

Peace is not an absence of war, it is a virtue, a state of mind, a disposition for benevolence, confidence, justice.
—Benedict Spinoza, *Theological-Political Treatise, 1670*

*Ef you want peace, the thing you've gut to du
Is jes' to show you're up to fightin', tu.*
—James Russell Lowell, *The Biglow Papers,* No. 2, 1848

I was not quite four years old when Pearl Harbor was attacked. I grew up in Portsmouth, Virginia, an area whose military density ranks among the highest in the world; the navy yard, a naval base, a couple of naval air stations, soldiers, sailors, air force types, and marines by the hundreds of thousands. Servicemen used to walk the streets, and make their presence known in many ways. At the height of World War II, our downtown streets resembled fields of marshmallows; groups of sailors in distinctive white caps bobbed and weaved along block after block, stopped in bars here, shopped in stores there. The fleet was always in, the navy was always on the prowl.

Early on in life, I was caught up in a wave of patriotism. It wasn't my wave, of course; truly, I did not know what was going on. However, I was a cute, cuddly, blond boy soprano suited up to look like Uncle Sam, complete with top hat and a glued-on cottonball beard. I made my debut as a professional singer (salary was ten dollars) with a one-song act: "The Chattanooga Choo-Choo." The lyrics has been rewritten (without regard to copyright) by a family member to reflect the fever of the war.

They brought me on to close the show. Family legend has it that this cute, cuddly, and blond Uncle Sam sang his war-inspired song, and audiences loved both of us, song and singer. I hardly remember those changed lyrics, only the last line, which went something like, "Wooo Wooo, Tokyo, here we come!"

It's just as well I can't remember more of the lyrics; undoubtedly today they'd be declared jingoistic and racist. It was, after all, a time of Us vs. Them.

I remember going back out on stage to sing an encore. I hadn't been asked, but I did it anyway. I didn't have a second song to sing, so I sang my revised "Chattanooga Choo-Choo" a second time. More applause. Finally, someone pulled me off the stage, otherwise, I probably would have sung it a third time.

Memory and time do strange things; Uncle Sam's cottonball beard has been replaced with an almost equally white one that's real.

The hardships and fervor of the times were everpresent but misunderstood emotions in my young life. Take rationing. To me, the rationing of gasoline meant that we had to use the trolley to go to the local amusement park or go fishing. We had a B ration, meaning that the family car was needed for work; it wasn't to be used for recreation. Meat rationing never really hit home, even though, officially, the government called for "Meatless Tuesday" and "Meatless Friday." A couple members of our family owned farms, which in the South meant that we seldom had a shortage of meat, certainly not pork. I once found a couple dozen round red meat ration points lying on the street; I took them home, proud to contribute to our family's larder. They weren't really needed. In addition to family farm ties, we may have bought meat on the black market, which wouldn't have been beyond some of my relatives.

With butter and sugar rationed, I got fewer cookies than I would have liked; however, someone came up with a substitute for jam—flour, water, and food coloring mixed with a little sugar. As I remember, it wasn't particularly good. Another family member concocted his own mayonnaise.

As a six year old, alcoholic shortages didn't bother me, not that a lack of legal booze ever stopped many other Americans, anyway. Prohibition wasn't long dead, so people remembered how to make their own.

Individuals who didn't use a particular product—say, coffee—could trade their ration coupons for others they *could* use—say, for shoes; with two growing boys in our family, we always needed new shoes. Women's stockings not only were rationed, generally they were just plain unavailable; some women even drew lines down the backs of their legs to give the appearance of wearing hose. After the war, of course, when stockings again became available, seamless stockings became all the rage.

We planted tomatoes, beans, collard greens (it was the South, remember), and corn. Through the summer and fall my grandmother canned vegetables. We never managed to consume them all. No, food rationing wasn't a problem for us, yet it remains the strongest memory of World War II for many Americans today.

It was not unusual in the early 1940s to see boys and girls wearing "uniforms." A family picture shows my brother and myself wearing pint-sized sailor suits, that is if the pints were rather rotund. Underweight we were not, and in fact, his wasn't a *costume* sailor suit but the real thing, cut down only in the sleeves and pant legs. He was larger than some members of the fleet, and the shore patrol once stopped him and made him take off the unit decorations and stripes. During the Korean War, he won decorations and stripes on his own, but the World War II shore patrol rightly figured that he was large enough to generate questions. At the time, he was about the age of Calvin Graham, America's youngest sailor at age twelve.

Friends and relatives, I realized, were gone to places I'd never heard of, gone to fight a war, and, on occasion, they never returned. In our front window, we hung a white banner with red fringe and two blue stars in the center, indicating that two of our family members, my mother's brothers, were on active military duty. Other such banners hung all along our street, some with blue stars, some with gold. Gold indicated that some soldier or sailor or airman had died while in service. The issue of blue versus gold wasn't yet clear in my mind, and I remember asking why our banner had only blue stars. Until I finally realized the difference, I was jealous of those gold stars. Such is childhood ignorance and innocence.

The war left me with memories strong enough to grab onto half a century later. My conscience twinges when I open a can of tuna fish and toss away the empty can. I'd often watch my grandmother perform the fine art of tin can opening, World War II style, never completely cutting off the top and bottom but leaving them as hinges. She'd strip off the paper label, wash the empty can, fold in the hinged lids, and, with the can on the floor, allow me to jump up and down on it to flatten it out. Into the pile it went, ready for what today we call recycling. Tin cans would win the war, I truly believed. We all have to stick together to win this one, you know.

We saved everything: fat—one pound contained enough glycerin to make a pound of gunpowder; scrap metal—iron from an old shovel could be recycled into a hand grenade; rubber—it took 124 salvaged used auto tires to build one 28-ton tank (rubber bands and pencil erasers were suddenly scarce). "Every attic, every garage, every farmyard is a mile of scrap metal," we were told in *Youth Goes to War,* a chest-thumping book aimed at high school boys and girls. "Every able bodied boy is destined at the appointed age for the armed services. The tempo of war is such that a complex college education is impossible."

We'd go to a movie and, before the feature, the house lights would be turned up and the National Anthem would be played. We'd stand at attention, hands over hearts, and sing about our pride. Can you imagine doing that today?

House lights still up, we'd be called on to contribute to the war effort by buying War Bonds and Stamps. Or as Bugs Bunny would sing in a still famous cartoon, "the tall man with the high hat and whiskers on his chin" wanted us to buy War Bonds. President Roosevelt purchased the first Series E bond on May 1, 1941. "Any bonds today?" Bugs Bunny asked. "Bonds for freedom. . . ." Part of the cartoon would be politically incorrect in the 1990s—Bugs in blackface doing an Al Jolson imitation: "Sammy, my Uncle Sammy. . ." The cartoon pitch ended with Bugs and Porky Pig and Elmer Fudd all in uniform, all marching our way, calling on us to help out the war effort. They set up War Bond and War Stamp booths in the theater lobby next to the popcorn stand.

These bonds were, of course, low-interest loans made to the U.S. government by private citizens. A $25 bond cost $18.75, and we'd make $6.25 profit after ten years. That was an annual interest rate of 1.8 percent, pretty low compared to the 4.25 percent interest on similar bonds issued in World War I, but we bought them anyway, more than $190 billion worth during World War II.

Tuesday was Stamp Day at school. Save enough 25¢ stamps, paste them in a War Bond book, and we'd get a $25 Series E War Bond.

One by one on Stamp Day we'd proudly walk up to the teacher's desk and plunk down palm-wet coins to buy stamps to pay for the fight. If we didn't have coins, we'd pretend; we'd knock on the teacher's desk, as if we were plunking down real money. No one was cruel to those who couldn't afford to buy War Stamps; at least my adult memory disclaims such cruelty.

"Any stamps and bonds today?" A penny saved on Stamps was more than a dollar earned on War Bonds, and we helped defeat Hitler with his funny mustache and Tojo with his shiny bald head. About fifteen years ago, I found a partially completed book of saving stamps tucked away in an old chest. I cashed it in for about five dollars. "The tall man with the high hat and whiskers on his chin" repaid my loan.

On May 7, 1945, we read in my hometown newspaper, the *Portsmouth Star.* "Germany Surrenders; End is Unconditional. Bulletin London, May 7—AP—The greatest war in history ended today with the unconditional surrender of Germany." A subheadline set everybody straight: "People Realize Big Task Ahead." The following day an ad in the *Norfolk Virginian-Pilot* from across the river spelled out just what that task was:

> Don't forget. . . We are still at war with the Japs.
> Stay at your job.
> Keep buying War Bonds so we can finish the Nips off in a hurry."

The finish came three months later with Hiroshima and Nagasaki.

On Sunday, August 12, an erroneous report interrupted the *American Album of Familiar Music* radio program, claiming President Harry S Truman had announced the Japanese surrender. Celebrators flooded streets, honking horns, and people everywhere cheered. In my hometown, someone started a crap game in the middle of the main street, but police were busy with serious incidents and didn't bother about it.

But the Sunday announcement was premature. Somehow, it got into the United Press wire and was sent throughout the country. We were still at war. Never mind, we'd celebrate again when the real end came. Two days later, the real end did come, and we did celebrate.

I was seven years old the summer of 1945, and I sold newspapers on the street corner. Gangs of us would buy papers for two cents a copy and sell them for a nickel each, a three-cent profit. Sell thirty-four papers and earn a dollar. A seven year old who ended the day with a dollar profit from selling newspapers on the street corner believed he was rich. I'd like to say I contributed my profits to the family coffers to help out when money was tight, but undoubtedly I devoted most of it to ice cream, a product to which I'm still inordinately devoted.

On the afternoon of August 14, I'd just bought my usual load of twenty-five copies of the hometown *Portsmouth Star*. I paraded up and down, calling out in my loudest boy soprano voice, "*Star* paper! *Portsmouth Star!* Getcha *Portsmouth Star!*" I'd sold only about half a dozen or so when sirens from the nearby navy yard went off and church bells pealed and people began running up and down the streets, running around in circles crying out, "It's over! The war is over! Japan has surrendered!"

No dummy, I instantly realized that the copies of the regular edition of the newspaper I had were worthless. They carried nothing about that day's end of the war, only broad hints that it was coming soon. I headed for the nearest trash barrel to toss them away, ready to run back to the newspaper distribution center. Good newspaperman that I was, I knew they'd be putting out an *Extra! Extra! War Ends!* edition about the end of the war.

Before I reached the trash barrel, a man saw me with newspapers under my arm and demanded to buy one. I hesitated only a second before handing one over in exchange for—"Praise the Lord and Pass the Ammunition!"—a whole dollar. My day was made. Then my customer saw that what he'd bought wasn't the anticipated *Extra!* but just the regular war-might-end-any-day-now edition. You cheated me, he said, or something to that effect, and he threw away his newly bought but worthless newspaper. However, he didn't ask for his dollar back, and I wasn't about to offer to return it. Ethics and honesty go only so far on the day a world war ends and you're seven years old.

Running to buy the *Extra!* edition that I knew would be coming out, I met my brother headed for the same destination. He's older than I, and it was he who first turned me on to the life of a street vendor. Now, the war was over and we were about to make childhood fortunes selling newspapers at exorbitant prices in the midst of growing chaos, confusion, and celebration.

The streets of that military town were full; thousands of those marshmallow-like sailor hats were being tossed into the air, picked up, and tossed again. Torn bits of paper filled the air. Telephone books, maybe even that regular edition of the *Star* I'd sold for a buck and seen thrown away. Office workers danced in the streets, strangers kissed strangers, even kissed a cute, cuddly, blond newspaperboy whose only thought was to get those *Extra!* editions and, if things worked out, maybe even make five whole dollars.

Radios blared from shops along the street, martial music and ecstatic annoucers: The war in the Pacific was over. Japanese emperor Hirohito had ordered the government of Japan to sue for peace. It came three months and seven days after Germany surrendered to the Allies. It was official, and we celebrated with car horns and street dancing and people cheering and, I hoped, with *Extras!* selling at outrageous prices.

Somewhere, a hand held down a siren and soon others joined in; noise grew to a cacophony. Streets were jammed by horn-honking cars, by cheering people, by sailors joining hands to dance. Seamen in their white pajama-like uniforms pulled women into their cavorting circles, and together they sang "Roll Out the Barrel, We'll Have a Barrel of Fun!"

The barrel was dry that day. The Virginia Alcoholic Beverage Control Commission (the ABC Board) had ordered all sales of liquor prohibited; bars and taverns were closed, so sailors sat on curbs or overturned garbage cans, passing brown bags of anonymous bottles back and forth.

Excited girls kissed sailors and sailors kissed them right back. In the heat of the celebration, a motorist driving through the heart of the downtown area stopped for a red light. A sailor stuck his head through the rolled-down car window, and asked the driver, "May I kiss your wife, mister?" He didn't wait for permission, and the wife didn't complain. Everywhere, snake-dancing soldiers, sailors, and civilians clogged the streets, drinking, kissing, and singing. Everyone had a helluva good time.

Extra! Extra! Extra! Read all about it! "Japan Surrenders, End of War!

Emperor Accepts Allied Rule; MacArthur Supreme Commander." Newspapers were rolling off the presses and my brother and I wanted to get our share. The celebration surrounded us until my uncle drove up in his black 1940 Ford. He pulled my brother and me off the streets for our own safety. Safety? What about the fortunes we were about to make selling EXTRA! EXTRA! EXTRA! WAR ENDS! Forget it, my Uncle Pete said; I'm getting you off the streets. It's not safe.

Across the nation, millions of wildly happy Americans celebrated the end of the war, and President Truman hadn't even made the announcement. That didn't come until seven that night, Washington time. The celebration continued for more than a day.

The officially sanctioned V-J Day, September 2, was more somber. In Tokyo bay that day, representatives of Japan and the Allied nations met on board the USS *Missouri*. The Japanese delegation was erect and formal in top hats and cutaway coats. The British were less formal in khaki uniforms and neatly knotted neckties. Most of the American brass were tieless, certainly those in General MacArthur's close circle. MacArthur himself wore no necktie. He had on the same old crushed hat he'd worn the day he escaped from the Philippines, the same one he'd worn the day he waded ashore on his return. He wore an open-collared uniform shirt and he used a thirty-year-old Parker fountain pen to sign the instrument of surrender.

It was really over. Only I wasn't out on the street trying to sell newspapers that day. My family made certain I was safe at home. And a safe home, after all, was what the war was all about.

A newspaper cartoon shortly after the end of the World War II shows a middle-aged man sitting in his easy chair, surrounded by young children. He tells his wife, "I'm giving them a history lesson. I'm teaching them the war wasn't fought for nylons, gas, and girdles."

Home, that's what we fought for.

Those stars my family proudly displayed on our front-window banner remained blue, never changed to the gold stars of death, I'm happy to say. Still, there were far too many gold stars flying on banners across America and England, over Germany and Japan.

It's over now, all over. Everyone suffered. Neither side was innocent, and that is the way of war. Enemies may now be friends and get on with life.

SELECTED BIBLIOGRAPHY

UNPUBLISHED SOURCES AND PRIMARY WORKS

Brown, John Sloan. "Draftee Division: A Study of the 88th Infantry Division, First All Selective Service Division Into Combat in World War II." Ph.D. Dissertation, Indiana University.

Personal interview with Roger Harris, August 8, 1997.

Personal interview with Richard L. Wright, December 25, 1975.

Selective Service System, Special Monogram No. 8., National Archives.

Congressional Record. Vol. 88.

"The Battle of the Coral Sea: Strategical and Tactical Analysis." U.S. Naval War College.

Shafer, Boyd and Underhill, H. Faber. "Military Training in World War II." U.S. Army Military History Institute.

"War Ration Book One." Office of Price Stabilization.

World War II archives, Franklin D. Roosevelt Library, Hyde Park, New York.

Audio archival recording of crash of Hindenburg, Chicago, Illinois, Museum of Broadcast Communication.

Poster collection, U.S. Naval History Institute.

Army Pearl Harbor Board records. National Archives.

Franklin Delano Roosevelt memo January 22, 1941 to Army Adjutant General memo RG407, entry 360, box 3. National Archives.

Off the record personal interview with Fr. Coughlin, November 1972.

Douglas MacArthur biography, Douglas MacArthur Memorial, Norfolk, Virginia. Personal communication May 27, 1997.

Earl Warren, U.S. House Select Committee investigating National Defense Migration Hearings. National Archives.

Western Defense Command and Fourth Army Wartime Civil Control Administration posters, dated April 1, 1942 and April 20, 1942. National Archives.

Photograph of window in Japanese-American store. Oregon Historical Society.

Sommers, Stan. "American Ex-Prisoners of War." *National Medical Research Committee*, No. 8. National Archives.

Prisoner of War Circular No. 2, October 30, 1943. National Archives.

Seventh Service Command, conference of POW camp commanders, Omaha, Nebraska, March 24, 1944. National Archives.

Evelyn Hobson, "Ernie Pyle Correspondent," October 1, 1991. Ernie Pyle Historic Site, Dana, Indiana.

General Orders, Head Quarters, Middle-Brook, June 6, 1777. Archives, Colonial Williamsburg Foundation, Williamsburg, Virginia.

Letter: Albert Einstein to FDR, August 2, 1939. National Archives.

Letter: Henry L. Stimson to A. J. Cornell, December 1, 1942. National Archives.

Interoffice Los Alamos Project memo: B. C. Brazier to J. G. Ryan, October 1943. National Archives.

Letter: Sgt. Ed Doty while at Los Alamos to his parents, August 7, 1945. National Archives.

Interoffice Los Alamos Project memo: Brig. Gen. Leslie R. Groves to Dr. J. R. Oppenheimer, July 29, 1943. National Archives.

"My Observations During the Explosion at Trinity on July 16, 1945. E. Fermi." Undated. National Archives.

Top Secret message: ADWAR, Washington to Tripartite Conference, Babelsbert, Germany. National Archives.

Interoffice Los Alamos project memo. "Memorandum: To All Concerned: Norris E. Bradbury, Director, December 5, 1945. National Archives

Memorandum: Chief of Naval Personnel to all Sea Frontier Commands, All Naval Districts, etc. Sub: "Negro Personnel confidential Report of Conference with regard to the Handling of." U.S. Naval Institute.

Letter: American Consul General Nadi to Department of State, February 3, 1943. National Archives.

Letter: Hon. F. M. Forde to Gen. Douglas MacArthur, May 21, 1942. Richard K. Sutherland Papers, National Archives.

Letter: Douglas MacArthur to H. B. Chandler, May 28, 1941. Richard K. Sutherland Papers, National Archives.

Memorandum: Egon W. Fleck and 1st Lt. Edward A. Tenenbaum, "Buchenwald, A Preliminary Report," Headquarters Twelfth Army Group, Publicity and Psychological Warfare, April 12, 1945. National Archives.

Official Records: British House of Parliament.

BOOKS

Agawa, Hiroyuki. *The Reluctant Admiral: Yamamoto and the Imperial Navy.* Tokyo: Kondansha, 1979.

Barker, A. J. *Pearl Harbor.* New York: Ballantine, 1969.

Beck, John Jacob. *MacArthur and Wainwright.* Albuquerque: University of New Mexico Press, 1974.

Beinhart, Larry. *American Hero.* New York: Pantheon, 1993; reprinted by Ballantine Books, 1994.

Bernbaum, Michael, ed. *Witness to the Holocaust: An Illustrated Documentary History of the Holocaust in the Words of its Victims, Perpetrators and Bystanders.* New York: Harper Collins, 1997.

Bernstein, Walter. *Keep Your Head Down.* New York: Henry Holt, 1945.

Berube, Allan. *Coming Out Under Fire: The History of Gay Men and Women in World War Two.* New York: Free Press, 1990.

Blum, John Morton. *V Was For Victory: Politics and American Culture During World War II.* New York: Harcourt, Brace, and Jovanovich, 1976.

Boatner, Mark M. III. *The Biographical Dictionary of World War II.* Novato, California: Presidio, 1996.

Bookman, John T. and Powers, Stephen T. *The March to Victory.* New York: Harper and Row, 1986.

Bourke-White, Margaret. *They Called It "Purple Heart Valley," A Combat Chronicle of the War in Italy.* New York: Simon and Schuster, 1944.

Boyne, Walter J. *Clash of Wings: World War II In the Air.* New York: Simon and Schuster, 1994.

Brienes, Wini. *Young, White, and Miserable: Growing Up Female In the Fifties.* Boston: Beacon, 1992.

Brinkley, David. *Washington Goes to War.* New York: Random House, 1988; reprinted by Ballantine Books, 1989.

Buchanan, A. Russell. *The United States and World War II.* 2 Vols. New York: Harper, 1964.

Butow, Robert J. C. *Japan's Decision to Surrender.* Stanford, California: Stanford University Press, 1954.

Caldwall, Oliver J. *A Secret War: Americans in China, 1944–1945.* Carbondale: Southern Illinois University Press, 1972.

Campbell, D'Ann. *Women At War With America: Private Lives In A Patriotic Era.* Cambridge: Harvard University Press, 1984.

Carey, John, ed. *Eyewitness to History*. Cambridge, Massachusetts: Harvard University Press, 1987.

Carlson, Lewis H. *We Were Each Other's Prisoners: An Oral History of World War II American and German Prisoners of War*. New York: Basic Books, 1997.

Churchill, Winston. *Memoirs of the Second World War*. 6 Vols. Boston: Houghton Mifflin, 1959; abridged 1987.

Clausen, Henry C. and Lee, Bruce. *Pearl Harbor: Final Judgment*. New York, Crown, 1992.

Cohen, Stan. *V For Victory: America's Home Front During World War II*. Missoula, Montana: Pictorial Histories Publishing, 1991.

Colville, John. *Winston Churchill and His Inner Circle*. New York: Wyndham, 1981.

Cutler, Thomas J. *The Battle of Leyte Gulf: 23–26 October 1944*. New York: Harper Collins, 1994.

Davies, Norman. *Europe: A History*. New York: Oxford University Press, 1996.

Davis, Burke. *The Billy Mitchell Affair*. New York: Random House, 1967.

Davis, Gavan. *Prisoners of the Japanese: POWs of World War II In the Pacific*. New York: Quill, 1994.

Davis, Kenneth C. *Don't Know Much About History*. New York: Crown, 1990.

Ding, Ignatius. *The Rape of Nanking*. Old Brookville, New York: Triumph, 1997.

Doolittle, Gen. James Harold. *I Could Never Be So Lucky Again*. Altglen, Pennsylvania: Schiffler Military Press, 1972; reprinted by Bantam, 1995.

Dunnigan, James F. and Nofi, Albert A. *Dirty Little Secrets of World War II*. New York: Quill, 1994.

Eisenhower, Dwight David. *Crusade In Europe*. Garden City, New York: Doubleday, 1948; reprinted by Permabooks, 1952.

Foner, Jack D. *Blacks and the Military in American History*. New York: Praeger, 1974.

Foy, David A. *For You the War Is Over: American Prisoners of War in Nazi Germany*. New York: Stein and Day, 1984.

Galbraith, John Kenneth. *A View From the Stands*. Boston: Houghton Mifflin, 1986.

Gallagher, Richard. *Malmédy Massacre*. New York: Paperback Library, 1964.

Gesensway, Deborah and Roseman, Mindy. *Beyond Words: Images From America's Concentration Camps*. Ithaca, New York: Cornell University Press, 1987.

Gilbert, Martin. *The Second World War: A Complete History*. New York: Henry Holt, 1989; revised edition, 1991.

Giovanitt, Len and Freed, Fred. *The Decision to Drop the Bomb*. New York: Coward McCann, 1965.

Glines, Carrol V. *Doolittle's Tokyo Raiders*. New York: Arno Press, 1980.

Goldberg, M. Hirsh. *The Blunder Book*. New York: Quill, 1984.

Goldhagen, Daniel Jonah. *Hitler's Willing Executioners: Ordinary Germans and the Holocaust*. New York: Knopf, 1996.

Gordon, Lois and Gordon, Alan. *American Chronicle: Six Decades in American Life, 1920–1980*. New York: Atheneum, 1987.

Groueff, Stephane. *Manhattan Project: The Untold Story of the Making of the Atomic Bomb*. Boston: Little, Brown, 1967.

Groves, Leslie R. *Now It Can Be Told: The Story of the Manhattan Project*. New York: Harper, 1962; reprinted by Da Capo, 1970.

Haberfeld, Caroline V., ed. *Fodor's Great Britain*. New York: Fodor's Travel Publications, 1991.

Hackett, David A., trans. *The Buchenwald Report*. Boulder, Colorado: Westview Press, 1995; original in German: Bericht über das Kanzentrationslager Buchenwald bei Weimar.

Hargrove, Marion. *See Here, Private Hargrove*. New York: Henry Holt, 1942.

Harris, Mark Jonathan; Mitchell, Franklin; and Schechter, Steven. *The Homefront: America During World War II*. New York: G. P. Putnam's Sons, 1984.

Hasting, Max. *Bomber Command: Churchill's Epic Campaign. The Inside Story of the RAF's Attempt to End the War*. London: Michael Joseph, Ltd., 1979; reprinted by Touchstone, 1989.

Hersey, John. *Hiroshima*. New York: Knopf, 1946; reprinted by Bantam, 1959.

Hewlett, Richard G. and Anderson, Oscar E., Jr. *The New World: 1939–1945*. University Park: Pennsylvania State University Press, 1962.

Holmes, W. J. *Undersea Victory: The Influence of Submarine Operations In the Pacific.* New York: Doubleday, 1966.

Hurley, Alfred F. *Billy Mitchell: Crusader For Air Power.* Bloomington: Indiana University Press, 1975.

Höss, Rudolf. *Commandant of Auschwitz: The Autobiography of Rudolf Höss.* London: Oxford University Press, 1959.

Hymes, James L., Jr., ed. *Early Childhood Education: Living History Interviews.* 2 Vols. Carmel, California: Hacienda Press, 1978.

James, D. Clayton. *The Years of MacArthur.* 3 Vols. Boston: Houghton Mifflin, 1972–1975.

James, D. Clayton and Wells, Anne Sharp. *From Pearl Harbor to VJ-Day: The American Armed Forces in World War II.* Chicago: Ivan Dee, 1995.

Kennett, Lee. *For the Duration: The United States Goes to War: Pearl Harbor–1942.* New York: Scribner's Sons, 1985.

———. *G.I.: The American Soldier in World War II.* New York: Scribner's Sons, 1987.

Kerr, E. Bartless. *Surrender and Survival: The Experiences of American POWs in the Pacific 1941–1945.* New York: Morrow, 1985.

Krammer, Arnold. *Nazi Prisoners of War in America.* New York: Stein and Day, 1979; reprinted by Scarborough House, 1996.

Kunhardt, Philip B., Jr., ed. *Life: The First Fifty Years-1936–1986.* Boston: Little, Brown, 1986.

Lech, Raymond B. *All the Drowned Sailors.* New York: Stein & Day, 1982; reprinted by Jove, 1991.

Lewis, Jon E., ed. *Eye-Witness to D-Day: The Story of the Battle By Those Who Were There.* London: Robinson, 1994; reprinted in the United States by Carroll & Graf, 1994.

Litoff, Judy Barrett and Smith, David C. *Since You Went Away: World War II Letters From American Women On the Home Front.* New York: Oxford University Press, 1991.

Lomax, Eric. *The Railway Man.* New York: W. W. Norton, 1995.

Lord, Walter. *Day of Infamy.* New York: Henry Holt, 1957.

MacArthur, Douglas. *Reminiscences.* New York: McGraw-Hill, 1964.

McCombs, Don and Worth, Fred L. *World War II: 4139 Strange and Fascinating Facts.* New York: Random House, 1983; reprinted by Wing Books, 1996.

McCullough, David. *Truman.* New York: Simon and Schuster, 1992.

McCutcheon, Marc. *Everyday Life From Prohibition Through World War II*. Cincinnati, Ohio: Writer's Digest Books, 1995.

McNeil, Bill. *Voices of A War Remembered: An Oral History of Canadians in World War II*. Toronto: Doubleday Canada, 1991.

Malone, John. *The World War II Quiz Book*. New York: Quill, 1991.

Marsden, M. H. E. *Khaki Is More Than A Color*. Garden City, New York: Doubleday, 1940.

Masters, Peter [Peter Arany]. *Striking Back: A Jewish Commando's War Against the Nazis*. Novato, California: Presidio, 1997.

Mauldin, Bill. *Bill Mauldin's Army: Bill Mauldin's Greatest World War II Cartoons*. New York: Sloan, 1949; reprinted by Presidio, 1983.

Meltzer, Milton. *Never to Forget: The Jews of the Holocaust*. New York: Harper and Row, 1976; reprinted by Dell, 1984.

Meyer, Agnes, E. *Journey Through Chaos*. New York: Harcourt, Brace, 1944.

Millett, Alan R. and Maslowski, Peter. *For the Common Defense: A Military History of the United States*. New York: The Free Press, 1984.

Montagu, Ewen. *The Man Who Never Was*. Philadelphia: J. P. Lippincott, 1954; reprinted by Time-Life, 1988.

Morison, Samuel Eliot. *The Oxford History of the American People*. New York: Oxford University Press, 1965.

Morse, Arthur D. *While Six Million Died: A Chronicle of American Apathy*. New York: Random House, 1968.

Morton, Louis. *The Fall of the Philippines*. Washington, D.C.: Office of the Chief of Military History, Department of the Army, 1953.

Moynihan, Michael, ed. *People At War: 1939–1945*. London: David & Charles, 1974; reprinted by David & Charles, 1989.

Nichols, David, ed. *Ernie's War: The Best of Ernie Pyle's World War II Dispatches*. New York: Random House, 1986.

Palmer, Robert R., ed. *The Procurement and Training of Ground Combat Troops*. Washington, D.C.: U.S. Government Printing Office, 1948.

Parramore, Thomas C. with Stewart, Peter G. and Bogger, Tommy L. *Norfolk: The First Four Centuries*. Charlottesville: University Press of Virginia, 1994.

Parris, Thomas. *The Ultra Americans: The U.S. Role in Breaking the Nazi Codes*. New York: Stein and Day, 1986; reprinted as *The American Codebreakers: The U.S. Role in Ultra* by Scarborough House, 1991.

Peattie, Mark R. *Ishwara Janki and Japan's Confrontation With the West.* Princeton: Princeton University Press, 1975.

Peckham, Howard H. and Snyder, Shirley A., eds. *Letters From Fighting Hoosiers.* Bloomington: Indiana University Press, 1948.

Perret, Geoffrey. *There's A War To Be Won: The United States Army in World War II.* New York: Random House, 1991.

Pogue, Forest C. *George C. Marshall: Ordeal and Hope 1939–1942.* 4 Vols. New York: Viking, 19, 63, 86.

Polmar, Norman and Allen, Thomas B. *World War II: The Encyclopedia of the War Years-1941–1945.* New York: Random House, 1996.

Reader's Digest *Illustrated Story of World War II.* Pleasantville, New York: Reader's Digest Association, 1969.

Risch, Erna A. *The Quartermaster Corps: Organization, Supply and Service.* Washington, D.C.: U.S. Government Printing Office, 1953.

Roeder, George H., Jr. *The Censored War.* New Haven, Connecticut: Yale University Press, 1993.

Rothberg, Abraham. *Eyewitness History of World War II: Siege.* New York: Bantam, 1962.

Ryan, Cornelius. *The Longest Day.* New York: Simon and Schuster, 1959.

Schlegel, Marvin W. *Conscripted City: Norfolk in World War II.* Norfolk, Virginia: Norfolk War Commission, 1951; reprinted by The Virginian-Pilot and The Ledger-Star, 1991.

Schlesinger, Arthur M., Jr., ed. *The Almanac of American History.* New York: Putnam Grosett, 1993.

Seidel, Robert W. *Los Alamos and the Development of the Atomic Bomb.* Los Alamos, New Mexico: Otowi Crossing Press, 1993.

Shenkman, Richard. *Legends, Lies & Cherished Myths of American History.* New York: Morrow, 1988.

Smith, R. Harris. *OSS: The Secret History of America's First Central Intelligence Agency.* Berkeley: University of California Press, 1972.

Snyder, Louis L. *Encyclopedia of the Third Reich.* New York: McGraw-Hill, 1976.

Spector, Ronald H. *Eagle Against the Sun: The American War With Japan.* New York: Free Press, 1984; reprinted by Vintage Books, 1985.

Spencer, Lyle M. and Burns, Robert K. *Youth Goes to War.* Chicago: Science Research Associates, 1943.

Springs, Holmes B. *Selective Service in South Carolina: An Historical Report*. Columbia: South Carolina Press, 1948.

Storry, Richard. *The Double Patriots: A Study of Japanese Nationalism.* Boston: Houghton Mifflin, 1957.

Sulzerger, C. L., ed. *The American Heritage Picture History of World War II.* New York: Forbes, 1966; reprinted by Houghton Mifflin as *World War II* in 1987.

Taylor, A. J. P. *The Origins of the Second World War.* New York: Atheneum, 1961; reprinted by Premier Books, 1963.

Terkel, Studs. *The Good War: An Oral History of World War Two.* New York: Pantheon Books, 1985.

Toland, John. *Infamy: Pearl Harbor and Its Aftermath.* Garden City, New York: Doubleday, 1982.

Treadwell, Mattie E. *The Women's Army Corps.* Washington, D.C.: Office of the Chief of Military History, 1954.

Tuttle, William M., Jr. *Daddy's Gone to War: The Second World War In the Lives of America's Children.* New York: Oxford University Press, 1993.

U.S. Bureau of the Census. *Historical Statistics of the United States: Colonial Times to 1970, Bicentennial Edition.* Washington, D.C.: U.S. Government Printing Office, 1975.

U.S. Strategic Bombing Survey: Final Report Covering Air Raid Protecting and Allied Subjects in Japan. Washington, D.C.: U.S. Government Printing Office, 1947.

Vlahos, Michel. *The Blue Sword: The Naval War College and the American Mission-1919-1941.* Washington, D.C.: U.S. Government Printing Office, 1980.

Vonnegut, Kurt. *Slaughterhouse Five.* Garden City, New York: Doubleday. 1966; reprinted by Dell, 1991.

Wedemeyer, Albert C. *Wedemeyer Reports!* New York: Henry Holt, 1958.

Weintraub, Stanley. *Long Day's Journey Into War: December 7, 1941.* New York: Dutton, 1991.

Whtwycky, Bohdan. *The Other Holocaust: Many Circles of Hell.* Washington, D.C.: Novak, 1980.

Willey, Roy De Verl and Young, Helen Ann. *Radio In Elementary Education.* Boston: D. C. Heath, 1948.

Wilson, Jane S. and Serber, Charlotte, eds. *Standing By and Making*

Do: Women of Wartime Los Alamos. Los Alamos, New Mexico: Otowi Crossing Press, 1993.

Wright, Gordon. *The Ordeal of Total War: 1939–1945.* New York: Harper and Row, 1968.

Yamazaki, James N. with Fleming, Louis B. *Children of the Atomic Bomb: An American Physician's Memoir of Nagasaki, Hiroshima, and the Marshall Islands.* Durham, North Carolina: Duke University Press, 1995; pre-publication uncorrected page proofs.

PUBLISHED ARTICLES

American Nurses Association, 50th anniversary booklet.

"Advanced Weaponry of the Start." *American Heritage of Invention & Technology,* spring 1997.

"Allowances For Servicemen's Dependents, 1942." *Monthly Labor Review.* August 1945.

Bossard, H. S. "The Hazards of War Marriages." *Psychiatry.* February 1944.

"Calling All Fathers." *Parents Magazine,* March 1945.

Conroy, Frank. "The Fifties: America in a Trance." *Esquire Magazine,* June 1983.

Deac, Wilfred P. "Amy Elizabeth Thorpe, Code-Named 'Cynthia,' Was a World War II Version of the Legendary Mata Hari," *World War II,* February 1996.

————"The Polish Submarine Orzel Escaped From Internment and Went on to Fight the Germans Against Long Odds." *World War II,* July 1996.

Haufler, Hervie. "Half A Century After the End of World War II, the 'Ultra Americans' Are Finally Piecing Together Their Wartime Story." *World War II,* March 1996.

Hoover, J. Edgar. "Wild Children." *American Magazine,* July 1943.

Janis, Irving L. "Psychodynamics of Adjustment to Army Life." *Psychiatry,* May 1945.

Jervey, Frank K. "The New Semiautomatic Rifle." *Army Ordnance,* XIX, 1938.

Maslowski, Peter. "Truman, the Bomb, and the Numbers Game." *Military History Quarterly: The Quarterly Journal of Military History,* spring 1995.

Morlock, Maud. "Babies on the Market." *Survey Midmonthly,* March 1945.

Palmer, Gretta. "Your Baby or Your Job." *Woman's Home Companion,* October 1943.

Pepper, Claude. "Senate Committee Report." *Wartime Health and Education,* 1943.

"The Plight of the Jew in Germany." *Current History,* 1939.

Porter, William C. "What Has Psychiatry Learned During the Present War?" *American Journal of Psychiatry,* May 1943.

Samuelson, Robert J. "The Great Postwar Prosperity." *Newsweek,* May 20, 1985.

Smith, Larry. "A Picture to Remember." *Parade,* May 25, 1997.

Smith, Robert Barr. "Justice Under the Sun: Japanese War Crime Trials." *World War II,* September 1996.

Steel, Ronald. "Life in the Last Fifty Years." *Esquire,* June 1983.

Vanzo, John P. "Saga of U-505: A Crewman's Story." *World War II,* July 1997.

Wilson, William R. "Code Talkers." *American History,* February 1997.

NEWSPAPERS

The Chicago Tribune, June 2, 1997.

The New York Times, October 30. 1939; July 1, 1942; June 30, 1943; October 17, 1943; November 21, 1943; October 15, 1943; November 7, 1943; December 26, 1944; January 17, 1945; April 13, 1945; August 7, 1945; October 25, 1955; December 5, 1946.

The Norfolk Virginian-Pilot, January 27, 1880; May 8, 1945.

Mexia (Texas) Daily News, June 30, 1971.

Portsmouth (Virginia) Star, May 7, 1945.

Rockford (Illinois) Morning Star, December 1, 1944.

Tulsa (Oklahoma) World, July 12, 1945.

The Los Angeles Times, February 25, 1942.

INDEX